Against Prediction

Against Prediction

Profiling, Policing, and Punishing in an Actuarial Age

BERNARD E. HARCOURT

THE UNIVERSITY OF CHICAGO PRESS   CHICAGO AND LONDON

BERNARD E. HARCOURT is professor of law and director of the Center for Studies in Criminal Justice at the University of Chicago. He is the author of *Illusion of Order: The False Promise of Broken Windows Policing* and *Language of the Gun: Youth, Crime, and Public Policy*.

The University of Chicago Press, Chicago 60637
The University of Chicago Press, Ltd., London
© 2007 by The University of Chicago
All rights reserved. Published 2007
Printed in the United States of America
16 15 14 13 12 11 10 09 08 07   1 2 3 4 5

ISBN-13: 978-0-226-31613-0 (cloth)
ISBN-13: 978-0-226-31614-7 (paper)
ISBN-10: 0-226-31613-0 (cloth)
ISBN-10: 0-226-31614-9 (paper)

Library of Congress Cataloging-in-Publication Data

Harcourt, Bernard E., 1963–
    Against prediction : profiling, policing, and punishing in an actuarial age / Bernard E. Harcourt.
        p.   cm.
    Includes bibliographical references and index.
    ISBN-13: 978-0-226-31613-0 (cloth : alk. paper)
    ISBN-13: 978-0-226-31614-7 (pbk. : alk. paper)
    ISBN-10: 0-226-31613-0 (cloth : alk. paper)
    ISBN-10: 0-226-31614-9 (pbk. : alk. paper)
    1. Racial profiling in law enforcement—United States.   2. Criminal behavior, Prediction of—United States.   3. Law enforcement—United States—Statistical methods.   I. Title.
    HV7936.R3H37   2006
    363.2'30890973—dc22

                                                    2006011178

⊗ The paper used in this publication meets the minimum requirements of the American National Standard for Information Sciences—Permanence of Paper for Printed Library Materials, ANSI Z39.48-1992.

FOR MIA RUYTER AND OUR CHILDREN, ISADORA AND LÉONARD

Contents

Prologue

Actuarial methods in criminal law *n. Abbr.* **The actuarial.** *Law.* The use of statistical rather than clinical methods on large datasets to determine different levels of criminal offending associated with one or more group traits, in order (1) to predict past, present or future criminal behavior and (2) to administer a criminal justice outcome. [From actuarial tables in the insurance industry used to predict mortality rates for different groups of insured persons and to set individual premium payments.]

"Predictability is feasible," declared Ernest W. Burgess in 1928.[1] The distinguished University of Chicago sociologist had just completed a study of three thousand inmates paroled in Illinois during the early 1920s and constructed one of the very first parole-prediction instruments in the United States—a twenty-one-factor test that would determine, based on group recidivism rates, the likelihood of success or failure of any inmate eligible for parole. Within a matter of years, the Illinois State Penitentiary at Joliet hired its first "actuary," Ferris F. Laune—former PhD student of Burgess—and by 1935, the "Burgess method" was being used in the carceral field. Laune would compile each man's information, administer the Burgess test, and prepare a report—officially titled a *prognasio*—to inform the Illinois parole board of the likelihood of the inmate's success if granted parole. Laune's *prognasios* ushered actuarial methods into the criminal law.

By 1951, Ernest Burgess was recommending that the same actuarial paradigm be extended to many other domains of the criminal law. "Although the predictive methods described in this book are limited to parole selection," Burgess wrote,

they are also applicable to several other fields of delinquency and criminality. They could now be introduced, at least experimentally and for demonstration purposes, in such additional areas as the identification of predelinquent children, the disposition of cases in the juvenile court, parole from institutional training schools and reformatories, and the selection of adults for probation. . . . Prediction may be just as important or even more important in parole supervision.[2]

Burgess's words would prove prescient.

Today, the actuarial permeates the field of criminal law and its enforcement. From the use of the IRS Discriminant Index Function to predict potential tax evasion and identify which tax returns to audit, to the use of drug-courier and racial profiles to identify suspects to search at airports, on the highways, and on city streets, to the use of risk-assessment instruments to determine pretrial detention, length of criminal sentences, prison classification, and parole eligibility, prediction instruments increasingly determine individual outcomes in our policing, law enforcement, and punishment practices. More and more, we use risk-assessment tools to identify whom to search, when to punish more, and how to administer the penal sanction.

Most of us view this trend with hope, rather than alarm. With the single and notable, but limited, exception of racial profiling against African Americans and Hispanics on the highways, most scholars, criminal justice practitioners, and public citizens embrace the turn to actuarial methods as a more efficient, rational, and wealth-maximizing tool to allocate scarce law enforcement resources. When we want to identify violent sexual predators, drug traffickers, tax cheats, or dangerous recidivists, we increasingly put our faith in actuarial instruments. The simple fact is, the police can detect more crime with the same resources if they investigate suspects who are more likely to offend, and courts can reduce crime more effectively if they imprison for longer periods convicted criminals who are more likely to return to crime. Most of us believe that the use of reliable actuarial methods in criminal law represents progress. No one, naturally, is in favor of spurious stereotypes and erroneous predictions. But to most of us, it simply makes common sense to decide whom to search based on reliable predictions of criminal behavior, or whom to incarcerate based on dependable estimates of future reoffending. It has become second nature to think about just punishment through the lens of actuarial prediction.

In this book, I challenge this commonsense view and set forth three compelling reasons why we should be skeptical of—rather than embrace—the new actuarial paradigm. First, the reliance on predictions of future criminality may undermine the primary goal of law enforcement, namely, reducing crime. Though this may sound counterintuitive, it is surprisingly correct: the use of probabilistic methods may increase the overall amount of targeted crime depending on the relative responsiveness of the profiled individuals (in comparison to the responsiveness of those who are not profiled) to the shift in the level of law enforcement. The ultimate effect on crime will depend on how members of the two different groups react to changes in policing or punishment: if the profiled persons are less responsive to the policy change, then the overall amount of profiled crime in society will likely increase. In other words, profiling on higher past, present or future offending may be entirely counterproductive with regard to the central aim of law enforcement—to minimize crime.

Second, the reliance on probabilistic methods produces a distortion in the carceral population. It creates an imbalance between, on the one hand, the distribution of demographic or other group traits among the actual offender population and, on the other hand, the distribution of those same traits among the population of persons with criminal justice contacts, such as arrest, conviction, probation, incarceration, parole, or other forms of supervision and punishment. Simply put, the profiled population becomes an even larger proportion of the carceral population—larger in relation to its representation among actual offenders—than the nonprofiled population. This in turn aggravates and compounds the difficulties that many profiled individuals have obtaining employment, pursuing educational opportunities, or simply leading normal family lives. These are significant social costs that are most often overlooked in the crime and punishment calculus—overlooked primarily because these people are *guilty* of a criminal offense.

Third, the proliferation of actuarial methods has begun to bias our conception of just punishment. The perceived success of predictive instruments has made theories of punishment that function more smoothly with prediction seem more natural. It favors theories of selective incapacitation and sentencing enhancements for offenders who are more likely to be dangerous in the future. Yet these actuarial instruments represent nothing more than fortuitous advances in technical knowledge from disciplines, such as sociology and psychology, that have no normative stake in the criminal law. These technological advances are, in effect, exogenous shocks to our legal system, and this raises very troubling questions about what theory of just punishment we would independently embrace and how it is, exactly, that we have allowed technical knowledge, somewhat arbitrarily, to dictate the path of justice.

These three arguments should temper our embrace of the actuarial in the field of crime and punishment. To be sure, the force of these arguments will resonate differently in different punishment and policing contexts. They are at their strongest in cases like the racial profiling of African American and Hispanic drivers on the nation's highways—for several reasons. First, given the likely differentials in offending rates and responsiveness to policing between the different racial groups, racial profiling on the highways probably increases the overall amount of criminal activity in society. The likely increase in drug and other offending among whites, as a result of their accurate perception that the police are focusing on African Americans and Hispanics, will probably exceed the potential reduction in drug offending among minorities. Second, racial profiling is likely to produce a ratchet effect resulting in a disproportionate representation of minorities with correctional contacts in relation to their representation in the offending population—a ratchet that operates along one of the most troubling lines, namely, race and ethnicity. It is precisely the type of ratchet that can only aggravate our tragic legacy of racial discrimination in this country. Third, profiling on the highways for drug contraband involves a law enforcement objective—the war on drugs—whose net benefits are, at the very least, debatable and, certainly, highly contested. Finally, racial profiling tends to distort our conception of just punishment, especially our shared ideal that similarly situated offenders should be treated similarly, regardless of skin color.

One or more of the arguments may be less persuasive in other punishment and policing contexts. In some situations, the comparative responsiveness of different groups to profiling may vary, as may the comparative offending rates, the seriousness of the crime, or the criminal justice objective itself. These differences may render one or more of the three arguments unpersuasive. In the case of profiling men in stranger-rape investigations, for instance, there may be a significant offending differential between men and women, so that there is, in effect, no room for a ratchet effect to operate on the profiled population. In the case of setting bail, for example, the criminal justice objective—ensuring a defendant's presence at trial—may originally have called for prediction, and, as a result, the use of actuarial measures may not distort our underlying conception of just punishment. In other cases, the seriousness of the crime—or lack thereof—and the problematic nature of the group trait that is being profiled may significantly affect the cost-benefit assessment. To many, race is unique and requires stricter scrutiny, though to many others, a ratchet that operates along the lines of class, gender, or sexual orientation—or even one that stigmatizes wearing tattoos, smoking cigarettes, or having a prior criminal record—may be just as troubling.

All these different dimensions will impact the force of the argument. But the central intuition remains intact: the mechanics that are triggered by the use of actuarial methods in the criminal law are problematic in the vast majority of cases—not just in the case of racial profiling. The mechanisms are prone to misfire. And as a result, the turn to actuarial methods in crime and punishment is not—or rather should not be—as natural and intuitive as it appears. This book sets forth three powerful arguments against using prediction methods but does not stop there. It also identifies the different dimensions that affect the force of these arguments. In this sense, it proposes a general framework to understand and assess the mechanisms that are triggered by the use of actuarial instruments.

Instead of embracing the actuarial turn in criminal law, I argue that we should celebrate the virtues of randomization. Random sampling, it turns out, is the only way to achieve a carceral population that reflects the actual offending population. It is thus the only way to fulfill a central moral intuition regarding just punishment, namely, that similarly situated individuals should have the same likelihood of being apprehended when they offend *regardless of race, ethnicity, gender, or class*. Randomization also avoids the risk that actuarial methods will increase the overall amount of crime in society where the targeted population is less responsive to policing.

Naturally, random sampling does not mean pulling prison sentences out of a hat or granting parole by lottery. Like the actuarial, randomization has a very limited and narrow definition: it means making criminal justice determinations blind to predictions of future dangerousness. In the policing context, randomization is simple: law enforcement should randomly sample IRS tax filings for audits or use numerical sequencing for consensual car searches on the highway. In the sentencing area, randomization means something quite different, but no less straightforward: it means imposing a sentence based on a proper and independent metric and then avoiding the effects of the actuarial by eliminating devices such as parole that are prediction-based. Randomization does not mean drawing names arbitrarily in deciding who to release: it means, instead, eliminating the effects of predictions of future offending.

The baseline presumption in the criminal law should favor *randomized* policing and punishment. Actuarial methods should be employed only when we are persuaded that they will promote the primary interest of law enforcement without imposing undue burden on the profiled groups and without distorting our conceptions of just punishment. Barring that, criminal law enforcement and correctional institutions should be blind to predictions of criminality based on group characteristics. We should adopt a presumption *against* prediction.

CHAPTER ONE

Actuarial Methods
in the Criminal Law

CASE I. In Kansas, the sentencing commission is required by statute an-
nually to prepare two-year projections of the expected adult prison population. When its projections exceed available prison-bed capacity, the
commission has to identify ways to either reduce the number of inmates
admitted to prison or adjust the length of their sentences. In fiscal year
2002, with dire projections of an unprecedented number of prisoners, the
Kansas legislature followed the lead of California and Arizona and insti-
tuted mandatory drug abuse treatment in lieu of incarceration for a designated group of drug offenders convicted after November 1, 2003.[1] Other
states faced with similar problems, such as Louisiana and Alabama, have
enacted early-release legislation. Those statutes make outright release
from prison possible in order to alleviate overcrowding.[2]

In general, candidates for early release or diversionary programs must
satisfy strict risk-of-reoffending criteria. For example, in Kansas, to be eligible for drug treatment in lieu of incarceration, the offender must have
been convicted of drug possession only. Drug sales or trafficking preclude
diversion, as do prior violent felonies and posing a significant threat to
public safety. To assess the latter, the Kansas legislature mandates that each
candidate for treatment be subject to what they refer to as "a statewide,
mandatory, standardized risk assessment tool."[3] That risk-assessment tool,
in Kansas, is the Level of Services Inventory-Revised—known in the business as the LSI-R—and the results of the assessment are incorporated into
the presentence investigation report submitted to the sentencing judge.
From November 2003 to mid-January 2004, 149 drug convicts in Kansas
were diverted to treatment.[4]

The LSI-R was developed in Canada in the late 1970s and is used today in nearly all of the United States and the Canadian provinces at some point in the postconviction process—for the security classifications of prison inmates, for levels of probation and parole supervision, or as a factor for determining eligibility for parole. In many states the LSI-R is administered for multiple purposes. It is championed as a versatile and cost-effective tool for predicting risk and assessing needs. So, for instance, in Pennsylvania the LSI-R score is a component of a number-based decision matrix for deciding whether to parole an inmate.[5] In Washington state the Indeterminate Sentence Review Board, assigned responsibility for determining parole eligibility for all offenders who committed their crimes prior to July 1, 1984, uses the LSI-R.[6] In North Dakota the parole board considers the results of the LSI-R when making its decisions to parole someone—along with the availability of treatment programs, the nature of the offense, the inmate's prior record, and an evaluation of how well the inmate did under the terms of any prior parole and probation supervision.[7] In Alaska the parole board may give the LSI-R score up to 35 percent weight in its decision,[8] and in Vermont the LSI-R is one of the primary factors in the decision of the parole board.[9] In Oklahoma active supervision of parole cannot be terminated without an LSI-R score below a designated number.[10]

The trend toward using prediction instruments in the parole context is visually dramatic, as shown in figure 1.1, which traces the historical use of such instruments by state parole authorities over the past hundred years. Illinois alone accounted for the only use of an actuarial instrument throughout the 1930s, '40s, and '50s. Ohio experimented with a risk-assessment tool in the 1960s, and California began using a prediction tool in the early 1970s—as did the federal government. While some states, such as Illinois and California, later stopped using actuarial methods when they abandoned parole, other states, such as Georgia, Iowa, Tennessee, South Carolina, Alabama, and Florida, began using risk-assessment tools in the late 1970s and early 1980s. Soon, many other states followed their lead—Missouri, Michigan, North Dakota, South Dakota, Washington, Arkansas, Colorado, Nevada, Maryland, Connecticut, New Jersey, Ohio, Vermont, Alaska, Idaho, Kentucky, Maine, Montana, Pennsylvania, Texas, Utah, and Delaware.

In 2004, twenty-eight states used risk-assessment tools to guide their parole determinations—approximately 72 percent of states that maintain an active parole system. As a leading parole authority association suggests,

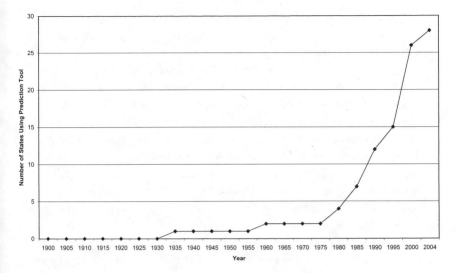

FIGURE 1.1 Historical trend in the number of states using parole-prediction instruments
Source: Survey conducted by Marylynne Hunt-Dorta in July and August of 2004. Hunt-Dorta surveyed the parole authorities of the fifty states to determine whether they used prediction instruments, which ones they used, and when they began using them. Documentation of the interviews is available upon request from the author.

"In this day and age, making parole decisions without benefit of a good, research-based risk assessment instrument clearly falls short of accepted best practice."[11]

CASE 2. The Internal Revenue Service receives approximately 130 million individual tax returns per year, but only has the resources to audit about 750,000 or 0.6 percent of those filings—about 1 in 170.[12] In order to enhance its ability to detect tax evasion, the IRS has developed a complex, top-secret computer algorithm that predicts likely cheating electronically. Each return is fed into a computer in Martinsburg, West Virginia, and the computer assigns a score based on the algorithm—an algorithm guarded like the Coca-Cola formula.[13] "The higher the score, the more likely a return will be selected for an audit," the IRS explains.[14]

The algorithm is known as the Discriminant Index Function, or DIF. The DIF is based on multiple-regression analysis of past audits intended to identify the key factors that are most likely to indicate tax fraud. The DIF was last updated in 1992 based on a regression analysis of approximately 50,000 tax returns that had been randomly audited in 1988. The

DIF is an expense-based scoring model that is based on the actual items on a tax return, rather than on failures to report items. (Another filter, the UIDIF, was developed around 2000 to pick up returns that fail to report items reported on other forms, such as W-2s, 1099s, and 1098s.)

The DIF compares the tax return under review with average returns in the same income bracket and profession, and identifies outliers. It assigns a number value to suspicious items on the tax return and then produces a score that represents the estimated probability of noncompliance. Typical items that may raise a red flag—according to leaked information—include high, above-average levels of itemized deductions and Schedule C filings. When the DIF score exceeds the IRS target, the tax return is reviewed manually by an IRS agent in order to determine whether it should be audited. Depending upon the problems detected, the return will be sent to an IRS Service Center or an IRS district office. Returns that fit the profile are the most likely to be examined.[15] The IRS uses the DIF system to select around 20–30 percent of the tax returns that are audited each year in the United States.[16]

CASE 3.   In September 1994, the governor of Virginia, George Allen, called a special session of the Virginia legislature to consider sweeping reforms to the state's felony sentencing system. Under the motto of "truth-in-sentencing," the governor and legislature abolished the existing parole system and imposed mandatory sentence-completion requirements. Convicted felons were now required to complete at least 85 percent of their prison sentences. And the sentences were lengthened: the reform package required that violent offenders serve prison terms two to six times longer than before. The governor and legislature also established a sentencing commission, the Virginia Criminal Sentencing Commission, to develop and eventually administer a new set of discretionary sentencing guidelines that would channel judicial discretion in sentencing.[17]

Along with these reforms, the Virginia governor and legislature placed a new emphasis on using empirically based, actuarial risk-assessment instruments. The Virginia legislature directed the new sentencing commission to develop a first actuarial instrument in the context of nonviolent offenders who could be diverted from the prison system at low risk. Specifically, the commission was asked to "study the feasibility of using an empirically based risk assessment instrument to select 25% of the lowest risk, incarceration bound, drug and property offenders for placement in alternative (nonprison) sanctions."[18] After examining a random sample of more than two thousand drug, fraud, and larceny cases, the commission produced an actuarial instrument—the Risk Assessment Instrument—that was put into effect in pilot sites in 1997.[19] A follow-up study by the National Center for State Courts of 555 diverted offenders in six judicial circuits in Virginia concluded that the program was a success and recommended the statewide expansion of risk assessment at the sentencing stage.[20]

The legislature then asked the commission in 1999 to develop an actuarial risk-assessment instrument to predict recidivism for sex offenders in order to enhance their sentences under the voluntary guidelines.[21] The commission conducted extensive empirical analyses of felony sex offenders convicted in the Virginia circuit courts.[22] Taking a random sample of 579 felony sex-offenders released from prison between 1990 and 1993, the commission reviewed narrative accounts in pre- and postsentence investigation reports, rap sheets, criminal background records, and other information on the offender and the offense. After two years of data collection and data analysis, the commission produced an actuarial risk-assessment tool.[23]

Virginia's Sex Offender Risk Assessment instrument became operational on July 1, 2001, and since then has been incorporated into the sentencing guideline system for sex offenders. The instrument uses a set matrix to produce a numeric score that is used to classify convicted individuals into one of four risk levels. To calculate the numeric score, judges and sentencing officials are referred to a simple, one-page, fill-in-the-blanks grid. In rape cases, the grid takes account of eight factors concerning the offender and the offense, including the age, education, and employment record of the convict; his relationship to the victim; the location of the offense; and his prior arrest, incarceration, and treatment record. In lesser sexual assault cases (including, for instance, molestation, but excluding "bestiality, bigamy, non-forcible sodomy, and prostitution"), a separate grid asks one additional question concerning the aggravated nature of the sexual battery. In all rape and other sexual assault cases, the responsible criminal justice official fills in the blanks on the worksheet and obtains a risk score that then translates into a risk level. Figure 1.2 shows an example of the grid in the rape cases.

Possible scores on the risk-assessment tool range from 0 to 65. For anyone scoring 28 or more, the sentencing guidelines have been adjusted to ensure that a term of imprisonment will always be recommended.[24] In addition, any score above 28 results in an increased maximum sentence recommendation (without affecting the minimum recommendation). The

Rape ❖ Section A

Offender Name: _____

◆ **Offender's Age at Time of Offense**

Younger than 35 years 12
35 to 46 years 4
Older than 46 years 0

◆ **Less than 9th Grade Education** — If YES, add 4 → [0]

◆ **Not Regularly Employed** — If YES, add 5 → [0]

◆ **Offender's Relationship with Victim**

Victim Under Age 10
Relative 0
Known to victim (not relative or step-parent) 4
Stranger 4
Step-parent 9

Victim Age 10 or more
Relative 2
Known to victim (not relative or step-parent) 3
Stranger 8
Step-parent 2

[0]

◆ **Location of Offense**

Place of employment 0
Shared victim/offender residence 3
Outdoors 3
Motor Vehicle 4
Victim's residence (not offender's) 5
Offender's residence or other residence 9
Location other than listed 3

[0]

◆ **Prior Adult Felony/Misdemeanor Arrests for Crimes Against Person**

Number: 0 Felonies
1 - 3 Misdemeanors 1
4+ Misdemeanors 8

1 Felony
0 - 2 Misdemeanors 5
3+ Misdemeanors 8

2+ Felonies
0 - 3 Misdemeanors 8
4+ Misdemeanors 15

◆ **Prior Incarcerations/Commitments** — If YES, add 3 → [0]

◆ **Prior Treatment**

Prior mental health commitment 0
Prior mental health treatment 2
Prior alcohol or drug treatment 3
No prior treatment 4

[0]

Risk Score →

Risk Level   ☐ 44 or more .... Level 1
(Risk Score)   ☐ 34 - 43 .... Level 2
                ☐ 28 - 33 .... Level 3
                ☐ up to 27 .... No Adjustment

Go to **Section C**

FIGURE 1.2 State of Virginia's sex-offender risk assessment for rape cases

increased sentence recommendation adjustments, based on those scores, are as follows:

0–27   No adjustment
28–33   Level 3   50% increase in upper end of the guideline range
34–43   Level 2   100% increase in upper end of the guideline range
44+   Level 1   300% increase in upper end of the guideline range

These risk levels are meant to "identify those offenders who, as a group, represent the greatest risk for committing a new offense once released back into the community."[25]

Virginia courts have begun to rely on the risk-assessment adjustment to enhance the sentences of convicted sex offenders. In 2004, 233 offenders were convicted of rape in Virginia. Of those, 118, or 50.6 percent, were classified as level 1, 2, or 3 offenders, receiving enhanced sentencing recommendations; the other half had scores under 28 and therefore received no recommended adjustment. Of the offenders classified as level 1, 2, or 3, approximately 20 percent actually received enhanced sentences as a result of their higher-risk status. Of the 166 lesser sexual assault offenders with level 1, 2, or 3 risk, 16.26 percent received enhanced sentences. In addition, in those lesser sexual assault cases, judges followed the recommendation for incarceration in 75 percent of the cases—resulting in a prison sentence rather than probation.[26]

Virginia has also led the country in the area of civil commitment of "sexually violent predators"—a term of art in today's criminal justice system that refers to sex offense recidivists who have been released from prison. John Monahan, a leading expert in the development and use of risk-assessment instruments, notes, "Virginia's sexually violent predator statute is the first law ever to specify, in black letter, the use of a named actuarial prediction instrument *and an exact cut-off score* on that instrument."[27]

That statute, Virginia's Sexually Violent Predators Act (SVPA), enacted in April 2003, provides for the civil commitment of sex offenders who have been convicted of a sexually violent offense and who are deemed likely to engage in sexually violent acts in the future. Offenders are identified for possible commitment based on an actuarial instrument, the Rapid Risk Assessment for Sex Offense Recidivism (RRASOR). This instrument is explicitly mentioned in the SVPA, which directs the commissioner of the Virginia Department of Corrections to identify for review all prisoners about to be released "who receive a score of four or more on the Rapid Risk Assessment for Sexual Offender Recidivism or a like score on a comparable, scientifically validated instrument."[28] The RRASOR consists of four items, scored as shown in table 1.1.[29] The RRASOR score is the sum of the four items. As John Monahan explains, the RRASOR was based on an empirical study of male offenders in Canada. A "score of 4 or more on the RRASOR was associated with a 5-year sex offense recidivism rate of 37 percent and a 10-year sex offense recidivism rate of 55 percent."[30]

The RRASOR is just one among a rash of new actuarial instruments that are intended to predict future sexual violence. Other instruments

TABLE 1.1   **Items and scoring of the Rapid Risk Assessment for Sex Offense Recidivism**

	Score
1. Prior sex offenses (not including index offense)	
None	0
1 conviction or 1–2 charges	1
2–3 convictions or 3–5 charges	2
4+ convictions or 6+ charges	3
2. Age at release (current age)	
More than 25	0
Less than 25	1
3. Victim gender	
Only females	0
Any males	1
4. Relationship to victim	
Only related	0
Any nonrelated	1

Source: Monahan and Walker 2006, 400.

that have recently hit the market include the more comprehensive Static-99, which builds on the RRASOR; the Violence Risk Appraisal Guide (VRAG); the Hare Psychopathy Checklist-Revised (PCL-R); the Minnesota Sex Offender Screening Tool (MnSOST-R); the Sex Offender Risk Appraisal Guide (SORAG); the Sexual Violence Risk-20 (SVR-20); and the HCR-20[31]—as well as, for the first time (released in 2005), violence risk-assessment software called the Classification of Violence Risk (COVR).[32]

These new actuarial instruments have become increasingly popular in civil commitment statutes for sexually violent predators.[33] As Carol Steiker notes, these statutes "were preceded by earlier 'sexual psychopath' or 'psychopathic personality' statutes, which were enacted in a large number of states between 1930 and 1960, but which mostly had been repealed or had fallen into desuetude by 1990."[34] That trend was rapidly reversed in the 1990s, first in Washington state in 1990 and then with a rash of statutes modeled on Washington's. The most notorious of these statutes is the Kansas Sexually Violent Predator Act, which led to the United States Supreme Court's decision in *Kansas v. Hendricks* (1997) upholding such statutes against constitutional challenge.[35] By 2004, sixteen states had enacted legislation similar to the Kansas statute.[36] Of those sixteen, in fact, fourteen enacted such laws in the 1990s.[37] For 2004, "1,632 people have

been adjudicated to be sexually violent predators and are currently confined in psychiatric facilities, with a further 846 people hospitalized for
evaluation and currently awaiting trial for commitment as sexually violent
predators."[38]

CASE 4.   In the early 1970s, DEA agents John Marcello and Paul Markonni started identifying the common characteristics of illegal drug couriers disembarking from planes at U.S. airports.[39] "The majority of our
cases, when we first started," Markonni explains, "[were] . . . based on
information from law enforcement agencies or from airline personnel.
And as these cases were made, certain characteristics were noted among
the defendants."[40] Those characteristics eventually became known as the
drug-courier profile, first implemented in a surveillance and search program at the Detroit airport in the fall of 1974.

The profiles first used in the Detroit experiment were based on empirical observations collected over eighteen months of surveillance at
the airport, observations that focused on the conduct and appearance of
travelers.[41] The experiment was deemed a success, and the program went
nationwide. Between 1976 and 1986 there were more than 140 reported
court decisions involving DEA stops of passengers at airports across the
country based on the drug-courier profile.[42] In the *Mendenhall* case, for
example, the suspect was stopped partly on the basis of the following profile attributes:

(1) The respondent was arriving on a flight from Los Angeles, a city believed
by the agents to be the place of origin for much of the heroin brought to Detroit; (2) the respondent was the last person to leave the plane, "appeared to
be very nervous," and "completely scanned the whole area where [the agents]
were standing"; (3) after leaving the plane the respondent proceeded past the
baggage area without claiming any luggage; and (4) the respondent changed
airlines for her flight out of Detroit.[43]

In 1982, the National Institute of Justice—the research arm of the Department of Justice—conducted a systematic study of the drug-courier
profile.[44] The study required DEA agents to fill out a report for all encounters they instigated and a log of passengers observed during an
eight-month period in 1982. Of about 107,000 passengers observed, the
agents approached 146. According to the report, most of the encounters
(120 of the total 146) were triggered by a combination of behavioral and

demographic peculiarities of the passengers—matches to a profile. The results were as follows:[45]

	Number	Percentage
Total passengers stopped	146	100
No search after questioning	42	29
Consent searches	81	55
Searches with warrant or incident to arrest	15	10
Contraband found or other evidence of crime	49	34

Many consider this study as proof that the drug-courier profile works.

The Rise of the Actuarial

These four episodes reflect one of the most striking trends in law enforcement and punishment at the turn of the twenty-first century: actuarial methods have grown exponentially in the criminal justice system. Risk assessment, algorithms, and criminal profiles now permeate the field of crime and punishment. The same trend is present in a number of other criminal law contexts, including the increased popularity of selective incapacitation, use of risk assessment for setting bail, predictions of future dangerousness in capital sentencing, and the notorious three-strikes laws passed in California and elsewhere.[46] As Jonathan Simon notes, actuarial risk assessment "has become a largely uncontested aspect of a much-expanded criminal process, and it has been entrusted to a range of criminal justice actors, including prosecutors, juries, judges, and administrative appointees."[47] Prediction of criminality has become de rigueur in our highly administrative law enforcement and prison sectors—seen as a necessity, no longer a mere convenience.

I label these methods "actuarial" in a very narrow and specific sense. They are actuarial in that they use statistical methods—rather than clinical methods[48]—on large datasets of criminal offending rates in order to determine the different levels of offending associated with a group or with one or more group traits and, on the basis of those correlations, to predict the past, present, or future criminal behavior of a particular person and to administer a criminal justice outcome for that individual. More formally, as defined by Paul Meehl in 1954, actuarial methods involve "the mechanical combining of information for classification purposes, and the resultant probability figure which is an empirically determined relative frequency"[49]—which explains why actuarial methods are sometimes called "mechanical prediction." Clinical methods, in contrast, rely on subjective expert opinion—or, more formally, "on the subjective judgment of experienced decisionmakers, who evaluate each applicant on an individual basis in light of the experience accumulated by the decisionmaker and his profession."[50]

In other words, actuarial methods in the criminal law use statistical predictions about the criminality of groups or group traits to determine criminal justice outcomes for particular individuals within those groups. The IRS Discriminant Index Function is actuarial in precisely this narrow sense: it uses the greater statistical likelihood of tax evasion among a group of tax filers in order to predict past or current behavior (namely tax evasion) of any particular tax filer and to decide a criminal justice outcome (namely whether or not to audit his or her tax return). The drug-courier profile is actuarial in the same sense: it uses the statistical likelihood of being a drug-courier based on group demeanor evidence in order to predict whether an individual is a drug trafficker and to decide whether to administer a police search. Similarly, parole-prediction instruments use group-trait statistics from large datasets of parolee violation rates to predict whether a particular inmate will violate parole and to determine whether or not to parole that inmate. Selective incapacitation uses group-trait statistics to identify how likely it is that a convict will reoffend, in order to determine how long to incarcerate that individual. The federal sentencing guidelines also qualify as actuarial insofar as they rely on prior criminal history to predict future criminality and to determine the proper length of sentence for each individual convicted of a federal offense.

I use the term *actuarial* in this narrow and limited sense so as not to include many other criminal justice outcomes that are also based on probabilities. The truth is, most criminal justice determinations rest on probabilistic reasoning. The jury's verdict at trial, for instance, is nothing more than a probabilistic determination of prior fact. So is a police officer's determination whether there is sufficient cause to search or arrest a suspect; a judge's decision whether a suspect was coerced to confess; or even a forensic laboratory's conclusion regarding a DNA match—or DNA exoneration. In all these cases, the decision maker renders a factual finding using some legal standard—"beyond a reasonable doubt," "probable cause," "a preponderance of the evidence," or "clear and convincing evidence"—that essentially translates a probability into a legal conclusion.

As Laurence Tribe correctly emphasized, "*all* factual evidence is ultimately 'statistical,' and all legal proof ultimately 'probabilistic,' in the epistemological sense that no conclusion can ever be drawn from empirical data without some step of inductive inference—even if only an inference that things are usually what they are perceived to be." [51]

These more general cases of probabilistic reasoning in criminal law, however, do not qualify as actuarial because they do not rely on statistical correlations between a group trait and that group's criminal offending rate. A jury's decision to overwhelmingly credit (for example, with 98 percent certainty) an eye-witness identification of height, race, and gender (for instance, that the offender was a tall, white male) does create three relevant group traits for purposes of the ultimate probabilistic determination of culpability. If the accused is indeed tall, white, and male, the jury will no doubt consider these group traits in deciding whether the accused is guilty beyond a reasonable doubt—but *not* because of any higher offending rates among tall, white males in general versus, for instance, women; that is, not because of any general correlation between the group trait and offending rates. The jury will use height, race, and gender because those categories help to delimit in probabilistic terms the pool of possible suspects. Similarly, DNA evidence does rely on group traits and group probabilistic determinations but does not concern itself with the offending rates of any particular group—only with probable membership in a group.

I reserve the term *actuarial,* then, for the narrower set of criminal justice determinations that do not rest simply on probabilities but on statistical correlations between group traits and group criminal offending rates. There is absolutely no way to avoid using probabilities in the larger category of criminal justice determinations. A jury's determination of prior fact or a police officer's determination of probable cause is and will always remain—at least in the foreseeable future—an odds determination. In contrast, it is possible—and I argue in this book advisable—to avoid reliance on probabilistic determinations of an actuarial nature.

Locating the Actuarial Debate

Many before me have identified the turn to more administrative and bureaucratic methods in the field of crime and punishment during the latter half of the twentieth century. The transformation of punishment into more regimented forms of discipline was a central theme in Michel Foucault's masterful book, *Discipline and Punish* (1976), and also played a central role in the work of David Rothman, especially *The Discovery of the Asylum* (1971). Prominent scholars and critics of our new disciplinary age have elaborated on these themes, including, most notably, sociologists of punishment such as Katherine Beckett, Stanley Cohen, Malcolm Feeley, David Garland, John Pratt, Nikolas Rose, Jonathan Simon, and Loïc Wacquant, as well as legal scholars such as Albert Alschuler and Paul Robinson.[52]

Much of this contemporary literature interprets the bureaucratic and disciplinary turn as a new and emerging form of political governance. From this perspective, the modern administrative state metamorphosed from a social welfare state in the 1960s and 1970s into a correctional administrative state at the turn of the twenty-first century—a state that manages the margins of society by means of social control and correctional supervision. Other work in this tradition locates the administrative turn within a generalized movement in society toward increased social control—what David Garland refers to as "a culture of control." In a prescient essay in 1992, Malcolm Feeley and Jonathan Simon specifically discuss the rise of actuarial methods as part of what they call an emerging language of "New Penology" that characterizes the entire field of corrections. In more recent research, Jonathan Simon and Tom Baker identify the trend as part of a new paradigm they call "embracing risk"—a cultural trend that is "a reaction against spreading risk" that "consists of various efforts to make people more individually accountable for risk."[53] Still other research associates the trend with new forms of disciplinary power and new means of oppression—what Loïc Wacquant refers to as the fourth and final stage of our "peculiar institutions" of racial oppression in the United States, following on the heels of, respectively, slavery, Jim Crow, and the urban ghetto.[54]

These scholars usually portray the trend toward more managerial and administrative measures in dark terms. But it is not always so. In the criminal profiling context, some researchers favor the use of actuarial methods as a more efficient means of policing. Specifically, in the racial profiling debate, there is an emerging consensus among a group of economists working on econometric models of racial profiling that disproportionate stops of racial minorities may not necessarily reflect invidious discrimination on the part of the police, but may result instead from an honest and good faith effort to increase the success rate of searches.[55] Here, the use of actuarial methods is valuable in enhancing the performance of law enforcement. So long as the differences in offending rates are not spurious, these economists assert, searching a disproportionate number of minorities is only demonstrably problematic (racist) if the rate of successful searches of minority suspects is *lower* than the rate of successful searches of white suspects. Otherwise, disproportionate searches of minorities are consistent with policing efficiency and do not prove invidious bias.

Others defend the rise of the actuarial in more general terms—while carving out specific exceptions for generalizations based on race, gender, or sexual orientation. Frederick Schauer, in his book *Profiles, Probabilities, and Stereotypes* (2003), offers a generalized, but nuanced, defense of actuarial reasoning. "In this book," Schauer explains, "I defend the morality of decision by categories and by generalizations, even with its consequent apparent disregard for the fact that decision-making by generalization often seems to produce an unjust result in particular cases."[56] Schauer defends the nonspurious generalizations that form the basis of many stereotypes and profiles on the ground that they tend to be prudent and efficient and, in many cases, morally appropriate.

Schauer sets aside generalizations based on race, gender, and sexual orientation as most often problematic, but argues that these are the exceptional cases of generalization and that it would be wrong to generalize from them to the vast majority of nonspurious generalizations. "[T]he problems with racial profiling are not problems of profiling, with race being merely an example. Rather," Schauer claims, "the problem is about race and not about profiling. Once we comprehend the ubiquity and inevitability of profiling, we see that the objection to racial profiling, when valid, will treat the racial component and not the profiling component of racial profiling as crucial."[57] A lot of profiles, Schauer suggests, are simply prudent and efficient ways of dealing with a complex world.

Schauer contends that he is in the minority and that, today, it is far more fashionable to favor the individual and frown on stereotypes. There has been a turn to the particular, he maintains, especially in law, where the focus is always on "this particular case" or "these particular facts": "The modern idea is that *this* particular case, or *this* particular event, is what is most important, and that making the right decision for *this* case or on *this* occasion is the primary building-block of just behavior."[58]

To be sure, Schauer is correct that the language of legal decision making is strongly case-specific. The common law method of applying precedent to the specific facts of a case in controversy *is* a particularistic endeavor. But outside the narrow confines of the judicial decision-making process, in the larger area of law and policy—in this case, in the area of criminal law enforcement, sentencing, and corrections—the vast majority of our judgments tend to fall in the category of the generalization, stereotype, and profile.

Moreover, except for racial profiling, we tend to be comfortable with such generalizations. The general public and most academics generally support the use of prediction in policing. To most, it is a matter of plain common sense. Why would we not use our best social science research and most advanced statistical methods to improve the efficiency of police investigations, sentencing decisions, parole practices, treatment efforts, and general correctional procedures? Why not deploy our wealth of new knowledge to fight crime more effectively? It would be crazy not to take advantage of what we now *know* about the propensity to commit crime.

Contrary to what Schauer suggests, his is the majority view. It has become, today, second nature to believe that actuarial methods enhance the efficiency of our carceral practices with hardly any offsetting social costs— with the exception, for some, at least publicly, of racial profiling. To most people, criminal profiling on a nonspurious trait simply increases the detection of crime and renders police searches more successful, which inevitably reduces crime rates. Although racial profiling may be suspect because of the sensitive issues surrounding race, other forms of criminal profiling—profiling the rich for tax audits, for instance—do not raise similar concerns. There, the calculus is self-evident: the detection of crime will increase, the efficiency of law enforcement will improve, and, through the traditional mechanisms of deterrence and incapacitation, crime rates will decrease. No one in their right mind—at least, no reasonable, law-abiding, and rational person—would oppose using the most rigorous and advanced social scientific methods where it matters most, namely, in preventing innocent victimization, injury, and harm. Most people believe this. In fact, even the staunchest and most vocal academic opponents of racial profiling today support criminal profiling more generally.[59]

Against Prediction

And they have it all wrong. This book challenges our common sense. It challenges the generally accepted view that most actuarial methods are beneficial to society. The problems that plague racial profiling, I contend, are problems about criminal profiling more generally. Actuarial methods in the criminal justice field produce hidden distortions with significant costs for society.

This book however does not simply identify, label, or trace the actuarial turn but goes on to argue *against* the actuarial turn. And the argument does not rest on the traditional value associated with individualized decision making or the importance of paying attention to the particular—it is not about the particular versus the general. Others, indeed, have engaged the debate at this level. Barbara Underwood, in her noted *Yale Law Journal* article, "Law and the Crystal Ball," argued that "The choice of a statistical method rejects the flexibility and individualized judgment of a clinical method in favor of general rules, explicit criteria for decision, lower administrative costs, and aggregate accuracy."[60] Others as well have engaged the discussion at this abstract level of debate—of individualization versus generalization. It would be wrong, however, to take the bait: the fact is that the actuarial impulse derives precisely—and very paradoxically—from the *desire to individualize*. The actuarial represents, in the eyes of its proponents, the highest fulfillment in the aspiration to respect the individual. It is the very concern or obsession with the individualization of punishment that led many down the actuarial path to the difficulties that we are in today. It is the desire to be more accurate *in the individual case* that triggered the turn to prediction.

No, this is not a debate about the particular versus the general. Not at all. Those categories are too closely woven together—and far too abstract philosophically to be of any use. This is a debate about mathematics, identifiable social costs, and social and epistemic distortions. Let me begin to sketch these in order.

First Critique: The Mathematics of Criminal Profiling

One of the strongest arguments for the use of actuarial methods in criminal law derives from rational-action theory and rests on both a deterrence and efficiency rationale: assuming that potential offenders respond rationally to the probability of being apprehended and punished, then focusing law enforcement efforts on members of a higher-offending group will both (1) decrease the offending rates of those higher-offending group members because it will increase the cost of their deviant behavior and (2) increase the efficiency of the police in detecting crime and apprehending offenders or increase the efficiency of sentencing authorities in meting out punishment and deterring future offending. In its purest form, the economic model of crime suggests that the government should target members of a higher-offending group until that group's offending rate has fallen to the same level as that of the general population. At that point, the government has maximized the effectiveness of its law enforcement practices by both detecting the maximum amount of crime and maximally reducing offending among the higher-offending group.

Policing and Law Enforcement

The trouble is, the deterrence and efficiency arguments in the policing context—and the associated criminal profiling model—rest on a crucial assumption that is unfounded and probably wrong in many circumstances, namely, that the different groups react similarly to the change in policing. This is what is called, in more technical jargon, the relative elasticity of offending to policing—or simply the elasticity—of the two groups. The elasticity of offending to policing is the degree to which changes in policing affect changes in offending. So, for instance, if the IRS targets drywall contractors or car dealers for audits—as they did in the mid-1990s[61]—we would expect less tax evasion by drywall contractors and car dealers. We assume that their tax evasion is elastic to policing and will fall with the enhanced scrutiny. It is the elasticity that reduces the offending of the targeted group—those identified by the actuarial method.

But even if we assume elasticity of offending to policing among drywall contractors and car dealers, society as a whole will only benefit from their decrease in tax evasion if the nonprofiled groups do not begin to evade their tax burden more, in absolute numbers, because they feel immune from scrutiny—in other words, because of *their* elasticity to reduced enforcement. Accountants, bankers, and CEOs, for instance, may realize that they are less likely to be audited, and may therefore cheat more on their taxes. What matters, then, is the *comparative elasticity* of the two groups—profiled (drywall contractors and car dealers) and nonprofiled (accountants and bankers). If the targeted group members have lower elasticity of offending to policing—if they are less responsive to policing than other groups—then targeting them for enforcement efforts will likely increase the overall amount of crime in society as a whole because the increase in crime by accountants and bankers would exceed the decrease in crime by drywall contractors and car dealers. In raw numbers, the effect of the profiling will be greater on the more elastic nonprofiled and smaller on the less elastic profiled.

To make matters worse, there is no good reason to assume that the higher-offending group is as responsive to policing as the lower-offending group. The two groups do, after all, offend at different rates—otherwise

the police are profiling on a spurious trait. Whether the different offending rates are due to different socioeconomic backgrounds, to different histories, cultures, or education, nonspurious profiling rests on the accurate
assumption that members of one group offend more than those of another, holding everything else constant. If their offending rates are different, then why would their elasticity be the same? If, for instance, they offend more because they are socioeconomically more disadvantaged, then
it would follow logically that they may also have less elasticity of offending
to policing because they have fewer alternative job opportunities. Some
drywall contractors, for instance, may only be able to pay their bills and
employees by evading taxes, whether because of their socioeconomic condition or because the tax laws were not written with the economics of
drywall contractors in mind.

I develop this first critique of the mathematics of the actuarial with
equations and graphs in chapter 4, but the intuition is simple: if the profiled group has lower elasticity of offending to policing, profiling that
group will probably increase the overall amount of crime in society. The
reason is that profiling the target group will reduce their offending rate
but will increase the offending rate of the nonprofiled group. Because of
the different elasticities and the fact that profiled groups are usually small
minorities, the raw increase in offending among the nonprofiled group
will be greater numerically than the raw decrease in offending of the profiled group. And the clincher is, we have no good idea how the elasticities
compare. We presume that the different groups have different offending
patterns, but we have no idea whether that also means they have different
elasticity. We have no knowledge—we're in the dark. So why, you might
ask, should we assume that profiling will be efficient in deterring crime?
Why should we assume that predictions of criminality and actuarial analyses will benefit society as a whole? There is no good reason. The fact that
we do believe tells us something about *us* rather than anything about *them*.
It tells us something about *our desire* to believe, *our desire* to predict, *our
desire* to know the criminal. We are predisposed to *wanting* the actuarial
model to be right—regardless of the empirical evidence.

Sentencing Matters

This first critique of the mathematics of actuarial prediction is intuitively
clear in the context of policing, racial profiling and, more generally, criminal profiling as a law enforcement tool. As long as there is reason to believe

that offending rates differ among different groups—whether racial groups, classes, or employment clusters—there is also reason to suspect different elasticities of offending to policing. And that's all it takes: if there are indeed lower elasticities among the profiled group, there is no good reason to believe that profiling will reduce overall crime in society.

It may be tempting to think that none of this applies to the situations of sentencing, parole, and punishment—or especially to the case of selective incapacitation. After all, lengthening the sentence of a likely repeat offender based on membership in a high-recidivist group is clearly not going to increase overall crime in society. By incapacitating that person for a longer period of time, we have *prevented* his future offending, not increased his future criminality. And certainly there is an important difference between the use of actuarial methods in the policing context on the one hand and in the sentencing context on the other. In the policing context—that of racial profiling, the IRS Discriminant Index Function, or drug-courier profiles—the actuarial tends to focus on predicting the *past or present* criminal behavior of a group in order to determine a criminal justice outcome, such as whether to search, audit, or investigate. In contrast, in the sentencing context—that of parole prediction, sentencing guidelines, or selective incapacitation—the actuarial methods tend to focus on predicting the *future* criminal behavior of a group in order to determine a criminal justice outcome, such as whether to parole or how long to sentence. Shouldn't this difference—however slight—change the crime and punishment equation?

Though perhaps counterintuitive, the answer is no. The very same problems with the deterrence and efficiency rationales plague the sentencing context as well. I want to be careful here to distinguish the argument in rational-action theory from the argument of incapacitation—which I address in my second critique and in more detail in chapter 5. Using actuarial methods will certainly have an incapacitation effect and prevent the likely recidivist from offending again in the future. This will have a favorable effect on overall crime rates, as well as a number of costs, which I discuss later. But for now, I intend to address only the deterrence and efficiency arguments, and in this respect, there is no difference between the policing and sentencing contexts. If we assume rational action and have reason to believe that different offending rates and elasticities exist between high-risk recidivist inmates and low-risk first-offender types, then the use of actuarial methods will affect them just as it does the different populations in the racial profiling example: low-risk first-offenders

are likely to offend *more* on a first-time basis if their sentences are relatively reduced as compared to average sentences, and their greater overall
offending is likely to outweigh the reductions in crime by less elastic,
high-risk recidivists, resulting in higher overall crime in society—if indeed
these first-offenders are more elastic to sentencing. The analysis is identical—though perhaps less intuitive. Let me slow this down and take it
frame by frame.

For purposes of this first critique, I am again assuming a rational-actor
model. I assume that people are deterred by more punishment, by a longer sentence, by the higher costs associated with conviction of a crime. In
terms of deterrence, the case of parole is in fact the perfect illustration
of increasing or decreasing the cost of crime. The parole determination
affects the length of the expected prison sentence: granting parole reduces it, and denying parole extends it. If offending is elastic to punishment—the core assumption of the economic model of crime pioneered
by Gary Becker and Richard Posner at the University of Chicago—then
we expect that, in response to parole profiling, offending by first-time offenders will increase (since they now expect relatively less punishment),
and offending by recidivists will decrease (since they now expect longer
punishment).

The case of parole prediction, it turns out, works in exactly the same
way as criminal profiling: overall crime in society would increase if the
elasticity of recidivists is lower than that of first-time offenders—which
is easy to assume if they do in fact have different offending rates. The
intuition, again, is simple: recidivists are a small minority of the population, and they may be less responsive to punishment; if so, first-time and
one-time offenders may engage in more criminal behavior overall due to
the comparatively reduced cost of crime, and their offending may outpace
any gains achieved with regard to the recidivists. Again, this assumes the
rational-action model: it assumes that individuals will commit more crimes
if the relative cost of crime declines. The result is exactly the same, and
the consequences equally troubling: depending on comparative elasticities, the use of actuarial measures, whether at sentencing or in policing,
may increase overall crime in society.

Second Critique: An Overlooked Social Cost

Now, not all proponents of the actuarial, however, believe in rational choice.
Many endorse the turn to actuarial methods on the basis of the incapacita-

tion rationale discussed in passing earlier: if we audit more tax filers who are more likely to be evading taxes, we will detect and punish more tax evaders; if we stop and search more motorists who are more likely to be transporting drug contraband, we will detect and punish more drug couriers; if we deny parole to more convicts who are more likely to reoffend, we will incapacitate more hard-core offenders. Setting aside the potential adverse deterrence effects on overall crime discussed in the first critique, incapacitation theory suggests there will simply be more detection of crime — and, correlatively, fewer undetected tax evaders, fewer drug-couriers on the highways, and fewer recidivists preying on society. In short, actuarial methods help to incapacitate more offenders with the same resources; and even more offenders with even more resources. Thus, regardless of whether actuarial instruments encourage or deter crime, their use is likely to increase the success rate of searches, audits, and parole decisions, and therefore produce enhanced incapacitation of criminal offenders. And this, of course, is a good thing.

But all good things come at a price, and the key question is, at what price? As a preliminary matter, in addressing the incapacitation argument, it is important to distinguish between, on the one hand, the more ordinary element of incapacitation that we achieve by shifting fixed resources from incarcerating "ordinary" citizens to incarcerating "recidivists" and, on the other hand, the massive, multibillion-dollar investment we have made and continue to make as a nation in *additional incapacitation*. The last quarter of the twentieth century witnessed an exponential increase in the number of persons in federal and state prisons and local jails, and under federal and state supervision. Federal and state prison populations nationwide grew from less than 200,000 in 1970 to more than 1,300,000 in 2001 with another 630,000 persons held in local jails. At the turn of the twenty-first century, more than two million men and women were behind bars in this country.[62] And the research of Steven Levitt and others has shown that this exponential increase in the prison population during the past thirty years has had an effect on crime.[63] The best evidence suggests that approximately one-fourth of the crime drop in America during the 1990s was attributable to the prison expansion.[64]

In discussing the benefits of incapacitation, then, it is crucial to differentiate between this massive social investment in prisons and the more ordinary, minor incapacitation effects flowing from the mere shift in resource allocation associated with the use of actuarial methods in parole or sentencing. With regard to the first—the infusion of resources associated with the exponential increase in prison populations—any analysis of the benefits of prediction must ask, first, what role prediction played in the equation, and, second, whether those resources could have been better spent on other crime-fighting practices, such as increased police presence, more drug-treatment programs, free abortions, mandatory military conscription, or other policies. If we as a society are willing to pour tremendous resources into fighting crime, then we have to weigh the role and use of actuarial methods against the provision of free abortions or whatever else apparently reduces crime. This is a much larger and more complicated calculus.

In contrast, the ordinary incapacitation effects are likely to be relatively small. Generally, they will be washed out by the effect of any change in offending: there is no incapacitation effect if you imprison a recidivist versus an ordinary citizen *once the rates of offending have equalized*. But what if the offending rates do not equalize? What if offenders are entirely irrational and completely unresponsive to policing?

Incapacitation in Policing and Law Enforcement

Even assuming that there are incapacitation gains, the question then is, at what price? The benefits—for instance, a marginal increase in the detection of tax evaders or drug couriers—are not achieved without an offsetting cost. An evaluation along these lines, naturally, calls for cost-benefit analysis. And here I would emphasize one particular cost that is generally overlooked—largely because it focuses on the guilty more than on the innocent. This is what I call the "ratchet effect."

Under normal conditions, the use of accurate prediction instruments will have a distortive effect on the targeted population, a distortion that ultimately operates as a ratchet. The distortion occurs when successful profiling produces a supervised population that is disproportionate to the distribution of offending by racial group. To give a quick illustration, if the targeted population represents 25 percent of the overall population, but 45 percent of the offending population—in other words, targeted persons are offending at a higher proportion than their representation in the general population, and the profiling is nonspurious—then if law enforcement profiles the targeted population by allocating, say, 45 percent of its resources to the targeted population, the resulting distribution of offenders will be approximately 67 percent targeted and 33 percent nontargeted individuals—as I demonstrate in chapter 5 with equations, illustrations, and graphs.[65] The disparity between targeted persons representing 45 percent of actual offenders but 67 percent of detected offenders represents a distortion that has significant negative effects on the minority population. This distortion will produce a ratchet effect if law enforcement then relies on the evidence of the resulting correctional traces—arrests, convictions, supervision—in order to reallocate future law enforcement resources. And the fact is, given the paucity of reliable information on natural offending rates, law enforcement relies heavily on arrest, conviction, and supervision data in deciding how to allocate resources. This, in turn, accelerates the imbalance in the prison population and acts like a ratchet. How serious the distortion and ratchet effect will be depends, again, on subtle variations in comparative elasticities and offending rates. But some distortion is practically inevitable.

The reason, in essence, is that when we profile, we are essentially sampling *more* from a higher-offending population. Instead of sampling randomly—which would net a proportional representation of the offending population—we are sampling in greater numbers from the pool of higher offenders and thereby skewing our sample results. Somewhat counterintuitively, the only way to produce a prison population that mirrors the offending population is to sample randomly from the general population—to engage in essentially random searches, or random audits, or random policing. Barring randomization, our results will be distorted.

What the ratchet effect does is to disproportionately distribute criminal records and criminal justice contacts, which has terrible effects on the profiled population. Disproportionate criminal supervision and incarceration reduces work opportunities, breaks down families and communities, and disrupts education. It contributes to the exaggerated general perception of the criminality of the targeted group in the public imagination and among law enforcement officers. This, in turn, further undermines the ability of the targeted group to obtain employment or pursue educational opportunities. It may also have a delegitimizing effect on the criminal justice system that may lead disaffected members of the profiled group to greater disregard of the criminal law in a kind of backlash against perceived or real prejudice. And it may corrode community-police relations, hampering law enforcement efforts as members of the profiled community become less willing to report crime, to testify, and to convict. In this sense, the use of actuarial methods in the criminal justice context can affect a person's life-course in extremely detrimental ways. It can result in self-fulfilling effects on employment, education, and family. And it powerfully reinforces what Dorothy Roberts eloquently describes as "America's longstanding association between blackness and criminality."[66] The ratchet effect is a significant cost of actuarial justice.

Punishment and Sentencing Matters

The ratchet effect is most clearly evident in the context of racial profiling—or criminal profiling in law enforcement more generally. There, disparities between the offending population and the prison population have significant symbolic effects: the black face of the incarcerated inmate, the silk stocking of the tax evader, the blue collar of the drywall contractor, these are all powerful symbolic products of the ratchet effect. It is less obvious, though, how this critique applies to the sentencing and punishment contexts—to the slightly different use of actuarial methods to predict *future* criminality or recidivism in determining sentencing outcomes. But here also—again somewhat counter-intuitively—the critique applies with equal force to these other forms of actuarial justice.

Consider the case of likely recidivists who are disproportionately denied parole or sentenced under enhanced statutes and are therefore disproportionately represented in prisons. The symbolic message associated with this disproportionate representation—that is, with the *correct* perception that prisons are "filled with recidivists"—is the following: "If you offend once, you are likely to offend again; if you offend twice, it's all over." The result is a powerful symbolic message that turns convicts into even worse offenders—in the public imagination, but also in the reentry context. This too will have the effect of a self-fulfilling prophecy, reducing employment and education opportunities upon reentry. In fact, there is no good reason to expect that the effect will be any different than the effect of racial profiling on the association between blackness and criminality.

There are, naturally, other costs to consider. I emphasize the ratchet effect, but only because others have properly emphasized other costs. Some point to the reduced obedience to law resulting from the perceived illegitimacy of the criminal justice system. Psychologist Tom Tyler has demonstrated how perceptions of the legitimacy of criminal justice procedures affect the willingness of citizens to abide by the law.[67] Other commentators have properly emphasized the link between targeted enforcement—particularly in the case of racial profiling—and increased police misconduct. So, for instance, the implementation of a targeted policing strategy focused on increased stop-and-frisk searches on the streets of New York

City in the 1990s resulted in disproportionate searches of African American and Latino citizens, as well as a sharp rise in the number of civilian complaints of police misconduct, including brutality.[68] Still others have focused on the direct costs to families and the incarcerated.[69]

These costs need to be weighed against the incapacitation effects. The fact is, the incapacitation argument—though incredibly powerful, given our recent experiment with exponential prison growth—is typically boundless. Standing alone, it is indiscriminate. It does not tell us *how much* incapacitation is socially optimal. It has no internal limiting principle. Taken to its extreme, the incapacitation argument favors full incarceration of, say, the entire male population between the ages of 16 and 24. That, of course, is absurd—or at least, should be absurd. But what it points to is that, ultimately, we must be willing to perform a cost-benefit analysis *on crime*. We must be willing to undertake a cost-benefit analysis to determine whether the potential reduction in crime attributable to an incapacitation effect outweighs the costs associated with the increased incarceration, including the possible ratchet effect.

Third Critique: Shaping Conceptions of Justice

There is one other troubling dimension to the actuarial turn—one that lends itself less easily to mathematical proof, to demonstration, to equations that show how the use of prediction instruments may actually increase the social cost of crime. This last dimension maps less easily onto graphs, formulas, and tables—to visual representations of ratchet effects and other externalities. But it is no less troubling.

The actuarial turn has begun to shape our conception of just punishment. The use of predictive methods has begun to distort our carceral imagination, to mold our notions of justice, without our full acquiescence—without deliberation, almost subconsciously or subliminally. Today, we have an intuitive but deep sense that it is just to determine punishment largely on the basis of an actuarial risk assessment. We have come to associate the prediction of future criminality with just punishment. This seems intuitively obvious, even necessary. Who on earth would object? From a social welfare perspective, it makes all the sense in the world to try to reduce social harm and injury—and thereby decrease the cost of crime—by using prediction instruments, by identifying ahead of time the more likely offender.

But, the fact is, we have *chosen* this conception of just punishment. We have chosen it from among a wide spectrum of theories of punishment. It is not natural, obvious, or necessary. We embrace it from a variety of equally attractive conceptions of justice. We chose it as against a rehabilitative model and as against a more strictly retributivist model.

Or rather, *it chose us*. Remarkably, what triggered the shift in our conception of just punishment from notions of reform and rehabilitation to notions of risk assessment in the late twentieth century is *the production of technical knowledge:* our progress in techniques of predicting criminality is what fueled our jurisprudential conception of just punishment. It is possible to trace the shift in our conception of justice to the popular rise of actuarial methods and their implementation. Incapacitation as the model of punishment grew in part because it is *what we began to know technically*.

What we have done, by and large, is to allow the actuarial to displace earlier conceptions of justice and just punishment. Today, the amount of punishment that we mete out is determined largely by the inmate's likelihood of reoffending. The criminal sentence is pegged primarily to prior criminal history and the likelihood of recidivism as measured by instruments such as the LSI-R or the Salient Factor Score, or by more intuitive metrics such as prior history of institutionalization and drug use.

If we had developed a way to measure intentionality—a thermometer for intent—there would likely be a push to punish based on moral culpability. If we had developed a way to measure deterrence, we would more likely see a push toward deterrence. If we had developed a more rigorous way to equate moral blame and punishment (through better measures of pain), there might be a renewed push toward retributivism. This is, in some sense, remarkable—and deeply troubling. It is deeply troubling because it demonstrates the influence of technical knowledge on our sense of justice. We have become slaves of our technical advances.

We have come to believe that it is just for punishment to relate primarily to the statistical probability of reoffending. This breaks the link between just punishment and the heinousness of the offense, and thereby attenuates the retributive element of punishment. It also breaks the link to the deterrent effect of punishment. Conceptually, one could imagine that more punishment may be necessary to deter the convict who is likely to reoffend, but this is purely speculative. There is no direct connection to a determination of the punishment necessary to deter the commission of the crime in question. It also attenuates the link to rehabilitation and reformation, especially where the actuarial method relies on static past indices such as prior criminal record.

What is left, from the perspective of punishment theory, is incapacitation (constrained by prison-bed capacity). This represents a negative form of incapacitation: the idea is not that we should compute optimal incarceration in order to efficiently incapacitate likely future offenders; instead, the idea is that we need to kick people out of prison, and we might as well send out those who are less likely to offend again. It is an incapacitation approach by default, in the absence of a better system.

Utilitarian theories of deterrence fall aside because there is no good measure of deterrence. It is not yet possible to calibrate properly the quantum of punishment necessary to deter any particular individual. There is no way to mete out punishment in a scientific way along these lines. We can argue about whether there should be more punishment generally or less, but these are crude arguments indeed. Retributive theories also subside for lack of a good metric. Here too, there is no technical knowledge on the subject. No thermometer to measure intent. No blood test for villainy. Rehabilitation proves inadequate because it cannot be shown to be technically right.

The only technical knowledge we have developed is simple binary prediction based on objective measures. Simplistic, basic, but predictive—it can be proven right. It can be validated, tested, replicated. It is a form of technical knowledge that makes possible "right" and "wrong" answers. In the end, it is this quest for technical knowledge that has helped shape our contemporary notions of justice. This is a story of technical knowledge taming just punishment.

This is true as well in the policing context more generally. What happens is that we begin to feel justified about punishing the members of the targeted group because they offend at higher rates. We begin to feel that they are legitimate targets of punishment not because of their offending activity, but because of the characteristic trait that we profile. Take, for example, the case of profiling the rich for IRS audits or minorities for drug searches. At some point, the lines begin to blur, and we begin to feel morally righteous about going after the rich for tax evasion or minorities for drug trafficking because we begin to associate the profiled trait with suspicion. Not everyone, of course, does this. But there is a tendency. It begins to alleviate our scruples, even if slightly. We are just a little bit less disturbed—even though we may be creating huge disparities in the prison or correctional contexts. We become a little bit less troubled by the collateral consequences, precisely because we begin to perceive these groups as more criminal.

Shades of Gray

Naturally, the force of these three critiques depends on a number of variables—or what I call dimensions in chapter 8. The first critique, for instance, rests predominantly on an assessment of the relative elasticities and offending rates between profiled and nonprofiled groups. As such, it is a powerful critique of racial profiling in the war on drugs. As I show in chapter 7, there is every reason to believe that the offending differentials, if any, are slim and that the profiled population—African Americans and Hispanics—is less elastic to policing than nonprofiled whites, primarily because of reduced employment opportunities. On the basis of these facts, a racial profiling strategy that communicates to the general public that the police will focus more intensely on minorities is likely to increase the overall commission of drug and other offenses, which of course undermines the entire law enforcement objective. On the other hand, where offending differentials are large and the nonprofiled group is inelastic to policing—as is true, for instance, with regard to profiling men in cases of stranger rape—the first critique may not apply.

Similarly, the second critique involves a cost-benefit weighing, and is stronger where the purported benefits relate to serious crimes—to severe physical and psychological injury or harm. Again, in the case of stranger rape, the benefits of crime reduction, if any, may outweigh the ratchet effect on men since the offense itself involves such serious physical injury. The force of the argument will also depend on the specific group trait that is being profiled. To many, the use of race or class may be problematic, though other profiles, such as marijuana-leaf bumper stickers or tattoos, may be less troubling. While the critiques developed in these pages apply with different force in different contexts, they raise questions and develop methods of analysis that apply to the use of all actuarial measures in the criminal law.

The arguments will also resonate differently among different audiences. The first argument, for instance, is addressed primarily to a rational-choice audience. It responds to the deterrence and efficiency rationales for using actuarial methods and, accordingly, assumes the premises of rational-action theory. Specifically, it accepts, for purposes of argument, that individuals will offend less if the potential cost of offending (here, the probability of being detected) increases. It is, in this sense, an internal critique of the rational-choice argument for using actuarial methods. Naturally, many are skeptical of the rational abilities of criminal offenders, especially when they act in the heat of passion or under the influence of drugs or alcohol. To many readers, the very premise of rationality may be questionable and the entire discussion of elasticities—of the responsiveness of individuals to police profiling—may sound off the mark. But this is only the first argument, one that is specifically addressed to a rational-choice perspective.

The second argument takes on the incapacitation rationale for using actuarial methods—namely, the idea that by investigating and enhancing the punishment of those most likely to offend, the police and courts will incapacitate a greater number of criminal offenders and thereby reduce future crime. This argument is indifferent to the assumptions of rational action, and focuses exclusively on costs and benefits: the ratchet effect represents a significant cost—one among others—that must be weighed against any potential benefits of crime reduction. While avoiding rational-action assumptions, it nevertheless embraces a consequentialist framework that assesses the advantages and disadvantages of using actuarial methods. Many readers may be skeptical of such a utilitarian approach and believe instead that certain jurisprudential or moral principles—what are often referred to as "deontological" principles—should trump the maximization of social welfare. I argue, however, that it is relatively easy to articulate these deontological claims within a consequentialist framework by spelling out the principle and locating it within the cost-benefit equation. So, for instance, in this book I expressly invoke a central moral intuition of the criminal law, namely, the idea that similarly situated offenders should be treated alike regardless of race, gender, or class. I privilege this principle of just punishment at the expense of selective incapacitation and also rehabilitation (both of which naturally derive from predictions of future criminality and dangerousness). I locate this principle within the structure of the cost-benefit equation, and argue that it often, though not always, favors resisting the actuarial. The second argument is thus neither purely consequentialist nor purely principled. But I recognize that it will sometimes resonate better with utilitarians and, at other times, better with deontologists.

The third argument raises larger issues of social theory, exploring whether the increased use of actuarial methods and the perception of their scientific objectivity have led us, as contemporary subjects, to embrace theories of just punishment that draw on prediction. It asks whether the technology itself and our desire to know the criminal have made more natural the act of sentencing convicted criminals on the basis of their predicted future dangerousness. It raises the specter and explores the possibility that the use of actuarial methods in punishment and policing promotes conformity in society—that it tends to shape social reality. Paradoxically, I argue, we are attracted to the actuarial in criminal law largely because we believe it helps us get closer to the truth, closer to reality, closer to knowing each individual, each delinquent. We believe that it helps us align our carceral practices with social reality. But surprisingly, quite the opposite is true: social reality aligns with our carceral practices. The reliance on actuarial methods actually ends up shaping the social world by accentuating and aggravating the correlations between group traits and criminality. The repeat offender, who indeed may have a higher risk of recidivism, is stigmatized by the profiling and thus has an even harder time with reentry, resulting in an even greater probability of reoffending. The black male youth, who may indeed have a higher risk of offending, is also stigmatized by the profiling and has an even harder time obtaining legitimate employment, resulting in an even greater probability of delinquency. The distortive effects of the ratchet become self-fulfilling prophecies that shape reality. Naturally, these social-theoretical questions do not lend themselves easily to a calculus of social welfare maximization. They do not translate well into consequentialist or even deontological arguments. As a result, the social theoretic explorations in the third critique may not resonate as well with an audience vested in rational-action theory, guided by welfare maximization, or adhering strictly to certain moral and jurisprudential principles.

Outline of the Book

My goal, however, is to address all three audiences. I realize this is ambitious, but I believe that it is possible to cast the debate in a way that speaks in one voice to different constituencies. In part, I try to achieve this goal by speaking with different audiences at different times. So, for instance, the first critique—internal to rational-action theory—expressly addresses rational-choice proponents, and I encourage those who do not subscribe to—or even bristle at—rational-action assumptions to be patient. The second critique does away with assumptions of rationality.

More importantly, I try to achieve my goal by deploying a transparent and loose consequentialist framework. I set out as explicitly as possible the consequences of believing any particular assumption and map out all the different interests and values that may be affected. So, for instance, I articulate how a ratchet might occur, along what lines it will tend to stigmatize, and what consequences it may have for those stigmatized. My goal is not to convince everyone that the costs associated with a particular ratchet necessarily outweigh the possible benefits, but to set up a framework that allows you, the reader, to weigh these costs and benefits according to your own judgment and assessment of social welfare, and according to the value that you place on any jurisprudential or moral principles. By deploying a flexible and transparent consequentialist framework, I hope to invite welfare-maximizers, deontologists, and social theorists to the table.

Part 1 of the book begins, then, by tracing the rise of the actuarial in the field of crime and punishment. Chapter 2 explores the birth of the actuarial in American criminal law, focusing on the development and use of the first actuarial instrument by Ernest W. Burgess in the late 1920s. Chapter 3 documents the ascendance of the actuarial paradigm, focusing on a wide range of predictive tools in criminal law and punishment. I explore the use of actuarial methods in the larger context of selective incapacitation and the resulting reliance on sentencing guidelines that mete out punishment based on prior criminal history. I also describe a gradual shift in law enforcement toward the increased use of criminal profiling—from the early instances of hijacker profiles developed in the 1960s to the more frequent use in the 1970s of drug-courier and alien-smuggler profiles and the more frequent use of profiling in the last quarter of the twentieth century. The historical trajectory reflects the breadth of the actuarial paradigm—from preliminary investigation, through sentencing, and ultimately to the prison-release decision.

Part 2 sets forth my three critiques of the actuarial turn. Chapter 4 critically analyzes the mathematics of profiling, with special attention to the assumption of equal elasticity at the heart of the economic models of racial profiling. Chapter 5 discusses the distortion and potential ratchet effect of targeted enforcement on profiled populations. Chapter 6 explores the relationship between technical knowledge and our conceptions of just punishment.

Part 3 then lays out the different dimensions that affect the force of the arguments and discusses the general implications for punishment and policing. In chapter 7, I examine the specific case of racial profiling on the highways. This area of actuarial policing has received the most sustained attention in the social science and policy literature, and as a result, it is the area where there is the most empirical evidence. In chapter 8, I present some generalizations about the force of the arguments and set forth a framework for analyzing the use of actuarial methods. The critiques are strongest in the case of profiling for less serious crimes and depend on the comparative elasticities and offending rates. I set out these different dimensions as a way to assess predictive instruments. I then briefly touch on what is perhaps today the most controversial contemporary debate in actuarial justice, namely the profiling of young, Arab-looking men in the international war on terror. Chapter 9 concludes the book by sketching the contours and benefits of a more randomized universe of crime and punishment.

My overarching goal in this book is to question the strong appeal of the actuarial and to excavate the virtues of the random. For it is only by randomizing law enforcement that we will promote the central moral intuition of just punishment, namely, that everyone who commits a crime should have the same likelihood of being apprehended, regardless of race, ethnicity, gender, class, or any other irrelevant group trait. Randomization is the only way to achieve a carceral population that reflects the offending population. It also avoids the risk that profiling will ultimately increase rather than decrease the overall amount of crime in society.

Like the term *the actuarial,* the term *randomization* has a very limited and narrow definition. Randomization does *not* mean pulling criminal sentences from hats or using a lottery to determine parole. In the context of policing initiatives, the idea is to use random sampling for investigatory purposes—for instance, to randomly sample IRS filings for purposes of auditing, or to use numerical sequencing for purposes of consensual car searches. In the context of sentencing and parole determinations, randomization means something quite different. It means eliminating the effects of predictions of future dangerousness.[70] It means imposing a sentence based on an independent standard—for example, the harm principle, retribution, the seriousness of the offense—and then avoiding the effects of prediction by eliminating any prediction-based device. The baseline presumption in the criminal law and its enforcement should favor randomized policing and punishment.

PART I
The Rise of the Actuarial Paradigm

It may be possible to date the birth of the actuarial in American criminal justice to 1933, the year that Ferris F. Laune, PhD, assumed the newly created post of Sociologist and Actuary at the Illinois State Penitentiary in Joliet. Ferris Laune would be the first to officially implement the "Burgess method" of parole prediction and to produce the first *prognasio,* a report based on group-trait offending rates evaluating an individual prisoner's probability of violating parole if released. Perhaps it was earlier, in 1927, the year the noted University of Chicago sociologist Ernest W. Burgess devised the prediction instrument that Laune would use, or even 1923, the year that Sam B. Warner, director of the Committee on Criminal Records at the Institute of Criminal Law and Criminology in Eugene, Oregon, set out to identify group factors that would predict individual success or failure on parole.[1]

Or perhaps the actuarial—the *rigorous* actuarial impulse—should be traced to a relatively unknown researcher laboring at the Iowa Child Welfare Research Station in 1923 by the name of Hornell Hart. His precursor, Sam Warner, had, after all, simply eyeballed the factors. He had failed to apply "accurate statistical tests," Hart insisted.[2] With the new tools and techniques of statistics, Hornell Hart claimed, it might be possible to do better, to create an actual prediction instrument, to produce "a prognostic score for each man coming up for parole."[3] With a little more rigor and state-of-the-art statistical methods, Hart wrote, a parole board might be able to devise and implement "the same scientific procedure employed by insurance companies when they estimate the probable cost of insuring new applicants on the basis of their experience with the past death rates of insured persons of similar characteristics."[4]

Ernest Burgess took note and would eventually lead the way.[5] In the next several decades, with Burgess at the helm, many of the great sociologists cut their teeth on prediction instruments. Albert J. Reiss Jr., the luminary University of Chicago sociologist, wrote his dissertation on the "Burgess method" of parole prediction.[6] Reiss's thesis, entitled "The Accuracy, Efficiency, and Validity of a Prediction Instrument," was itself a statistical analysis of prediction instruments completed in 1949 under the supervision of Professor Burgess himself. Lloyd Ohlin, the noted sociologist and, later, professor at Harvard Law School, updated the Burgess method and published the first manual for parole prediction in 1951.[7] Daniel Glaser, the reputed University of Southern California sociologist, wrote his dissertation, "A Reformulation and Testing of Parole Prediction Factors," [8] in 1954, under the supervision of both Burgess and Reiss.

Numerous others wrote dissertations on the topic of prediction instruments. George B. Vold's 1931 dissertation, "Prediction Methods and Parole," landed him a position at the University of Minnesota.[9] Courtlandt Churchill Van Vechten Jr. wrote his dissertation, "A Study of Success and Failure of One Thousand Delinquents Committed to a Boys' Republic," under the supervision of Burgess and Edwin Sutherland in 1935.[10] Ferris Laune, the first actuary, called his dissertation "A Technique for Developing Criteria of Parolability," and dedicated it "To Professors Ernest W. Burgess, Edwin H. Sutherland, Arthur J. Todd in Gratitude for Aid and Encouragement." [11] Also in 1935—a fertile year for such treatises—Charlotte Ruth Klein at the University of Chicago wrote "Success and Failure on Parole: A Study of 160 Girls Paroled from the State Training School at Geneva, Illinois." [12] George A. Lunday in 1949 wrote his dissertation, "A Study of Parole Prediction," under the supervision of Ernest Burgess with guidance from Albert Reiss, Clifford Shaw, and Henry McKay.[13]

Parole-prediction research had become an engine of scholarly production—of dissertations, conference papers, journal articles, and monographs. The sociology department at the University of Chicago and the Illinois Department of Corrections were at the epicenter of the research, and the state of Illinois was at the forefront of practice, implementing the very first actuarial parole-prediction instrument in the early 1930s and pioneering the methods throughout the next three decades. The expansion and gradual nationalization of the actuarial movement was a much slower process. It was not before the 1960s—about thirty years later—that a second state would decide to experiment with a parole-prediction instrument. In the early 1970s, the federal parole authorities developed and implemented the Salient Factor Score, a leaner, seven-factor prediction tool, stimulating greater interest in using prediction instruments. California followed suit, bringing with it a tidal wave of adoptions in the late 1980s through the 1990s. Although the historical sequence is somewhat disrupted in the 1970s by the "truth in sentencing" movement and the repeal of parole in many states, still, by 2004, twenty-eight states used risk-assessment tools to decide whether an inmate should receive parole. Of the thirty-two states that still maintained an active parole system for new convictions in 2004, twenty-three, or 72 percent, used a parole-prediction instrument.

In the two chapters of this first historical section, I trace the development of the actuarial in American criminal justice, beginning with the earliest experiments in parole prediction. I explore the parallels and links to the other actuarial methods that developed during the later part of the twentieth century, especially sentencing reform and, in the area of policing, criminal profiling, starting with the airline-highjacker profile in the 1970s and running through the drug-courier profile of the 1990s. The federal government's intervention in the parole area in the 1970s—especially its development of the Salient Factor Score—heavily influenced research and practice in the areas of federal sentencing, as well as, more generally, state sentencing, "three-strikes" laws, and enhancement statutes. I demonstrate how all these apparently disparate developments— from parole decision making to sentencing guidelines and street-crime profiling—use similar methodology with common antecedents. Parole-prediction research in the 1930s may well have been the precursor, but it spawned a whole series of prediction techniques and triggered growing interest in the area of group prediction and individual forecasting. The methods and approaches that laid the foundations for parole prediction fueled developments in many other areas of sentencing and policing, creating a large field of actuarial methods in crime and punishment.

Locating the Actuarial

Before proceeding, though, it is important to locate this turn to actuarial methods within the larger context of the nineteenth and twentieth centuries. Somewhat paradoxically, the actuarial impulse was an outgrowth of a turn to individualization in law at the dawn of the twentieth century—not a turn to the general, but a turn to the particular. The desire to predict human behavior in the criminal context, surprisingly, grew out of a new aspiration to individualize punishment—an aspiration that marked the early twentieth century in Europe and the United States.

On the Continent, Raymond Saleilles, a prominent French jurist, published an influential book, *The Individualization of Punishment,* in 1898
that advocated what its title suggests: "[T]here is today," Saleilles declared,
"a general movement having as its object the goal of detaching the law
from purely abstract formulas which seemed, to the general public at least,
to divorce the law from human contact."[14] This general movement represented a new orientation of judicial institutions and practices toward the
individualization of punishment. "One cannot fix punishment in advance
in a rigid or strict manner, nor legally regulate it in an inflexible manner,
since the purpose of punishment is an individual one that must be achieved
by means of specific policies appropriate to the circumstances, rather than
by the application of a purely abstract law ignoring the varieties of cases
presented," Saleilles explained. "This adaptation of punishment to the individual is what we call, today, the individualization of punishment."[15]

A similar development characterized British penality at the beginning
of the twentieth century, as others have noted.[16] The modern break in
England—a break from the Victorian penal system—can be traced to the
period 1895–1914. The earlier Victorian penal system, well in place by the
1860s, increasingly relied on the prison as the primary mode of sanction-
ing, but its focus on the prison was not individually tailored to the convict.
"[A]lthough Victorian prisons exhibited a close and detailed form of *discipline* or 'dressage,' they did not manifest a concern with *individualisation.* On the contrary, each individual was treated 'exactly alike,' with no
reference being made to his or her criminal type or individual character."[17]
It was also marked by a legal-formalist view: punishment in the period
was viewed exclusively as a legal event that made no room for other disciplinary knowledges like psychiatry, sociology, medicine, or economics.[18]
This Victorian model was displaced during the early twentieth century
by penological modernism.[19] The range of sanctions was expanded to include probation and various types of reformatory institutions, and new
agencies were created to administer these forms of correction. The objectives of the penal system diversified, and there developed "a general
objective . . . of *assessment and classification.*"[20] Psychiatric and medical
judgments were allowed to inform these processes. The goal, however,
was to individualize punishment. This produced "a move *from individualism to individualisation,* which alter[ed] the penal field fundamentally."[21]

In the United States, leading legal scholars and positivist criminologists
joined efforts to identify the causes of crime and to prescribe individualized treatment. The National Conference on Criminal Law and Criminol-

ogy, held in Chicago in 1909, marked this turn to individualization. In a statement representing the views of the core legal academics, law professors Ernst Freund and Roscoe Pound of the University of Chicago and several eminent colleagues announced a new era of individualized, remedial, penal treatment that would address the individual causes of crime in each and every delinquent.[22] According to Freund and Pound, the new science of crime had deep implications for criminal law: "Modern science recognizes that penal or remedial treatment cannot possibly be indiscriminate and machine-like, but must be adapted to the causes, and to the man as affected by those causes," they declared. "Thus the great truth of the present and the future, for criminal science, is the individualization of penal treatment—for that man, and for the cause of that man's crime."[23]

Roscoe Pound wrote an introduction to the American translation of Raymond Saleilles's book, *The Individualization of Punishment,* which appeared in 1911 and announced the need for greater individualization of punishment in the United States. "What we have to achieve, then, in modern criminal law is a *system* of individualization," Pound declared. "More recently throughout the world there has come to be a reaction against administration of justice solely by abstract formula," Pound explained. "In the United States it is manifest in a tendency toward extra-legal attainment of just results while preserving the form of the law. . . . The movement for individualization in criminal law is but a phase of this general movement for individualizing the application of all legal rules."[24]

This turn to individualization rested precisely on statistical progress, which appeared to increase the ability to predict human behavior—an outgrowth of the developments in statistics and data collection from the nineteenth century. As Ian Hacking persuasively demonstrates in *The Taming of Chance,* the laws of probability had largely displaced the laws of necessity in much of Western discourse by the late nineteenth century, especially in the area of crime and punishment.[25] This paradigm shift would allow for more individualization through increased knowledge and predictability. Somewhat paradoxically, the turn from natural law to probabilistic reasoning allowed for more control over the individual. It served to discipline uncertainty, as Nikolas Rose suggests, "by bringing uncertainty under control, making it orderly and docile."[26] Rose explains:

> Risk thinking tames chance, fate, and uncertainty by a paradoxical move. By recognizing the impossibility of certainty about the future, it simultaneously makes this lack of certainty quantifiable in terms of probability. And once one

has quantified the probability of a future event's occurring, decisions can be made and justified about what to do in the present, informed by what now seems to be secure, if probabilistic, knowledge about the future.[27]

Predictive knowledge about the future—the laws of chance—allowed for more control over individual behavior.[28] "The cardinal concept of the psychology of the Enlightenment had been, simply, human nature," Hacking explains. "By the end of the nineteenth century, it was being replaced by something different: normal people."[29] And by the dawn of the twentieth century, the laws of chance had become autonomous in many political and social milieus, in the sense that they could be used to predict and to explain phenomena.

Most of these laws of chance were first observed, recorded, and publicized in the area of delinquency—crime, suicide, madness, prostitution. Adolphe Quetelet, the great Belgian statistician, would write as early as 1832 of the statistical regularities concerning crime. He described the phenomenon as a "kind of budget for the scaffold, the galleys and the prisons, achieved by the French nation with greater regularity, without doubt, than the financial budget."[30] Karl Pearson, the famous statistician and eugenicist who assisted Charles Goring at the turn of the twentieth century, would summarize Goring's findings about "the English criminal as he really is" as "not absolutely differentiated by numerous anomalies from the general population, but relatively differentiated from the mean or population type, because on the average he is selected from the physically poorer and mentally feebler portion of the general population." "The criminal," Pearson explained, "is not a *random* sample of the general population, either physically or mentally. He is, rather, a sample of the less fit moiety of it."[31] Many years before that, Madame de Staël would observe that "there are cities in Italy where one can calculate exactly how many murders will be committed from year to year."[32]

The first inroads into chance were made in the area of crime and punishment. The proliferation of numbers helped create the categories of the normal, criminal, and pathological in the nineteenth century.[33] And the laws of chance were precisely what grounded the turn to the individualization of punishment at the turn of the twentieth century. The movement was premised on the new science of crime—on the idea that there are identifiable causes of crime that we can discover and study. The notion of individualization of punishment rested on the newly discovered correlations between criminality and home conditions, physical traits, genetic makeup, and neighborhood environment. These correlations offered an alternative to the classical, or utilitarian, model of crime, which emphasized the rational decision-making process of the delinquent and the need to calibrate the cost of crime against the expected gain from the delinquent behavior.

The National Conference of 1909, which gave rise to the American Institute of Criminal Law and Criminology, was an outgrowth of the statistical discoveries emerging from positive criminology. As Freund, Pound, and their colleagues explained, "This truth [the statistical laws of criminality] opens up a vast field for re-examination. . . . And it means that the effect of different methods of treatment, old or new, for different kinds of men and of causes, must be studied, experimented and compared. Only in this way can accurate knowledge be reached, and new efficient measures be adopted."[34] The development and refinement of criminology in the nineteenth century fueled the movement toward individualized punishment, which in turn energized the actuarial impulse.

The individualization movement, in sum, rested on a probabilistic model that attempted to predict the likely success of different treatment interventions on the basis of inferences from an accumulation of data points about a particular individual. This new era of individualization gave rise to departments of corrections, the juvenile court, and treatment and rehabilitation programs—and to the actuarial model. By 1970, the desire for individualized sentencing had led practically every state to adopt a system of indeterminate sentencing. Legislatures would set maximum sentences, inmates would become eligible for parole after serving about a third of the maximum sentence, and parole boards would decide when inmates were released. Minimum sentences imposed by the legislature were rare and generally frowned upon.[35] The stage had been set for actuarial instruments.

CHAPTER TWO

Ernest W. Burgess
and Parole Prediction

The actuarial impulse was strong in the 1920s, especially at the University of Chicago in both the departments of sociology and law. There was a thirst for prediction—a strong desire to place the study of social and legal behavior on scientific footing. A certain euphoria surrounded the prediction project, reflecting a shared sense of progress, of science, of modernity. One after another, in measured tones, professors and researchers preached the mantra of prediction. Doctoral students seemed mesmerized. George Vold, a sociology PhD student at the University of Chicago, captured well, in reasoned and deliberate cadence, the sentiment of the times: "The principle of predicting future human conduct . . . seems sound and worthwhile. Insurance companies have built up large business enterprises on this principle of predicting the future from the past. The present study, in common with those of Burgess and of the Gluecks, seems to establish the validity of that general principle for other phases of human conduct as well."[1]

One of the leading masterminds behind this turn to prediction, Ernest W. Burgess, expressed the sensibility and aspirations of the older generation when he declared, "[T]here can be no doubt of the feasibility of determining the factors governing the success or the failure of the man on parole."[2] Burgess, at the time, was emerging from the shadow of his preeminent colleague and coauthor, Robert Park, and from the Chicago ecological paradigm. Drawing on sociology's new statistical rigor, Burgess helped refocus the study of sociology on the individual and was a leading figure in the structural transformation that took place in the discipline during the 1930s and 1940s. As Andrew Abbott and James Sparrow suggest, "by the mid 1950s large portions of sociological writing were not socio-logical at all in the older sense. They were not studies of social groups, group conflict, or group relations. Rather they were studies of atomized individuals characterized by variable properties and located in a larger and indefinite field—'the collectivity,' 'the social group,' 'the society.'"[3] Burgess's research on prediction—not only in the context of parole, but also later with regard to marital and occupational success—helped steer sociology in that direction.

The First Inroads into Chance

A similar movement toward the individual occurred in the practice of cor-rections and criminal law. By the 1920s, the ideal of individualized pun-ishment was being carried out predominantly by means of indeterminate sentencing and delegation of authority to parole boards. Judges essen-tially extricated themselves from the day-to-day business of individualiza-tion by sentencing convicted offenders to a wide range of imprisonment and affording corrections administrators and parole boards wide discre-tion to decide about rehabilitation and release. This created the possibil-ity of a natural experiment: collect data on the convicts who are paroled and those who are not, figure out what factors led to parole, and then test whether those factors correlated with success or failure on parole.

Ernest Burgess was not the first to get the idea. That distinction prob-ably goes to Sam B. Warner, who in 1923 published a study on the factors determining parole at the Massachusetts Reformatory and their correla-tion with success on parole.[4] To be sure, some earlier studies had begun to tackle the task of predicting success or delinquency. Some had attempted to link success to measures of intelligence, race, age, previous record, and length of stay in the institution. Researchers Pinter and Reamer had made a study in 1918 of 26 delinquent girls, trying to link their future success to coefficients of mental ability; and F. L. Heacox, a year earlier, had studied 143 paroled, delinquent boys to see whether their success correlated with race, age, prior criminal record, home conditions, length of stay in refor-matory, or mental intelligence.[5] But Warner was the first to try to measure on a very large sample the specific factors that lead to success or failure on parole.

Warner, who was at the University of Oregon Law School at the time, reviewed the parole records of former inmates of the Massachusetts refor-

matory for young men in the period 1912–1921 and selected 680 records
of former inmates—300 cases of parole success, 300 cases of parole failure, and 80 cases of prisoners not paroled.[6] At the time, Massachusetts
law did not prescribe which factors the board of parole should consider
in determining whether to grant parole, but the board had promulgated
rules that listed the nine factors it would consider. From his review of the
files, Warner determined that the board actually relied on only four pieces
of information: the nature of the offense, the convict's conduct in the reformatory, his prior criminal history, and the length of time he had spent
in the reformatory.[7] Warner compared the parole outcomes—with failure
defined as violating parole and all other cases defined as successes—with
sixty-six background characteristics that he was able to obtain from the
parole and reformatory records.[8] Most of these characteristics involved
information that the parole board had but did not consider in making
their decisions. For each factor, Warner tabulated the percentage distribution within the three categories of successful parolees, failed parolees,
and prisoners not paroled. So, for instance, for race, Warner created the
following tabulation:[9]

	Successes	Violators	Not Paroled
15. *Color*			
White	96	96	91
Black	3	3	9
Not answered	1	1	0

Warner then eyeballed all the factors—literally just looked them
over—and concluded that they tended not to have much predictive value.
About sixty of the traits that were collected by the department of corrections but ignored by the parole board were, in his words, "worthless as
a basis of parole."[10] "[P]oor as the criteria now used by the Board are,
the Board would not improve matters by considering any of the sixty-odd
pieces of information placed at its disposal, which it now ignores." Of the
four traits that the board did consider, Warner only credited one: prior
criminal record. The type of crime, the conduct in the reformatory, and
the length of time in the reformatory all turned out to be useless when it
came to predicting success. The only "true, but by no means infallible,
criterion of success on parole" was the prisoner's prior criminal history.
Warner's conclusion: "By and large, the more crimes a man has committed, the more likely he is to commit another."[11]

Ultimately, Warner did not take the next step and either statistically analyze the discrepancies or create a prediction table. These tasks were taken up by Hornell Hart, who replicated Warner's study with an eye to creating a prediction tool—what he called "a prognostic score."[12] Unfortunately, Hart had none of the underlying data and thus had to rely on the Warner's summary tables. As a result, Hart could only hypothesize about the predictive tool and could not test it against other sets of parolees. Nevertheless, Hart's work was insightful and laid the statistical groundwork for the later Burgess study. Hart, in effect, produced the first prognostic parole-prediction tool. As Sheldon and Eleanor Glueck observed in 1930, "So far as we have been able to ascertain, Hornell Hart was the first person to suggest the possibility of adapting to penology the methods used in the insurance field for predictability."[13] Walter Argow of Yale University would also trace the idea of actuarial devices in the parole context to Hart: "The idea of the use of statistics for the prediction of success on parole was first brought forth by Hornell Hart in an article in . . . 1923."[14]

At the time, Hart was a researcher at the Iowa Child Welfare Research Station with a particular expertise in new and emerging statistical methods. He believed that "through scientific utilization" of the data already collected by Warner, the parole board in Massachusetts could reduce by one half the percentage of parole violations. Hart was a harsh critic of Warner, casting Warner as statistically ignorant and flat-out wrong: whereas Warner had concluded that the available information could not improve the success rate of parole and that new methods of data collection were necessary, Hart declared that "both of these conclusions are in error, and . . . the Board could greatly improve its parole results by proper utilization of the information already at its disposal." The real problem, Hart emphasized, was Warner's "failure to apply accurate statistical tests."[15]

Hart used Warner's summary tables. Applying what were then new statistical methods, Hart determined that the chance was less than 1 in 1,000 that there would be a 4 percent disparity as between successful and failed parolees on a single factor. He then assembled a list of thirty factors for which "the probability that the observed contrast is due to chance is less than about one in 100."[16] On the basis of these thirty factors, Hart proposed constructing a "prognostic score" for each inmate, which would allow the board, in his words, to read a report that would say something like this:

Jim Jones has a prognostic score of 93 points. In the past experience of the Board among the men with prognostic scores in the neighborhood of 93 points, only 19 percent have violated their parole.

Will Smith has a prognostic score of 21 points. In the past experience of the Board among men with diagnostic scores close to 21 points, 80 percent have violated their paroles.[17]

On the basis of these predictions, Hart argued, the board could then grant or deny parole, producing in the process a much lower rate of recidivism.

Warner and Hart's work stimulated research in the following years, some following the path of Warner, others that of Hart. Among the former was a sociologist by the name of Helen Leland Witmer of the University of Minnesota who studied the parole system of the state of Wisconsin, publishing her findings in 1927. Her sample was drawn from both a prison and a reformatory for men, and consisted of 443 successful parolees and 164 failed parolees over the period 1917–1925. Witmer looked at fifteen characteristics and created separate tables with subcategories of degree or values.[18] She used the same method as Warner, comparing the percentage of the successful inmates against the failure rates in each subcategory of all the tables, looking for significant disparities, and using the "eyeball" approach. Not surprisingly, Witmer referred to Warner's article, but not to Hart's.

Among those following Hart was Howard Borden, a director of statistics at the Department of Institutions and Agencies in Trenton, New Jersey. Borden published a study in 1928 inspired, in his own words, "by the critique by Hornell Hart."[19] Borden looked at data on 263 consecutive parolees from a reformatory for young men who were paroled between 1923 and 1924. Borden created tables for about twenty-six factors, and then offered separate tables for twenty-six characteristics showing the tabulation of the interrelations with success. Borden reached some surprising conclusions, including, for instance, the fact that "the lower the intelligence the more likely a boy is to succeed."[20] Ultimately, though, Borden did not attempt to formulate an expectancy table or a prognostic tool. But the groundwork was laid.

Professor Ernest W. Burgess

In 1927 and 1928, Ernest W. Burgess, law professor Andrew Bruce of Northwestern University, and Dean Albert Harno of the University of Illinois College of Law conducted extensive research on parole procedures at the request of the chairman of the Illinois parole board. Two other researchers—who would play important roles in the subsequent history of

parole in Illinois—were part of the research team: John Landesco, described as "an expert in vocational education and an experienced student
in criminology," was appointed field-worker in the study, and Clark Tibbitts was selected "as research assistant upon certain special phases of the
subject." [21] The research project involved extensive interviews, a study of
parole records, a review of the entire criminal and penal records of 3,000
paroled men, and physical visits to the penal institutions. It resulted in
a 306-page report published in May 1928 in the *Journal of the American
Institute of Criminal Law and Criminology*. [22]

Parole in Illinois

In Illinois, indeterminate sentencing replaced fixed sentencing gradually
over the course of the late nineteenth century. The first experiment occurred in the context of a juvenile reform school for boys in 1867, and indeterminate sentencing was formalized for male juvenile offenders in 1891
and for female juvenile offenders in 1893. For adults, good-time credits
began to surface around 1863, and a general adult parole system was enacted in 1895. Indeterminate sentencing was enacted by the Illinois legislature in 1917 (for crimes other than treason, murder, rape, and kidnapping)
to make the parole system effective. [23] By the time the Burgess report was
written in 1928, the idea of indeterminate sentencing was well established.
As law professor Andrew Bruce declared, somewhat enthusiastically,

> The wisdom of the policy of indeterminate sentence and the parole, if properly
> administered, is now almost universally recognized, not only in America, but
> throughout the civilized world. The policy can hardly any longer be classed as a
> product of unenlightened sentimentalism.
>   In 1922 only four states of the American Union were without either the in-
> determinate sentence or the parole system. In 1925 the laws of forty-six of the
> forty-eight American states made definite provision for the release of prisoners
> on parole, only Mississippi and Virginia having no such laws.
>   In 1925 also, the International Prison Commission, meeting in London with
> fifty-three nations represented, adopted a resolution favoring the indeterminate
> sentence and the parole laws and recommending their adoption to the Govern-
> ments of the civilized world. [24]

The parole system, however, was marred from its inception by a lack of
resources and adequate staffing. The Illinois parole system was severely

understaffed until at least 1927. The 1897 act that created indeterminate sentencing in Illinois provided for the creation of a state board of pardons consisting of three persons who were charged with overseeing all paroles in the Illinois system.[25] This lasted until 1917 when the legislature created a Department of Public Welfare and incorporated the board of pardons and paroles as a subdivision.[26] However, the legislation did not state who should compose the parole board, and the responsibility for determining parole fell entirely onto the supervisor of paroles and three appointed assistants.[27]

In 1920, the state began performing psychiatric examinations of prisoners and using those evaluations to aid in the parole decision. As Ferris Laune explains, "Men were classified into different personality-groups, and on the basis of this classification modified by general impressions obtained during the course of the interview plus a general interpretation of the prisoner's background, a prognosis was made." This was, however, most often a formality. The real decision was based on an interview. Laune continues, "The principal method of selection, however, was the Parole Board interview—thorough or superficial as the case might be—with the type of crime dictating, to a large extent, the term of incarceration, and no logical bases being employed to account for the impressionistic opinions formed."[28]

With more than seven thousand persons incarcerated in the mid-1920s, the parole process was haphazard at best. The board was not able to review all the cases and would only cursorily review those it did, spending two or three minutes with the inmate and reading primarily the state's statement and the synopsis of the case. The parole board had little time to spend with any one case, and the materials they received were often a jumbled mess. The report indicates that researchers

> found the material in the "jackets" in confusion. No effort had been made to file in orderly sequence and no list or inventory was kept with the "jackets" of the documents and papers they contained. All the material was merely jammed in together.... [O]ften it took a member of the [research team] a day, sometimes two and even three days, to disentangle the mass of material in one of these jackets, to rearrange it, and to read and digest it.[29]

According to the Burgess report, few inmates were paroled, and those who were, were "'guessed out of' prison."[30] "The responsibility imposed on the Supervisor and the labor required of him by such numbers was too great. It was resulting," the report concluded, "in superficiality."[31]

Lack of resources and short staffing were not unique to Illinois; they were common among state parole agencies. The parole system in California, for instance, was initiated around 1893. Although parole began to be used increasingly—with the percentage of releases through parole increasing from 7 percent in 1907 to 35 percent in 1914—it was not until 1914 that a state parole officer was appointed.[32] It took another fifteen years to assemble a field staff.[33] "In California supervision was largely a matter of paperwork since there was no real field staff until the 1930s, except for the single parole officer headquartered in San Francisco."[34] Most other states suffered from understaffed, resource-deprived parole organizations that did not fulfill the promise of rehabilitation. As David Rothman has written regarding the parole system in the Progressive Era,

> No sooner does one plunge into the realities of parole than the question of its persistence is further complicated, for one uncovers almost everywhere a dismal record of performance. Neither of the two essential tasks of parole, the fixing of prison release time or post-sentence supervision, was carried out with any degree of competence or skill. Amateurs on parole boards reached their decisions hastily and almost unthinkingly, while overworked and undertrained parole officers did little more than keep a formal but useless file on the activities of their charges. Whatever the reasons for the survival of parole, they will not be found in the efficient or diligent administration of the system.[35]

In Illinois, the legislature passed a bill in 1927 at the urging of the supervisor of paroles, directing that the parole board consist of a supervisor and nine members. A separate appropriation was made for this board, which allowed for, among other things, investigators to conduct fieldwork on the outside regarding parole candidates.[36] This expanded board formed subcommittees of three members that sat three days a week at the three separate primary institutions in Illinois—Joliet, Menard, and Pontiac.[37] The subcommittees at the institutions, and then the full committee reviewing the recommendation, would consider whether parole was appropriate.

When these additional resources and staff were made available, the decision to parole began to approximate a clinical judgment. It rested on empirical data and represented a subjective judgment as to whether an inmate would be a good candidate for parole. In response to the question "On what principally do you base your judgment in granting or refusing a parole?" the chair of the parole board explained,

First, the man's history; his education; his apparent mentality; his physical condition; his attitude towards discipline and toward society, as evidenced by his institutional record. In addition to that, his former habits; his associates; the environment under which he grew up; all the facts and circumstances relating to the man's history before he committed the crime, so far as it is available to us, his commission of the crime and his conduct since and while being punished; and his learning of one or more useful trades while confined. His attendance at school or church in the institution, and finally our own conclusion after talking to the prisoner in great detail and examining him several times before he is given a final parole.

It is very rarely the case that we talk to a prisoner less than three or four times now before he is given his final parole, so your question is a hard question to answer. It is the net collected judgment of the ten men after reviewing all the facts and circumstances with reference to the individual. In other words, we try to fit the punishment and the scheme of reformation to the individual and not the crime after the inmate or the prisoner has served what is believed to be a reasonable punishment, as a deterrent to others, or other would-be criminals, for the crime committed.[38]

To give the flavor of the written rationale offered by the board, here are two examples of the reports from the subcommittees:

A member of this Committee [research team] has read several hundred of the subcommittee's reports. The following may be taken as typical: "(No.) ——, (Name) ——. Received ——, 1923, from —— County upon a plea of guilty to burglary and larceny. Paroled, conditional that he be deported to Canada and that the authorities come after him. He is a Canadian. Did one term in the Ontario prison. Has been in this institution more than four years and we believe he is now entitled to release. There is in the record the necessary order for his deportation to Canada, both our own government and the Canadian government having consummated arrangements for bringing that about whenever he is released by the Illinois authorities.

"(No.) ——. (Name) ——. Received ——, 1926, from —— County upon plea of guilty to burglary and larceny. Not ready for parole. Young —— has done a term at the Vandalia State Farm, was once tried and acquitted for the killing of his step-father. He is regarded by the authorities as a pretty bad young man. We have paroled his associate ——, because he has had no previous record, but we feel that this boy should have a substantial lesson to the end that he will learn that he cannot do the things that he has been doing so flagrantly."[39]

These typical subcommittee reports are revealing. The parole decision turned largely on the state attorney's statement to the parole board. As the Burgess report noted, "[N]o recommendations, evidence or other material that come before the Parole Board have greater influence with it than the statements concerning prisoner coming from the trial judges and the State's Attorneys."[40] And these statements from the judge and state's attorney were, in the view of the research team, most often inadequate to address issues of rehabilitation and often factually wrong. In addition, a decision to parole had an important political dimension. The research team found that a large number of the jackets contained evidence of lawyers employed to obtain favorable parole decisions or "of a prominent politician at work on the case." "[T]here is abundant evidence in the records that the efforts of those who are induced to champion the cause of the prisoner are often placed upon other grounds than those of the facts."[41]

Recommendations

The research team expressed some skepticism about the parole board's functioning, suggesting that some of its rationales and written reports "lacked discrimination" and were somewhat impressionistic. Dean Harno recommended "respectfully" that the parole board members "become thorough students of the theory of parole" and that "the mastering of the theory will materially enrich their judgment." The research team hinted that the data on which the parole board made its decisions were often "very scanty" and suggested that the board conduct more independent investigation to obtain a full dossier on the individuals. "With more funds at its disposal than formerly," Dean Harno emphasized, "the Board needs to put skilled investigators with training in sociology and social work on the job to get this information. The Committee commends this to the Board as an essential feature supplementing the other material it has at its disposal."[42]

The Burgess Study

Ernest Burgess went further, however, and recommended a more scientific approach. Burgess conducted a study of three thousand inmates paroled in the four-to-five years prior to December 31, 1924,[43] and sought to find a statistical relationship between success on parole (as defined by the limited achievement of not violating parole) and some two dozen independent variables. The idea was to see which factors were associated with the likelihood of success on parole—as Warner and Hart had done before.

The twenty-two variables included such things as an inmate's father's race or nationality, social type, mental age, personality type, and psychiatric prognosis, in addition to the circumstances of the crime and prior criminal records.[44] With regard to national origin, Burgess discovered "the smallest ratio of violations among more recent immigrants like the Italian, Polish and Lithuanian," and "the highest rates of violation among the older immigrants like the Irish, British and German."[45] Burgess did not report any correlations along race lines, other than to observe that "[t]he group second in size was the Negro with 152 at Pontiac, 216 at Chester, and 201 at [Joliet]."[46] Burgess also relied on a number of other unique variables, including social type and psychiatric personality type. Burgess's table from the report regarding social type is shown in table 2.1. Table 2.2 shows the data regarding psychiatric personality type.

Burgess concluded that the parole board could use identifiable factors to achieve much greater predictive abilities. "[T]here can be no doubt of the feasibility of determining the factors governing the success or the

TABLE 2.1 **Social type in relation to parole violation: Violation rate by institutions**

Social type	Pontiac	Menard	Joliet
All persons	22.1	26.5	28.4
Hobo	14.3	46.8	70.5
Ne'er-do-well	32.8	25.6	63.0
Mean citizen	—	30.0	9.5
Drunkard	37.5	38.9	22.7
Gangster	22.7	23.2	24.1
Recent immigrant	36.8	16.7	4.0
Farm boy	11.0	10.2	16.7
Drug addict	4.3	66.7	83.3

Source: Bruce, Burgess, and Harno 1928, 261.

TABLE 2.2 **Psychiatric personality type in relation to parole violations: Violation rate by institutions**

Personality type	Pontiac	Menard	Joliet
All persons	22.1	26.5	28.4
Egocentric	24.3	25.5	38.0
Socially inadequate	20.0	24.7	22.6
Emotionally unstable	8.9	—[a]	16.6

Source: Bruce, Burgess, and Harno 1928, 269.
[a]number of cases insufficient for calculating percentage.

failure of the man on parole," Burgess wrote. "Human behavior seems to be subject to some degree of predictability."[47] He elaborated as follows:

> Many will be frankly skeptical of the feasibility of introducing scientific meth-
> ods into any field of human behavior. They will dismiss the proposal with the
> assertion that human nature is too variable for making any prediction about
> it.... [But i]t would be entirely feasible and should be helpful to the Parole
> Board to devise a summary sheet for each man about to be paroled in order for
> its members to tell at a glance the violation rate for each significant factor.[48]

Burgess recommended that the parole board create a multifactor test to determine the likelihood of parole success. This Burgess did himself, creating a twenty-one-factor test to grade each inmate, and applying the test to his sample of three thousand cases. He assigned points for each factor on which an inmate was above the average (high likelihood of success) and then ran an analysis to determine the percentage of violators. Those with the highest number of above-average factors (16–21) had the lowest violating rates (1.5 percent), and those with the lowest number of above average factors (2–4) had the highest offending rates (76 percent).

"[P]redictability is feasible," Burgess declared. "The prediction would not be absolute in any given case, but, according to the law of averages, would apply to any considerable number of cases."[49] He recommended that the parole decision be based on a multifactor analysis using these variables, and urged the supervisor of paroles to create an actuarial table of success expectancy. On the basis of his research, the full research team declared in its final recommendations to the chair of the parole board:

> [T]he Committee recommends that the Parole Board seriously consider the
> placing of its work on a scientific basis by making use of the method of statisti-
> cal prediction of the non-violation of parole both in the granting of paroles and
> in the supervision of paroled men. One competent statistician could compile
> the necessary information from the records and still further develop the ac-
> curacy of prediction by this new method.[50]

Actuarial Implementation

Burgess's actuarial system was tested almost immediately by the criminologist at the Joliet penitentiary in the period 1932–1933. As Laune reported in 1936, "Some application of the Burgess findings for purposes of prediction was made during 1932–1933 by the Division of the Criminologist for the State Department of Public Welfare at the Joliet Penitentiary."[51] Clark Tibbitts conducted additional research and tweaked the Burgess system slightly.[52]

Then fortune struck. "With the nation-wide Democratic landslide in the elections of 1932, Illinois elected a Democratic Governor, Henry Horner. Among the early appointments of Governor Horner's administration was that of John Landesco as a member of the Parole Board."[53] Recall that Landesco had been one of Burgess's research assistants.[54] At Landesco's urging, the Illinois legislature passed a bill in 1933 providing for the hiring of sociologists and actuarians "to make analyses and predictions in the cases of all men being considered for parole."[55]

Ferris F. Laune, PhD, was hired as sociologist and actuary at the Illinois State Penitentiary at Joliet.[56] As Laune explained, "It was definitely understood that the work of these men would be something more than mere routine application of the experience tables already developed by Burgess and Tibbitts; they were expected to engage in further research for the purpose of expanding these tables, to refine the factors which had gone into them, and to improve the methods of prediction in any other way which seemed possible."[57]

By 1935, the Burgess method was being used in the field. In fact, it was the only parole-prediction tool being used at the time in the country.[58] By 1939, the Illinois parole board was assisted by three sociologists and actuaries—as well as five investigators and approximately sixteen stenographers, file clerks, and watchmen.[59] There was also a division of parole supervision with fifty-four employees in Chicago and a slightly smaller office in Springfield.[60] The actuaries would compile the inmate's information and prepare a report—a "prognasio"—that predicted the likelihood of success on parole. The prognasio was "based on the revised Burgess 'probability' scale."[61]

The Burgess model was relatively primitive, insofar as it merely added up the variables to produce a score rather than using a weighted system of multiple-regression analysis. Nevertheless, it set the precedent that heavily influenced other models, including the later federal parole decision-making method.[62]

The Burgess-Glueck Debates

Burgess's prediction instrument triggered an outpouring of research papers and dissertations, and much debate ensued over what became known as the "Burgess method." One important trend in the subsequent research reflected the desire to reduce the number of factors and focus on a narrower actuarial model with a smaller set of predictive variables—to make the model more parsimonious. University of Chicago sociologist and heir to Burgess, Albert J. Reiss Jr., strenuously advocated limiting the number of factors in prediction instruments: "[V]alid predictions are made from a prediction instrument when a small number of stable items from efficient factors having a relatively high association with the criterion are used as predictors," Reiss maintained.[63] Another prominent sociologist, Lloyd E. Ohlin, researched the Burgess tables that were in use at the penitentiary in Joliet, Illinois, in the early 1950s and produced a modified Burgess model with a reduced number of variables that was implemented at that penitentiary.[64] Daniel Glaser, who worked on the prediction tables used at the penitentiary at Pontiac, Illinois, in 1954 and 1955, focused on only seven predictive factors, two of which involved prior criminal history. Beginning in the 1970s, the federal government adopted more narrowly focused parole guidelines. The United States Parole Commission relied on the Salient Factor Score as an aid in predicting parole performance. That method used seven predictive factors, and the majority of those seven factors related to prior delinquency. California adopted an actuarial model that also focused more intensely on prior criminality. The first California Base/Expectancy Score focused more narrowly on four factors.[65]

Much of the ensuing debate revolved around narrowing the actuarial instruments, largely because of the principal competing model of prediction, which was developed and published in 1930 by Sheldon and Eleanor Glueck in their work, *Five Hundred Criminal Careers*.[66] At the time, Sheldon Glueck was an assistant professor of criminology, and Eleanor Glueck was a research assistant in criminology; both were at the Harvard Law School.[67] Their educational, teaching, and research backgrounds crossed several disciplines—including education, law, criminology, sociology, social work, and psychology.[68] As a result, they advocated an interdisciplinary approach that tended to put them in tense relationship with many sociologists, especially the noted criminologist Edwin H. Sutherland. As outsiders to the sociological field—or club—the Gluecks and their method became the foils against which much of the sociological theorizing took place. Sutherland scathingly criticized the Gluecks' research at the time for being overly focused on individual determinants and failing to recognize the larger social influences on behavior, which Sutherland himself developed into the theory of differential association.[69] Interestingly, Ernest Burgess did not suffer the same fate or receive similar critical attention, even though he too focused his research so intensely on predicting behavior on the basis of individual traits. Burgess avoided the wrath of Sutherland because of his earlier collaborative work with Robert Park in urban sociology, resulting in the famous mapping of Chicago neighborhoods by concentric circles,[70] the heart and soul of the Chicago ecological paradigm. Nevertheless, there is an interesting parallel, in the sense that Burgess's prediction work on parole is relatively marginalized in the history of the Chicago School—reflecting a similar bias against the more individually focused work. But the impact was far more powerful for the Gluecks. Today, as John Laub and Robert Sampson note, "despite their seminal contributions to the field, the Gluecks' works have been either ignored or criticized—especially by sociologists. As a result, contemporary researchers rarely, if ever, read their original studies. And when perfunctory citations do appear, their purpose is usually to allege fatal flaws in the Gluecks' position."[71] At the time, though, in the 1930s, their prediction model was the leading alternative to the Burgess method.

The Gluecks based their research on more laborious data collection and refined their prediction tool to a narrower set of factors. With regard to their methods, the Gluecks conducted extensive investigation into the lives of 510 inmates whose criminal sentences expired in 1921 and 1922. They focused on the parolees' experience during the first five years after their release. The Gluecks reviewed information about home life prior to the time spent in the institution, conducted interviews of the ex-convicts, and gathered information from parole agencies—a huge enterprise of data collection.[72] From that data, the Gluecks made four prediction tables that relied on a variety of pre-reformatory and reformatory statistics—one prediction table for an initial sentencing judge, one for parole, one for continued parole supervision, and one for sentencing recidivists.

Their parole-prediction instrument had seven factors,[73] and, unlike Burgess, they weighted each factor using a simple method based on the subcategories for each factor. If, for instance, there was a 43 percent failure rate for industrious workers and a 68 percent failure rate for poor workers, an inmate who was industrious got 43 points, and a poor worker got 68 points. The other factors were scored in a similar way and added to each other, with the overall score reflecting the total probability of success or failure—the lower the score, the better. Each person's score reflected the percentage of failures in each of the subcategories into which he fell.

The Gluecks criticized the Burgess method on a number of grounds, several of which are not particularly important here—for instance, the fact that some records from the parole agency were unreliable, that the time horizon was short (only during parole, not post-parole), and that no prediction instrument was available for judicial sentencing. But the major methodological differences—and disagreements—involved the number of and the weighting of factors: Burgess gave equal weight to all twenty-two factors, whereas the Gluecks weighted their seven factors according to some approximation of importance. Despite these "serious defects," the Gluecks observe that "Professor Burgess must be credited with having made a beginning in this important field and having been among the first to recognize its possibilities."[74]

Like Burgess, the Gluecks were true believers when it came to the science of human behavior and the possibility of prediction. The value of a prediction instrument, they asserted, "cannot be sufficiently emphasized."[75] They were also true believers in their own approach, and the ensuing competition between the Burgess and Glueck methods generated a tremendous amount of research from the 1930s through the 1950s, much of which was focused on narrowing the number of factors in the models and weighting them.[76]

Clark Tibbitts was one such researcher. The assistant to Ernest Burgess on the Illinois parole study, Tibbitts published additional research in 1931 that formed the basis of Ferris Laune's enthusiasm. He replicated Burgess's study, using a sample of three thousand youths paroled from the Illinois reformatory at Pontiac over a seven-year period from 1921 to 1927 and added a few factors.[77] Tibbitts settled on twenty-three,[78] but then reduced them to the twenty-two factors that he found most significant. He employed the Burgess method, reporting the comparison of percentages of the group that were successes or failures for each subcategory. The subcategories that contained a larger number of successes than violators were deemed favorable and vice versa. The number of favorable and unfavorable factors was counted for each parolee and an expectancy table was formulated.

Tibbitts used slightly different language for his model, referring to "white marks" and "black marks." So, he wrote,

> A record of no work . . . which shows a violation rate of 38.5 percent would be an unfavorable sign or what we have chosen to call "a black mark," while a good work record with only 5.6 percent failure would be favorable or "a white mark." The rates of violation either above or below the average permit the factors to be listed . . . according to whether they are favorable or unfavorable, "white" or "black."[79]

Not surprisingly—though one has to wonder whether Tibbitts caught the lack of irony—being "American (Colored)" was a "black mark" and being "American (White)" was a "white mark."[80]

The same year, 1931, George Vold, then assistant professor of sociology at the University of Minnesota, published his PhD dissertation on the factors associated with parole violation and success. Vold had received his master's degree in sociology at the University of Chicago, and had studied with Edwin Sutherland, receiving his doctorate at the University of Minnesota. In the preface to his dissertation, Vold traces his intellectual lineage to both Burgess and the Gluecks: "Students in the field will recognize the writer's heavy indebtedness to the pioneer studies of Professors Burgess and Glueck for fundamental methodology and approach. This is particularly true of Professor Burgess's earlier study of parole prediction in Illinois."[81]

Vold criticized the Burgess method on a number of grounds that mirrored those of the Gluecks—for instance, that Burgess had confined himself only to official records during the official parole period and had used equal weights on all factors.[82] Vold also criticized Burgess for using categories that were too subjective, which is interesting because it became a bit of a leitmotif in the ensuing debates. Ultimately, though, Vold used the same types of categories that he had criticized as excessively subjective.

As for the Glueck method, Vold started out by suggesting that "[t]hough this is a far more intensive and painstaking study than that of Burgess, the fundamental method is basically the same."[83] His principle critique of the Gluecks is that they overemphasized the role of prior criminality in the prediction tool. As noted earlier, in terms of predicting success for purposes of parole (in contrast to post-parole issues), the Gluecks identified seven factors. Vold writes, "Examination of the seven factors used in their parole prediction table makes it clear that there is heavy weighting of the factors of past criminality. Four out of the seven factors have reference to the violation of law or of prison regulations. May not this be giving too much weight to the assumption 'once a criminal, always a criminal?'"[84]

Vold's study reviewed the records of 542 men paroled from a Minnesota state prison and 650 men paroled from the reformatory in St. Cloud over a five-year period from 1922 to 1927. He originally looked at forty-four factors. He drew on the statistical method of the contingency tables developed by Karl Pearson, which are particularly suited to qualitative categories—what Vold refers to as "the Pearsonian r."[85] Pearson's method calculates the likelihood that the distributions in a contingency table vary from a random distribution within the table. He created scatter diagrams for each of the factors studied and compared the frequencies in the matrices in the subcategories of the first classification with the subcategories of the second.

Vold thereby obtained contingency coefficients for each of the forty-four factors.[86] Remarkably, the single most predictive factor was prior criminal history. "It will be noticed," Vold comments, "that the factor apparently most definitely associated with outcome on parole is the fact of prior criminal record."[87] Of the forty-four factors, only thirty-four referred to "traits, circumstances, or conditions of the man's life *prior to parole*."[88] Not sure whether to go with Burgess, who used all factors that predicted parole success, or the Gluecks, who used only the seven strongest predictors, Vold cut the baby in half and decided to use one-half of the predictive factors, namely the seventeen highest pre-parole factors. Vold divided his sample in two and created an "operating group," from which he derived the factors, and a "control group" to test his methods. Vold then tested both a Burgess model and a Glueck method of scoring the samples, and used different collections of factors to compare which models predicted best.

In the end, Vold never endorsed either the Burgess or Glueck model wholeheartedly, nor did he ultimately state an unequivocal preference for either. He adopted the selectivity of the Glueck model, but the unweighted approach of Burgess—noting at one point that, because the two methods yielded essentially similar distributions, he would skip applying the Glueck method: "The Glueck method is somewhat more laborious, calling for the use of an adding or calculating machine and really requiring two people to do the scoring—one to locate and call off the percentages, the other to operate the machine and record the results. With the Burgess method, however, one person can readily score the data rapidly and accurately."[89] Ease of application triumphed.

The very next year, in 1932, Elio Monachesi published his PhD dissertation, also on prediction, also from the University of Minnesota, and also using the method of contingency tables and the Pearson *r*-square—but he examined probation rather than parole. Monachesi would have been a contemporary of Vold's—working on his PhD at the University of Minnesota from 1928 to 1931 while Vold published his PhD dissertation in 1931—but being one year junior in the rapidly evolving world of prediction made him a student of Vold's as well. "To Professor George B. Vold," Monachesi wrote, "the writer is greatly indebted. Professor Vold was most patient and always ready to discuss with the writer the problems which arose in the preparation of this study."[90]

Monachesi was self-consciously following in the footsteps of Burgess, the Gluecks, and now Vold.[91] He reviewed the files of 1,515 probationers (896 cases of juvenile delinquents placed on probation and 619 adult cases) from the period 1923–1925, and used 60 files to create the major categories—54 for juveniles and 45 for adults.[92] He figured out the numerical distribution of cases for each factor and then tabulated the distributions and calculated the percentage of violators and nonviolaters for each factor. He compared the average rate of violation to the percentage violation rate for each factor and constructed prediction tables based on both the Burgess and Glueck models in order to compare them. His conclusion: the Burgess method was just as good and easier to administer. "Relatively comparable prediction results are obtained by weighting preprobation factors equally or by assigning different weight values to preprobation factors. (The simplest scoring method (Burgess) gives the most satisfactory results.)"[93] Naturally, Monachesi found that prior criminal history was "of special interest in that it shows the relation between violation rates and criminal record."[94]

Another PhD dissertation—this one also slightly outside the parole context—was produced at the University of Chicago in 1935 by a student of Ernest Burgess and Edwin Sutherland, Courtlandt Churchill Van Vechten Jr.[95] Van Vechten had also worked with Clark Tibbitts and Ferris Laune, and, not surprisingly, had spent two years making parole predictions at the Illinois state penitentiary at Pontiac.

Van Vechten appears to be one of the first to have taken seriously an important critique of prediction tools—namely, the question of "the intercorrelation of factors considered."[96] His conclusion was that "the problem of intercorrelation is merely an aspect of the problem of weighting, and that while agreement or non-agreement with other studies may alter the a priori basis for the acceptance of an apparent relationship as a valid one, it is not in itself a criterion of validity."[97] In his own study, Van Vechten used the records of one thousand problem boys between ten and seventeen years of age who were admitted to Ford Republic, a private reformatory in Michigan, during a period of about seven years ending in 1929. At the time of the study, some of the boys—thirty-eight, to be precise—were still in the institution, and others had only been out a short time. As a result, he defined success and failure slightly differently than previous studies had done, with a large allowance for "unknown." Successful cases were those of boys who, after leaving the reformatory or while still in, were getting along well and making an acceptable social adjustment—not just in terms of noncriminality, but also in terms of work and home. Van Vechten then evaluated each child on two hundred factors and constructed four different prediction tools. Ultimately, he adopted a modified Burgess approach. He wrote that the Burgess method "is easier in actual practice than the Glueck method. . . . With the significance of factors established before they are used, the Burgess many-factor method permits the inclusion of much valuable material ignored by the Glueck method."[98]

Several other contributions and attempts to refine the Burgess and Glueck models appeared in the following years. Ferris Laune devised a complicated tool intended to tap into the "hunches" of fellow inmates.[99] The idea was that a peer inmate might have a better sense of the probability of success on parole than practically anyone else, so Laune tried to objectify the subjective judgment of inmates. He spent three years working with two prisoners in Illinois and found that their hunches were based on fifty-four unit factors.[100] These factors, he argued, would give an outsider the same information that formed the hunch of a fellow inmate.[101] Laune's approach, however, ultimately proved to be no more successful than the Burgess method—and a lot more complicated.[102] United States Attorney General Homer Cummings commissioned a large survey of parole practices in 1936, culminating in a multivolume study that included a statistical analysis of factors that predict success on parole. The analysis reviewed more than ninety thousand federal parole cases.[103] Among its findings were that "whites had better records on parole than Negroes," that "unmarried persons [were] less likely to succeed on parole than married persons," and that "first offenders were found to be better risks for parole than recidivists."[104] R. L. Jenkins and his colleagues in 1942 sought to incorporate more personal psychiatric and psychological factors into their prediction tables, such as "shamelessness," "assaultive tendencies," "bullying," "daydreaming," "impudence," "jealousy," and "active homosexuality."[105] Michael Hakeem in 1948 validated the Burgess method, adding a few factors.[106] Bernard Kirby in 1954 experimented with multiple regression as an alternative to the unweighted Burgess model.[107]

Lloyd Ohlin updated the Burgess model and published the first manual for parole prediction in 1951.[108] Ohlin's research—the culmination of more than twenty years of experimentation and study—was based on the records of more than seventeen thousand prisoners paroled from Joliet and Menard between 1925 and 1945. Ohlin's method was to choose a factor and secure a violation rate for each of the subclasses of that factor. He then tested the significance of the violation rates to determine if that particular factor was valuable. Ohlin divided the subclasses into "favorable," "unfavorable," and "neutral." From a list of twenty-seven factors, Ohlin found twelve that were reliable.[109] In his method, each parolee got one point (favorable, unfavorable, or neutral) for each factor. Subtracting the unfavorable points from the favorable ones yielded a final score. Ohlin was optimistic about the effect of these experience tables, and so was his mentor. Burgess wrote an introduction to Ohlin's book, noting that "These Illinois materials have permitted the preparation of the first manual on parole selection in which the theory and methods of parole prediction have been set forth in a form that can be applied in other states."[110] Ohlin himself remarked that "[s]ince the setting up of a routine prediction system in Illinois in 1933, there has been a steady decline in violation rates," and added that "a detailed study in 1937 led to the conclusion that the prediction information played a significant part in selecting better risks for parole, and that this improved selection was a major factor in the decline of the violation rate."[111] The 1937 report, entitled "Parole and the Indeterminate Sentence," was written by none other than Ernest Burgess. Ohlin's model, which had a reduced number of predictive variables, was then implemented at the Illinois penitentiary.

Albert Reiss intervened at about this time, and his intervention was important because he, more than others, explicitly argued for narrowing the prediction instruments. In his dissertation, published in 1949, and his 1951 article in the *American Journal of Sociology*, Reiss argued that more precise prediction tools use smaller numbers of factors.[112] Another researcher, Louis Guttman, arrived at a similar conclusion at around the same time: the marginal benefit of adding factors decreases, and sampling errors increase after a certain point, so that adding factors may ultimately decrease the predictiveness of the instrument.[113] Other researchers were concluding at around that time that prior criminal history was the most predictive factor. J. L. Gillin, reviewing a number of studies conducted on Wisconsin records, concluded that criminal record was the only valid predictor found consistently correlated with parole and probation violation.[114]

These trends heavily influenced Daniel Glaser, who completed his PhD dissertation at the University of Chicago in 1954. Glaser had started his research much earlier, in September 1940, when he was employed as an actuary for the Illinois Parole and Pardon Board.[115] He had worked closely with Lloyd Ohlin, and his dissertation committee included Ernest Burgess and Albert Reiss, as well as Leo Goodman, the noted University of Chicago statistician and prediction-instrument theorist. Glaser strove for better predictive factors rather than improved statistical techniques. He believed that everyone had both criminal and conventional values and that their allegiance to both shifted through time. Influenced by Sutherland's criminological theory of differential association, Glaser believed that the chance of success on parole varied with the parolee's interaction with these good or bad influences and with the set of opportunities available to the parolee. Following Sutherland, Glaser dubbed his theory a "differential identification" approach.[116] He hypothesized that success or failure on parole would vary as follows:

1. Directly with the parolee's previous total identification with persons whose influence would be in support of conventional values.
2. Inversely with his identification with persons who are unconventional in that they regard themselves as criminals or have grossly disorderly recreational interests.
3. Directly with his probable economic opportunities and acceptance by conventional associates on parole.[117]

Glaser started his research with the traditional twenty-seven factors used at Joliet and Menard. He tested them and also searched for stronger factors. His sample consisted of 4,448 parolees from Pontiac between 1940 and 1950. Ultimately, relying on "differential identification," Glaser identified seven factors that were the most predictive. These were associated primarily with the potential for positive or negative identification and peer influence—as well as, of course, prior criminal record.[118] The number, though, was important: like Reiss, Glaser narrowed down the predictive tool to seven factors. Glaser's modified Burgess model was implemented at Pontiac in about 1955.

Several other predictive models were developed for other criminal justice purposes. Walter Argow at Yale University created a "criminal-liability index" to predict rehabilitation.[119] Monachesi, discussed earlier, worked on probation, and Van Vechten on youth adjustment. Elizabeth Redden, another PhD student in the department of sociology at the University of Chicago, created prediction tables for embezzlement crimes in 1939.[120] Ashley Weeks created prognostic tables in 1943 to predict the delinquency of juveniles.[121] In all of this research, the central battle lines were between the Burgess unweighted, multiple-factor model and the Glueck weighted, few-factor model.[122]

The Theory-Practice Divide

Despite all the research and academic papers, few states were actually using statistical prediction methods as part of the parole decision-making
process at the time. According to the 1939 *Attorney General's Survey,*
Illinois in fact was the only state to use a prediction tool.[123] A historical
survey conducted in the United Kingdom and published in 1954 similarly
reports that Illinois was still then the only state to implement a parole-
prediction tool, though it suggested that, "after this had gone to Press, we
have been informed by Professor Norman S. Hayner of the University of
Washington, Seattle, that the State of Washington Board of Prison Terms
and Paroles, of which he is a member, has for the past few years been
using prediction techniques in an experimental way and that it is hoped
to use them in the near future as a matter of routine."[124] A survey of the
parole boards of the fifty states conducted in August 1961 revealed that
two states (Illinois and Ohio) were using predictive models, that two states
(California and Colorado) were developing prediction statistics, and that
one other state (Minnesota) had experimented with but was no longer
using prediction tables.[125]

Although prediction instruments were not in place, there is good evidence that parole authorities were effectively relying on similar predictive
factors anyway. The 1939 *Attorney General's Survey,* for instance, discovered that in the federal parole system, "White persons are more likely to
be granted parole than Negroes" and simultaneously that race is a good
predictor of success on parole. Similarly, it found that "[u]nmarried persons are not as likely to be paroled as married persons" and that marriage
correlates with success; and also that "recidivism seems to have a marked
association with selection for parole" and that recidivists do poorly on
parole.[126] According to the report, "The data indicate that the Federal Parole Board gives considerable weight in parole selection to the factors of
the inmates' criminal histories. . . . Analyses of all the factors of criminal
history indicated that the Federal Parole Board granted parole sparingly
to persons in the classes which were associated with high violation rates
on parole and conditional release." In fact, the survey rejected the idea
of moving more aggressively toward a parole-prediction tool, at least in
1939, because their "commonsense" approach of taking these factors into
account was so successful.[127] Here is what the survey had to say:

> The conclusion to be reached from this summary of the data is that the Fed-
> eral Parole Board, using a common-sense approach to the problem of parole

selection, in effect takes into consideration the general traits which, as shown by the preceding analyses, are associated with the "good risks" and the "poor risks" for parole. It should be pointed out that the common-sense approach does not necessarily mean that the Board makes a conscious effort to select parolees according to the factors which the violation rates, as classified in this report, show to be associated with good records on parole. The policies followed by the Federal Parole Board are based upon careful study of individual case histories and the availability of acceptable parole plans. In this way the Board is able to recognize these general traits which are associated with "good risks" for parole.[128]

The Federal Salient Factor Score

Beginning in the 1970s, though, the actuarial approach became more widely accepted, and the key factor for predicting success or failure on parole became prior criminal history. The federal government adopted more narrow, more focused parole guidelines. The United States Parole Commission relied on the Salient Factor Score as an aid in predicting parole performance, an instrument that was developed on the basis of the Burgess model.[129]

Peter B. Hoffman, director of research, and James L. Beck, research assistant at the United States Board of Parole, explained their decision to adopt the Burgess method in the following terms:

A recent and rather comprehensive study by Simon (1971), which compared the predictive power of a number of mathematical methods for combining predictive items, indicates that the method commonly known among criminological researchers in the United States as the "Burgess" method (Burgess 1928), using a number of equally weighted dichotomous items, tends to predict as well on validation samples as the newer and more mathematically sophisticated methods (such as multiple regression or configural analysis). A smaller but similar study by Wilbanks and Hindelang (1972) produced a similar conclusion. That is, while the more sophisticated methods produce a higher correlation on the construction sample, there tends to be considerably greater shrinkage when applied to a validation sample. As the purpose of a predictive device, by definition, is to predict to future samples, it is the validation results that are important. Given this equality in predictive power, the "Burgess" method was chosen because of its simplicity and ease of calculation in "field" usage. . . . As the "Burgess" method requires only dichotomous (or in this case, trichotomous) coding and simple addition, the probability of coding or tabulation error is reduced.[130]

Hoffman and Beck's major methodological contribution to the Burgess method was to reduce the number of factors to nine (and later to seven), and to focus heavily on prior criminal history. Hoffman and Beck drew their samples from persons released from federal prisons in 1970. They used a sample of 902 cases to construct the prediction tool, and then samples of 919 and 662 to validate it. Hoffman and Beck started out with sixty-six factors and a two-year follow-up period, and narrowed their factors down to nine on the basis not only of predictive ability, but also of ethical choices and sound judgment.[131] They then constructed an instrument of the Burgess-method type, using the nine factors, departing slightly in that some factors were trichotomous rather than dichotomous. The nine factors were (1) prior convictions; (2) prior incarcerations; (3) age at first commitment; (4) auto theft; (5) prior parole revocation; (6) drug history; (7) education grade achieved; (8) employment; and (9) living arrangements on release.[132]

The nine factors were used to create a zero-to-eleven-point scale (recall that two of the factors were trichotomous). The Board of Parole then collapsed the eleven-point scale into four categories of risk, and used those categories combined with six categories of offenses to create a four-by-six matrix guideline, very similar in effect to the federal sentencing guidelines. These were "explicit parole selection policy guidelines—a four by six (risk by severity) matrix which displayed a customary range of time to be served before release for each matrix cell."[133]

According to Hoffman and Beck,

These guidelines are intended to structure discretion in order to provide more rational, consistent, and equitable parole selection decisions. If an examiner panel wishes to make a decision outside of the guidelines, it is required to explain its decision and obtain the approval of an additional examiner. Also included is a provision for clinical override of the Salient Factor Score. That is, if the examiner panel feels that the Salient Factor Score is substantially inaccurate, it may substitute its clinical judgment provided it gives a written explanation and justification.[134]

In 1974, Hoffman and Beck reported that

[t]his Salient Factor Score has been in use as an aid in Federal parole selection decisions throughout the United States since November 1, 1973, when it

replaced an earlier version. Board members and hearing examiners have made over 3,000 decisions using this instrument to date and appear well satisfied with its performance. Operationally, the Salient Factor Score requires no special skills to compute and can be completed in a short time; thus, it does not impose an undue administrative burden.[135]

At around the same time, California adopted an actuarial model that also focused more intensely on prior criminality. The first California Base/ Expectancy Score focused on four factors. One of them was prior commitments; another was race; and the other two were offense type and number of escapes.[136] For its part, after having a leadership role in developing actuarial parole guidelines, Illinois ultimately abolished parole release and adopted determinate sentencing in the late 1970s.

Ongoing Methodological Debates

The debates over methodology, though, continued to rage. While many, like the federal parole authorities with their Salient Factor Score, endorsed the Burgess method, others continued to argue for multiple-regression analysis or other tools. In 1978, for example, Lawrence Brown argued for the superiority of multivariate analyses over univariate approaches like the Burgess method. "Our findings," Brown declared, "highlight the deficiency of using univariate techniques to model parole performance. . . . The results of this study suggest that multivariate analysis, when properly applied and interpreted, is capable of yielding results which hold up well when tested with validation samples."[137] Nevertheless, a consensus developed in the 1970s and 1980s that the Burgess method was simpler to administer and that it was often better at predicting violation rates: while multiple regression was more accurate on the sample, it was often less predictive on the test group.

As a result, the actuarial models developed in the parole context evolved over the course of the twentieth century, focusing on a narrower set of factors and especially on the prior criminal history of the incarcerated. The development of parole prediction began with actuarial aspirations but a clinical approach by default; it then emerged in multifactored tests produced by sociologists; and ultimately led to narrower and narrower prediction instruments that relied heavily on the criminal record of the convict. Though its evolution is reflected well in the literature—from the writings of Professors Ernst Freund and Roscoe Pound on the individual-ization of punishment to the research and predictive model of Professor Ernest Burgess and ultimately to the nine- or seven-factor Salient Factor Score developed for federal parole determinations—the scholarly debate rarely resulted in actual implementation.

We can observe the narrowing of prediction factors and the lack of implementation in table 2.3, which traces the history of most of the

TABLE 2.3 **Parole-prediction models, 1923–1978**

Year	Name	No. of factors considered	No. of factors in model	Actuarial method	Used?	Subject location
1923	Warner	66	n.a.	Zero-order correlation (looked for informa-tion to be positively or negatively correlated with outcome)	No	MA
1924	Hart	66	30	Advocated use of multi-ple linear regression	No	MA
1927	Witmer	15	n.a.	Zero-order correlation	No	WI
1928	Borden	26	n.a.	Zero-order correlation	No	NJ
1928	Burgess	22	21	Zero-order correlation; then created tool that added or subtracted 1 point of score for any item found to be positively or negatively correlated with outcome. Factors are not weighted.	Yes	IL
1930	Glueck	52	7	Zero-order correlation, looking for compara-tive correlations with success post-parole. Created a parole predic-tion tool with 7 factors. Weighted the factors.	No	MA
1931	Vold	34	25	Used contingency table and Pearson r-square to determine predictive factors. Tested Burgess and Glueck methods. Ultimately created various predictive tools using hybrid approach.	No	MN
1931	Tibbitts	25	22	Used Burgess method.	No	IL

(*continued*)

TABLE 2.3   (*continued*)

Year	Name	No. of factors considered	No. of factors in model	Actuarial method	Used?	Subject location
1932	Monachesi	54	n.a.	Followed Vold but as applied to probation: used contingency tables to create categories. Tested Burgess and Glueck models. Developed approach for probation.	No	MN
1935	Van Vechten	225	n.a.	Used a modified Burgess method on data about successful adjustment of delinquent boys; created four different prediction tables. Reviewed about 225 individual factors.	No	MI
1935	Argow	37	n.a.	Created a prediction tool regarding general disposition to rehabilitation using 37 factors and contrasting percentage of first offenders and recidivists	No	CT
1935	Laune	54	n.a.	Tried to discover objective factors associated with the "hunches" of prison inmates about success on parole. Interviewed people still in prison, instead of tracking released prisoners.	No	IL
1939	Redden	22	20	Tried to predict white-collar crime of embezzlement	No	MD
1939	Survey of Release Procedures	82	n.a.	Looked at the factors of people who were paroled and then looked to see if prediction methods based on those factors would have been useful	No	Federal parole cases
1942	Jenkins et al.	95	n.a.	Sought to include more personal psychiatric and psychological factors in the prediction tools	No	NY
1943	Weeks	14	n.a.	Prediction tool for juvenile delinquency	No	WA

TABLE 2.3   *(continued)*

Year	Name	No. of factors considered	No. of factors in model	Actuarial method	Used?	Subject location
1948	Hakeem	27	27	Replication study of the Burgess method of parole prediction for purposes of validation. Used a different sample of cases and a different set of factors, but the method was straight Burgess.	No	Un-known
1951	Ohlin	27	12	Used the Burgess method (sociologist at the IL prison updating the Burgess system)	Yes	IL
1954	Glaser	27+	7	Developed a set of factors based on parolees' interaction with good and bad influences—based on Sutherland's theory and dubbed "Differential Identification." More dynamic set of factors. Used the Burgess model.	Yes	IL
1954	Kirby	33	n.a.	Used multiple regression on factors determined using a Burgess approach. Weighted system.	No	Federal parole cases from WA
1967	Carney	14	14	Prediction for recidivism	No	MA
1973	Hoffman and Beck	66	9	Used the Burgess method to construct a 9-factor prediction tool that was adopted by the federal parole-board	Yes	Federal parole cases from WA
1976	Heilbrun, Knopf, and Bruner	10	10	Used chi-square tests on frequency data	No	GA
1978	Brown	10	10	Used multiple-discriminant analysis, a form of multiple regression, rather than the univariate approach of Burgess	No	48 states

important parole-prediction models developed from 1923 through 1978. A bibliography of the literature on parole prediction appears in appendix A.

The narrowing of the prediction instruments can be visualized by plotting the number of factors used in parole-prediction models over time and drawing a regression line through the plot, as shown in figure 2.1. This graph illustrates well the narrowing of the prediction models. But the models, for the most part, remained academic.

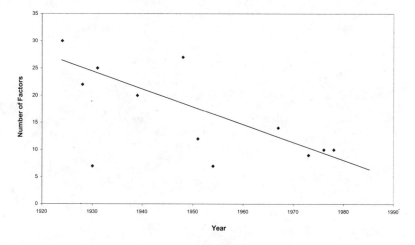

FIGURE 2.1 Number of factors in prediction models, 1923–1978

CHAPTER THREE

The Proliferation of Actuarial Methods in Punishing and Policing

The academic status of parole-prediction models changed rapidly in the last decades of the twentieth century: at an increasing rate, more and more states began using risk-assessment instruments to determine whether inmates should be released on parole. The trend is visually dramatic and is well illustrated in figure 1.1.

By 2004, twenty-eight states were using a risk-assessment tool as part of their parole decision-making process. Illinois was the only state to use an actuarial instrument during the 1930s, '40s, and '50s, and Ohio experimented with them in the 1960s, but many other states turned to prediction tools after California and the federal government adopted them in the 1970s. Georgia, Iowa, Tennessee, South Carolina, Alabama, and Florida began using risk-assessment instruments in the late 1970s and early 1980s, and other states—including Connecticut, Michigan, New Jersey, Ohio, Pennsylvania, and Texas—followed suit. Marylynne Hunt-Dorta's 2004 survey and the time-line shown in figure 1.1—which are corroborated by other surveys conducted in 1939, 1961, and 1994[1]—reflect an exponential increase in the use of actuarial methods at the turn of the twenty-first century.

What is especially remarkable about this exponential trend is that it coincided with the relative demise of parole. The number of states offering parole declined steadily from about 44 in 1979 to about 32 in 2003. Despite this decline, the number of states *with* parole that used an actuarial method increased from about 1 in 1979 to 23 in 2004.[2] In other words, of the 28 jurisdictions using prediction instruments in 2004, 5 no longer had parole for new convictions but used an actuarial method to determine parole for grandfathered sentences. All the other 23 jurisdictions using actuarial methods still had parole.

The trend here is dramatic as well, especially if one looks at the proportion of states using an actuarial method *of the states that maintain an active parole system.* The graph shown in figure 3.1 represents the proportion of states that actively grant parole that also use an actuarial parole-prediction instrument.

The states that use prediction instruments vary greatly in their choice of tools. The most popular risk-assessment instrument is the Level of Services Inventory-Revised (LSI-R), used by eight states. Three states use the Salient Factor Score, developed for the federal parole board. Several states have developed their own risk-assessment tools. In addition, some states utilize a guideline method that incorporates risk-assessment factors. Table 3.1 summarizes the different prediction instruments in use in 2004.

The LSI-R is the most popular prediction tool in the United States and is also used abroad, for instance, by probation departments in England, Wales, and Northern Ireland.[3] The instrument was developed in Canada in the late 1970s by two Canadian researchers, and it asks fifty-four questions targeting both static and dynamic risk factors. Static risk factors include prior criminal history and other unchanging or historical factors like employment and educational history. Dynamic factors are more forward-looking, less tangible, and subject to change. They include, for instance, emotional and personal factors or attitude and orientation. The interviewer administering the LSI-R has some leeway in asking the questions in order to build rapport with the interviewee, but essentially asks questions

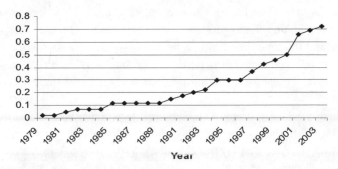

FIGURE 3.1 Historical trend in proportion of states using parole-prediction instruments among states that actively grant parole
Source: Survey conducted by Marylynne Hunt-Dorta in 2004, which inquired not only into the use of actuarial measures but also into parole.

TABLE 3.1 **Prediction instruments used in different states (2004)**

State	Does state use parole in new cases?	Does state use prediction instrument?	Name of prediction instrument	When did state start using this instrument?
Alabama	Yes	Yes	Alabama Risk Assessment Tool	1985
Alaska	Yes	Yes	Risk Factor	2002
Arizona	No	No		
Arkansas	Yes	Yes	Post-Prison Board Transfer Risk Assessment	1994
California	No	No		
Colorado	Yes	Yes	Colorado Actuarial Risk Assessment Scale	1993
Connecticut	Yes	Yes	Salient Factor Score	1999
Delaware	No	Yes	Delaware Parole Board Risk Assessment	1996
Florida	No	Yes	Salient Factor Score	1983
Georgia	Yes	Yes	Parole Decision Guidelines	1979
Hawaii	Yes	No		
Idaho	Yes	Yes	LSI-R	2001
Illinois	No	No		
Indiana	No	No		
Iowa	Yes	Yes	Iowa Parole Board Risk Assessment	1981
Kansas	No	No		
Kentucky	Yes	Yes	Kentucky Parole Guidelines Risk Assessment Instrument	2003
Louisiana	Yes	No		
Maine	No	Yes	LSI-R	2001
Maryland	Yes	Yes	Uniform Assessment Policy, Uniform Sexual Offense Policy	1997
Massachusetts	Yes	No		
Michigan	Yes	Yes	Parole Guidelines	1992
Minnesota	No	No		
Mississippi	Yes	No		
Missouri	Yes	Yes	Salient Factor Score	1991
Montana	Yes	Yes	Risk Assessment	2001
Nebraska	Yes	No		
Nevada	Yes	Yes	Guidelines and Recommended Months to Serve	1994
New Hampshire	Yes	No		
New Jersey	Yes	Yes	LSI-R	1998
New Mexico	No	No		
New York	Yes	No		
North Carolina	No	No		
North Dakota	Yes	Yes	LSI-R	1990
Ohio	Yes	Yes	Parole Board Guidelines	1998
Oklahoma	Yes	No		
Oregon	No	No		
Pennsylvania	Yes	Yes	LSI-R	2001

(continued)

TABLE 3.1 *(continued)*

State	Does state use parole in new cases?	Does state use prediction instrument?	Name of prediction instrument	When did state start using this instrument?
Rhode Island	Yes	No		
South Carolina	Yes	Yes	Parole Risk Assessment	1985
South Dakota	No	Yes	Wisconsin Risk and Needs Assessment	1990
Tennessee	Yes	Yes	Parole Grant Prediction Scale and Guidelines	1982
Texas	Yes	Yes	Risk Assessment Instrument	2001
Utah	Yes	Yes	LSI-R	2001
Vermont	Yes	Yes	LSI-R	2000
Virginia	No	No		
Washington	No	Yes	LSI-R, VRAG, MSOFT, MMPI, MSI	1991
West Virginia	Yes	No		
Wisconsin	No	No		
Wyoming	Yes	No		

like "How do you do in your job?" and "Do you have a lot of friends?"
Some of these questions seem odd in the parole-decision context—especially, for example, the question "Are you sexually dissatisfied?"—but the
instrument is nevertheless popular for parole decision making. The fifty-
four questions are grouped into ten substantive areas:

1. Criminal history (10 items)
2. Education and employment (10 items)
3. Financial (2 items)
4. Family and marital (4 items)
5. Accommodations (3 items)
6. Leisure and recreation (2 items)
7. Companions (5 items)
8. Alcohol and drugs (9 items)
9. Emotional and personal (5 items)
10. Attitude and orientation (4 items)

Interviewees are asked to answer yes or no to the series of questions or
are scored on a range from 0 to 3. The interviewer scores the instrument
and determines the offender's risk level. The scores are effectively translated into odds of reoffending within a defined period. So, for instance,

a score in the 30 range translates to a low-to-moderate risk with about a 48 percent chance of reoffending within a one-year time frame.[4]

The range of areas covered by the LSI-R reflects another major change from the trend toward the narrowing of prediction factors discussed in chapter 2. The LSI-R takes a multifactor approach that resembles more closely the early Burgess-type approach that included factors related to family, marriage, socioeconomic conditions, and emotional outlook. The list of questions in the LSI-R appears in table 3.2.

TABLE 3.2 **The multiple factors in the LSI-R prediction instrument**

I. Criminal History
1. Any prior convictions?
2. Two or more prior convictions?
3. Three or more convictions?
4. Three or more present offenses?
5. Arrested under age 16?
6. Ever incarcerated upon conviction?
7. Escape history from a correctional facility?
8. Ever punished for institutional misconduct?
9. Change made for probation/parole suspended during prior community supervision?
10. Official record of assault/violence?

II. Education/Employment
11. Currently employed?
12. Frequently unemployed?
13. Never employed for a full year?
14. Ever fired?
15. Less than regular grade 10?
16. Less than regular grade 12?
17. Suspended or expelled at least once?
18. Participation/performance
19. Peer interactions
20. Authority interactions

III. Financial
21. Problems?
22. Reliance upon social assistance?

IV. Family/Marital
23. Dissatisfaction with marital partner or equivalent?
24. Non-rewarding, parental
25. Non-rewarding, other relative
26. Criminal family/spouse?

V. Accommodations
27. Unsatisfactory
28. Three or more address changes last year?
29. High-crime neighborhood?

VI. Leisure/Recreation
30. Absence of recent participation in an org. activity?
31. Could make better use of time.

VII. Companions
32. A social isolate?
33. Some criminal acquaintances?
34. Some criminal friends?
35. Few anti-criminal acquaintances?
36. Few anti-criminal friends?

VII. Alcohol/Drug Problem
37. Alcohol problem, ever?
38. Drug problem, ever?
39. Alcohol problem, currently?
40. Drug problem, currently?
41. Law violations?
42. Marital/family?
43. School/work?
44. Medical?
45. Other indicators?

IX. Emotional/Personal
46. Moderate interference?
47. Severe interference, active psychosis?
48. Mental health treatment, past?
49. Mental health treatment, present?
50. Psychological assessment indicated?

X. Attitudes/Orientation
51. Supportive of crime.
52. Unfavorable toward convention.
53. Poor, toward sentence?
54. Poor, toward supervision?

This return to the multifactor approach can be attributed to efficiency gains. The LSI-R, for instance, is used for classification at the inception of the prison term, but the results are often recycled for other uses. In the state of Washington, the LSI-R, administered once a person is convicted of a crime, is also a major component in deciding what level of supervision a prisoner needs.[5] The LSI-R is administered again directly before a person is released from prison and is used to determine the terms and conditions of release.[6] Similarly, the Hare Psychopathy Checklist-Revised (PCL-R) is used not only for parole determinations but also for civil commitment of violent sexual predators, for juvenile transfers to adult court, for sentencing enhancement, as mitigation, in death penalty sentencing, in hearings on competence to stand trial, and even in cases terminating parental rights.[7] In Vermont, a person who is convicted of a crime is given two tests, the Supervision Level Assessment and the LSI-SV (the eight-item short version of the LSI-R). A person who scores low may be given probation or put in a low-security facility. A higher score requires administration of the LSI-R, and that score is used to determine prison classification.[8] The same test results are available to determine release supervision—in some cases, the tests are readministered and compared to earlier results. In Oklahoma, the level of community supervision is determined primarily by the LSI-R score.[9] In Alaska, the LSI-R score determines the level of post-release supervision: a low score means that the person does not have to come in for supervision at all; with a medium-range score, the person must come in monthly; and with a high range score, the person must come in weekly.[10] BI, Inc., is a company that assists twenty-five hundred probation and parole agencies across the country to monitor and treat offenders living in the community. BI uses the LSI-R to determine the levels of surveillance and support required for each individual it monitors.[11]

The versatility of the LSI-R probably accounts for its popularity and explains the reversal of the earlier trend toward fewer predictive factors. It does not, however, assure accuracy. Although the LSI-R appears to be one of the best instruments for predicting recidivism,[12] the reliability and validity of the LSI-R are questionable. The Pennsylvania Board of Probation and Parole, which uses the LSI-R, commissioned a study of Pennsylvania examiners and inmates to assess the reliability and validity of the LSI-R. The first of the reliability assessments, completed in October 2000, was disappointing. It found that only eighteen of the fifty-four items on the LSI-R (33 percent) had an inter-rater consistency score at or above an 80 percent threshold, and that "there was substantial disagreement between the two interviewers regarding the risk level (high, medium, and low). In total, the interviewers agree[d] on the assessed risk level in 71 percent of the cases."[13] With additional staff training, a second reliability test found that thirty-four of the fifty-four items (63 percent) met the 80 percent inter-rater consistency threshold. Regarding validation, on a sample of 1,006 Pennsylvania prisoners, the study found that only eight of theLSI-R items were associated with recidivism, and they tended to be static measures related to prior criminal history and prior drug use. The study concluded that "The LSI-R as tested in [the Pennsylvania] institutional setting had problematic reliability. These results do not warrant its use by the [Pennsylvania Board of Probation and Parole] as a method for assessing risk at the time of a parole review. Instead a more succinct instrument [focusing on the eight static items] would be more effective for the Board's risk assessment."[14]

Another study conducted by the Home Office of the United Kingdom found similar disparities. The Home Office showed 83 percent inter-rater reliability between two officers using the LSI-R. Regarding validity, the study found that the LSI-R predicted accurately in 65 percent of the cases assessed. However, according to the study, the LSI-R did not predict reconviction for serious offenses or for offenses attracting custodial sentences "well enough to make [it] appropriate for use as the main method of assessing dangerousness."[15]

Despite this, a number of states use the LSI-R in the parole decision-making process. So, for instance, in 1997, Pennsylvania was chosen to participate in a multistate, two-year project called Structured Release, funded by the National Institute of Corrections. The project developed new parole guidelines that included, at their core, an assessment of future risk using the LSI-R. As a result, today in Pennsylvania, the LSI-R score is a component of a number-based decision matrix for deciding whether an inmate is to be paroled.[16] In Washington State, the Indeterminate Sentence Review Board determines parole eligibility for all offenders who committed their crimes prior to July 1, 1984. The Washington board is "specifically charged not to release an inmate on parole prior to the expiration of his/her maximum term unless satisfied of his/her rehabilitation and fitness for release." In order to satisfy this mandate, the board, in its words, "remains behavior-focused in making individual risk assessments."[17] It uses the LSI-R. In North Dakota, the parole board considers the results of the LSI-R when making the decision to parole someone—along with treatment programs, nature of offense, prior record, and previous parole and probation supervision.[18] In Alaska, the parole board gives the LSI-R score anywhere between 5 and 35 percent weight in the decision.[19] In Vermont, the LSI-R is one of the primary factors in the decision of the parole board.[20]

There are several other general risk-assessment instruments, including the Violence Risk Appraisal Guide (VRAG), the General Statistical Information on Recidivism Scale (GSIR), and the Psychopathy Checklist Revised (PCL-R), as well as specialized risk-assessment instruments for certain categories of crime, especially sex offenses and domestic abuse, such as the Minnesota Sex Offender Screening Tool (MSOST), the Rapid Risk Assessment for Sexual Offense Recidivism (RRASOR), and the Spousal Assault Risk Assessment Guide (SARA). In addition, there are state-specific instruments. In Colorado, for instance, juvenile offenders must take the Colorado Youthful Offender–Levels of Supervision Inventory (CYO-LSI) in order to determine levels of probation supervision. The CYO-LSI is an automated, standardized assessment that was developed in Colorado for probation supervision, treatment, and placement decisions. The assessment measures risk of reoffending, identifies needed services, and is also used as a reassessment tool to measure juveniles' progress while on probation.[21] The Salient Factor Score discussed earlier was developed for use in the federal parole context and is popular today in three states. It focuses primarily on prior criminal history and history of incarceration—that is, on static factors.

In most states, the risk-assessment instrument is ultimately woven into a guideline procedure, sometimes using a "matrix" model and sometimes a "sequential" model. These are the dominant models among state parole boards that have moved toward more policy-driven approaches to parole— referred to as "guideline" models—and away from individualized, clinical decision making. The first model—the matrix approach—was pioneered by the federal parole board in the 1970s. Under the matrix approach, the parole authorities first use a risk-assessment instrument—the Salient Factor Score, for instance—and then use a grid based on the severity of the sentence and the risk assessment to determine length of sentence prior to parole. The two determinants, then, are the length of the original sentence imposed and the risk assessment. In Maryland, for instance, a violent offender who is "good risk" on the Salient Factor Score will serve 50–58 percent of his sentence before being paroled, whereas a "poor risk" will serve 68–75 percent of the original sentence. The actual term in months is set out in the grid. The grid used in Maryland is shown in figure 3.2.

The second approach is referred to as a "decision tree" or "sequential model." Using this approach, parole authorities fill in a table with scores that relate to different factors for parole and tally the score to determine

Parole Eligibility of 50% for Violent Crimes

Pursuant to the *Correctional Services Article, § 7-301 and 7-101(m),* applicable for an inmate who has been sentenced to the Division of Correction after being convicted of a violent crime committed on or after October 1, 1994.

I. The commission of, or attempt to commit, any of the following offenses :

- Abduction
- Arson in the first degree
- Carjacking and armed carjacking
- Kidnapping
- Manslaughter (except involuntary manslaughter)
- Mayhem and maiming
- Murder
- Rape
- Robbery and robbery with a deadly weapon
- Sexual offense in the first and second degrees
- Use of a handgun in the commission of a felony or other crimes of violence, or

II. The commission of :

- Assault in the first degree
- Assault with intent to murder
- Assault with intent to rape
- Assault with intent to rob
- Assault with intent to commit a sexual offense in the first degree
- Assault with intent to commit a sexual offense in the second degree
- Burglary in the first, second, or third degree.

Maryland Parole Commission
Stuart O. Simms, Secretary
Patricia K. Cushwa, Chairperson
6776 Reisterstown Rd., Suite 307
Baltimore, MD 21215
410-585-3200   fax 410-764-4355

5/2000

Risk Assessment Instrument

A.   Prior convictions/adjudications (adult and/or juvenile)
None = 3   One = 2   Two or Three = 1   Four or more = 0   ☐

B.   Prior commitment(s) of more than thirty days (adult and/or juvenile)
None = 2   One or Two = 1   Three or more = 0   ☐

C.   Age at current offense/prior commitments
26 or older = 2*   20 - 25 = 1*   19 or younger = 0

* exceptions. If five or more prior commitments of more than 30 days (adult and/or juvenile), place "x" here ____ and score item = 0   ☐

D.   Recent commitment-free period (three years)
No prior commitment of more than thirty days (adult and/or juvenile) or released to the community from last such commitment at least three years prior to the commencement of the current offense = 1   Otherwise = 0   ☐

E.   Probation/parole/confinement/escape status violator this time
Neither on probation, parole, confinement, or escape status at the time of the current offense; nor committed as a probation, parole, confinement, or escape status violator this time = 1   Otherwise = 0   ☐

F.   Substance abuse
No history of substance abuse = 1   Otherwise = 0   ☐

Total Score _____

Offender Category / Risk Rating			
6 - 10 points	Good Risk	Category I
3 - 5 points	Fair Risk	Category II
0 - 2 points	Poor Risk	Category III

Other Crimes

This table applies to inmates who are eligible for parole after serving twenty-five percent (25%) of their term of confinement.

(Nonviolent crimes and violent crimes committed before October 1994)

The parole decision range for terms of confinement of less than 4 years is from parole eligibility to mandatory supervision release or release via expiration of sentence.

Sentence in Months	Category I 25% - 36%	Category II 37% - 48%	Category III 49% - 60%
48-53	12-17	18-23	24-MSR*
54-59	13-20	21-26	27-MSR
60-65	15-22	23-29	30-MSR
66-71	16-24	25-32	33-MSR
72-77	18-26	27-35	36-MSR
78-83	19-28	29-37	38-MSR
84-89	21-30	31-40	41-MSR
90-95	22-32	33-43	44-MSR
96-101	24-35	36-46	47-MSR
102-107	25-37	38-49	50-MSR
108-113	27-39	40-52	53-MSR
114-119	28-41	42-55	56-MSR
120-125	30-43	44-58	59-MSR
126-131	31-45	46-60	61-MSR
132-137	33-48	49-63	64-MSR
138-143	34-50	51-66	67-MSR
144-149	36-52	53-69	70-MSR
150-155	37-54	55-72	73-MSR
156-161	39-56	57-75	76-MSR
162-167	40-58	59-78	79-MSR
168-173	42-60	61-81	82-MSR
174-179	45-65	64-84	85-MSR
180-185	45-65	66-86	87-MSR
186-191	46-67	68-89	90-MSR
192-197	48-69	70-92	93-MSR
198-203	49-71	72-95	96-MSR
204-209	51-73	74-98	99-MSR
210-215	52-76	77-101	102-MSR
216-221	54-78	79-104	105-MSR
222-227	55-80	81-107	108-MSR
228-233	57-82	83-109	110-MSR
234-239	58-84	85-112	113-MSR
240-245	60-86	87-115	116-MSR

Mandatory Supervision Release

Violent Crimes

This table applies to inmates who are eligible for parole after serving fifty percent (50%) of their term of confinement (Article 27, Section 643B Crimes or Burglary in the first, second, or third degree committed on or after October 1, 1994).

The parole decision range for terms of confinement of less than 4 years is from parole eligibility to mandatory supervision release or release via expiration of sentence.

Sentence in Months	Category I 50% - 58%	Category II 59% - 67%	Category III 68% - 75%
48-53	24-28	29-32	33-MSR*
54-59	27-31	32-36	37-MSR
60-65	30-35	36-40	41-MSR
66-71	33-38	39-44	45-MSR
72-77	36-42	43-48	49-MSR
78-83	39-45	46-52	53-MSR
84-89	42-49	50-56	57-MSR
90-95	45-52	53-60	61-MSR
96-101	48-56	57-64	65-MSR
102-107	51-59	60-68	69-MSR
108-113	54-63	64-72	73-MSR
114-119	57-66	67-76	77-MSR
120-125	60-70	71-80	81-MSR
126-131	63-73	74-84	85-MSR
132-137	66-77	78-88	89-MSR
138-143	69-80	81-92	93-MSR
144-149	72-84	85-96	97-MSR
150-155	75-87	88-100	101-MSR
156-161	78-90	91-105	106-MSR
162-167	81-94	95-109	110-MSR
168-173	84-97	98-113	114-MSR
174-179	87-101	102-117	118-MSR
180-185	90-104	105-121	122-MSR
186-191	93-108	109-125	126-MSR
192-197	96-111	112-129	130-MSR
198-203	99-115	116-133	134-MSR
204-209	102-118	119-137	138-MSR
210-215	105-122	123-141	142-MSR
216-221	108-125	126-145	146-MSR
222-227	111-129	130-149	150-MSR
228-233	114-132	133-153	154-MSR
234-239	117-136	137-157	158-MSR
240-245	120-139	140-161	162-MSR

Mandatory Supervision Release

FIGURE 3.2 State of Maryland sentencing grid: (top) risk-assessment instrument; (bottom) guidelines matrix

whether the inmate is likely or unlikely to be paroled. In Pennsylvania, for instance, the four factors in the table include whether the offense was a violent or nonviolent crime, the LSI-R score, institutional adjustment, and institutional behavior. Depending on the total score, the inmate is found to be either "likely to parole" or "unlikely to parole."[22] Both the matrix format from Maryland and the sequential model from Pennsylvania rep-

---

PENNSYLVANIA BOARD
OF PROBATION AND PAROLE

PAROLE DECISION MAKING GUIDELINES

Name _____

Parole No. _____ SID No. _____ Institution No. _____

Date of Interview _____ Institution _____

Interview Type ___ Minimum ___ Review ___ Reparole Review ___ Parole Application

---

Violence Indicator

1. Instant Offense

Violent ☐ +3
Non-Violent ☐ +1

(1) Murder, Voluntary Manslaughter, Aggravated Assault, Robbery, Arson, Burglary (Residential), Assault by Prisoner, Assault by Life Prisoner, Kidnapping, Extortion Accompanied by Threats of Violence, all Sex Crimes, and criminal attempt, criminal conspiracy, and/or criminal solicitation to commit any of the above-noted offenses.

Risk/Needs Assessment

2. Level of Service Inventory - Revised   **Sex Offender Risk Assessment (Static 99)**

Raw Score: _____   Raw Score: _____

High Risk ☐ +3   High Risk ☐ +3
Medium Risk ☐ +2   Medium Risk ☐ +2
Low Risk ☐ +1   Low Risk ☐ +1

*(All offenders considered for parole shall be assessed using the Level of Service Inventory - Revised ("LSI-R"). Offenders convicted of a sex offense shall be assessed using the LSI-R as well as the Sex Offender Risk Assessment Instrument. **The higher level of risk shall be used for all sex offenders.***

Institution Adjustment

3. Institutional Programming

Unacceptable Program Compliance ☐ +3
Reasonable Efforts (2) ☐ +2
Currently Involved ☐ +1
Completion of Required Programs (3) ☐ +0

(2) No access or on waiting list.
(3) Includes offenders who are currently involved and will complete prior to release

resent structured approaches to parole decision making that place significant emphasis on risk assessment. These two guideline approaches use
easy-to-administer, fill-in-the-box guidelines. The matrix format is shown
in figure 3.3.

These grids and matrices reflect what Paul Robinson refers to as a fundamental shift in our criminal justice system during the last decades of
the twentieth century: a shift "from punishing past crimes to preventing
future violations through the incarceration and control of dangerous offenders"—or, more succinctly, "the shifting of the criminal justice system
toward the detention of dangerous offenders."[23]

---

4. Institutional Behavior

Any of the following acts which occurred: while incarcerated on the instant offense;
and, within one year of the parole interview date or since the date of last review.

1. Crimes Code Violation - *Criminal charges pending in which probable cause has
   been established or a conviction has occurred from an offense that was committed
   while serving sentence currently under consideration for parole; and/or*   □ +5

2. Drug/alcohol offense - *Determined to be in possession of any controlled substance
   and/or positive test result of drugs or alcohol; and/or*

3. Assaultive behavior - *Verbal or physical aggression which is documented by the
   Department of Corrections or the Board of Probation and Parole; and/or*

4. CCC failure - *Return to institution as a result of inappropriate behavior occurring
   while in prerelease status; and/or*

5. Pattern of institutional misconducts - *Three or more class II, two class II and one
   class I, or two or more class I misconducts.*

No occurrence within one year of the parole interview date
or since date of last review.

                                                                                            □ +0

Notate cumulative score
from first four components _____   Likely to Parole   □ 2 to 6
                                    Unlikely to Parole   □ 7 or greater

FIGURE 3.3 State of Pennsylvania sentencing matrix
Source: Handbook for New Parole Board Members 2003, 39.

Selective Incapacitation

The meteoric rise of parole-prediction instruments—and especially the development of the federal Salient Factor Score—coincided with a more general turn to actuarial methods in a number of other criminal justice arenas. One such area was the development of selective incapacitation. Selective incapacitation is based on the central insight that a small subset of repeat offenders is responsible for the majority of crime and that incapacitating that small group would have exponential benefits for the overall crime rate. As defined in one of the seminal reports on selective incapacitation, written by the RAND Corporation for the National Institute of Justice in 1982, "Selective incapacitation is a strategy that attempts to use objective actuarial evidence to improve the ability of the current system to identify and confine offenders who represent the most serious risk to the community."[24]

The theory of selective incapacitation, in its modern version, generally traces to a seminal study by Marvin Wolfgang, Robert Figlio, and Thorsten Sellin published by the University of Chicago Press in 1972.[25] Earlier studies had collected extensive data on the background and characteristics of young and adult offenders. (Recall the early research of Sheldon and Eleanor Glueck from the 1930s.) These early studies generally relied on collecting longitudinal criminal justice data, including arrests, convictions, and prison terms, from a sample of youthful delinquents or prisoners, or conducting self-report surveys from among known offenders or delinquents. The Wolfgang, Figlio, and Sellin study pioneered a new approach that became known as the "cohort study": they collected data on every single male youth born in 1945 who lived in Philadelphia between the ages of 10 and 18.[26] This turned out to be a large group of boys, 9,945 in total.

Their study revealed that a large number of the youths—3,475, or 35 percent of the total cohort—had at least one recorded police contact by the age of 18.[27] However, only a much smaller subset—627 youths, or 6.3 percent of the cohort—constituted chronic offenders, having committed more than four violations. This much smaller subset was responsible for more than 50 percent of the crimes committed by the total cohort.[28] In other words, about 6 percent of these youths in Philadelphia were committing 50 percent of the crime. A follow-up study by Figlio, Wolfgang, and Paul Tracy of a 1958 cohort, also from Philadelphia, similarly showed that a disproportionately small group of youths were committing most of the crime. That study revealed that high-rate offenders made up 7.5 percent of the group but accounted for 61 percent of the crimes committed by the total group.[29]

The modern idea of selective incapacitation grew from this insight: locking up those 6 percent could cut crime in half.[30] The problem became how to identify the 6 percent of chronic offenders. And the solution, naturally, was to turn to actuarial methods. In the 1970s, Kristen Williams, a researcher at the Institute of Law and Social Research, conducted a study of 4,703 subjects arrested in Washington, D.C., and identified positive and negative factors associated with recidivism.[31] Some of those factors included race, gender, and age—with higher recidivism rates for black male youths. Williams organized twenty-one of the factors into a numerical scale and developed a prediction instrument. When tested against actual records, the instrument proved moderately successful: "[O]f the offenders the prediction model estimated to be in the worst 10 percent of the recidivists, 29 percent were in fact correctly identified."[32]

These developments led, in the 1980s, to more sustained attention to sentencing—to identifying the higher-risk offenders for purposes of sentencing determinations—rather than investigation or prevention. The RAND Corporation began a Habitual Offender Project that would eventually come to define selective incapacitation in sentencing.[33] The idea of focusing on sentencing derived from studies of California prisons showing that there were no real differences between prison sentences for low- and high-rate offenders. The idea behind the RAND project was to reshuffle inmate sentencing: by locking up for longer periods the high-rate offenders, a state could both reduce its crime rate and simultaneously its prison population. At about the same time, in 1983, a blue-ribbon panel of the National Academy of Sciences was convened to explore the available research on selective incapacitation. Chaired by Alfred Blumstein, the panel's stated mission was "to evaluate the feasibility of predicting the future course of criminal careers, to assess prediction instruments in reducing crime through incapacitation (usually by incarceration), and to review the contribution of research on criminal careers to the development of fundamental knowledge about crime and criminals."[34]

Peter Greenwood, with Allan Abrahamse, issued a RAND report in 1982 that set forth the most fully articulated plan for implementing a strategy of selective incapacitation. Greenwood and his colleague based their study on self-report surveys from 2,100 male prison and jail inmates from California, Michigan, and Texas in 1977.[35] The study focused on robbery and burglary offenses, and excluded more serious crimes such as murder or rape because these low-rate crimes are so extremely difficult to predict.

The researchers developed a seven-factor test to identify the high-rate offenders that relied on three primary categories: prior criminal record, history of drug abuse, and employment history. More specifically, the seven
factors focused on the following information regarding the defendant:

1. Incarcerated more than half of the two-year period preceding the most recent
   arrest.
2. A prior conviction for the crime type that is being predicted.
3. Juvenile conviction prior to age 16.
4. Commitment to a state or federal juvenile facility.
5. Heroin or barbiturate use in the two-year period preceding the current arrest.
6. Heroin or barbiturate use as a juvenile.
7. Employed less than half of the two-year period preceding the current arrest.[36]

Notice that the first four of the seven factors focus on prior criminal history and dominate the prediction instrument.

Greenwood and his colleague assigned each offender a score from 0
through 7: a positive response on any one of the seven factors resulted in
one point on the offender's score. The resulting score was used to distinguish between low-, medium-, or high-rate offenders—here, burglars or
robbers. When the researchers tested the prediction instrument, it was better at identifying low- and medium-rate offenders than high-rate offenders: 91 to 92 percent of those scoring 0 or 1—the lowest possible scores—
turned out to be low- or medium-rate offenders. In contrast, 50 percent
of those scoring 5, 6, or 7 turned out to be high-rate burglars or robbers.[37]

Nevertheless, Greenwood and his colleague concluded their study on
an optimistic note: "Increasing the accuracy with which we can identify
high-rate offenders or increasing the selectivity of sentencing policies can
lead to a decrease in crime, a decrease in the prison population, or both.
Selective incapacitation is a way of increasing the amount of crime prevented by a given level of incarceration."[38]

Another study,[39] also for the Institute of Law and Social Research, produced a slightly different prediction instrument that relied on factors such
as "a history of alcohol abuse or heroin use, the age of the offender, the
character of the offender's most recent offense, and a number of factors
derived from the offender's criminal record."[40] Drawing on a sample of
1,708 persons convicted of federal offenses released during 1970 and 1971,
this study noted the following results: "Eighty-five percent of the offenders classified as probable recidivists were rearrested for a serious offense

within five years of release, as opposed to only thirty-three percent of those identified as noncareer criminals."[41]

The approach should sound familiar, as it had so much in common with the parole-prediction instruments developed many years earlier. It borrowed method and insight from the Burgess models and, later, the Salient Factor Score. The trouble for the proponents of these methods in sentencing is that the false positive rate was high, and resistance developed to imposing a sentence—rather than parole release—based on an approach with such high rates of false positives. The American Law Institute would eventually take this view, recommending the sentencing provisions of the Model Penal Code be revised to move away from strict adherence to prediction instruments.[42] An influential note from the *Harvard Law Review* reflecting this general perception: "[T]he results of efforts in the late 1960's and early 1970's to predict violence or 'dangerousness' among former convicts were almost uniformly discouraging, with rates of 'false positives'—individuals who were mistakenly classified as dangerous—ranging between fifty-four and ninety-nine percent."[43]

The solution that emerged was essentially to fall back on prior criminal history as a proxy for future dangerousness. All the studies—from parole prediction to selective incapacitation contexts—showed that prior correctional contacts (arrests, convictions, and incarcerations) were the single best predictor of recidivism. The result was the development of sentencing schemes that were more simplistic but easier to administer, relying predominantly on prior criminal history, such as sentencing guidelines, mandatory minimums, and "three-strikes" laws that enhanced punishment for prior offenders. Paul Robinson, a former commissioner on the United States Sentencing Commission and a professor of law at the University of Pennsylvania, explains that the "[n]ew sentencing guidelines increase the sentence[s] of offenders with criminal histories because these offenders are seen as the most likely to commit future crimes."[44] Robinson goes on to say, "The rationale for heavy reliance upon criminal history in sentencing guidelines is its effectiveness in incapacitating dangerous offenders. As the Guidelines Manual of the United States Sentencing Commission explains, 'the specific factors included in [the calculation of the Criminal History Category] are consistent with the extant empirical research assessing correlates of recidivism and patterns of career criminal behavior.'"[45] As another commentator suggests, "[C]riminal history is seen as a crucial component of the determination of an offender's sentence because of its use as a predictor of future criminality."[46]

Habitual-offender enhancement statutes specifically grew out of this simplifying trend. The California "three-strikes" law is perhaps the most notorious of these enhancement statutes—described by commentators as "the single toughest penal statute in state history"[47] and "the toughest anti-crime law in the nation."[48] Adopted in 1994 and patterned on Washington State's Persistent Offender Accountability Act, California's three-strikes law provides that a person with one prior serious or violent felony conviction must receive double the punishment for a second felony conviction; and someone with two or more such convictions must receive three times the sentence for a new conviction or a minimum of twenty-five years to life.[49] The rationale behind California's three-strikes statute is, very simply, selective incapacitation.[50] As Erik Luna explains in detailing the history of its adoption and its justifications, the California law is based primarily on the theory of selective incapacitation.[51]

Though California's law is the best known, most states have enacted enhancement statutes for habitual offenders. Some states, such as Massachusetts and Virginia, have had these statutes since the early colonial period;[52] and numerous other states adopted recidivist statutes between 1920 and 1945.[53] By mid-century, more than twenty states and the federal government had adopted laws mandating or permitting life imprisonment for felons convicted of two, three, or four prior offenses—laws that were named after the sponsor, New York legislator Caleb Baumes.[54] Those numbers would increase, though, with the advent of selective incapacitation, and, by 1980, habitual-offender statutes were in place in forty-four states, at the federal level, and in the District of Columbia, Puerto Rico, and the Virgin Islands.[55] Many of these statutes are severe, such as those in Texas, Washington, and West Virginia, which require mandatory life sentences for a third felony conviction.[56] At the close of the twentieth century, forty-seven states, the federal government, and the District of Columbia had some version of an antirecidivist law on their books.[57] Though these laws vary by jurisdiction, they essentially provide longer sentences for prior felony offenders. In fact, more than 80 percent of the statutes in effect at the close of the twentieth century required a life sentence for habitual offenders, and the majority of those states preclude parole.[58]

The Federal Sentencing Guidelines

The emergence of fixed sentencing guidelines is intricately interwoven with the historical development of parole-prediction instruments and parole-decision guidelines. On one hand, the developments in parole decision making prompted the effort to systematize sentencing. As the United States Sentencing Commission recognized in the report proposing the initial federal guidelines, "[T]he use of guidelines in the federal parole system led to suggestions that similar guidelines be developed for use by federal trial judges in their sentencing decisions. Also, a number of state parole authorities developed guidelines systems, and several states used their experience with parole guidelines as a springboard for the development of sentencing guidelines."[59] On the other hand, the development of federal sentencing guidelines coincided with the demise of parole in the 1970s.

The break was somewhat abrupt and sharp. As Michael Tonry explains, "Beginning with Maine's abolition of parole in 1975, nearly every state has in some ways repudiated indeterminate sentencing and recast sentencing policies to set standards for judges' and parole boards' decisions and thereby to narrow or eliminate their discretion."[60] Led by Minnesota and Pennsylvania in the 1970s, and then by the federal government in 1984, most jurisdictions turned to sentencing guidelines or other mechanisms—such as statutory determinate sentencing—to constrain judicial sentencing. In 1994, Congress enacted legislation making billions of dollars in grants to states depend on whether they had adopted sentencing guidelines, eliminated parole, and ensured that individuals would serve at least 85 percent of their sentences. By 1996, "[f]ifteen jurisdictions had adopted sentencing guidelines to limit judicial discretion; more than ten had eliminated parole release; another twenty-five had adopted parole guidelines; many had narrowed the ambit of good time; and all had enacted mandatory minimum sentence legislation (often requiring minimum ten-, twenty-, or thirty-year terms and sometimes mandatory sentences of life-without-possibility-of-parole)."[61] The new constraints on discretion in place today include mandatory minimum penalties, firearm and other sentencing enhancements, fixed sentencing guidelines, and a system of guidelines for state parole authorities, as well as repeat-offender statutes such as three-strikes laws and habitual-offender enhancements.[62]

At the federal level, the sentencing guidelines were the product of a contentious process within an institution—the federal sentencing commission—which can only be fairly described as an "organization in disarray."[63] The commission had no particular strategy for developing guidelines, so different commissioners went off in different directions trying to develop their own ideas for a guideline system. Commissioner Paul Robinson tried to develop a system based on "detailed comparative assessments of offenders' culpability," which focused first on offense elements (mental and physical components) and then on a complicated scheme of incremental punishment units relying, in part, on the square and cube roots of property values.[64] This, the commission found, was "unworkable."[65] Too much complexity, the commission noted, would make the guidelines unworkable, and would undermine fairness because the different variables might interact in unexpected ways:

> Complexity can seriously compromise the certainty of punishment and its deterrent effect. The larger the number of subcategories, the greater the complexity that is created and the less workable the system. Moreover, the factors that create the subcategories will apply in unforeseen situations and interact in unforeseen ways, thus creating unfairness. Perhaps most importantly, probation officers and courts, in applying a complex system of subcategories, would have to make a host of decisions about whether each of the large number of potentially relevant sentencing factors applied. This added fact-finding would impose a substantial additional burden on judicial resources. Furthermore, as the number and complexity of decisions that are required increases, the risk that different judges will apply the guidelines differently to situations that in fact are similar also increases. As a result the very disparity that the guidelines were designed to eliminate is re-introduced.[66]

Even if it were workable, the commission noted, a complex system could not be properly devised.[67]

Commissioners Michael Block and Ilene Nagel tried to devise a different set of guidelines based on research on deterrence and incapacitation. "Penalties would be set that would either have optimal deterrent effects or cost-effectively incapacitate those at highest risk for future crimes."[68] This, too, proved unsuccessful. The commission also considered but rejected a simpler, broad-category approach like those used in some states, which feature a few simple categories and narrow imprisonment ranges. And it considered and rejected "employing specific factors with flexible adjustment ranges (e.g., one to six levels depending on the degree of damage or injury)."[69]

By the time the commission rejected the Robinson proposal and then abandoned two subsequent drafts, time was running out. According to Andrew von Hirsch, "It was only in the winter of 1986 that other commissioners were drawn actively into the process. The final draft was written at a late date in some haste to meet the submission deadline."[70]

The commission ultimately chose a system that focuses primarily on prior criminal record and level of offense, with few additional variables, to achieve the twin objectives of uniformity and proportionality—uniformity among similar criminal conduct by similar offenders, and proportionality between different types of offenses. As a commentator notes, the U. S. Sentencing Commission "accepted that these past offenses could serve as reliable predictors of future criminal conduct."[71]

In order to achieve its goals, the commission conducted a statistical analysis of a dataset consisting of detailed observations regarding about 10,500 convictions, as well as less-detailed data regarding about 100,000 convictions. The guiding intuition was to use the statistical analyses to estimate current sentencing practices in order to replicate what then-commissioner Stephen Breyer referred to as "typical past practice."[72]

The Administrative Office of the United States Courts provided the basic data, which consisted of all defendant records—felony and misde-meanor—leading to convictions from (apparently) mid-1983 to late 1985 that were in the Federal Probation Sentencing and Supervision Infor-mation System.[73] The basic information included in this data consisted of offense description, defendant's background and criminal record, case disposition (trial or appeal), and sentence. A sample of 11,000 defendants from approximately 40,000 defendants convicted in fiscal year 1985 was then taken, and the data for 10,500 of those cases were supplemented with additional information concerning (1) the corresponding presentence in-vestigation reports; and (2) the actual or likely sentence to be served. The commission then posed several questions of the data:

> How much time on average is served currently by convicted federal defendants? How does this average vary with characteristics of the offense, the background and criminal history of the defendant, and the method of disposition? How much of the variation about these averages cannot be attributed to the crime and the defendant; that is, how disparate is sentencing? What is the rate at which defendants are returning to prison following a parole revocation? How long do defendants remain in prison following revocation?[74]

The key question—referred to as the "baseline question"—concerned the sentence of a first-time offender who was convicted at trial. Naturally, there were few of those in the dataset. So the commission used standard multi-variate statistical analysis (multivariate maximum likelihood estimation) to draw inferences about the sentences received by first-time defendants convicted at trial.[75] The commission developed two "levels tables" from the data that assisted them in setting guideline ranges. The first table is entitled "Estimated Time Served for Baseline Offenses: 1st Time Offenders, Sentenced to Prison, Adjusted for Good Time" and, as its title suggests, gives the estimated length of sentences by offense and the estimated number of persons sentenced to prison. The second table, entitled "Estimated Level Adjustment," reports the adjustments in estimated length of sentence associated with different aggravating or mitigating factors. The factors in the second table include the level of participation in the offense (leader or lesser role), whether a weapon was used, whether the crime involved additional planning, organized crime, hostage taking, infliction of injury, importation of drugs, blackmail, planned or permanent injury; whether the institution or person victimized was a nonfederal facility, the postal service, a government victim, an especially vulnerable victim, or a law enforcement officer; whether the defendant cooperated, pleaded guilty, was a drug user, was unusually cruel, or perjured himself; and whether the defendant generated income primarily from crime.

An Actuarial Proxy: Criminal History

What emerged as the most important dimension of the guidelines was prior criminal history, which was incorporated into the federal guidelines system as a proxy for the prediction of future offending. The commission specifically studied a number of the more reliable prediction instruments, such as the Salient Factor Score from the parole context and the Inslaw Scale for Selecting Career Criminals for Special Prosecutions.[76] Drawing on these instruments, the commission developed certain ranges of criminal history called Criminal History Categories. These categories were intended to replicate the predictive instruments and maximize the predictive power of the guidelines:

> In selecting elements for the criminal history score, the Commission examined a number of prediction instruments, with particular attention to the four prediction instruments recently reviewed by the National Academy of Sciences Panel on Criminal Careers. Two of these four prediction instruments, the United States Parole Commission's "Salient Factor Score" and the "proposed Inslaw Scale for Selecting Career Criminals for Special Prosecution," were developed using data on federal offenders. Four of the five elements selected by the Commission for inclusion in the criminal history score are very similar to elements

contained in the Salient Factor Score. The remaining element was derived from an element contained in the Proposed Inslaw Scale.[77]

By deriving the criminal history elements directly from the Salient Factor Score and the Inslaw Scale, the commission guaranteed maximum predictive power for the guidelines. In fact, they expressly stated as much in their report:

> The indirect evidence available to the Commission strongly suggests that the criminal history score will demonstrate predictive power comparable to that of prediction instruments currently in use. Using its augmented FPSSIS (Federal Probation Sentencing and Supervision Information System) data, the Commission has verified that, as anticipated, there is a close relationship between the criminal history score and the Salient Factor Score, a prediction instrument used by the United States Parole Commission as part of its system of parole guidelines for nearly fifteen years. The predictive power and stability of the Salient Factor Score have been firmly established.[78]

"From a crime control perspective," the commission emphasized, "a criminal history component is especially important because it is predictive of recidivism."[79] The commission quoted extensively from the most current and reliable social scientific literature on prediction instruments, including the 1986 article by Stephen Gottfredson and Don Gottfredson, "Accuracy of Prediction Models," in Alfred Blumstein's edited volume *Criminal Careers and "Career Criminals"*:

> [O]ne of the best predictors of future criminal conduct is past criminal conduct, and the parole prediction literature amply supports this fact. From the earliest studies to the latest, indices of prior criminal conduct consistently are found to be among the most powerful predictors. . . . This generalization tends to hold regardless of the measure of prior criminal conduct used or of specific operational definitions of the conduct.[80]

In this sense, the idea of relying so heavily on prior criminal history was precisely to capture the selective incapacitation effect without complicating the guidelines with the problem of false positives. The commission expressly recognized this, writing that "[p]rimary reliance on criminal history to predict recidivism limits the tension between a just punishment and a crime-control philosophy."[81] Relying on the ABA Standards for

Criminal Justice, the commission noted that "confinement based on predicted risk is a troubling concept. . . . [But it] can be averted because to a substantial extent the factors that best distinguish high-risk from low-risk offenders also are factors that make the former group more culpable than the latter (e.g., prior convictions, prior incarcerations, etc.)." [82] The commission went on to quote Peter Hoffman, who developed the Salient Factor Score in the parole context, who proposed that "items compatible with 'desert' [are] those concerning . . . the frequency, seriousness, and recency of prior offenses. Prior criminal history items [also] tend to be among the items found most predictive of recidivism. Thus, in practice, there is likely to be considerable overlap between a 'predictive' dimension and a 'desert' dimension." [83]

In sum, the commission chose to focus on prior criminal history as an actuarial proxy for the likelihood of future offending. As the commission expressly recognized, "The particular elements that the Commission selected have been found empirically to be related to the likelihood of further criminal behavior." [84]

The Guidelines in Operation

In practice, the guidelines break down criminal history into six categories, entitled Category I through Category VI. A defendant is assigned a given number of points—ranging from one to three—for prior criminal convictions, based solely on the length of the prior imposed sentence. In other words, the point system does not depend on the offense level of the prior offense, but on the actual length of the sentence imposed. The defendant is assigned three points for a sentence longer than thirteen months, two points for any sentence longer than sixty days but less than thirteen months, and one point for any shorter sentence, with additional points for defendants who were under supervision at the time of the crime.[85] Certain older prior offenses as well as many juvenile and other special convictions are excluded from the computation. The points are then used to calculate the category, with only a few further refinements:

> The rate of increase in severity among the criminal history categories is carefully balanced. The Sentencing Commission fashioned the criminal history categories so that the rate at which a sentence increases from Criminal History Category I to Category II, or from Category II to Category III, is equivalent to a one-level increase in the base offense level. Reflecting the greater seriousness

of more substantial criminal records, the Commission designated that a move from Category III to Category IV, Category IV to Category V, or Category V to Category VI, would represent a more Byzantine change in the offense level, because these categories include much broader ranges of criminal history points.

Interestingly, the Sentencing Commission designed the criminal history categories in this fashion so that the relative increase is actually greater for less serious offenses. While this seems somewhat counterintuitive—the notion being that the increase in categories actually ought to be greater for more serious offenses—a system of this sort would thus more heavily penalize those at the top of the criminal history categories. The Commission, however, based its decision on sociological research indicating that the crime-preventive benefits of imprisonment decline with age. As a consequence, the Commission reasoned that "adding any given number of years to a five-year sentence, for example, is likely to be more effective in decreasing the overall level of crime than adding the same number of years to a twenty-year sentence." In other words, the marginal benefit of adding more years to lengthen sentences at the top-end of the guidelines was thought to be small.[86]

Naturally, the commission also made political choices once it had established these categories. The commission "raised substantially" the sentences for crimes involving actual (rather than merely threatened) violence, such as murder, aggravated assault, and rape.[87] Though the data revealed lower sentences for white-collar offenses (embezzlement, fraud, and tax evasion) than for larceny, the commission decided to ignore the disparities and treat them essentially identically. Also, in light of the Anti-Drug Abuse Act, the commission imposed guidelines for drug offenses that were "much higher than in current practice."[88] But at the heart of the federal guidelines lies a crude proxy of an actuarial instrument: the criminal history categories.

State Guidelines

It is important to note that most of the state guidelines and sentencing mechanisms also use two-dimensional grids that focus primarily on prior criminal history as well as, naturally, the severity of the crime. As Michael Tonry explains,

> Reduced to their core elements, all sentencing guidelines grids are fundamentally the same: two-dimensional tables that classify crimes by their severity along

one axis and criminal records by their extent along the other. Applicable sentences for any case are calculated by finding the cell where the applicable criminal record column intersects with the applicable offense severity row. Guidelines grids vary in details. Although most divide crimes into ten or twelve categories, some use more. . . . They vary in ornateness. Although most, like Washington's, provide a range of presumptive sentences such as "twenty-one to twenty-seven months" for any offense severity/criminal record combination, those in North Carolina (1994) and Pennsylvania (1994) contain a range for "ordinary cases" and separate ranges for cases in which aggravating or mitigating considerations are present. Finally, they vary in severity.[89]

States vary in the way in which they treat prior criminal history in their guideline grids. Some simply tabulate the total number without differentiating the type of prior offense. Others categorize the priors into violent or nonviolent and calibrate the sentence accordingly. Pennsylvania falls in the former category: "[A]ll prior convictions are included in the computation of the criminal history score, although some offenses are weighed more heavily than others. Because the focus is on the number of prior offenses, little distinction is made between types of offenders."[90] Oregon, in contrast, falls in the latter category: it uses "a typography classification of offenders that focuses not on the number of prior convictions, but, instead, the type of prior offenses committed with violent offenders and repeat non-violent felony offenders . . . targeted for longer sentences."[91]

What is clear from the development of these state and federal guidelines is that prior criminal history has become one of the principal axes of sentencing, and that it has become so dominant because it serves as a proxy for the likelihood of future offending. Most sentencing guidelines represent, in this sense, a crude actuarial device.

Capital Sentencing and Future Dangerousness

The death penalty in the United States also experienced an actuarial turn, as a number of states began to use future dangerousness as an aggravating circumstance militating in favor of imposing a capital sentence. Texas was the leader.

In the wake of the United States Supreme Court's decision in *Furman v. Georgia* (1972)[92]—holding unconstitutional death-penalty sentencing measures that rested on unguided jury discretion—the state of Texas enacted a more determinate capital punishment sentencing scheme. Under Texas's new death penalty statute, Texas juries were required to impose a sentence of death if they found that the defendant convicted of capital murder acted deliberately and posed a risk of future dangerousness and, if he had acted with provocation, that his conduct was an unreasonable response to that provocation.[93] On the future dangerousness prong, Texas juries were to be asked whether the defendant was likely to commit future acts of violence that would constitute a continuing threat to society. If a capital sentencing jury responded yes to all three questions, then a sentence of death automatically would be imposed. In a series of subsequent challenges to the Texas statute—including *Jurek v. Texas* (1976)[94] and *Barefoot v. Estelle* (1983)[95]—the United States Supreme Court upheld the use of future dangerousness as a factor in capital sentencing as well as the introduction of psychiatric testimony to prove future dangerousness.

Following the lead of Texas, a number of other states began using future dangerousness as an important factor in death-penalty sentencing.[96] At the turn of the twenty-first century, twenty-one states included the risk of future dangerousness as an aggravating circumstance to be considered at the death-penalty phase of a capital trial, with Oregon—along with Texas—requiring that the jury predict future dangerousness if they were to impose a sentence of death; in addition, federal capital prosecutions often rely on future dangerousness as a nonstatutory aggravating circumstance.[97] In other states, the death-penalty statutes rely on prior criminal history as a proxy for future dangerousness (e.g., Arkansas, Oklahoma, and California). California, for instance, does not include future dangerousness as an aggravating circumstance, and the courts there have determined that the introduction of evidence of future dangerousness is reversible error. Nevertheless, California includes prior criminal history as an aggravating circumstance.[98] In other states, like Maryland, the lack of future dangerousness is explicitly considered a mitigating circumstance and is included in the statutory definition of mitigation.[99] As a result, the concept of future dangerousness seems to have permeated the public's imagination in death-penalty cases. Recent empirical evidence, based on interviews of capital jurors, suggests that the issue of future dangerousness is on the mind of most jurors in capital cases, regardless of whether it is introduced as an aggravating factor by the prosecution.[100]

For many years, the states' primary method of demonstrating future dangerousness was to call expert psychiatrists to convince the jury in layman's terms based on their expert clinical opinion and years of experience.

Often the expert psychiatrists would never have interviewed or met the capital defendant prior to sentencing, but would opine on the basis of hypothetical questions regarding prior criminal history and demeanor at trial. This became something of a *cause célèbre* in Texas, when one particular psychiatrist, Dr. James P. Grigson, commonly known as "Dr. Death," testified repeatedly that he was "one hundred percent" certain—in some cases "one thousand percent" certain—that the defendant at sentencing would be dangerous in the future.[101] Dr. Grigson notoriously testified in the capital case leading to *Barefoot v. Estelle*. As was his habit, Dr. Grigson had not interviewed the defendant, but asserted that, having examined between thirty and forty thousand individuals, with enough information he could give an opinion "within reasonable psychiatric certainty as to the psychological or psychiatric makeup of an individual."[102] By 1994, Dr. Grigson had appeared on behalf of the state in at least 150 capital trials, and his predictions of future dangerousness had been used to sentence at least one-third of all Texas death row inmates.[103]

More recently, though, and increasingly, prosecutors in death-penalty cases are turning to actuarial rather than clinical evidence. And so, increasingly, government psychiatric experts testify not only in layman's terms about their clinical judgments, but also about the more technical results of prediction instruments. At the 1998 federal capital trial of Aquilia Barnette in North Carolina,[104] for instance, the government expert recounted to the jury the results of the Psychopathy Checklist-Revised (PCL-R) to substantiate his opinion that the defendant presented a risk of future dangerousness.[105] In fact, the actuarial evidence included not only the Psychopathy Checklist-Revised, but also "an actuarial analysis comparing Barnette to groups of people with characteristics similar to him."[106] In ultimately allowing the evidence to reach the jury, the federal court declared that the expert opinion was admissible precisely because it was based in part on "the actuarial approach; and the research on predicting future dangerousness."[107]

The turn to actuarial methods in the death-penalty context is heating up. Two other federal courts of appeals—the Eighth and the Fifth Circuits—have deemed admissible PCL-R evidence as proof of future dangerousness in death-penalty cases.[108] In a recent influential article, Mark Cunningham and Thomas Reidy argue for a more rigorous actuarial approach. In their work, they review the best available data and point toward an actuarial future: "Actuarial follow-up data on the violent recidivism outcome of capital murderers in prison and post-release has been compiled and synthesized in this paper with the hope that capital sentencing risk assessment testimony will be more empirically based and thus will more closely reflect the probabilities demonstrated by this group of offenders."[109]

Criminal Profiling

Another significant area that witnessed a turn to actuarial measures in the late twentieth century is the field of policing and, especially, criminal profiling. Criminal profiling emerged as a formal law enforcement tool at midcentury in the United States,[110] although it arguably had antecedents in the early-twentieth-century eugenics movement. Criminal profiling became more frequent in the 1970s with drug-courier profiles and alien smuggling profiles, and its use increased in the last quarter of the twentieth century.[111]

The basic idea of profiling is actuarial and simple: to develop correlations between specific group-based traits and group-based offending rates in order to help law enforcement officers identify potential suspects for investigation. One of the first well-known uses of criminal profiling involved the hijacker profiles developed in the 1960s to disrupt the hijacking of American planes. The Federal Aviation Administration put in place a hijacker profile beginning in October 1968. The profile was based on a detailed study of the known characteristics of identified airline hijackers, and it highlighted approximately twenty-five characteristics, primarily behavioral.[112] The list of profiles that have been developed is long, and includes many crime-specific profiles like the "drug smuggling vessel profile, the stolen car profile, the stolen truck profile, the alimentary-canal smuggler profile, the battering parent profile, and the poacher profile."[113]

The turn to profiling reflects an overall shift from the earlier reform model of "professional" policing. This earlier model traced back to August Vollmer's tenure as police chief in Berkeley beginning in 1905 and to the 1931 Wickersham Commission report condemning police corruption and brutality.[114] It was characterized by a strategy of rapid response to 911 calls. And it was displaced by the crime-prevention models of the late twentieth century—what I have referred to elsewhere as the "order-maintenance" approach to criminal justice.[115] The order-maintenance approach relies heavily on offender profiles to target stop-and-frisk encounters and misdemeanor arrests, to disperse gang-members, to stop drug couriers and illegal immigrants, and to control the disorderly.

The several different types of criminal profiling mechanisms can be arrayed along several dimensions.[116] One dimension has to do with the type of data upon which the profiles are based. Some profiles are derived from external, observable characteristics that are identifiable in law enforcement reports and arrest records: clothing, hair-style, facial hair, demeanor, nervousness, luggage, and so forth. The drug-courier profile is an example of this type. Other profiles are based primarily on psychological data: mental health and counseling reports, analyses of family and social relationships, and interviews of friends and family. These tend to be clinical rather than actuarial. The school-shooter threat-assessment model and serial killer profiles fit in this category.[117] Another dimension has to do with the timing of the profile—whether it is assembled *ex ante* from previous arrests in order to identify future suspects for investigation, or whether the crime has been committed and a profile is being assembled from the known facts to identify a suspect. Drug-courier profiling fits in the first category. An ongoing homicide investigation might fit in the second, particularly where a serial killer profile is being developed from the evidence. It is possible to categorize these different types of profiling in a two-way matrix:

	Mental	Physical
Ex ante	School shooter	Drug courier
Ex post	Homicide investigation	Witness ID

The drug-courier profile, discussed in the introduction to this book, is one of the more prominent examples of a criminal profile. The profile was developed through DEA agents' experience, and it is, in this sense, the product of a combination of clinical and statistical findings. It consists of personal observations from a large number of cases involving subjective judgment built over many years. "In theory, the drug courier profile seeks to incorporate the subjective judgments of experienced narcotics agents into a statistical model that uses predetermined profile characteristics based on an analysis of prior cases." [118]

Most students of the drug-courier profile trace it back to two former DEA agents, John Marcello and Paul Markonni, who are considered the "godfathers" of the profile.[119] They and other DEA agents started identifying the common characteristics of illegal drug couriers in airports. Much of this began on the basis of tips from informants or airline personnel. "Before developing the drug courier profile, DEA agents learned the *modus operandi* of cross-country drug distributors and couriers through conversations with undercover operators, informants, and cooperative defendants—those arrested on drug charges as well as convicted codefendants who turned state's evidence."[120] Most of the evidence about these profiles comes from litigation on motions to suppress or for selective enforcement. The information, though, was not made public but was reviewed *in camera* so as not to disclose the behavioral model that the DEA agents had developed.[121] The airplane hijacker profile was also an important source of information, because stops based on that profile often netted persons in possession of drugs.[122]

"At some point in time the DEA apparently undertook a nationwide effort to draw a composite picture of those persons likely to carry illegal drugs."[123] This effort was not successful. As the United States government declared in its petition for *certiorari* filed with the Supreme Court in the *Mendenhall* case, "[T]here is no national [drug-courier] profile; each airport unit has developed its own set of drug courier characteristics on the basis of that unit's experience. . . . Furthermore, the profile is not rigid, but is constantly modified in light of experience."[124]

Several scholars, David Cole in particular, have compiled lists of the drug-courier profile characteristics, which are often internally contradictory.[125] With time, the profiles have proliferated. As Charles Becton explains,

> Not only does each airport have a profile, but a single DEA agent may use multiple profiles of his or her own. Paul Markonni, the person most often credited with developing the drug courier profile, and clearly the agent most often listed in drug courier profile cases, has articulated several slightly varying profiles in reported cases. One court has used different profiles for incoming and outgoing flights. The United States Court of Appeals for the Ninth Circuit in *United States v. Patino* made reference to a "female" drug courier profile. The United States Court of Appeals for the Fifth Circuit referred to a regional profile in *United States v. Berry,* and a profile associated with particular agents in *United States v. Elmore.* And, contributing to the proliferation of the drug courier profile, state and local law enforcement agencies have instituted their own profile programs.[126]

How much credence should we give these drug-courier profiles? Opinions differ widely. According to former Justice Lewis Powell, concurring in *Mendenhall,* the drug-courier profile is a "highly specialized law enforcement operation."[127] In the *per curiam* opinion in *Reid,* the Supreme Court referred to the drug-courier profile as "a somewhat informal compilation of characteristics believed to be typical of persons unlawfully carrying narcotics."[128] Former chief Justice William Rehnquist has referred to the profile as "the collective or distilled experience of narcotics officers concerning characteristics repeatedly seen in drug smugglers."[129] According to David Cole of Georgetown University, the drug-courier profile "simply compiles the collective wisdom and judgment of a given agency's officials. Instead of requiring each officer to rely on his or her own limited experience in detecting suspicious behavior, the drug-courier profile gives every officer the advantage of the agency's collective experience."[130]

As noted earlier, though, a 1982 National Institute of Justice study found a 34 percent success rate based on 146 encounters with passengers.[131] The study has been offered as empirical support for the profiling method.

The Actuarial versus the Clinical

Overall, the rise of the actuarial also coincided with a gradual perception within the scientific community that actuarial methods were more reliable than clinical approaches. During the second half of the twentieth century, it is fair to say, a consensus emerged within the social scientific community that actuarial instruments were generally more accurate at predicting future events than clinical methods.[132] Paul Meehl's work in this area was pathbreaking and extremely influential,[133] and Meehl is most often cited as the person who single-handedly displaced the clinical paradigm. His research and writings are referred to as a "devastating critique of clinical judgment":[134] "The empirical support for Meehl's thesis has been demonstrated repeatedly over the ensuing decades, with recent contributions noteworthy for their clarity and persuasiveness."[135] To give just a little flavor of the discourse, the National Center for State Courts, for example, declares that "Beginning with Paul Meehl's early, highly influential study, *Clinical versus Statistical Prediction* (1954), preponderant evidence shows that statistical techniques of risk assessment are clearly superior to clinical assessments."[136] John Monahan and his colleagues, referring back to Meehl, similarly suggest that "[t]he general superiority of statistical over clinical risk assessment in the behavioral sciences has been known for almost half a century."[137]

As a result, there is today, even among skeptics, a general recognition of what Thomas Litwack calls an "increasingly widespread academic view that actuarial assessments of dangerousness are superior to clinical assessments." Litwack, a clinician at John Jay College of Criminal Justice and a skeptic of the actuarial, acknowledges that "Today, one routinely finds statements in the literature suggesting that actuarial assessments of dangerousness have proven to be superior to clinical assessments, or at least, to unstructured clinical assessments."[138] To be sure, the consensus is not completely uncontested,[139] but it is solid and pervasive. And it has had tangible consequences: in most areas of criminal law, the actuarial takes precedence over the clinical. "Although there are exceptions," as Jonathan Simon observes, "classical clinical prediction has been replaced almost everywhere with more or less structured and standardized instruments that incorporate, in style and partially in substance, the actuarially weighted and validated instruments famously used in setting insurance premiums as well as in functions like college admissions."[140]

The Actuarial Paradigm

Looking back over the twentieth century, it becomes clear that the actuarial paradigm underwent significant structural transformations. In the parole and sentencing area, the actuarial models first focused on the prior criminal history of the accused and then widened out in order to serve multiple purposes. In the context of indeterminate sentencing, the model gradually shifted from trying to find the most appropriate rehabilitative remedy—which is extremely hard to operationalize—to focusing on one key factor on a grid: prior criminal history. In the field of guideline sentencing, the models first tracked parole-prediction instruments and then focused more simplistically on criminal history. But although the models may have evolved and changed over time, what runs through all these variations is the larger trend favoring the actuarial, which is reflected in the exponential increase in the use of prediction instruments in the parole context. It is the movement toward criminal profiling along so many dimensions, from race, to tax deductions, to drug couriers. And it is one of the most important trends in criminal law at the turn of the twenty-first century.

PART II
The Critique of Actuarial Methods

Many critics of the actuarial today associate the rise of statistical models with a loss of individualization—with a movement toward generalization and away from what Frederick Schauer calls the "primacy of the particular."[1] These commentators locate the actuarial in opposition to individualism. Legal scholar Albert Alschuler, for example, laments the increased use of aggregation in criminal sentencing precisely because it undermines the traditional focus on the individual. In a 1991 article subtitled *A Plea for Less Aggregation,* Alschuler writes, "Increased aggregation seems characteristic of current legal and social thought, and . . . now seems to threaten traditional concepts of individual worth and entitlement."[2] Alschuler places the rise of aggregation in criminal law alongside the emergence of group rights as a new strategy for social reform. Aggregation has led to a new group-based penology: "Judges determine the scope of legal rules, not by examining the circumstances of individual cases, but by speculating about the customary behavior of large groups," Alschuler explains. "We seem increasingly indifferent to individual cases and small numbers."[3]

These criticisms reflect in part the original contribution of Malcolm Feeley and Jonathan Simon, who coined the phrase "New Penology" in the early 1990s.[4] The New Penology referred precisely to a mode of discourse and to technologies for the management of dangerous persons that replaced the earlier language of individual moral culpability, clinical diagnoses, and treatment interventions. The New Penology represented, in their words, an "actuarial language of probabilistic calculations and statistical distributions applied to populations" that "seeks to regulate levels of deviance, not intervene or respond to *individual* deviants or social malformations."[5]

Frederick Schauer, in his book *Profiles, Probabilities, and Stereotypes* (2003), joins the debate at exactly this juncture, but, in contrast, he sings the praise of aggregation as opposed to individualization. "My aim in this book," Schauer emphasizes, "is to challenge the primacy of the particular."[6]

It is, however, far too simplistic for either side to characterize the turn to the actuarial as a movement away from the individual or from individualization. The actuarial is better understood, instead, as the culmination or the zenith of the turn to the individualization of punishment. It is the crowning glory of Raymond Saleilles's *The Individualization of Punishment* and of Ernst Freund and Roscoe Pound's "*system* of individualization."[7] It grows out of the desire to better individualize and tailor our law enforcement practices to the reality of *this particular individual*. Though decision by categories may cause error in an identifiable percentage of cases, multiplying the categories and identifying the most powerful predictors is precisely intended to make possible better outcomes for each individual convict.

It makes no sense, then, to debate the merits or demerits of individualization versus generalization at such an abstract level. The contrast between the categories is not instructive because both serve the same master—namely, the more accurate individualization of punishment. Instead, in order to properly evaluate the turn to the actuarial, we need to adopt the tools, the instruments, and the methods of aggregation: mathematics, prediction, and data analysis. We need to *model* the actuarial. Only then will we be in a position to properly assess claims of deterrence, of efficiency, and of progress. I turn first to the mathematics of prediction.

CHAPTER FOUR

The Mathematics of Actuarial Prediction: The Illusion of Efficiency

One of the strongest arguments for the use of actuarial methods is the economic argument based on deterrence and efficiency: assuming that people respond rationally to the costs and incentives of policing, using predictions based on group offending rates will result in greater detection of crime. By maximizing the detection of crime, law enforcement will deter the higher-offending targeted population. This is the most efficient allocation of law enforcement resources.

A number of able economists have turned their attention to demonstrating this more rigorously. They are developing models of criminal profiling and demonstrating that using actuarial methods may be an efficient way to engage in law enforcement—in fact, that profiling based on group offending rates may be the *most* efficient way to allocate police resources. They are laying out the rational-action argument for profiling and actuarial methods in its most pristine form. The basic idea is that law enforcement should use group offending rates in order to make inferences about individual offending: for example, to pick motorists for searches based on their offending rates by race. They argue that this will reduce the offending of higher offenders and maximize the success rate of police searches. This in turn is viewed as the most efficient allocation of resources. Let me begin by setting forth the economists' models.

The Economists' Intervention

Drawing on Gary Becker's groundbreaking work on tastes for discrimination,[1] a group of economists—notably John Knowles, Nicola Persico, and Petra Todd at the University of Pennsylvania, and Jeff Dominitz at Carnegie Mellon University—are developing econometric models of racial profiling. The models would apply to any form of profiling but are being developed in the context of racial profiling largely because there are a lot of new data on police practices broken down by the race of the person stopped. The goal of the models is to test police behavior in order to distinguish between efficiency and racial animus in policing. That is, they aim to test whether a situation involving potentially disproportionate searches of minority motorists reflects efficient discrimination—also called statistical discrimination—resulting from the desire to maximize the number of successful searches of suspects, or raw racial prejudice.

The fact that police disproportionately search minority suspects is not, in itself, proof of racism, the argument goes. What matters instead is the rate of successful stops or searches—those that lead to arrests or the discovery of contraband. This is most frequently referred to as the "hit rate": the rate at which police interventions are successful in detecting criminality.

The models of racial profiling suggest the following: when the hit rates are the same across racial or ethnic lines, the police are not bigoted in their searches because they have no incentive to search more or fewer suspects of any particular race.[2] At equilibrium, the police have achieved a racial balance, though perhaps one with a racial imbalance at its heart, that they are unwilling to change on the basis of race—unless, of course, they have a taste for discrimination.

Accordingly, when the data reveal equal hit rates for different racial groups, these economists conclude that the disproportionate searches of minority suspects do not reflect a taste for discrimination but an attempt to maximize successful searches. When the data reveal lower hit rates for minority suspects, they reason that bigotry against minority suspects explains the disparity, and when the data reveal higher hit rates for minority suspects, they conclude that reverse racism is at work—in other words, bigotry against white suspects.

Explaining the Model: A Few Key Premises

The economic models rest on a few core premises of rational-choice theory. The first premise is that police officers seek to maximize the success rate of their stops and searches, given the cost of these interventions. In this sense, police officers are rational utility-maximizers who derive greater utility when they detect criminal activity. The second premise is that the suspects are also rational and try to maximize their own payoff associated with criminal activity: people who might, say, transport contraband will seek to maximize the payoff of carrying that contraband. If they face a negative payoff, they will not transport contraband. The third premise—the core theoretical premise that draws on Gary Becker's notion of a taste for discrimination—is that racism is reflected in the fact that the racist police officer experiences a lower cost for stopping or searching minority suspects than for searching white motorists. These three premises drive the model.

There is one more stipulation that drives the application of the model to current law enforcement practices and statistics: namely, that minorities offend at higher rates than whites under conditions of color-blind policing, in other words, in the absence of racial profiling. The model does not require this assumption. The model would also work if offending rates were the same among racial groups or if whites offended more as a group. But the interpretation of the model as applied to the case of racial profiling is based on the assumption that minorities offend at a higher rate overall under conditions of no racial profiling.

Given these premises, the economic model of racial profiling predicts that police officers will target the higher-offending group (minorities), for police searches because they will achieve better hit rates for their stops and searches. Profiling the higher-offending group and searching them disproportionately, however, will increase the cost of offending for members of this higher-offending group and thus eventually reduce their rate of offending. As the search rate of minority suspects increases, for instance, their payoff for transporting contraband will decrease, so that fewer minority suspects will carry contraband.

Police officers will continue to search members of the higher-offending group disproportionately until the point of equilibrium, where minority and white offending is at the same level. At that point, it will be possible to distinguish between the efficient, nonracist police officer and the racist officer who has a taste for discrimination. The efficient, nonracist police officer will maintain the distribution of searches at the equilibrium point. In fact, maintaining that equilibrium will demonstrate that the police officer is efficient rather than racist. It will also maximize the likelihood that the next search will be successful: if the police were to search proportionally more minorities, their offending rate would fall below that of whites, and the police would be targeting a pool of suspects with a hit rate below the one they could achieve by searching an additional white motorist. On the other hand, if the police were to search proportionally more whites,

then their offending rate would correspondingly fall below that of similarly situated minorities, thus reducing overall efficiency.

Given a relatively fixed level of law enforcement resources, there is
only one equilibrium point that will maximize hit rates if the police officer
is not racist, and that is the point at which the hit rates are the same across
racial lines. At that equilibrium, the police officer is engaged in maximally
efficient searches. In contrast, the racist police officer will continue to
target more minorities because his cost of searching minority suspects is
lower. In other words, at the point of equilibrium of the nonracist police
officer—the point of equal hit rates—the racist police officer will be able
to maximize his utility (search success rate minus cost) by searching more
minority suspects. Depending on how great a taste for discrimination this
racist police officer has, he will find his own point of equilibrium at some
distribution where the hit rate of minority suspects is below the hit rate
of white suspects.

The hit rate of searches, then, indicates whether the police officer is
purely efficient or bigoted. Knowles, Persico, and Todd, the leading economists working on racial profiling, explain that

> The key implication of the model is that if a police officer has the same cost
> of searching two subgroups of the population and if these two subgroups are
> searched at equilibrium, then the returns from searching will be equal across
> the subgroups. For example, suppose that searching one subgroup of motor-
> ists yielded a higher return. Then police would always search these motorists,
> who would in turn react by carrying contraband less often, until the returns to
> searching are equalized across groups.[3]

The economic model of racial profiling can be represented in a graph.[4]
The graph—shown in figure 4.1—visually represents the relationship between the internal rate of searches conducted within each racial group
(on the x-axis) and the offending rate of the different racial groups (on
the y-axis). At Time 1, the police are engaged in color-blind policing: assuming a certain level of searches, the police are searching both the white
population and the minority population at the same internal search rate of
10 percent. If minorities represent 20 percent of the total population, then
the police would be conducting 20 percent of its searches on minorities
and 80 percent of its searches on whites. And we are assuming at Time 1
that minorities are the higher-offending group—that, barring racial profiling, minorities offend at a higher rate as a group than whites. Figure 4.1

reflects this, in that minorities are offending at a higher rate than whites—
6 percent versus 4.5 percent—resulting in higher hit rates for minority
searches.

Given the higher marginal hit rate for minority suspects, the police begin to search minorities disproportionately, in far greater numbers than
their share of the population. They begin to search, say, 11 percent of the
minority population, then 12 percent; and, assuming relatively fixed law
enforcement resources, the police are searching a lower and lower percentage of the white population. Now, as the proportion of searches targeting
minority suspects increases, their group offending rate decreases. Crime
now costs minorities more because they are more likely to be detected.

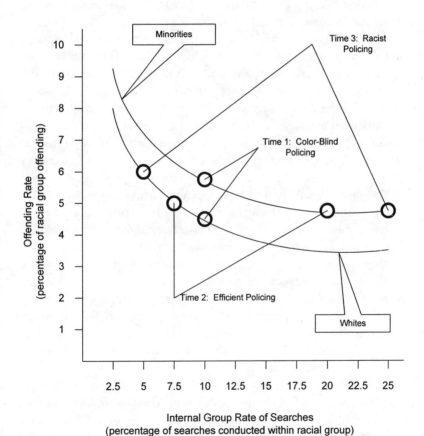

FIGURE 4.1 The economic model of racial profiling

They are being searched more, and therefore the overall payoff of criminal activity marginally decreases. The police continue to search marginally more minority suspects until Time 2, when the offending rates for
whites and minorities are the same—in this example, 5 percent.

At Time 2, the police are using race in the decision to search. The police are searching 20 percent of the minority population and 7.5 percent
of the white population, resulting say in a hypothetical total distribution
of searches of 60 percent minority and 40 percent white suspects. At that
distribution of searches, the offending rates are similar—and, one can infer, so are the hit rates. And at that distribution, the efficient police officer
has no reason to change the racial distribution of searches: the officer
has no incentive to search more minority suspects than the 60/40 total
distribution, which produces the different internal group search rates of
20 percent for minorities and 7.5 percent for whites.

If the police officer searches proportionally more minority suspects,
at Time 3 the offending rate of minorities will edge lower than that of
whites—in this example, 4.8 percent versus 6 percent. If this happens, then
the police officer must be racially bigoted. The only reason for an officer
to search more minority suspects than at the Time 2 equilibrium—that is,
say, 70 percent minorities and 30 percent whites, instead of the Time 2 distribution of 60 percent minority and 40 percent whites—would be that the
officer had a *taste* for discrimination resulting in higher utility even though
fewer minorities are offending.

The three hypothetical distributions of searches—20/80, 60/40, and
70/30—correspond to three different sets of internal group rates of
searches within the different racial groups. These three scenarios, graphi-
cally represented in figure 4.1, correspond to the three equilibrium points
for the color-blind, the efficient, and the racist police officer.[5]

The several basic premises discussed earlier are reflected well in this
graph. First, police officers are trying to maximize their utility and increase the efficiency of their interventions when they shift the distribution
of their searches from Time 1 to Time 2. In this sense, they are responding
to the likelihood of successful searches, targeting their searches at populations with higher hit rates.

Second, ordinary citizens are responding to the changes in police practices and corresponding changes in the cost of committing crime. As that
cost increases for minorities, their offending decreases, and as that cost decreases for whites, their offending increases. Individuals, whether minority
or white, are assumed to reduce their criminality when the police increase

the proportion of searches conducted on members of their racial group. As John Knowles and Rubén Hernández-Murillo explain, "The key assumption in the analysis is that while motorists differ in their propensity to carry contraband, those who face a high probability of being searched will tend to reduce their probability of carrying contraband in the vehicle."[6] This is what is generally referred to in more technical terms as the elasticity of offending to policing, or sometimes by the shorthand "elasticity." A core theoretical premise of the economic model of crime—of rational-choice theory—is that individuals are elastic to policing: their offending will vary depending on the likelihood of being detected—in other words, depending on the cost of crime.

Third, racist police officers continue to profile minorities past the point of equal hit rates because their cost of searching minorities is lower than the cost for a nonracist police officer: they have a taste for discrimination that results in disproportionately more minority stops and searches and therefore an even lower hit rate for minorities. In effect, racism manifests itself through the lower cost for racist police officers of searching minority motorists. It is in this sense that the crux of the economic models is derived from Gary Becker's work on discrimination, specifically from the central insight that "tastes for discrimination lead to lower profits for the discriminators."[7] By assuming that all police officers seek to maximize the search success rate minus the cost of searching, and that racism enters the picture by means of the cost of conducting a search, the economic models are able to factor out of the analysis all the other traits that lead police officers to search motorists—such as, for instance, age, tinted windows, bumper stickers, car model, and so forth. As Knowles, Persico, and Todd explain, "If the returns to searching are equal across *all* subgroups distinguishable by police, they must also be equal across *aggregations* of these subgroups, which is what we can distinguish in the data. Thus equality of the returns to searching can be tested without knowing all the characteristics observed by the police."[8] As discussed below, this is both a strength and weakness of the economic models.

Finally, the key stipulation reflected in the graph is that African Americans have a higher rate of transporting contraband, all other things being equal. If it takes such disproportionate searches of African Americans and whites (hypothetically here 60 percent versus 40 percent) to achieve comparable success rates for searches (5 percent in figure 4.1), this assumes that African Americans would offend at a much higher rate than whites if they were being stopped in proportion to their representation on the road. As Knowles, Persico, and Todd explain, "Our model implies that at equilibrium, both races should have the same probability of carrying drugs, but one race may be searched more often than another. In fact, searching some groups more often than others may be *necessary* to sustain equality in the proportions guilty across groups."[9] In other words, these groups offend more under natural (nonracial profiling) conditions, and only profiling will bring their offending rate into line with that of whites.[10]

Illustrations: Putting Some Real Numbers on the Model

It may be helpful here to put a bit of this in perspective with some real data, and fortunately there is a lot of it in the area of racial profiling. New reporting requirements and data-collection efforts by more than four hundred law enforcement agencies across the country—including entire states such as Maryland, Missouri, and Washington[11]—are producing a continuous flow of new evidence on highway police searches, as well as a lot of new research on the problem of "racial profiling."[12] In many cases, the data show disproportionate searches of African American and Hispanic motorists in relation to their estimated representation on the road.

The evidence from Maryland is illustrative. Samuel Gross and Katherine Barnes, in their article "Road Work: Racial Profiling and Drug Interdiction on the Highway,"[13] present data that cover stops and searches conducted by the Maryland State Police on Interstate Highway 95 from 1995 through mid-2000—a total of 8,027 searches, broken down by location, direction of travel, types of searches, quantities and types of drugs discovered, among other variables, though the data omit the number of persons stopped but not searched.[14] Approximately 40 percent of motorists searched by the Maryland State Police were African American, and 4.4 percent were Hispanic (663, table 1). On the specific corridor of I-95 that has been singled out in the racial profiling litigation, 60 percent of the persons searched were African American, and 6 percent were Hispanic (663, table 1). By contrast, African American motorists comprise about 17 percent of drivers and 17.5 percent of traffic violators (664, table 2).

With regard to a narrower corridor of I-95 from the Baltimore City limit to the Delaware border, more specific data cover stops and searches between May 1997 and April 2000. African Americans comprised 27.8 percent of the motorists stopped and 51.3 percent of the motorists searched. Hispanics comprised 1.3 percent of the motorists stopped and 6 percent of the motorists searched (665, table 3). In effect, African American drivers "were almost twice as likely to be stopped as white drivers; and more than five times as likely to be searched" (666).

One of the key statistics for purposes of the economic models of profiling is the hit rate—the rate at which searches discover contraband. The hit rates in Maryland were as follows: across the entire state, 37.4, 30.6, and 11.9 percent, respectively, for whites, African Americans, and Hispanics. On the I-95 corridor, 40.3, 37.8, and 15.8 percent, respectively, for whites, African Americans, and Hispanics (668, table 6). Gross and Barnes also break down the data by drug, location, type of search (consent search versus probable cause, with ground given for request, such as Grateful Dead stickers or nervousness). They find, for example, that "[c]ocaine and crack were found most often in cars with black drivers; heroin and 'other' drugs in cars driven by whites" (669).

Data have been collected from other states as well. These statistics have been rehearsed in leading law review articles and books. In Volusia County, Florida, on a stretch of I-95 in the mid-to-late 1980s, for instance, 70 percent of the persons stopped were minority motorists, and 80 percent of the cars searched belonged to minority motorists, even though minorities represented only 5 percent of motorists.[15] In Illinois in the early 1990s, under "Operation Valkyrie," 30 percent of state police searches involved Hispanic drivers, even though Hispanics comprised only about 8 percent of the state population.[16] In litigation in New Jersey, the state court credited defense experts' findings that suggested absolute disparities of 32.7 percent (46.2 percent of stops were of African Americans, 13.5 percent of drivers were African American) and 22.1 percent (35.6 percent stops of African Americans, 13.5 percent African American drivers) based on stops at different intervals of the New Jersey Turnpike.[17] In other policing contexts, the racial disparities are often also very high.[18] Now, let's see how these economic models work on the data.

Knowles, Persico, and Todd (2001)

In *Racial Bias in Motor Vehicle Searches: Theory and Evidence,* John Knowles, Nicola Persico, and Petra Todd develop a model of the behavior of police officers and citizen motorists to test whether recent empirical data concerning police searches of vehicles on Interstate 95 in Maryland reflect efficient policing—what they call "statistical discrimination"—or racial animus. Their model of citizen and police behavior uses the rationality assumptions discussed above; the ultimate determination of whether the police are racially prejudiced, then, turns on whether the hit rates are lower for minority motorists. "[I]f police are prejudiced," Knowles, Persico, and Todd explain, "the equilibrium returns to searching members of the group that is discriminated against will be below average."[19]

Knowles, Persico, and Todd apply their model to the Maryland data.[20] The police in Maryland disproportionately target African Americans for searches of their vehicles. Between January 1995 and January 1999, 63 percent of the persons stopped and searched by the state police along I-95 were African American, and 29 percent were white (of a total 1,590 observations).[21] The assumed proportion of African American drivers on the road was roughly 18 percent (204). In contrast, both groups have nearly equivalent offending rates based on those searches. With regard to African Americans, 34 percent of the searches turn up some evidence of drug carrying; with regard to whites, 32 percent of the searches turn up such evidence (222).

Based on data concerning the raw number of drug seizures, Knowles, Persico, and Todd conclude that there is no evidence that the police officers are displaying a taste for discrimination. They write that "[a]lthough African-American motorists are much more likely to be searched by police, the proportion of guilty motorists among whites and African Americans whose cars are searched is nearly identical (0.32 vs. 0.34)—a result that is consistent with the hypothesis of no racial prejudice" (219). In contrast, they do find racial prejudice against Hispanics because the success rate of searches is far lower—11 percent (222).[22] In other words, far more Hispanics are being stopped than would be necessary to get them to offend less (assuming they had higher natural offending rates).

Based on data concerning drug seizures of amounts that exceed the felony threshold (225–26), however, Knowles, Persico, and Todd find racial discrimination but discover that the prejudice works against whites. They find that African Americans are significantly more likely to be found guilty than white motorists—13 percent versus 3 percent. The authors conclude as follows:

> In our data, vehicles of African-American motorists are searched much more frequently than those of white motorists. However, the probability that a searched driver is found carrying any amount of contraband is very similar across races. Thus we cannot reject the hypothesis that the disparity in the probability of being searched is due purely to statistical discrimination and not to racial prejudice. When we look at the probability that a searched driver is carrying contraband in excess of a high threshold, this probability is higher for African Americans. Under our model, this would imply a bias against white motorists. (206–7)

Hernández-Murillo and Knowles (2003)

In *Racial Profiling or Racist Policing? Testing in Aggregated Data,* Rubén Hernández-Murillo and John Knowles apply the Knowles, Persico, and Todd model to aggregated Missouri data and their findings are consistent with racial prejudice rather than statistical discrimination. The dataset from Missouri consists of aggregated data by race and police force from an annual report published by the State of Missouri, the "2001 Annual Report on Missouri Traffic Stops," mandated by the recently revised Traffic Regulation Laws.[23]

The core data reveal the following. The proportion of each group stopped in Missouri is 31.5, 43.1, and 31.7 percent, respectively, for whites, African Americans, and Hispanics. The proportion of stops that lead to a search is 6.5, 11.4, and 12.9 percent respectively for whites, African Americans, and Hispanics. The hit rate for drugs is 19.7, 12.3, and 9.8 percent respectively.[24] Based on these aggregated data, Hernández-Murillo and Knowles "reject statistical discrimination as an explanation of the higher search rates of African-Americans and Hispanic motorists in Missouri," because searches of minority motorists "are less likely to be successful, with significantly lower probability of turning up drugs or other contraband." They calculate that 18 percent of the excess search rate of African Americans would be eliminated "if search rates were set so as to equalize success rates across racial groups."[25]

Because the data are aggregated and not individual observations, the authors are not able, strictly speaking, to hold other relevant variables—for instance, type of search—constant. The State of Missouri in fact argues in the report that the lower hit rates for African Americans and Hispanics may stem from higher rates of arrest and mandatory search,[26] but Hernández-Murillo and Knowles use sophisticated (nonparametric) statistical methods in an effort to take account of this variable (given that they have the relative arrests/searches rate), and they contend that this factor does not account for the racial differentials. They conclude, "We found strong evidence in support of racial bias against African-American motorists, even when controlling for sex and age."[27]

Borooah (2001)

In *Racial Bias in Police Stops and Searches: An Economic Analysis,* Vani Borooah develops a similar model of police behavior intended to distinguish between bigotry and efficiency, which he calls "business necessity," and applies it to data from the British Home Office on stops and searches of citizens in ten police areas in England. He finds wide disparities in the proportion of the racial groups searched, but far fewer disparities in the rates of success, and concludes that the only discrimination is "on grounds of business necessity." Borooah deduces that the racial disparities in stops are "untainted by racism" and have contributed positively to the efficiency of policing.[28]

Borooah's enthusiasm rests partly on his belief that "statistical discrimination [business necessity], untainted by bigotry, is optimal from a policing perspective because it maximizes the number of arrests consequent upon a given number of persons stopped."[29] But he realizes that there is a trade-off between efficiency and the appearance of fairness with regard to the stops, and that the ultimate decision is a normative one. Borooah is agnostic about questions of fairness. He recognizes that societies may prefer to equalize the likelihood of being stopped and searched or to equalize the rate of success of searches. As he suggests, "The conflict between the two types of equality arises because they represent different perspectives to the welfare aspects of police stops."[30]

In sum, then, the models are in agreement. When the data reveal equal hit rates for different racial groups—as in Maryland between African American and white motorists or in the ten police areas in England—these economists conclude that the disproportionate searches of minority drivers do not reflect a taste for discrimination; rather they are an attempt to maximize successful searches. When the data reveal lower hit rates for minority motorists—as in Maryland between Hispanic and white motorists or in Missouri between African American and Hispanic motorists on the one hand and white motorists on the other—these economists reason that bigotry against minority motorists explains the disparity. And when the data reveal higher hit rates for minority motorists—such as in Maryland regarding large hauls of drugs—these economists conclude that reverse racism is at play—in other words, bigotry against white motorists.

A Critique of the Economic Models of Racial Profiling

These economists are right that profiling on a nonspurious group trait that predicts higher offending will maximize the law enforcement goal of detecting criminal activity and, if we buy the premises of rational-action theory, will decrease crime among the higher-offending group. In the stop-and-frisk context or the IRS audit context, profiling on a predictive trait will likely increase the success rate of searches or tax investigations. Similarly, in the sentencing context, using an accurate parole-prediction tool will likely increase the success rate of parolees.

But this will only increase the general welfare of society if it has the effect of decreasing overall crime in society, and this will only happen if the members of the higher-offending targeted group have the same or greater elasticity of offending to policing. The overall effect on crime in society will depend entirely on the relative elasticity of the two groups to the profiling. If on the other hand, the targeted population is less responsive to the change in policing, then the profiling will *increase* overall crime in society.

In essence, there is a hidden assumption in the economic model of racial profiling. That hidden assumption is that the two groups have the same elasticity of offending to policing. Yet the economists are prepared to stipulate that minorities offend more. If they do in fact offend more, there is every reason to believe that they may also be *less* elastic to policing. Whether the different offending rates are due to socioeconomics, history, cultural forces, or path dependence, the fact is we are prepared to stipulate that there is a difference in offending. Nonspurious racial profiling rests on the nonspurious assumption that members of one racial group offend *more* than members of another racial group, holding everything else constant. If their offending is different, then why would their elasticity be the same? If they are, for instance, offending more because they are socioeconomically more disadvantaged, then it would follow logically that they may also have less elasticity of offending to policing because they have fewer alternative job opportunities. The bottom line, then, is that there is every reason to believe that nonspurious racial profiling would actually increase crime in society.

In effect, the problem with the economic model of racial profiling is that it does not properly specify what counts as "success" for purposes of a highway drug-interdiction program. The models assume that a nonracist police officer seeks to maximize the rate of successful searches that discover drug contraband. That, however, is simply the wrong objective. The proper goal for the police is to minimize the social cost of crime—in this case, to minimize the transportation of drug contraband on the highways and the social cost of policing. And the fact is that, under certain identifiable conditions, minimizing the social costs of crime is at odds with maximizing search success rates. Under certain conditions, statistical discrimination leads to *higher* overall social costs associated with the profiled crime and the costs of searches.

Ironically, the detection of criminal activity is not necessarily the primary goal of law enforcement. To be sure, high search success rates, high audit success rates, and high arrest rates are good, but they are not a good in themselves. The primary goal of law enforcement is to decrease the rate of crime—not to detect crime. And unfortunately—somewhat paradoxically—these two goals may conflict. When members of the profiled group are less responsive to changes in policing, auditing, or length of sentence, but the members of the nonprofiled group are very much more responsive to decreased policing, auditing, or length of sentence, then profiling on a nonspurious trait may actually increase the rate of the targeted crime. Depending on the comparative elasticities of the two groups, the narrowly "efficient" outcome may actually increase the overall crime rate. This is true not only in the criminal profiling context, but also, perhaps somewhat counter-intuitively, in the parole context. Denying parole to likely parole violators effectively increases their prison sentence and, relatively speaking, decreases the sentence of those who are more likely to succeed on parole and who are therefore released. If the parole-success types are more elastic to sentencing, then the use of the prediction tool may actually increase overall crime in society.

In sum, the economic models focus the definition of policing efficiency exclusively, and too narrowly, on maximizing search success rates. Knowles, Persico, and Todd, for instance, draw the line between efficiency and racial bigotry in the following terms: "Police may use race as a criterion in traffic stops *because they are trying to maximize successful searches* and race helps predict criminality or because they prefer stopping one racial group over another."[31] The only other factor that the authors take into account—other than the success rate of searches—is "the cost of searching motorists" in terms of police time, effort, and taste for discrimination.[32]

What is absent from the models is the effect of racial profiling on the absolute number of motorists transporting illicit drugs.[33] The long-term consequences on the *amount* of the profiled crime are simply not factored into the economic models. This is problematic because the two objectives—maximizing search success rates and minimizing crime—may conflict under certain conditions. If the police shift their allocation of resources away from white motorists and toward minority motorists, the offending rate among minority motorists may well decrease, but simultaneously the offending rate among white motorists may increase. The problem is, of course, that there are more white motorists. Depending on the relationship between the comparative elasticity of offending to policing of white and minority motorists and the comparative offending rates, the total increase in absolute numbers of offending by white motorists may outweigh the total decrease in absolute numbers of minority offending.

Some Mathematics

What follows is a bit technical and mathematical. If your eyes glaze at numbers, I demonstrate this in far simpler terms in the next section. Here, though, I will use equations. Assuming fixed law enforcement resources, racial profiling will reduce total crime only if the ratio of the minority to white motorist population is greater than the differential of the change in offending by race. Whether this condition is satisfied or not, however, depends entirely on comparative elasticities and offending rates. In terms of notation, let $r \in \{M, W\}$ denote the race of the motorists, either minority or white. Let Pop_r denote the representation of each racial group in the total population. Let O_r denote the offending rate of each racial group. Let ΔO_r denote the absolute value of the change in the offending rate of the racial group from Time 1 to Time 2.

Racial profiling will be beneficial from a long-term crime-fighting perspective only if total crime at Time 1 (pre–racial profiling) is greater than total crime at Time 2 (with racial profiling). This happens if

$$Pop_M O_M + Pop_W O_W > [Pop_M(O_M - \Delta O_M)] + [Pop_W(O_W + \Delta O_W)]. \quad (1)$$

We can rewrite this equation as follows:

$$\frac{Pop_M}{Pop_W} > \frac{\Delta O_W}{\Delta O_M}. \quad (2)$$

From equation (2), racial profiling will decrease overall crime only if the ratio of the populations of minority and white motorists—the "population differential"—is greater than the ratio of the absolute value of the change in offending by whites to the absolute value of the change in offending by minorities—the "differential of the change in offending by race."

If we assume that minority motorists comprise approximately 20 percent of the motorists on the road—in Maryland, for example, research reveals that 17 to 18 percent of motorists are African American—we can substitute estimated values for the population differential. What this suggests is that racial profiling is effective as a long-term crime-fighting strategy only if

$$0.25 > \frac{\Delta O_W}{\Delta O_M}. \tag{3}$$

In other words, for racial profiling to work, it must be true that the change in the offending rate of minority motorists is more than four times *greater* than the change in the overall offending rate of white motorists. If the minority representation is smaller than 20 percent, the required differential in the change of offending must be even greater. By the same token, if the minority representation is larger, then the required differential in the change in offending need not be as large. To put some numbers on this, if the minority population is 12 percent of the total population, then the change in the minority offending rate must be at least 7.4 times greater than the change in the offending rate of white motorists. If the minority population is 28 percent of the total population, then the change in the minority offending rate must be at least 2.6 times greater. The smaller the minority population, the larger the required differential in the change of offending rates.

Whether this ratio is satisfied depends on the relative elasticity of offending to policing and the relative offending rates of the two racial groups. If minority motorists have the same constant elasticity of offending to policing as white motorists, then racial profiling will work if the offending rate of minority motorists is greater than the offending rate of white motorists at Time 1 (under conditions of no racial profiling). As I demonstrate in a more technical appendix (see appendix B), the reason is that, by definition, if the elasticity is the same and constant between racial groups and there are resource constraints, the change in offending of the two racial groups will reflect the population differential. From appendix B, if elasticity is the same, then the following will also be true:

$$\frac{\Delta O_W}{\Delta O_M} = \frac{O_W}{4 O_M}. \tag{4}$$

If we substitute this into equation (3), then racial profiling will reduce crime only if the offending rate of minority motorists (O_M) is greater than the offending rate of white motorists (O_W) under conditions of no racial profiling. The same is true if minority motorists have higher elasticity of offending to policing than white motorists.

But if minority motorists have *lower* elasticity than white motorists, then racial profiling will decrease the profiled crime only if the offending-rate differential at Time 1 is greater than the difference in elasticity. Let E_r denote the elasticity of each racial group. If E_M is less than E_W, we can denote the relationship in the following way:

$$xE_M = E_W, \text{ where } x > 1. \tag{5}$$

If we assume that minority motorists have lower elasticity by a factor of x, then, by definition and substituting into equation (3), racial profiling will decrease the profiled crime only if the following condition holds true:

$$O_M > xO_W. \tag{6}$$

In other words, if minority motorists have *lower* elasticity than white motorists, racial profiling will decrease the amount of profiled crime only if minority-motorist offending is greater than white-motorist offending times the elasticity differential. If, for example, white-motorist elasticity is two times greater than minority-motorist elasticity, then racial profiling will reduce crime only if minority-motorist offending is more than two times greater than white-motorist offending.

As a result, the key statistics for purposes of determining the effect of racial profiling on the profiled crime are the elasticity and offending differentials. If minority motorists have lower elasticity, racial profiling may well increase overall profiled crime. The problem with the narrow definition of efficiency—maximizing search success rates—is that it may effectively mask racial prejudice. If a police officer or police department engages in disproportionate searches of minority motorists in order to maximize the success rate of searches and pays no attention to the consequences on long-term trends in the transportation of drug contraband—that is, if we as modelers and policymakers focus on narrow efficiency—then the police may endorse a scheme of racial profiling that may in fact promote more crime in the long run. The police may promote, whether intentionally or unwittingly, a policy that discriminates on the basis of race and increases overall crime. That would not be efficient, and it would, in effect, be racially prejudiced.

What is most troubling is that we have good reasons to suspect that minority and white motorists may have different elasticities of offending to policing and that the elasticity of minority motorists may be *less* than that of white motorists. Elasticity depends largely on the existence of legitimate work alternatives, as well as on different cultural scripts and community norms. Economist Nicola Persico suggests that, as a theoretical matter, the elasticity for African Americans may be less than for whites because they may have fewer job opportunities and therefore fewer alternatives to crime. As Persico explains, "The amount of criminal activity—and hence also the elasticity of crime to policing—depends on the distribution of legal earning opportunities."[34] This may affect the transportation of illicit drugs for personal use as well as the substitutability of drug couriers.

Another issue relates to the perception among minority motorists of the police and the criminal justice system. As Tracey Meares explains, "Legitimacy matters more to compliance [with the law] than [do] instrumental factors, such as sanctions imposed by authorities on individuals who fail to follow the law or private rules."[35] Tom Tyler's research on legitimacy and obedience to the law suggests that disproportionate searches of minority motorists may take a toll on minorities' perception of the overall fairness of the system, which might in turn lead to *more* rather than less offending. If minorities believe that they are going to be harassed by the police or supervised regardless of what they do, minority motorists may lose faith in the system and ultimately become less law-abiding.[36] This mechanism could produce different rates of elasticity between racial groups, as well as an upward-sloping offending curve at the tail end for minority motorists.

Here are a couple of additional observations. First, the analysis has assumed fixed law enforcement resources. This is, after all, the most realistic, reasonable, and conservative assumption, since the police budget is fixed by political processes that have little to do with hit rates or effects on profiled crime. Nevertheless, even if we relax the assumption of resource constraint, the same analysis would apply to the allocation of the additional police resources. Under conditions of lower elasticity, maximizing search success rates may possibly increase overall crime.

Second, it is important to emphasize that the problem with the economic models of racial profiling is *not* that the economists overvalue efficiency.[37] The problem is that they do not define efficiency properly in the policing and criminal justice context. A proper model of police behavior would assume that police departments and police officers seek first and foremost to minimize the number of persons carrying drug contraband on the highway. If searches are the most effective way to promote this objective—more effective, for instance, than advertisements or public announcements—then, and only then, should the police seek to allocate resources to maximize search success rates minus the cost of searching cars.

An Illustration of This Phenomenon

This discussion has been somewhat technical and abstract, but I can make the point more directly with a simple hypothetical case. Assume a city with a population of 1,000,000 residents, of which 20 percent, or 200,000, are minorities and the other 80 percent, or 800,000, are majorities. Let's assume that the police engage in 10,000 stops and searches each year, effectively searching 1 percent of the population, and that, at Time 1, the police stop and search randomly. They engage in no profiling. In order to make the profiling at Time 2 nonspurious, assume also that minorities offend at a higher rate, say 8 percent, than majorities, who offend at a rate of 6 percent across the board. Under these assumptions, the searches will prove successful in 8 percent of the 2,000 minority searches (or 160 minority searches) and 6 percent of 8,000 majority searches (or 480 majority searches). As for the total criminal population in the city, it would consist of 16,000 minorities (8 percent of the total 200,000 minority population) and 48,000 majorities (6 percent of the total 800,000 majority population)—or a total of 64,000 offenders overall. I present these simple assumptions and results in table 4.1.

Now, assume in Year 2 that law enforcement decides to profile minorities for searches because they have a higher offending rate and profiling would be more efficient. The idea, of course, is that the increased searches of

TABLE 4.1   **Time 1 assumptions**

	Total	Minority	Majority
City population	1,000,000	200,000 (20%)	800,000 (80%)
Police searches	10,000	2,000 (20%)	8,000 (80%)
Searches (% of relevant population)	1	1	1
Offending rate (%)	6.4	8	6
Successful searches	640	160 (8% of 2,000)	480 (6% of 8,000)
Number of offenders	64,000	16,000 (8% of 200,000)	48,000 (6% of 800,000)

minorities will decrease their offending rate since they will find offending more costly and, therefore, less attractive (assuming rational action on the part of these offenders). On the flip side, we must also assume that majorities will offend more now that they are being searched less, because, after all, we are assuming rational action on the part of these offenders as well.

Suppose, then, that the police decide to search twice as many minorities and that, since they have the same amount of police resources, they still only search 1 percent of the population. The police search four thousand minorities and six thousand majorities. Moreover, the police profile to this point because it is the most efficient point from a search perspective—the point, according to the best economic analysis, where the offending rates will become the same for minorities and majorities. Assume that the two groups have different elasticities of offending to policing—like their offending rates, their elasticities are different, holding everything else constant. Minorities do not have very elastic offending to policing because of more challenging socioeconomic conditions; majorities are more elastic because they have more opportunities and flexibility. Therefore, minority offending goes down to 7 percent and majority offending goes up to 7 percent. The effect on successful searches and on total crime is shown in table 4.2, which is the same as table 4.1 but uses the new values.

The use of profiling has indeed increased the efficiency of the police searches. The same number of searches has produced a higher number of successful searches that have discovered contraband. In fact, this is the optimally efficient allocation of resources from the perspective of successful searches because it is the point where the hit rates are the same. Unfortunately, the profiling has also increased the overall criminal element in the city. Whereas before there were 64,000 offenders in the city, now there are 70,000 offenders.

Why? Because the elasticity of minorities is less than that of majorities. The shift in policing has reduced the offending of minorities, but in-

TABLE 4.2 **Time 2 effects**

	Total	Minority	Majority
City population	1,000,000	200,000 (20%)	800,000 (80%)
Police searches	10,000	4,000 (40%)	6,000 (60%)
Searches (% of relevant population)	1	2	0.75
Offending rate (%)	7	7	7
Successful searches	700	280 (7% of 4,000)	420 (7% of 6,000)
Number of offenders	70,000	14,000 (7% of 200,000)	56,000 (7% of 800,000)

creased the offending of majorities—and there are more majorities in the
city. In other words, the increased efficiency of the targeted policing has
also increased the overall criminality of the population. The intuitive logic
is as follows: the effect on the majorities is greater because they are more
elastic and they greatly outnumber the minority. The combination is what
makes profiling counterproductive.

The relative elasticities and offending rates are visually represented in
the graph shown in figure 4.2—which helps make sense of what is going
on. Notice, in this graph, that as long as the hit-rate equilibrium exceeds

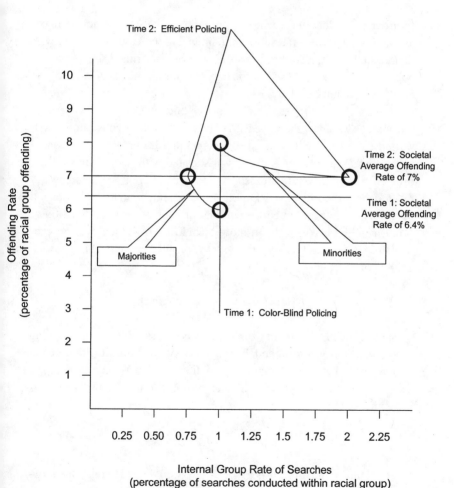

FIGURE 4.2 Racial profiling where minorities have lower elasticity

6.4 percent—which was the offending rate for the total population at Time 1—the profiling will be more efficient in terms of successful searches, but counterproductive in terms of total crime in society. Total crime in society will *increase* because of the more efficient policing. In essence, so long as the equilibrium point in offending at Time 2 is achieved *above* the average offending rate at Time 1, the profiling will produce increased crime in society.

An Alternative Model

In order to model police behavior properly, we must focus not on maximizing search success rates, but on minimizing the costs associated with the profiled crime, including the social costs of the crime itself and of the policing technique.[38] In this section, again a more technical one, I propose an alternative model.

Here, we need not assume fixed police budgetary resources, because the analysis would be the same with or without resource constraints. First, we must minimize the costs to society defined in terms of the profiled crime. Let D denote the social loss associated with one instance of the profiled crime, namely, the transportation of illicit drugs on the highway.[39] Let I_r denote the rate at which motorists are being searched. O_r (defined earlier as the internal rate of offending for each group) is a function of I_r and is noted accordingly. In more technical terms, then, we can capture the cost to society associated with the profiled crime by the following expression:

$$D[O_M(I_M)Pop_M + O_W(I_W)Pop_W]. \tag{7}$$

Second, we need to minimize the social costs associated with searching motor vehicles for contraband. For purposes of notation, let Q denote the cost associated with one instance of a police search.[40] We can capture the cost to society associated with the searches of automobiles by the following expression:

$$Q[I_M Pop_M + I_W Pop_W]. \tag{8}$$

To minimize the total costs to society, we would need to take the derivative of the total cost function, denoted as C_r, which would be a function of I_r and would contain both equations (7) and (8). We can express the total cost function as follows:

$$C_M(I_M) + C_W(I_W) = D[O_M(I_M)Pop_M + O_W(I_W)Pop_W] \\ + Q[I_M Pop_M + I_W Pop_W]. \tag{9}$$

Using partial differentiation to resolve separately for the two racial groups, if we were to minimize the social costs, we would have the following:

$$C'_r(I_r) = D[O'_r(I_r)Pop_r] + QPop_r. \tag{10}$$

Rewriting the equation, we obtain the following:

$$-[Q/D] = O'_r(I_r). \tag{11}$$

Since we are assuming that Q and D are the same for white and minority motorists—that is, we are assuming nonracist police officers—minimizing total social costs produces the following first-order condition:

$$O'_M(I_M) = O'_W(I_W). \tag{12}$$

Since $O'_r(I_r)$ is the slope of O_r at point I_r, or $[\partial O_r/\partial I_r]$, we can rewrite this first-order condition as follows:

$$\frac{\partial O_M}{\partial I_M} = \frac{\partial O_W}{\partial I_W}. \tag{13}$$

We can rewrite this as follows, multiplying both sides by 1:

$$\frac{\partial O_M}{\partial I_M}\frac{I_M}{O_M}\frac{O_M}{I_M} = \frac{\partial O_W}{\partial I_W}\frac{I_W}{O_W}\frac{O_W}{I_W}. \tag{14}$$

Given the definition of elasticity, and using E_r to denote elasticity, we can express the first-order condition as follows:

$$E_M \frac{O_M}{I_M} = E_W \frac{O_W}{I_W}. \tag{15}$$

This first-order condition must be satisfied to minimize the total social costs associated with the illicit transportation of drug contraband on the highways. Whether the condition is satisfied will depend on the comparative elasticities, natural offending rates, and search rates. It is possible to construct a three-by-three table to identify the conditions under which the police should search different racial groups at different rates. Table 4.3 summarizes the nine findings. The two cells where the results are not clear represent situations where racial profiling may *increase* total social costs. Where minority motorists have lower elasticities of offending to policing and higher natural offending rates, and, similarly, where minority motorists have higher elasticities but lower natural offending rates, racial profiling may increase overall social costs depending on the relationship between the relative offending and search rates. Note that this result does not even take into account the ratchet effect discussed in chapter 5.[41]

The foregoing underscores the myopia of an efficiency analysis that looks solely for equal hit rates and elides elasticities and offending differentials. As the model makes clear, minimizing the costs to society entails a distribution of searches between white and minority motorists that depends on the relative elasticities of offending to policing and on the relative natural offending rates. In other words, the equilibrium point is not defined by the *equality of hit rates,* but instead depends on *comparative elasticities and the relationship between offending and search rates.* As a result, the analysis should focus on the size and characteristics of the group of persons at the margins who are most likely to be influenced one way or the other carry illicit drugs on the highway for personal or commercial purposes. In this sense, the analysis calls not only for modeling skills and better data on overall elasticities and offending rates, but also for sociological and ethnographic studies of the groups of individuals who are most likely to respond to shifts in the allocation of police resources.

TABLE 4.3 **Minimizing total social costs**

	$E_M = E_W$	$E_M < E_W$	$E_M > E_W$
$O_M = O_W$	$I_M = I_W$ (No racial profiling)	$I_M < I_W$ (Profile whites)	$I_M > I_W$ (Profile minorities)
$O_M > O_W$	$I_M > I_W$ (Profile minorities)	$I_M < I_W [O_M/O_W]$ (Not clear)	$I_M > I_W$ (Profile minorities)
$O_M < O_W$	$I_M < I_W$ (Profile whites)	$I_M < I_W$ (Profile whites)	$I_M > I_W [O_M/O_W]$ (Not clear)

The economic modelers may respond that they are merely trying to distinguish between the racist and the success-maximizing police officers. And, to be sure, some police officers may measure success by the narrow metric of successful searches. This response, though, does not square with basic assumptions of rationality or police behavior. The broader notion of efficacy—associated with the long-term effects on the profiled crime— makes far more sense from the perspective of police officers and police departments. The bottom line for policing is crime rates, not hit rates. In fact, if the police focus exclusively on narrow efficiency, the economic models are completely irrelevant to the contemporary criminological and policing debates. A finding that the police conduct themselves in a narrowly efficient manner is orthogonal to the larger question whether racial profiling is racist. It may point to a principal-agent problem in policing. But it does not resolve the key question of racial profiling. If targeting minority motorists *increases* long-term offending on the highways or the overall costs to society, then it is *in effect* racially prejudiced. It may be inadvertent and mistaken, but it is effectively racist.

The bottom line is that criminal profiling may be entirely counterproductive to the crime-fighting goal—and in fact, several economists, including Nicola Persico, John Knowles, Jeff Dominitz, and Charles Manski now recognize this.[42] John Knowles and his coauthor, Jeff Dominitz, in a paper written in 2005, four years after the development of the original Knowles, Persico, and Todd model, acknowledge that "policies that are optimal under [the hit-rate maximization hypothesis] can actually lead to maximization of crime."[43] Knowles and Dominitz specifically recognize that the traditional assumptions about offending rates "are not sufficient to allow inference of racial bias from observation of search rates and hit rates, when police are known to minimize crime."[44]

As a result, we need to know more about the relative elasticities and offending rates of different groups in society before engaging in actuarial policing. To be sure, in a limited number of cases the likely differential elasticities and offending rates will favor profiling. In a traditional case of rape, for instance, there is little doubt that profiling males will not increase the overall incidence of rape in society. The reason, very simply, is that the offending-rate differential is extremely large, with practically little or no offending by women, and the elasticity of women—that is, the nonprofiled group—is also practically nonexistent. Profiling men does not appear to create a sharply elastic response among women. In this case, the elasticity of the profiled group (men) is far greater, as is the offending, and actuarial profiling is likely to have positive effects on rape rates. But these are the rare cases. In the more traditional cases of profiling, whether run-of-the-mill street crime or white-collar crime, any offending differential is likely to be accompanied by *lower* elasticity for the profiled group, resulting in adverse consequences on overall crime levels. In all cases, though, there must be proper analysis of these different factors—comparative elasticities and offending rates—before the police should engage in any form of actuarial policing.

Other Problems with the Economic Models

The bottom line is that criminal profiling may well have the adverse effect of increasing crime in society. Does this make sense? How would we understand it, in commonsense terms? Well, here is an illustration.

Assume, as the IRS has found, that tax fraud is more common in drywall contracting than in other trades. And assume that the IRS starts profiling drywall contractors—and that this information leaks out. Well maybe, just maybe, other subcontractors—painters, roofers, electricians, plumbers, floor specialists, tuck-pointers, and landscapers—start thinking that their cost of cheating on their taxes has decreased, and they begin to underreport their income. Pretty soon, all of the other trades are skimming on their tax returns. Meanwhile, the drywall contractors find it difficult to reduce their illicit activities because they have a poor cash-flow situation. They are, say, less elastic to the policing. So it takes a lot of audits and policing of the drywall contractors to bring their offending down, and meanwhile all that reallocation of law enforcement resources is triggering a strong reaction among the other tradespeople. Might tax evasion go up in society? Yes. It all depends on elasticities.

There are other problems with the economic models, especially their reliance on hit rates, that should temper any attempt to gauge racism based on those rates. These other problems are minor compared to the issue of elasticities, but they are worth mentioning here. Briefly, there are two. First, the police may be engaging in more careful and deliberate subsearches of stopped motorists depending on their race—and this may skew the interpretation of hit rates.[45] The police may, because of a reduced "cost of thoroughness," call canine units more often or engage in more intrusive visual inspection, closer scrutiny of documents, or more heavy-handed interrogation with disfavored categories of motorists. These subsearch techniques may affect hit rates in a statistically invisible way. And they are not accounted for in the economic models of racial profiling. As Knowles, Persico, and Todd write,

> [O]ur model abstracts from the issue of the thoroughness of searches. Suppose that it were the case that police search African-American motorists more thoroughly than whites, because of a lower "cost of thoroughness." As a result, searches of African Americans would not necessarily be more successful, because of the equilibrium reaction of motorists. In fact, we may expect searches of African Americans to be less successful since in equilibrium police equate the (lower) cost of searching thoroughly to the expected benefit from searching. Testing a model that takes into account thoroughness requires data on effort spent searching. In the absence of such data, we leave this question for future research.[46]

The differential application of subsearch processes, however, may significantly distort any interpretation of hit rates.[47]

Second, some ambiguity also surrounds the selectiveness with which the police use race and other search criteria for purposes of searching members of different racial groups. This concern is similar to the application of subsearch processes, but applies to the original decision to search—and, similarly, raises questions about interpreting hit rates. There is, after all, good reason to believe that a police officer who is racist is going to use race differently in the decision to search a minority motorist than in the decision to search a white motorist. A racist police officer might decide, for instance, to search all available African American motorists, but to search only young drivers in late-model cars with tinted windows and counterculture bumper stickers when it comes to white motorists. In other words, the racist police officer may use other search criteria more or less selectively depending on whether the motorist is white or minority. If the police are more or less selective when it comes to minority motorists, then the equal *official* hit rates would mask different *actual* offending rates among African American drivers. If so, the fact that there are equal official hit rates would not signal narrowly efficient policing.

The fact is that the police do not profile on race alone. They also profile on car models, vehicle attributes, rental cars, stickers, location, direction, motorist appearance, age, and so on.[48] The police use these various attributes—and possibly race as well—to narrow down the pool of likely suspects.[49] We know that they are doing this successfully—at least some of the time. The pool of motorists who are being searched are carrying drugs at high rates, far in excess of the rates for the population as a whole. In Maryland, for instance, about 34 percent of African American and 32 percent of white motorists searched are carrying drugs.[50] That is far higher than rates of personal drug use among surveyed adults, and far higher than success rates at nondiscretionary road blocks (about 4.7 percent in Indianapolis in 1998).[51] It is also higher than success rates in Missouri (12.3 percent for African Americans and 19.7 percent for white motorists).[52] By not stopping elderly motorists on their way to religious services, the police successfully narrow down the pool of suspects.

What we do not know, however, is how efficient the racist police officer is with regard to his racism. The economic models assume, in effect, maximal efficiency. This is Gary Becker's brilliant insight—to operationalize racism through the taste for discrimination—and it may work remarkably well as a way to capture unconscious racism. But it may not work as well if we relax slightly the assumption of rationality and assume instead that the blatantly racist police officer operates on a more simplistic heuristic — something like "I'll search any minority motorist that I stop for speeding, and search any white 'druggie' motorist that I stop for speeding. By white 'druggie' motorist, I mean young white male with a fancy car and drug stickers or other paraphernalia." If the racist police officer operates in this way, then the economic models cannot use hit rates to distinguish between the racist and narrowly efficient police officer, because the hit rates do not have the meaning attributed to them by the economic models.

This raises, naturally, the most interesting question—namely, How does racism express itself? The economic model defines efficiency as the leading objective for *all* police officers. Yet there is no good reason to assume that the blatantly racist police officer is *also* maximally efficient in her racism. Racism and narrow efficiency—that is, racism and rationality—may be mutually exclusive. In fact, the police officer might search more minority motorists and improve the overall hit rates—which is what she would do *if* she were perfectly efficient and knew that the other characteristics were accurate predictors across race. Yet the racist police officer may continue to select differentially on other search criteria out of racism. This is, possibly, the paradox of inefficient racism. Her racism may be masked *to us* by the equal hit rates, and it may mask *to her* the fact that she could search more minorities. In any event, this form of racism would distort the interpretation of hit rates.

The bottom line is that, when the hit rates are 34 percent for African American motorists and 32 percent for white motorists along Maryland

I-95, we do not know if the police have searched African American motorists simply because of their race and searched white motorists because of five other suspicious traits. If that is true, clearly, the African American motorists have actually far higher average hit rates than the average white motorist. Alternatively, this might be offset by differential subsearch techniques, which would increase the hit rate. Lower or equal official hit rates would mask much higher real offending rates.[53]

The result is that hit rates are far more difficult to interpret than many economists suggest, given that we know little about the selectiveness with which other search criteria are used or, for that matter, about elasticities and offending rates. The new data from across the country do not contain *any* evidence concerning these key quantities of interest, without which it is practically impossible to interpret the hit rates reliably. So even if we were interested only in narrow efficiency, the fact of lower, equal, or higher hit rates tells us very little. Multiple interpretations are possible in each case.

The problem of selectivity renders it impossible to know how the official hit rates really compare. The real offending rate for minority motorists may be higher or lower than the official hit rate because of greater or lesser selectivity or subsearching. As a result, the equal official hit rates might mask offending rates that were actually lower or higher among minorities, which, under assumptions of elasticity and higher offending among minorities, translates into racial prejudice rather than narrow efficiency. And the masking effect applies across the board: official lower hit rates could also mask actual equal offending rates. In other words, lower hit rates could reflect not racism but narrow policing efficiency (equal real hit rates) plus selectivity. This distortion seriously undermines our ability to make accurate inferences from the emerging data on hit rates.

Punishment and Sentencing

In sum, the economic models and the rational-action argument concerning "policing efficiency" are *maximizing the wrong thing*: Instead of maximizing the success rate of searches, the police should seek, first and foremost, to maximize the reduction in the profiled crime and associated policing costs—in other words, to minimize the social costs associated with the profiled crime and profiling technique. As a result, the economic models *track the wrong statistic*: Rather than focusing on hit rates, the models should focus on the overall amount of profiled crime and costs to society of the searches.

To compound this error, the new data on police searches on the high-way—and most data on the prediction of criminality—do not contain enough information to address the narrow question of whether racial profiling maximizes the success rate of searches, nor the larger question of whether it reduces the amount of profiled crime. The data contain only two of at least four necessary quantities of interest: first, the number and proportion of drivers searched by race and, second, the success rate of searches by race. (There is also more detailed information about types and amounts of drugs seized, location, type of searches, and so forth, which can produce more refined but not fundamentally different analyses.) The data, however, are entirely silent regarding the *comparative* elasticity of offending to policing and the *comparative* natural offending rates by racial group. Without this information, the data can say little *empirically* about the narrow efficiency of racial profiling or about the impact of racial profiling on the profiled crime and the profiled population. Thus, we have no good reason to believe that criminal profiling will reduce crime in society—our main goal in law enforcement.

This mathematical critique of the use of actuarial methods is intuitively clear in the context of racial profiling and, more generally, of criminal profiling. As long as we have some reason to believe that offending rates differ between different groups—whether racial groups, classes, or employment clusters—then we may also expect different elasticities of offending to policing. And if there are indeed different elasticities, we have no good reason to believe that the profiling will reduce overall crime in society.

At first glance, it may be tempting to think that none of this applies to the situation of sentencing, parole, or selective incapacitation. After all, lengthening the sentence of a likely repeat offender is certainly not going to increase overall crime in society. And there is surely a difference between the use of actuarial methods in policing and in the sentencing context. In the policing context—that of racial profiling, the IRS Discriminant Index Function, or drug-courier profiles—the actuarial tends to focus on predicting *past or present* behavior in order to determine the criminal justice outcome, such as whether to search, audit, or investigate. In contrast, in the sentencing context—parole prediction, sentencing guidelines, or selective incapacitation—the actuarial methods tend to focus on predicting *future* criminal behavior in order to determine a criminal justice outcome, such as whether to parole or how long to sentence. But this difference does not change the crime and punishment equation. The difference between predicting future events and past events is not significant for mathematical analysis. "Insofar as the relevance of probability concepts is concerned," as Laurence Tribe suggested many years ago, "there is simply no inherent distinction between future and past events."[54]

Though it is somewhat counterintuitive, the fact is that the very same problem plagues the punishment and sentencing contexts. If we assume rational action and have reason to believe that offending rates and elasticities differ between high-risk recidivist inmates and low-risk, first-offender types, then the use of actuarial methods will affect them in the same way it affects the different populations in the racial profiling example: low-risk, first-offenders are likely to offend more on a first-time basis if their sentence is relatively reduced, and their greater overall offending is likely to outweigh the reductions in crime by less elastic, high-risk recidivists, resulting in higher overall crime in society.

For purposes of this first critique, we are again assuming a rational-actor model. We assume that people are deterred by more punishment. In this sense, the parole decision-making example is the perfect illustration of increasing or decreasing the cost of crime: granting parole reduces the length, and denying parole extends the length of the expected sentence. If offending is elastic to punishment, then we would expect that, in response to parole profiling, offending by first-time offenders will increase and offending by recidivists will decrease. The case of parole prediction, then, works in exactly the same way as criminal profiling: overall crime in society would increase if the elasticity of the recidivists is lower than the elasticity of the first-time offenders. Again, a graph based on a simple hypothetical case will demonstrate the possible effect.

Imagine that the world is made up of two types of people. Members of one group are characterized by lower rates of criminal offending and the likelihood that if they do offend and are caught, they will not likely reoffend—I will call these "ordinary" citizens. Members of the second group are characterized by higher overall rates of offending, partly because they are likely to reoffend even after they have been incarcerated—I call these "recidivists." Increasing the length of prison sentences for recidivists—either at sentencing or later by denying them parole—is likely to increase the cost of criminal behavior to those individuals. Assuming rational action, the most efficient distribution of punishment would entail lengthening the sentences of the recidivists until the point where their offending rates fall to the same rate as that of ordinary citizens. At that point, there will be no benefit to imposing lengthier sentences on members of either group. Here too, though, the overall effect on crime will depend on the relative elasticities of members of the two groups to punishment.

Let me illustrate this too with a simple numerical hypothetical case—rather than mathematical equations—to show the proof. Assume an adult population of 200 million residents and a prison population of 2 million. Assume also that about 30 million violent and property crimes are committed each year (to put this in context, in 2003, the National Crime Victimization Survey reported approximately 24 million violent and property crimes); that less than half of those offenses are reported to the police, or about 12 million (in 2003, the Uniform Crime Reports reported about 12 million violent and property crimes); that about 20 percent of those—or 2.4 million offenses—are cleared by arrest (in 2001, 19.6 percent of serious crimes were cleared by arrest);[55] and that about 600,000 are sent to the penitentiary per year (in the late 1990s new admissions to state prison alone reached almost 550,000 per year).[56] Let's also assume that about one half of the prison population (1 million people) are "recidivists"—people who have offended on at least two previous occasions and will probably reoffend within a year of their release from prison (in 2001, as many as 25 percent of state prisoners were convicted again and resentenced within the three years following release).[57]

These recidivists are the targeted group: those with a higher likelihood of offending if released and who will be denied parole—as soon as the parole authorities adopt a policy of targeted parole release. Suppose that there are 60 million of them in the total population and that they account for 20 million of the crimes committed each year; under these assumptions, they would have an offending likelihood of 33.33 percent. The rest of the population has a 10/140 likelihood of offending, or 7.14 percent.

On these assumptions, at Time 1 in figure 4.3, total crime in society is 30 million offenses per year, for a societal offending rate in the total population of 15 percent, composed of 33.33 percent for recidivists and 7.14 percent for ordinary citizens. At Time 2, we target the recidivists and impose lengthier sentences (say, by paroling ordinary offenders but not the recidivists). The idea of targeting the recidivists, from a rational-action perspective, is to make their sentences longer so that their cost of offending goes up and they offend less. As noted, the optimal length of incarceration occurs when their offending rate matches that of ordinary citizens. The net effect on total crime from shifting resources in this way, though, will depend entirely on the elasticity of the different groups. If their elasticity is such that the equality point is above 15 percent, then there will be more crime in society as a whole. In this hypothetical case, the total offending rate in Time 2 is now 16 percent, resulting in higher overall crime in society. This is clear from table 4.4, which is visually represented in figure 4.3. The first half of table 4.4 describes the Time 1 assumptions; the second describes the Time 2 effects. As figure 4.3 demonstrates, different group elasticities can affect overall crime: if the equal offending rate at Time 2 (here 16 percent) exceeds the average society-wide offending rate at Time 1 (here 15 percent), parole prediction will *increase* overall crime.

The bottom line is that, at Time 2, society-wide crime has increased—compare the total number of annual crimes in the two parts of table 4.4. And the clincher is that we have no good idea of how the elasticities compare. So why, then, should we assume that parole prediction would

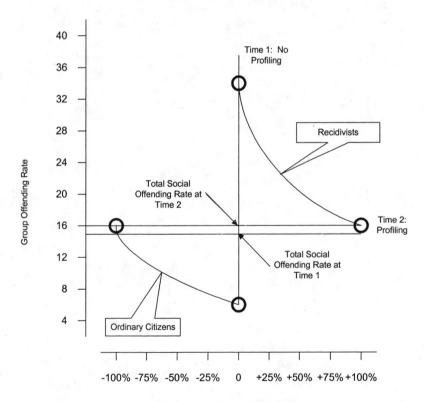

FIGURE 4.3 Actuarial methods as applied to criminal sentencing

represent the optimal way to deal with punishment? Why would we think it is the most efficient way to deter crime? There is no good reason. The fact that we *do* believe tells us about our *desire* to believe, our *desire* to predict, our *desire* to know the recidivist. We are, it seems, predisposed to wanting the actuarial model to be right. But more on that later. I turn now to the incapacitation argument.

TABLE 4.4 **Time 1 assumptions and Time 2 effects**

	Ordinary citizens	Recidivists	Total
Time 1 assumptions			
Population	140,000,000	60,000,000	200,000,000
Prison population	1,000,000	1,000,000	2,000,000
Free population	139,000,000	59,000,000	198,000,000
Offending rate (%)	7.14	33.33	15 (average)
Annual crimes	9,924,600	19,666,666	29,591,266
Time 2 effects			
Population	140,000,000	60,000,000	200,000,000
Prison population	0	2,000,000	2,000,000
Free population	140,000,000	58,000,000	198,000,000
Offending rate (%)	16	16	16 (average)
Annual crimes	22,400,000	9,280,000	31,680,000

The Ratchet Effect:
An Overlooked Social Cost

The use of actuarial methods does not withstand scrutiny on rational-theory grounds. Profiling may actually encourage, rather than deter, the overall commission of the targeted crime. But deterrence, naturally, is not the only argument for using instruments that predict criminality. A second and equally powerful argument relies on the incapacitative effect of group prediction: actuarial methods will increase the success rate of searches, audits, parole decision making, and other criminal justice decisions, and therefore enhance our ability to incarcerate criminal offenders. Put simply, if we search more high-offending motorists, we will detect more contraband; and if we deny parole to more likely recidivists, we will prevent them from reoffending. The use of actuarial measures will mean more tax evaders paying their fair share of national expenses, more drug traffickers behind bars, and more recidivists locked up in prison.

As noted in the introduction, the incapacitation argument is compelling, especially in light of the radical drop in crime experienced throughout the United States during the 1990s and 2000s. Many sociologists and economists attribute the sharp drop in crime—or at least, a significant portion of that drop—to the increase in the number of prison inmates in this country. Steven Levitt's research demonstrates that the massive investment in prisons contributed to the drop in crime:[1] the best evidence suggests that almost a fourth of the crime drop during the 1990s was attributable to prison expansion.[2]

In evaluating the argument from incapacitation, however, it is crucial to distinguish our recent experience with prison growth from the more ordinary amount of incapacitation that can be achieved by shifting fixed law enforcement resources in the direction of actuarial prediction. It is important to compare apples to apples and oranges to oranges. Any evaluation of the first—the massive, multibillion-dollar investment in prison expansion and incarceration—requires a full assessment and comparison of alternative crime-fighting measures. The investment in the first case is truly extraordinary: if we assume that it costs approximately $25,000 per year to imprison an adult,[3] given a prison population in excess of two million people, the cost exceeds $50 billion in one year. In order to properly evaluate this massive investment, we would need to explore other proven crime-fighting techniques—such as increased police presence or drug treatment programs—and to estimate their likely effect on crime at a similar investment. Such analysis is essentially orthogonal to the question at hand here, namely, whether shifting relatively fixed law enforcement resources toward actuarial measures is advantageous from a cost-benefit point of view.

With regard to the second issue—the more ordinary incapacitation effects associated with the use of actuarial methods in policing, parole, or sentencing—the incapacitation benefits are likely to be relatively small. For anyone who believes in rational-action theory, the benefits actually wash out completely: there is no incapacitation effect once the hit rates equalize—that is, once the offending rates become the same. If you believe in deterrence, there is no long-term incapacitation effect. There is no gain from imprisoning the recidivist longer than the ordinary citizen once their rates of offending are about the same. There is, in effect, no longer any distinction between the recidivist and the ordinary citizen.

This is an important point, and it is worth emphasizing: in the economic model of criminal profiling, there are no selective incapacitation gains to be had at the Time 2 equilibrium (e.g., in fig. 4.1) by incarcerating higher offenders or more likely recidivists, because, at that point, there is no longer a differential in offending between the different groups. If you believe in rational-action theory—if you believe in deterrence—then there is no argument for selective incapacitation of members of higher-offending groups.

But again, not everyone believes in rationality, especially in the field of crime and punishment. So let's do away with the theoretical premises of rational action theory. What if the offending rates do not equalize? What if the members of the higher-offending group continue to offend at higher rates despite the actuarial measures? Then there are benefits to be had from the selective incapacitation effects of investigating the higher offending-group, right? Yes. Naturally. But then the proper question is, at what cost? Any analysis here calls for cost-benefit weighing. And in answering this question, we tend to overlook one cost. I call it the "ratchet effect," and it takes center stage in this chapter.

By ratchet effect, I have in mind a very specific social phenomenon that occurs in multiple stages. In simple terms, it is a disproportionality that grows over time. The disproportionality in question is between the makeup of the offending population and the make-up of the carceral population—that is, the population that has criminal justice contacts such as arrest, conviction, fine, probation, imprisonment, parole, or other supervision. So, for instance, if drywall contractors comprise 10 percent of actual tax evaders but 40 percent of persons convicted of tax evasion, there is an imbalance between the offending population and the carceral population. If the IRS then uses the carceral proportion to allocate more resources to drywall contractors, that imbalance will increase. Over time, this process of increasing disproportionality represents what I call a ratchet.

Under ordinary conditions, assuming no rational-action feedback, the use of actuarial methods will have a distortive effect on the targeted population that will operate as a ratchet over time. The distortion occurs when profiling produces a supervised population that is disproportionate to the distribution of offending by racial group. I begin by illustrating this in the policing context.

Policing and Law Enforcement

The logic of the ratchet in the policing context is simple: if the police dedicate more resources to investigating, searching, and arresting members of a higher-offending group, the resulting distribution of arrests (between profiled and nonprofiled persons) will disproportionately represent members of that higher-offending group. The basic intuition is that policing is like sampling: when the police profile frequent offenders, they are essentially sampling *more* among members of the higher-offending group. Instead of sampling randomly, which would be the only way to achieve a proportional representation of the offending population, the police are sampling in greater numbers from within the higher-offending group, thereby skewing the sampling results in favor of frequent offenders.

An analogy may be useful here. Imagine that the fishing boats from a village in southern Spain troll at random two bodies of water—the Atlantic ocean, where cod are relatively sparse, and the Mediterranean, where sea bass are plentiful. The waters are far more dense with fish in the Mediterranean, and an average day's catch nets twice as many bass as a day in the Atlantic nets cod. When the captains fish in an entirely uncoordinated and random manner, the catch of the day in the village includes both cod and sea bass. However, if the captains coordinate and decide to fish a lot more in the more dense Mediterranean, then, at the end of the day, the catch will be larger in overall quantity and will contain proportionally far more sea bass. By shifting more fishing to the higher-density Mediterranean, the captains both increase the overall catch and skew it toward sea bass.

In this illustration, the catch of the day no longer represents a random sampling of the fish population within a certain radius of that port town in southern Spain. To obtain such a random sampling, the captains would need to revert to their earlier practice of fishing at random in an uncoordinated manner (over many months). By targeting the Mediterranean, the catch of the day is now skewed toward sea bass. A tourist visiting the Spanish town, strolling down to the waterfront, and reading the restaurant menus along the port would be misled into thinking that there's nothing but sea bass in the adjacent waters.

The same is true in the policing context. The sea bass, imagine, are the more dense criminals in the higher-offending group; the cod are the more scarce criminals in the lower-offending group. If the police stop and search individuals randomly, regardless of their group membership, then they will dedicate resources evenly across the different groups in relation to their representation in the overall population—say 80 percent of searches of low-offending group members and 20 percent of searches of high-offending group members. The resulting carceral population—persons with correctional traces, whether arrest, conviction, fine, probation, incarceration, or parole—will be a random sampling of the offending population and, naturally, will depend on the rate of offending within each group. As a random sampling of the offending population, the carceral population will reflect perfectly the distribution of offenders between the two groups in society.

If, however, the police profile the higher-offending group members, the resulting carceral population will be skewed toward members of the higher-offending group: these profiled persons will represent a larger proportion of the carceral population than of the offending population. Jails and prisons will be populated by members of the higher-offending population in a manner that is disproportionate to their contribution to the offending population: there will be far more members of the higher-offending population in jail and prison then there are even among the offending population. Just like the Spanish port town, a visitor walking through the criminal justice system will think that the only kind of offenders present are members of the higher-offending group—the only kind of fish in the offending population is the sea bass.

This disproportion produces a distortive effect on our carceral populations and has a tendency to perpetuate itself. When the disproportion increases, it produces a ratchet effect with potentially devastating consequences for members of the higher-offending group.

Before discussing those detrimental consequences—the hidden costs of using actuarial methods—let me first illustrate the ratchet effect itself with some simple, hypothetical numbers. My purpose is to demonstrate how actuarial measures, by necessity, create the potential for increasing disproportionality between carceral and offending populations. To make things easy, I will use the same hypothetical figures used in chapter 4 to discuss the rational-action model in the policing context. Assume, then, the same city population of 1 million residents, of which 20 percent, or 200,000, are minorities, and the other 80 percent, or 800,000, are majorities. Recall also that we assumed—in order to make any profiling nonspurious—that minorities offend at a higher rate, say 8 percent, versus majorities, who offend at a rate of 6 percent across the board. If the police engage in the same number of random stops and searches the first year, namely, 10,000, effectively searching 1 percent of the population, then under these assumptions we arrive at Time 1 (i.e., no racial profiling) at the same point as earlier: 8 percent of the 2,000 minority searches (or 160 minority searches) will prove successful, and 6 percent of 8,000 majority searches (or 480 majority searches) will prove successful. As for the total criminal population in the city, it would consist of 16,000 minorities (8 percent of the total 200,000 minority population) and 48,000 majorities (6 percent of the total 800,000 majority population)—or a total of 64,000 offenders overall. These simple assumptions and results are reflected in table 5.1.

Several important observations arise from these initial assumptions at Time 1: first, the higher-offending minority group represents 20 percent of the overall population, but 25 percent of the offending population. This makes sense: the higher-offending group makes up more of the offending population than it does the overall population. In fact, it is precisely this disparity that reflects the fact that the higher-offending minority group is offending at higher levels than the majority. Second, a random distribution

TABLE 5.1   **Results of police searches at Time 1**

	Minority	Majority	Aggregate (total)
Group population	200,000	800,000	1,000,000
Distribution of the population (%)	20	80	100
Group offending rate (%)	8	6	6.4
Number of offenders	16,000 (8% of 200,000)	48,000 (6% of 800,000)	64,000
Distribution of offenders (%)	25	75	100
Police searches	2,000	8,000	10,000
Searches (% of relevant population)	1	1	1
Successful searches leading to carceral contact	160 (8% of 2,000)	480 (6% of 8,000)	640
Distribution of carceral contacts (%)	25	75	100

of stops and searches yields a delinquent population—what I call a carceral population—that is 25 percent higher-offending minority and 75 percent lower-offending majority. Again, this makes intuitive sense: if the police engage in random stops and searches—as if they were sampling randomly from the population—then they will achieve a carceral population that reflects perfectly the offending population. Notice that, at this point, everyone in the general population who is offending has the same likelihood of being apprehended: here, a 1-in-100 chance of being caught by the police as a result of a random police search.

Visually representing all this requires some imagination, but it is helpful and useful. As noted earlier, we are assuming here no deterrent effect—no rational response to the change in policing—since we are addressing only the incapacitation argument; however, we can relax this assumption slightly here, for purposes of the graph, and assume a little elasticity—everyone, after all, believes in a least a modicum of rationality. For purposes of this visual representation, I measure the elasticity in terms of the distribution of total resources allocated to the different groups. In other words, instead of graphing offending rate by the internal search rate for the group, I use the comparative search rate for each group—that is, as compared to the other group. Depending on the size of the population and the overall percentage searched, it would be easy to convert this graph to one that measures elasticity by the internal search rate. For purposes of the ratchet discussion, however, it is more appropriate to use comparative group search rates. So, instead of plotting the internal group search rate (the rate of searches within each group) on the *x*-axis, the graph plots the

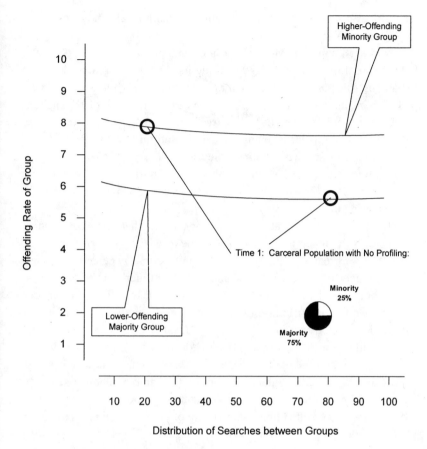

FIGURE 5.1 Basic model of profiling

total distribution of searches between the two groups. Let's also assume, naturally, that the higher-offending minority group is offending consistently at higher rates than the majority. On the basis of these assumptions, I can represent a simple model of policing at Time 1, with no criminal profiling, by the graph shown in figure 5.1.

As the graph shows, if the police engage in random policing and, as a result, are taking a random sample of the total population, then the police will stop and search approximately 20 percent minority and 80 percent majority members. Their searches will then reflect the offending rates of each group, so that the new carceral population—persons apprehended and touched by the criminal justice system—will be distributed 25 percent minority and 75 percent majority. This is a natural reflection of the offender distribution.

Now, let's continue with our earlier assumptions. Assume at Time 2 that law enforcement decides to profile higher-offending minorities for searches. The purpose of the profiling is not to decrease the offending rate of higher-offending minorities, but to incapacitate more of the higher-offending group. As we did earlier, we assume here, then, that the police decide to search twice as many minorities, and that, since they have the same amount of police resources, they still only search 1 percent of the population. The police search four thousand minorities and six thousand majorities. Table 5.2 shows the effect on successful searches and on total crime, using the new values.

Table 5.2 reveals the ratchet in operation: notice that the distribution of new carceral contacts has shot up from Time 1—where it reflected perfectly the offender breakdown of 25/75—and now stands at 47 percent members of the higher-offending minority and 53 percent members of the lower-offending majority. The disparity between the distribution of offenders (25/75) and the distribution of carceral contacts (47/53) is precisely the distortion created by using actuarial methods. It is what begins the ratchet.

Continuing with our earlier analogy to the Spanish port town, notice that the "catch of the day" is bigger: whereas at Time 1 the searches netted 640 new carceral contacts, at Time 2 the same number of searches nets 680. In addition, more of those catches, proportionally, are members of the higher-offending minority group. Thus, if the police engage in criminal profiling based on the higher offending rates of the minority

TABLE 5.2   **Results of police searches at Time 2**

	Minority	Majority	Aggregate (total)
Group population	200,000	800,000	1,000,000
Distribution of the population (%)	20	80	100
Group offending rate (%)	8	6	6.4
Number of offenders	16,000 (8% of 200,000)	48,000 (6% of 800,000)	64,000
Distribution of offenders (%)	25	75	100
Police searches	4,000	6,000	10,000
Searches (% of relevant population)	2	0.75	1
Successful searches leading to carceral contact	320 (8% of 4,000)	360 (6% of 6,000)	680
Distribution of carceral contacts (%)	47	53	100

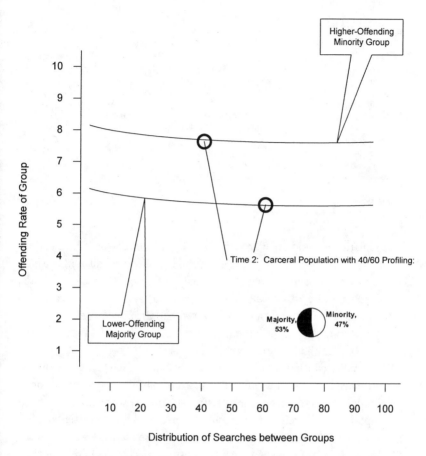

FIGURE 5.2 Criminal profiling at Time 2

group members, the carceral distribution will become skewed. Figure 5.2
provides a visual representation of table 5.2.

Now, if the police then rely on these statistics to reflect the actual breakdown of the offending population and engage in more profiling of the minority group, the distortion will increase. This is illustrated in table 5.3,
where the police distribute their stops and searches along the lines of the
latest carceral distribution at Time 2 (fig. 5.2)—47 percent of stops and
searches of the higher-offending minority group and 53 percent of the
lower-offending majority. Notice in table 5.3 that at Time 3 the distribution of carceral contacts becomes even more disproportionate to the actual offending distribution.

TABLE 5.3   **Results of police searches at Time 3**

	Minority	Majority	Aggregate (total)
Group population	200,000	800,000	1,000,000
Distribution of the population (%)	20	80	100
Group offending rate (%)	8	6	6.4
Number of offenders	16,000	48,000	64,000
	(8% of 200,000)	(6% of 800,000)	
Distribution of offenders (%)	25	75	100
Police searches	4,700	5,300	10,000
Successful searches leading to carceral contact	376	318	694
	(8% of 4,700)	(6% of 5,300)	
Distribution of carceral contacts (%)	54	46	100

Again, the overall "catch" has increased—up from 680 at Time 2 to 694 at Time 3. In addition, again, the distribution of new carceral contacts has become more disproportionate to the distribution of offenders. At both times the offending distribution is at 25/75, but at Time 2 the carceral distribution was 47/53, and at Time 3 it is 54/46. Criminal profiling, under these assumptions of no or minimal rational action, leads ineluctably to a ratchet effect on the carceral population.[4]

If the police continue to use prior carceral data to update their resource allocation, chasing the new offending distributions, the disparity will simply continue to increase. So, for instance, at Time X, when police officers are stopping and searching 60 percent higher-offending minorities and 40 percent lower-offending majorities, the disparity in the new carceral population will increase to 66.66 percent minority and 33.33 percent majority, as shown in table 5.4, where the police distribute their stops and searches 60/40—60 percent of stops and searches of the higher-offending minority group and 40 percent of the lower-offending majority. Notice that the distribution of carceral contacts becomes even more disproportionate to the actual offending distribution. Figure 5.3 provides a visual representation of table 5.4.

In sum, this illustration reveals two important trends. First, the efficiency of the police stops is increasing: each year, the police detect more offenders based on the same number of stops. Second, the group distribution of the newly apprehended offenders becomes increasingly out of proportion with the offending ratio. Criminal profiling, when it works, is a self-confirming prophecy. It aggravates over time the perception of a correlation between the group trait and crime. What I call a ratchet effect

TABLE 5.4 **Results of police searches at Time X**

	Minority	Majority	Aggregate (total)
Group population	200,000	800,000	1,000,000
Distribution of the population (%)	20	80	100
Group offending rate (%)	8	6	6.4
Number of offenders	16,000	48,000	64,000
	(8% of 200,000)	(6% of 800,000)	
Distribution of offenders (%)	25	75	100
Police searches	6,000	4,000	10,000
Successful searches leading to carceral contact	480	240	720
	(8% of 6,000)	(6% of 4,000)	
Distribution of carceral contacts (%)	66.66	33.33	100

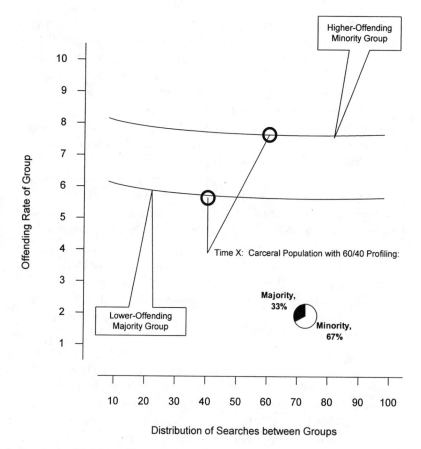

FIGURE 5.3 Criminal profiling at Time X

could be called a "compound" or "multiplier" effect of criminal profiling: profiling may increase disparities in the carceral population.

The important point of this thought experiment is that criminal profiling accentuates the apparent correlation between the group trait and criminality by skewing the carceral population, which is what we all use to proxy criminality. And it does so even if all the underlying assumptions are correct—namely, that the higher-offending group is in fact offending at a higher rate, and that the practice of criminal profiling is entirely justifiable. Naturally, we would see the same effect if the assumptions were wrong and the profiled group did not in fact offend more. Criminal profiling would also create a ratchet under those conditions: the same result, namely, increased disproportionality in the balance of the incarcerated population, would obtain if all groups had the same offending rate, but we allocated *slightly more* of our law enforcement resources to one minority group than their representation in the general population would warrant. Others have underscored this point: if you spend more time looking for crime in a subgroup, you will find more crime there.[5] The point here, though, is that the same type of effect will likely occur even on the assumption of differential offending—even if we accept fully the assumptions offered to justify criminal profiling and, in many cases, racial profiling. This will be especially true for the more unreported types of crime such as drug possession, gun-carrying, or tax evasion.

The distortive effect of criminal profiling on the new carceral population will produce a ratchet whenever law enforcement relies on the evidence of correctional traces—arrests or convictions—in order to reallocate future law enforcement resources. And, given the paucity of reliable information on natural offending rates, law enforcement often does rely heavily on arrest, conviction, and supervision rates in deciding how to allocate resources. As Peter Verniero, Attorney General of New Jersey, explains, "To a large extent, these statistics have been used to grease the wheels of a vicious cycle—a self-fulfilling prophecy where law enforcement agencies rely on arrest data that they themselves generated as a result of the discretionary allocation of resources and targeted drug enforcement efforts."[6] This accelerates the imbalance in the prison population and aggravates the secondary impact on the profiled population.

One other very important point: the same ratchet effect applies under assumptions of rational action. If, for instance, 60 percent of minority drivers on the highway must be searched to achieve equal hit rates for minority and majority drivers—which is apparently what is going on in Maryland (see chapter 4) if we assume that the rational-actor model explains the equal hit rates—then there is undoubtedly a ratchet: given the exact same hit rates, minority drivers will comprise 60 percent of the new carceral population—persons with negative police contacts resulting in some correctional trace, whether simply an arrest or more serious carceral supervision. There is hardly any chance, however, that minority drivers comprise 60 percent of the offending population. No one suggests as much. The difference between targeted persons representing more than their share of actual offenders, yet 60 percent of persons with a correctional trace reflects a ratchet effect that will only be aggravated with time if law enforcement relies on that 60 percent metric.

The ratchet effect, in other words, operates just as much under conditions of elasticity—under the assumptions of rational choice. The extent of the ratchet, in fact, will depend on the amount of elasticity within each group and on the relative offending rates. This can be demonstrated, again, using the earlier illustration. Assume here that the criminal profiling has produced some deterrence among the higher-offending group. The Time 1 table (table 5.1) and graph (fig. 5.1), naturally, remain the same since, at Time 1, the police are not engaged in criminal profiling. However, at Time 2.1 (a modified Time 2 with racial profiling), the situation looks as shown in table 5.5.

Table 5.5 reveals, again, the ratchet in operation: notice that the distribution of new carceral contacts has increased from Time 1—where it

TABLE 5.5   **Results of police searches at Time 2.1**

	Minority	Majority	Aggregate (total)
Group population	200,000	800,000	1,000,000
Time 1 offending rates (%)	8	6	6.4
Time 1 distribution of offenders (%)	25	75	100
Police searches	4,000 (40%)	6,000 (60%)	10,000 (100%)
Time 2.1 offending rates (%)	7.5	6.5	6.7
Time 2.1 offending population	15,000 (7.5% of 200,000)	52,000 (6.5% of 800,000)	67,000
Time 2.1 distribution of offenders (%)	22.4	77.6	100
Successful searches leading to carceral contact	300 (7.5% of 4,000)	390 (6.5% of 6,000)	690
Distribution of carceral contacts (%)	43.5	56.5	100

reflected perfectly the offender breakdown of 25/75—and now stands at 43.5 percent members of the higher-offending minority and 56.5 percent members of the lower-offending majority. The disparity between this distribution of new carceral contacts (43.5 percent minority; 56.5 percent majority) and the new distribution of offenders in the general population (which is now 22.4 percent minority and 77.6 percent majority, reflecting the change in offending rates associated with deterrence) is precisely the ratchet. This is the distortion created by using actuarial methods. Thus, even assuming rational action, if the police engage in criminal profiling based on the higher offending rates of the minority group members, the new carceral distribution will become skewed. Figure 5.4 provides a visual representation of table 5.5.

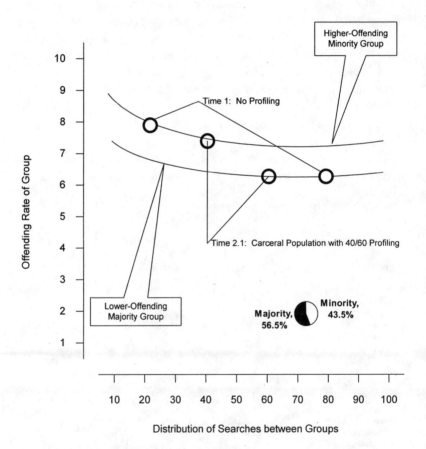

FIGURE 5.4 Criminal profiling assuming elasticity

As noted earlier, the extent of the ratchet will depend on the comparative elasticities and offending rates of the two groups. One final illustration captures this well, making very different assumptions about offending and elasticities. Assume, then, an even larger differential in offending—making criminal profiling even more attractive to its proponents—and lower elasticity for the higher-offending group. And suppose that, at Time 2.2, the police engage in heavy profiling, searching 60 percent minority members. Table 5.6 reflects these assumptions.

Under these assumptions, the ratchet effect is gigantic. As table 5.6 demonstrates, the disparity between the distributions of offenders and carceral contacts is extremely large: at Time 2.2, members of the higher-offending group are 26.4 percent of the total offending population, they are 68.3 percent of the new carceral population. The exponential growth in the disparity is the result of the greater differential in offending and elasticity between the two groups. Figure 5.5 is a visual representation of table 5.6.

To be sure, at some point the ratchet will no longer operate. If the differential in offending becomes too big, and members of the profiled population are the only ones offending, then there will be no room for a ratchet. If the higher-offending group is committing 99 percent of the offenses, there is no real possibility of a ratchet. So, for instance, if men are perpetrating practically all traditional rape offenses, then profiling

TABLE 5.6   **Results of police searches at Time 2.2**

	Minority	Majority	Aggregate (total)
Group population	200,000	800,000	1,000,000
Time 1 offending rates (%)	12	6	7.2
Time 1 offenders	24,000	48,000	72,000
Time 1 distribution of offenders (%)	33.33	66.66	100
Police searches	6,000 (60%)	4,000 (40%)	10,000 (100%)
Time 2.2 offending rates (%)	11.5	8	8.7
Time 2.2 offenders	23,000 (11.5% of 200,000)	64,000 (8% of 800,000)	87,000
Time 2.2 distribution of offenders (%)	26.4	73.6	100
Successful searches leading to carceral contact	690 (11.5% of 6,000)	320 (8% of 4,000)	1,010
Distribution of carceral contacts (%)	68.3	31.7	100

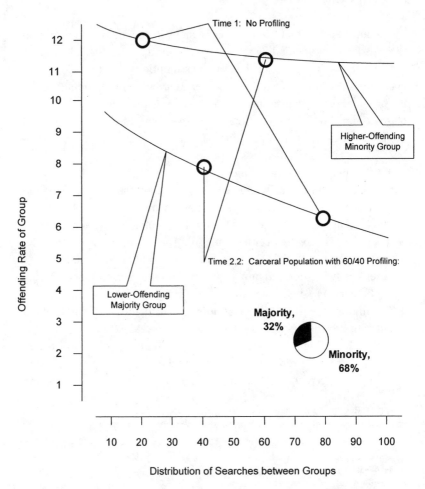

FIGURE 5.5 Criminal profiling assuming large differentials in offending and in elasticity

men in a rape case is unlikely to create any greater disproportionality. However, such cases are rare. In most cases where profiling is used, the offending disparities are less extreme, and, in combination with the elasticity differentials, they are more likely to produce significant ratchets.

The Ratchet and Its Cost

The distortion and eventual ratchet disproportionately distribute criminal records and criminal justice contacts, with numerous secondary implications for members of the profiled group in terms of their education, employment, and family lives. Disproportionate criminal supervision and incarceration reduces work opportunities, breaks down families and communities, and disrupts education.

The pernicious effects of overrepresentation of African Americans in our prisons—especially among incarcerated felons—have been detailed and documented by many scholars, including Tracey Meares, Dorothy Roberts, David Cole, Michael Tonry, and Loïc Wacquant, to name but a few.[7] Widespread conviction and incarceration affect not only the targeted individuals but their communities—producing feedback effects on them and others. Drawing on insights from the Chicago School of urban sociology—specifically, on the social disorganization theory of Clifford Shaw and Henry McKay[8]—Tracey Meares describes well the devastating effects of high incarceration rates on the convicts and on their communities—on "the vitality of families, the life chances of children left behind, and the economic circumstances of African-American communities."[9] Meares writes,

> The status of "convict" severely compromises the released felon's ability to make investments in human capital. A released convict may perceive further investment in human capital to be useless because he may understandably reason that sinking money and time into education and training will not overcome the stigma of a felony conviction on a job application. When he makes the decision to refrain from further investment, he weakens existing relationships he has with people who will be less likely to depend on him, because his ability to provide them with benefits through interaction is compromised. Additionally, the individual who decides not to make further investments in education, skills and training cuts himself off from potential useful relationships with others who have no incentive to form relationships with him. . . . The basic point is this: all unemployed populations are not equal, and any incremental increase in the proportion of convicts among the unemployed population of the ghetto portends incrementally worse consequences for the vitality of the community.[10]

Lower employment opportunities not only harm the released prisoner on reentry, but also erode the social fabric of the community. The deadly combination of prison and unemployment fuels a cycle of detrimental consequences for the community that then feed back on the community members. These include "fewer adults to monitor and supervise children" resulting in "increased opportunities for children to become involved in delinquency and crime," more broken families, and deepening poverty, all of which produce severe disruptions in African American communities.[11]

The ratchet also contributes to an exaggerated general perception in the public imagination and among police officers of an association between being African American and being a criminal—between, in Dorothy Roberts's words, "blackness and criminality."[12] As she explains,

> One of the main tests in American culture for distinguishing law-abiding from lawless people is their race. Many, if not most, Americans believe that Black people are "prone to violence" and make race-based assessments of the danger posed by strangers they encounter. The myth of Black criminality is part of a belief system deeply embedded in American culture that is premised on the superiority of whites and inferiority of Blacks. Stereotypes that originated in slavery are perpetuated today by the media and reinforced by the huge numbers of Blacks under criminal justice supervision. As Jody Armour puts it, "it is unrealistic to dispute the depressing conclusion that, for many Americans, crime has a black face."[13]

Roberts discusses one extremely revealing symptom of the "black face" of crime, namely, the strong tendency of white victims and eyewitnesses to misidentify suspects in cross-racial situations. Studies show a disproportionate rate of false identifications when the person identifying is white and the person identified is black. In fact, according to Sheri Lynn Johnson, "this expectation is so strong that whites may observe an interracial scene in which a white person is the aggressor, yet remember the black person as the aggressor."[14] The black face has become the criminal in our collective subconscious. "The unconscious association between Blacks and crime is so powerful that it supersedes reality," Roberts observes: "it predisposes whites to literally see Black people as criminals. Their skin color marks Blacks as visibly lawless."[15]

This, in turn, further undermines the ability of African Americans to obtain employment or pursue educational opportunities. It has a delegitimizing effect on the criminal justice system that may encourage disaffected youths to commit crime. It may also erode community-police relations, hampering law enforcement efforts as minority community members become less willing to report crime, to testify, and to convict. The feedback mechanisms, in turn, accelerate the imbalance in the prison population and the growing correlation between race and criminality. Borrowing and adapting slightly from Dorothy Roberts' work,[16] I can represent the negative impact of the ratchet effect in tabular form as follows:

Police Conduct →	Social Meaning →	Social Norm →	Impact on Community
Racial profiling that produces a ratchet effect on the carceral population.	Blacks are suspect, require police supervision, and are entitled to fewer liberties.	Presumed black criminality.	Blacks are perceived as criminals and experience more discrimination.

And the costs are deeply personal as well. Dorothy Roberts discusses the personal harm poignantly in a more private voice in her brilliant essay, *Race, Vagueness, and the Social Meaning of Order-Maintenance Policing*, sharing with the reader a conversation that she had with her sixteen-year-old son, who is African American:

In the middle of writing this Foreword, I had a revealing conversation with my sixteen-year-old son about police and loitering. I told my son that I was discussing the constitutionality of a city ordinance that allowed the police to disperse people talking on the sidewalk if any one of them looked as if he belonged to a gang. My son responded apathetically, "What's new about that? The police do it all the time, anyway. They don't like Black kids standing around stores where white people shop, so they tell us to move." He then casually recounted a couple of instances when he and his friends were ordered by officers to move along when they gathered after school to shoot the breeze on the streets of our integrated community in New Jersey. He seemed resigned to this treatment as a fact of life, just another indignity of growing up Black in America. He was used to being viewed with suspicion: being hassled by police was similar to the way store owners followed him with hawk eyes as he walked through the aisles of neighborhood stores or women clutched their purses as he approached them on the street.

Even my relatively privileged son had become acculturated to one of the salient social norms of contemporary America: Black children, as well as adults, are presumed to be lawless, and that status is enforced by the police. He has learned that as a Black person he cannot expect to be treated with the same dignity and respect accorded his white classmates. Of course, Black teens in inner-city communities are subjected to more routine and brutal forms of police harassment. Along with commanding them to move along, police officers often make derogatory comments, push them around, or throw them against the patrol car. As my son quickly noted, the Chicago ordinance simply codifies a police practice that is already prevalent in Black communities across America. But . . . the power of the police to enforce their orders with arrest, conviction, and incarceration powerfully validate[s] the harmful message of presumed Black criminality.[17]

These harms, I suggest, can be traced directly to a ratchet effect—to the disproportionality between the carceral population and the offending population and the significant symbolic meaning of prison demographics. Note, however, that the ratchet effect, while extremely troubling in the case of race, is not *only* troubling because of race. The ratchet is an abstract mechanism that is equally troubling in other contexts. The same problem plagues the actuarial profiling of persons with prior criminal records, with a similar, detrimental effect on recidivists who are reentering society—what I will call "recidivist criminality." Here the ratchet effect accentuates the symbolic meaning of prison and incarceration: it compounds the perception that a prison record means that the convict is more likely to reoffend. To be sure, there may well be a correlation. Again, as in all the cases in this book, I am assuming that the prediction is *correct*. The statistical correlation is presumably reliable, not spurious. What the ratchet does, though, is aggravate precisely that correlation: whereas prior offenders may represent, hypothetically, 40 percent of the offending population, *profiling* prior offenders will result in their representing, again hypothetically, 65 percent of the prison population. This differential represents a ratchet effect with heavy symbolic meaning. It leads the general public to think that prior offenders are even more prone to future criminality than they really are. And this has devastating effects on the possibilities and the reality of reentry.

It is what makes reentry so terribly difficult for prior felons: it is what reduces their employment opportunities and their ability to reintegrate into society. It is what renders them suspicious to us all—less trustworthy. They are the first to be investigated when a crime is committed—the first to be suspected when something is missing. It is what makes it even harder for someone returning from prison to go back to school, find a job, make friends, be trusted. And this too feeds a vicious cycle. As Robert Sampson and John Laub observe, imprisonment has "powerful negative effects on the prospects of future employment and job employment. In turn, low income, unemployment, and underemployment are themselves linked to heightened risks of family disruption. Through its negative effects on male employment, imprisonment may thus lead indirectly through family disruption to increases in future rates of crime and violence."[18]

Even under ordinary conditions, reentry is extremely difficult. The statistics are striking. Offenders who are released from prison face a high likelihood of returning to a cell. Several studies by the Bureau of Justice Statistics (BJS) and by state authorities consistently document high rates of rearrest, reconviction, and reincarceration. One BJS study of prisoners released from eleven states in 1983 revealed that 63 percent were rearrested for a felony or serious misdemeanor within a three-year follow-up period.[19] Another BJS study of prisoners released from fifteen states in 1994 revealed that 69 percent were rearrested within three years, with a reconviction rate of 47 percent.[20] State studies in Illinois, Texas, Kentucky, and Pennsylvania document three-year reincarceration rates ranging from a high of 50 percent to a low of 31 percent.[21] Part of the problem, naturally, has been our failure to manage reentry properly. As Jeremy Travis, one of the nation's leading thinkers about reentry, notes, "our system of justice lacks the organizational capacity to manage the reintegration of released offenders."[22]

These problems are *compounded* by the existence of a ratchet, which further accentuates the symbolic dimension of prior criminality. These are the costs of "recidivist criminality"—and they are no different than the costs of "black criminality." To be sure, there is no "recidivist community" like the African American communities that bear the brunt of these policies. But the effects are similarly devastating to the individual: even greater difficulties with employment, housing, and family reintegration. These represent a tremendous cost. And notice that the problem is not race. It is the mechanics of profiling. It involves the mathematical dimension of profiling that is marked by race in one context but prior criminality in the other.

One natural question is, Have we experienced such a ratchet in our criminal justice system? Has the increased use of actuarial methods in criminal justice contributed, for instance, to the growing racial imbalance in our carceral populations? Clearly, a combination of practices closely associated with criminal profiling has contributed to these national trends. These practices include drug-interdiction programs at ports of entry and on interstate highways, order-maintenance crackdowns involving aggressive arrest policies for misdemeanors, gun-oriented policing in urban areas focusing on stop-and-frisk searches and increased police-civilian contacts, as well as other instances of profiling, ranging from the drug-courier, street-dealer, gang-member, and disorderly profiles all the way to profiles of disgruntled former federal employees or outcast and bullied high school youths. The investigatory search-and-seizure jurisprudence that has grown out of *Terry v. Ohio,* especially cases such as *Whren v. United States*—where the Supreme Court upheld the use of a pretextual civil traffic violation as a basis for a stop-and-frisk procedure triggered by suspicion that the driver and passenger were engaged in drug trafficking—has likely facilitated the emergence of these practices.[23]

As to whether or to what extent the increased use of actuarial methods *itself* has contributed to any type of ratchet, it would be important to parse our criminal justice data to explore which portion of the national trends are attributable to offender differentials, to targeted law enforcement disproportionate to group representation, and to a possible ratchet effect, as well as to measure any possible feedback and incapacitation effects. The point of the previous thought experiment is that actuarial methods—including criminal and especially racial profiling—should logically contribute to a ratchet. How much is unclear. But it is clear that the criminal justice trends in the twentieth century were, at the very least, consistent with a ratchet effect.

The two largest criminal justice trends of the late twentieth century mirror the two lessons of the ratchet discussion. First, the United States witnessed a continuously increasing—in fact, exponential—rise in the prison population. As noted earlier, this was due largely to the massive social investment in prisons and incarceration. But the overall increase, or at least some small portion of that increase, is also entirely consistent with the first observation from the ratchet discussion: that criminal profiling increases the overall efficiency of police interventions. Criminal profiling means that the same number of stops and searches nets a larger number of

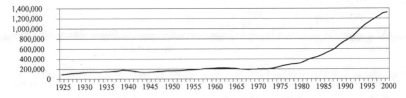

FIGURE 5.6 Sentenced prisoners under jurisdiction of state and federal correctional authorities on December 31 (U.S., 1925–2000)
Sources: U.S. Bureau of Justice Statistics 2001a, table 6.27, and 2002a, 2.

offenders: the "catch of the day" increases in overall size. This observation is consistent with the overall trend in prison population during the last third of the twentieth century, when criminal profiling began to flourish. Figure 5.6 traces the state and federal prison population growth discussed earlier: the prison population nationwide grew from less than 200,000 in 1970 to more than 1,300,000. This does not include the more than 630,000 persons held in local jails in 2001.

The second lesson from the ratchet discussion—namely, that criminal profiling likely produces an increasing imbalance between the offending and carceral populations—is also highly consistent with data from the criminal justice system. During the twentieth century, African Americans comprised a consistently increasing proportion of the new and overall supervised population. Since 1926, the year the federal government began collecting data on correctional populations, the proportion of African Americans newly admitted to state prisons has increased steadily from 23.1 percent to 45.8 percent in 1982. It reached 51.8 percent in 1991, and stood at 47 percent in 1997. Figure 5.7 illustrates this trend. In 1997, 9 percent of all adult African Americans were under correctional supervision in this country, in contrast to 2 percent of European Americans.[24] The trend from 1985 to 1997 is reflected in figure 5.8, which shows the percentage of the adult population in state and federal prisons and local jails by race and gender as a proportion of their representation in the general population.[25] Naturally, I do not contend that these trends verify the ratchet effect. They are merely consistent with a ratchet effect operating against African Americans in the U.S. criminal justice system.

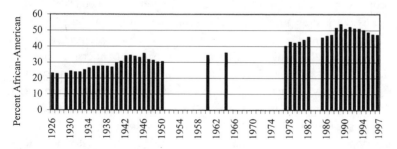

FIGURE 5.7 Percentage of new admissions to state prisons who were African American, 1926–1997
Sources: For statistics from 1926 to 1982, see Langan 1985, 666–67; for statistics from 1985 to 1989, see U.S. Bureau of Justice Statistics 1997, table 1.16; for statistics from 1990 to 1997, see U.S. Bureau of Justice Statistics 2000a, table 1.20.

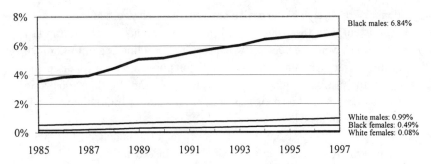

FIGURE 5.8 Percentage of U.S. adult population in state or federal prisons or in local jails, by race and gender, 1985–1997
Source: U.S. Bureau of Justice Statistics 2000a, fig. 1.

The Ratchet Effect in the Sentencing Context

The idea of a ratchet effect operating in the context of criminal profiling, especially racial profiling, makes intuitive sense. Many of us are familiar with the consequences for the supervised population. The black face of the street suspect, the suit and tie of the insider-trader, the blue collar of the drywall contractor—these are all powerful symbols produced by the ratchet effect. But make no mistake: the ratchet effect applies with equal force in the sentencing and punishment contexts.

As I hinted in the introduction, the ratchet also applies to recidivists and to those sentenced under habitual-enhancement statutes. How and to what effect? In precisely a parallel manner: likely recidivists are disproportionately denied parole or sentenced under enhanced statutes and, as a result, are disproportionately represented in the prison population. If sentencing and parole authorities use an actuarial method to predict likely future offending, and thus focus on repeat offenders, the authorities will target habitual offenders for increased incarceration and supervision. Deliberately increasing the punishment for this group of habitual offenders means that its members will make up a larger proportion of the prison population—larger, proportionally, than their share of the offending population. The important symbolic message associated with their disproportionate incarceration will be that prisoners are likely to reoffend—a message resembling this: "If you offend once, you are likely to offend again; if you offend twice, you will definitely reoffend again and again." This powerful symbolic message will have a detrimental effect on prisoners returning to their communities upon release, probably reducing their employment and educational opportunities, and further complicating their integration into family and neighborhood life.

Other Social Costs

The use of actuarial measures has other costs as well—aside from the ratchet effect. As I mentioned in the introduction, the perception that the criminal justice system is unfairly targeting certain groups—reflected, for instance, in expressions like "driving while black" or even "walking while black"—may have adverse effects on respect for the law. Tom Tyler's research demonstrates this link between perceptions of legitimacy and obedience to the law. Tyler's book *Why People Obey the Law* and his writings on procedural fairness and institutional legitimacy, including his essay "Trust and Democratic Governance," rest precisely on the idea that individuals derive a strong sense of identity from their relationship to legal authority. When the relationship is positive and respectful, a form of social trust—a concept closely linked to the idea of social capital made popular in Robert Putnam's book, *Bowling Alone,* as well as to the notion of collective efficacy in the work of Robert Sampson—develops and promotes obedience to the law. "[S]ocial trust," Tyler contends, "is linked to creating a commitment and loyalty to the group and to group rules and institutions."[26] This commitment and loyalty to the group translates into greater obedience to the law. When this loyalty is undermined, so too is obedience to the law.

In addition, aggressive targeting of higher-offending groups often goes hand in hand with increased complaints of police misconduct. This was the case in New York City in the early to mid-1990s.[27] It is not always easy, however, to measure these costs or to weigh them against one another. Often, the result is one or more instances of police brutality that are difficult to quantify.

The work of Jon Gould and Stephen Mastrofski offers a troubling illustration in this regard.[28] Their research closely tracked the search practices of officers in a top-ranked police department during a period of targeted, aggressive policing. The searches were systematically observed by trained field observers and coded by Gould, Mastrofski, and a team of researchers—including a state appellate judge, a former federal prosecutor, and a government attorney—to determine whether there were any Fourth

Amendment violations. Their research documented astonishingly high rates of unconstitutional police searches. By their conservative estimate, 30 percent of the 115 police searches they studied violated the Fourth Amendment. The vast majority of the unconstitutional searches—31 out of 34—were invisible to the courts, having resulted in no arrest, charge, or citation. In fact, the rate of unconstitutional searches was highest for suspects who were released—44 percent versus 7 percent of arrested or cited suspects. Focusing exclusively on stop-and-frisk searches, an even higher proportion—46 percent—were unconstitutional.[29]

The data also suggest that the police officers were engaged in racial profiling. Fully eighty-four percent of their searches—96 of the searches studied—involved African American suspects. Although we do not know the exact demographic breakdown for Middleberg,[30] the fictitiously named, medium-size American city where the study was conducted, it is practically inconceivable that the police could reach 84 percent searches of black suspects without any racial profiling. The message is clear: targeted aggressive policing comes at a cost. It may be incidences of police misconduct. It may be the loss of legitimacy and, with it, less obedience to the law. These are hard to quantify. But given, in addition, the distortion and ratchet effect—costs that are so often ignored in the crime-and-punishment calculus—the burden should be on proponents of the actuarial to justify the costs and demonstrate that they do not in fact outweigh the benefits.

Costing Out the Benefits

All of these costs need to be quantified and weighed against any potential benefit of incapacitation on crime. As noted earlier, if you believe in rational-choice theory, the benefits from incapacitation are washed out by the deterrent effect: once the hit rates equalize, there is no incapacitation gain to be had. Under these circumstances, the calculus reverts to whether the deterrence gains are outweighed by the different elasticities of the groups—that is, whether the use of actuarial methods actually reduces overall crime, which turns on comparative offending and elasticities.

Even assuming no rational response, the benefits of incapacitation must be weighed against these costs. I have emphasized the ratchet effect here because others have discussed other costs. But they all must be considered. The fact is, the incapacitation argument has no internal limiting principle.

It is typically boundless. It does not tell us *how much* incapacitation is socially optimal. It thus falls on us to perform the cost-benefit analysis.

In this cost-benefit analysis, the burden of proof and persuasion, I argue, must rest on those who would like to use actuarial methods. If the predictive factor behind the actuarial measure is indeed race—as in racial profiling—then the Equal Protection Clause requires that the proponents—in most cases government law enforcement and sentencing authorities—carry the burden of proving a compelling state interest. But I suggest, precisely because of the ratchet effect, that the same should be true in the case of classifications based on gender, class, wealth, and other troubling group traits. The ratchet effect is so problematic that it warrants shifting the burden of proof and persuasion to the proponents of the actuarial. The presumption should favor randomization; the default should be color-blind or, more generally, prediction-blind. And we should only move away from this presumption if the advocates of profiling can demonstrate that the distortion and possible ratchet effect will not be unduly burdensome.

CHAPTER SIX

The Pull of Prediction: Distorting Our Conceptions of Just Punishment

There is yet one other trouble with the actuarial turn—a more fundamental problem that goes beyond, or perhaps beneath, the equations, graphs, and tables. The fact is that today, we have begun to visualize just punishment through the lens of actuarial probability. The social shift in our conception of just punishment from rehabilitation in the 1950s and '60s to incapacitation in the 1980s and '90s can be traced specifically to the popular rise of actuarial methods and their implementation. To be sure, many other factors are involved as well—factors that David Garland describes powerfully in his work, *The Culture of Control*. But one important factor—one that has received less attention—is precisely the development of technical knowledge and, as the driving force behind it, the will to know the criminal.

The structural transformation of our conception of just punishment at the end of the twentieth century is a case study in justice conforming itself to our developing technical knowledge. It is a case of philosophical and legal notions of justice *following* technical progress. And what is remarkable is that the impulse, the original catalyst, the stimulant in all this was exogenous to the legal system. It came from the field of sociology and from the positivist desire to place human behavior on a more scientific level— from the desire to control human behavior, just as we control nature. The rise of the actuarial itself was born of the desire to know the criminal *scientifically,* and this scientific drive produced the technical knowledge that colonized our jurisprudential conception of just punishment.

The Desire to Know the Criminal

Social theorists have offered a number of theories to help understand the rise of actuarial methods. Some suggest that it is the product of a fundamental shift in our democracy from a social welfare to a penal state—a state that manages the underclass no longer through welfare programs but by means of incarceration.[1] Managing the underclass, in today's world of bureaucracy and modern management, requires the accounting, statistics, and categorization that produce actuarial judgment—the kinds of skills, metrics, and institutions that produce this new mode of bureaucratic management of crime, this new probabilistic or actuarial *episteme* involving a style of thought that emphasizes aggregation, probabilities, and risk calculation.[2]

One factor that has contributed importantly but received less attention is what I call the "will to know the criminal"—the desire to predict criminality. It is the drive to operationalize and model future behavior in the most parsimonious way, the quest for more efficient ways to anticipate crime. It is the same drive that inspired the development of statistics in the eighteenth and nineteenth centuries.

Ian Hacking's research, especially his book *The Taming of Chance,* reveals the close relationship between the birth and development of statistical methods on the one hand, and the fascination with delinquency, crime, and suicide on the other. In part, of course, the connection initially had to do with the ready availability of data on death and other vital statistics. It is there, naturally, that bureaucrats first began keeping track of numbers, colleting data, assembling the facts. But Hacking's research also reveals how the actuarial impulse led to increased control. The erosion of determinism—of conceptions of the laws of nature, of natural law—during the nineteenth century did not give way to chaos or indeterminism but to the laws of probability. It gave rise to the bell-shaped curve and, with it, even greater control over the physical and social environment. The domination and control of nature were achieved precisely by means of statistical regularity. As Hacking explains,

> The more the indeterminism, the more the control. This is obvious in the physical sciences. Quantum physics take[s] for granted that nature is at bottom irreducibly stochastic. Precisely that discovery has immeasurably enhanced our ability to interfere with and alter the course of nature. A moment's reflection shows that a similar statement may be attempted in connection with people.

The parallel was noticed quite early. Wilhelm Wundt, one of the founding fathers of quantitative psychology, wrote as early as 1862: "It is statistics that first demonstrated that love follows psychological laws."[3]

The desire to count, to predict, to know—the desire, in Hacking's words, to *tame chance*—reflects precisely this desire to control the future. And this same desire inspired the turn to the individualization of punishment in the early twentieth century. It is what motivated Ernst Freund, Roscoe Pound, and their colleagues at the University of Chicago to call for a new vision of criminal law based on science. The National Conference of 1909, discussed in chapter 2, was itself an outgrowth of the statistical discoveries emerging from positive criminology—of this desire to know the criminal. As Freund, Pound, and their colleagues explained,

> This truth [namely that there is a statistical regularity to criminality] opens up a vast field for re-examination. It means that we must study all the possible data that can be causes of crime,—the man's heredity, the man's physical and moral make-up, his emotional temperament, the surroundings of his youth, his present home, and other conditions—all the influencing circumstances.... Only in this way can accurate knowledge be reached, and new efficient measures be adopted.[4]

Freund, Pound, and their colleagues lamented the time it had taken for American criminal jurisprudence to embrace the statistical paradigm. "All this has been going on in Europe for forty years past, and in limited fields in this country. All the branches of science that can help have been working—anthropology, medicine, psychology, economics, sociology, philanthropy, penology. The law alone has abstained. The science of law is the one to be served by all this."[5]

This thirst for knowledge—this desire to render the study of human behavior scientific—appears as well in the writings of the sociologists working on parole prediction in the early twentieth century. It is clear in the resounding declarations of Professor Ernest W. Burgess that prediction is feasible and that the parole system must be put on a scientific footing. "Prediction is the aim of the social sciences as it is of the physical sciences."[6] Prediction is not only "feasible" but, as Laune would add, it is *necessary*. "Prediction as to probable success on parole is," Laune declared in 1936, "a self-evident necessity."[7]

The development of prediction reflected, in this sense, the best of scientific progress. "In the past two decades," Burgess reported in 1951, "social scientists have made significant progress in their efforts to find out which prisoners succeed on parole and which fail. . . . Out of their research has grown a conviction that, notwithstanding the difficulties involved, it is possible to predict to some extent how prisoners will behave on parole."[8]

This desire to know the criminal scientifically also appears in the aspirations of the practitioner collaborators. Here is Joseph Lohman, chairman of the Illinois department of corrections, in his 1951 preface to Lloyd Ohlin's *Manual of Parole Prediction*: "Illinois has been a leader in the United States in the systematic, scientific investigation of crime, and in the application of social science knowledge and techniques to the treatment of the convicted offender," Lohman declared. "We in Illinois shall continue to avail ourselves of the privilege of using our universities and their scientific resources in advancing knowledge about crime and its treatment."[9]

Listen carefully to Sheldon and Eleanor Glueck's ode to prediction and science in their masterful book *Five Hundred Criminal Careers,* first published in 1930:

> Workers in the fields of criminology and penology, as well as far-sighted lawyers and judges, have occasionally conceived of the need for some prognostic instrument whereby they might be enabled to predict with reasonable certainty the future of history of various types of criminal offenders. The probable value of such a device cannot be sufficiently emphasized. It would make the process of criminal justice articulate. It would compel judges to think in terms of the future results of the dispositions they make of the cases before them for sentence. It would furnish some objective, scientific guide for the sentencing function. Such an instrument would, for example, enable judges to decide, with much more wisdom than is manifest today, what types of criminals might be expected to do well on probation, which offenders are more suited to different forms of institutional control, and how to deal with various types of recidivists.
>
> A prognostic device would likewise prove of great value to a parole board in determining in a specific case whether a prisoner should be released on parole—that is, whether, according to past experience with similar cases, he will probably do well on parole and thereafter. Practically, it would aid such a board in deciding whether a prisoner should be paroled for an entirely indeterminate period or only for a brief span sufficient to bridge the gap between the penal institution and unsupervised freedom. It would, moreover, be of value in determining the type of parole supervision best adapted for certain cases.
>
> In addition, such an instrument of predictability would be of great value to

social workers and forward-looking legislators in establishing beyond cavil the actual value of existing punitive or reformatory institutions and devices, and in suggesting practical needs and modifications. Finally, a prognostic device scientifically conceived and executed would be extremely useful in the study of crime causation and in suggesting needed experimentation with new correctional methods.

Can such an instrument be devised? If so, how would it actually be utilized by judges and parole boards? Would it be really practicable? Answers to these questions are attempted in the following pages.[10]

The answers, naturally, were yes.

The Gluecks, Burgess, Laune—these researchers viewed themselves as part of a progression toward scientific truth and certain knowledge. They were putting parole on a scientific level. They were learning to *know* the criminal, the deviant, the delinquent.

And they were simply overcome with enthusiasm about the prospect of predicting parole success and failure. Listen to how George Vold, sociology PhD student at the University of Chicago, presents his work in the introduction to his dissertation:

The change from the early "common sense" observations of parole officers and other interested persons to the elaborate quantitative analyses of Burgess and of the Gluecks would seem to represent a step of some significance in the development of a beginning-to-be scientific criminology. The process has been marked by much fumbling and many deviations. Appeals to humanitarian sentiment have played their part; striking "case histories" have had their day; the traits of the individual have come in for their share of study; intelligence tests, psychiatric prognosis, and emotional questionnaires have been used; all have been important, all have had some significance, but none has given any very satisfactory answer to the question of how to judge in advance a man's probable conduct on parole. The important point has been demonstrated in study after study, that no one thing, nor any combination of a few things, is very important in determining a man's conduct on parole. With the recent studies by the Gluecks and by Burgess, the principle has been given practical recognition that the cumulative effects of many factors, individually of little significance, may become very important when operating together.

The present study has been made in full recognition of this principle and seeks to apply it to the parole situation in Minnesota. It is hoped that the present effort may become one more step in the chain of studies indicating the development of a more scientific method in the study of crime and penal administration.[11]

"A more scientific method"; "scientifically conceived and executed"; an "objective, scientific guide for the sentencing function"—the call of science was overwhelming, and it generated a contagious enthusiasm that knew no bounds. The scientific method could and should be applied to parole and everything else criminal. Recall Hornell Hart, one of the first to use rigorous statistical measures. As his enthusiasm for his project grew, he soon advocated applying prediction instruments "not only to the problem of parole, but also to the determination of whether a man should be put on probation, or if he is to be sentenced, to the problem of the length of the sentence which should be imposed."[12]

Here is Ernest Burgess again, in his first foray into prediction in 1928:

> Not only will these rates be valuable to the Parole Board, but they will be equally valuable in organizing the work of supervision. For if the probabilities of violation are even, it does not necessarily mean that the prisoner would be confined to the penitentiary until his maximum was served, but that unusual precautions would be taken in placing him and in supervising his conduct. Less of the attention of the parole officers need in the future be directed toward those who will succeed without attention and more may be given to those in need of assistance.[13]

Two decades later, in 1951, Ernest Burgess would recommend expanding the reach of prediction instruments to "several other fields of delinquency and criminality," including "the identification of predelinquent children, the disposition of cases in the juvenile court, parole from institutional training schools and reformatories, and the selection of adults for probation. . . . Prediction may be just as important or even more important in parole supervision."[14]

George Vold concludes his dissertation in 1931 in a similar tone, suggesting that similar prediction instruments could and should be developed for *all* aspects of the criminal law:

> There would seem to be no reason why a "prediction" technique, comparable to the one discussed in this study, should not be applied to a great many other fields of activity. Thus, criminal courts could presumably apply it at the time of the trial and pronounce sentence accordingly. Probation departments already

have the essential information in their files and would only need to systematize it in some such manner as was done for the parole records in this study to apply the method to their problems.[15]

There is a universalizing tendency in the prediction research, an imperialist impulse that reflects the ebullient moment of discovery, the enthusiasm of mastery, and the deep desire not only to control future behavior, but also to colonize other disciplines.

In this sense, the scientific quest to render parole more scientific was also a struggle *against* other disciplines. Prior to Burgess's intervention in the area, the mental health field—psychology and psychiatry—dominated parole decision making. The model was clinical, not actuarial. As Ferris Laune explains, "[T]he psychiatrist in the Division of the Criminologist in Illinois has included a prediction of prognosis as to the probable extramural adjustment of each inmate upon whom a report was written for the Parole Board."[16] This went against the grain for sociologists, as evidenced by these caustic remarks Laune made in 1936:

> Prognoses as to future behavior by a psychiatrist, whose education and training are those of a doctor of medicine, seem to imply that criminality is a medical problem. This appears to be an unwarranted assumption. Criminality is rather a social problem, and psychiatrists without training in sociology are as little qualified to diagnose and evaluate the factors contributing to criminality as sociologists with no psychiatric training are qualified to cope with mental disease.
>
> The Burgess system, then, seems to be the first to furnish any form of objective measurement of parolability.[17]

Criminality could be predicted, Laune argues here, not just diagnosed. It was a matter for sociologists, not psychiatrists. It was the domain of statistics, not clinical judgment. The difference was crucial, and it had everything to do with the division of labor between disciplines.

The sociologists, as disciplinary leaders, were also up against the parole authorities as practical experts. Dr. George Kirchwey, a former warden at Sing Sing and dean of the Columbia Law School, spoke for the practitioners when he said, "I would trust the judgment of a prisoner in whom I had confidence, regarding the probability of a successful parole, more than the judgment of a psychiatrist or of a parole board, and far more than the score derived from any prediction method."[18] Walter Argow at Yale

University expressed a similar sentiment, referring to the "morass of statistics and detailed elaboration" that "bogs down" the practitioner in the field. "The muddy road of theory is long and deep; and while the scientist labors along trying to find a bottom, the man in the field loses interest and turns aside. He wants something material with which he may work," Argow complained. "Hence he, the man in the field, conceives a method all his own which may or may not be based on valid foundations; or, what is even more likely, consigns the whole idea of scientific measurement to the waste basket and continues along the path of his own convictions."[19]

In the ongoing struggle between theory and practice, the Attorney General's survey in 1939 is particularly interesting. What the survey revealed was that the federal parole board took into account the *same* factors that were used in prediction instruments, but took them into account in a "common-sense" way:

> From an analysis of data derived from the official records of Federal institutions it seems that the Federal Parole Board is able, on the basis of a common-sense approach to the problem of parole selection, to recognize many of those general traits which are associated with 'good risks' and 'poor risks' for parole. Since this is the most that a parole-granting agency could hope to do by using a quantitative prediction device, it does not seem that the introduction of such a device into the Federal parole practice would bring about any substantial improvement in its selective policies, especially in view of the rather serious limitations in the quantitative prediction devices now available.[20]

Clearly, there was resistance and conflict. The rise of the actuarial is not a story of uninterrupted or unimpeded progress. But the hurdles, if anything, seem to have fueled the desire to know the criminal. The resistance and the competition both from other disciplines and from practice served to stimulate the impulse to dissect, categorize, and predict.

The Urge to Categorize

The desire to know the criminal went hand in hand with an urge to categorize—to put people into the right box, to fit them into the right rubric. It is amazing, and often surprising, to look at the categories that were developed. Recall Burgess's categories of the "ne'er-do-well," "farm boy," and "mean citizen." These would be recycled over the next few decades—

always criticized for being too vague or subjective, but then redeployed, so lovingly.

There developed in the prediction literature a categorical way of interpreting reality—a sensibility that was at once slightly skeptical and yet embracing. Listen, for instance, to George Vold criticizing the subjectivity of Burgess's categories in his 1931 dissertation:

> It uses categories of information that are in many cases highly subjective and overlapping. Thus, for example, the category of "social type" includes such subclasses as "hobo," "ne'er-do-well," mean citizen, drunkard, gangster, recent immigrant, farm boy, and drug addict. The same individual could presumably easily be a hobo, a ne'er-do-well, a drunkard, a drug addict and a gangster at one and the same time. In that case the particular classification under which a man is entered would seem to be very much a matter of chance. At best it would probably be impossible for another individual to classify 1,000 cases in the same way that Burgess did.[21]

Vold criticized Burgess, poring over the problems of subjectivity in his dissertation. Yet he too ultimately embraced very similar categories in his research design. The "ne'er-do-well" reappeared, this time alongside the "irresponsible youngblood," the "weak character," and the "country bully." Vold spelled out the definitions with care, but they too were hardly any different—"hobo," "drifter," or "tough guy." Notice how Vold's labels and their accompanying definitions categorize along strongly moral dimensions:

9. Responsible and substantial citizen (banker, lawyer, merchant, farm owner, etc., who occupies a position of trust and responsibility in the community and whose integrity has been unquestioned)

8. Respected workman (a settled, well established, regular "working man." Less prominent than the "responsible and substantial citizen," presumably of just as unquestioned integrity)

7. Irresponsible youngblood (youth of good substantial family, well brought up, who needs to "settle down")

6. Recent immigrant (adult immigrant in this country less than 10 years; "greenhorn" who gets into trouble largely through ignorance of ways and language)

5. Weak character (youth of poor responsible family who has never amounted to anything; not especially vicious, just "nothing there")

4. Ne'er-do-well (older than the "weak character"; applied to men of about 30 or

more who belong to the nondescript category of "harmless no good's;" differs
from the "transient" in that this group has fairly fixed residence)

3. Transient worker (hobo or drifter; no permanent connections and no role in
   any community)

2. Small town or country "bully" (rural "tough guy" with belligerent attitude
   towards community, police, and control; fighter involved in minor squabbles of
   many kinds)

1. City tough (runs with a bad crowd and has a definite bad record; rather definitely
   identified with a continuous delinquent and criminal career) [22]

Vold was not alone. Most researchers were well aware of the subjective nature of the classifications and yet continued to embrace them.
Ferris Laune in 1936 wrote that "[s]ome of the classifications are so am-
biguous that it is almost fortuitous when a given inmate receives the
same classification from two different investigators. For example, it is
often difficult to determine whether, under 'Social Type,' a man should
be classified as 'Gangster,' 'Socially Inadequate,' 'Ne'er-do-well' or even
'Farm Boy.'"[23] Yet Laune and many others returned to these very same
categories. Here is Lloyd Ohlin writing in 1951, embracing the subjectivity critique: "The subclass *ne'er-do-well* failed to meet [objective reliabil-
ity] tests, and *sex deviant* included too few cases to permit any confidence
in the results."[24] Regarding the overarching factor "social type," Ohlin
wrote that "When a sample of cases on this factor was restudied a year
after the first classification, there was 83 percent agreement between the
two classifications. This percentage of agreement was the lowest for any of
the 12 factors and reflects the presence of a subjective element in the judgment of the investigator."[25] Yet ultimately, he too would fall in line and
endorse the "social type" factor, as well as the "ne'er-do-well," the "erring
citizen," and many other loaded categories. Here is the list of categories
that Ohlin used in his research. Notice how outcome-determinative some
of these categories are, notably the first:

1. *Erring citizen*: An older man who has apparently been entrusted with responsibility; a substantial and reliable citizen, but one who erred on this occasion.

2. *Marginally delinquent*: A borderline classification between an erring citizen
   and a socially inadequate person.

3. *Socially inadequate*: An offender who has failed to establish a place for himself
   in conventional society, by virtue of mental deficiency, irresponsibility, or an
   unstable personality. He does not exhibit steadiness in his work history or responsibility in his family relationships.

4. *"Farmer"*: A rural-type person who generally leads a normal social life but becomes easily involved in situations that lead to trouble.

5. *Ne'er-do-well*: An irresponsible person who seldom seeks work, lives by the easiest way possible, and is considered to have a bad reputation in the community as a thief, gambler, drunkard, etc.

6. *Floater*: A man who drifts about the country, rides freights, lives in jungles, gets tagged for vagrancy, and frequently commits minor crimes en route.

7. *Socially maladjusted*: A person who cannot adjust himself to conventional society by virtue of strong criminal orientation or serious personality disturbances.

8. *Drunkard*: An offender who continually loses his job because of drinking, frequents saloons constantly, and works only to keep drinking. Generally he has a reputation for being an alcoholic and his crime is related to his drinking.

9. *Drug addict*: A person who has acquired the habit of using narcotics and whose crimes are generally related to this habit.

10. *Sex deviant*: A man who engages in recognized deviant sex behavior as a common practice.[26]

Despite all the introspection and criticism about the subjectivity of these categories, Ohlin and others recycled similar labels in their own research. Dan Glaser, in his 1954 study, would redefine the "social types" into "seven general life patterns toward which the subjects seemed to be developing prior to their offense," yet nevertheless retain the "ne'er-do-well" category, as well as the "floater" and the "dissipated."[27] The urge to categorize and the attraction to these labels was simply overwhelming.

The Impulse to Insure

Another strong impulse was the desire to mimic the actuarial supremacy of the insurance industry. In his first study in 1928, Ernest Burgess had emphasized that "[t]he practical value of an expectancy rate should be as useful in parole administration as similar rates have proved to be in insurance and in other fields where forecasting the future is necessary."[28] Practically all of the subsequent literature would express this leitmotif.

The comparison to the insurance industry served, in part, to normalize the research and to mainstream its application. The comparison was meant to reassure parole board members. After all, the insurance industry had been using these methods successfully for many years; parole boards did not need to fear them. The analogy to insurance was intended, at least in part, to assuage parole board members, to make sure that they could sleep at night. This is apparent, for instance, in the *Handbook for New Parole Board Members* published by the Association of Paroling Authorities International:

> Every parole board member is concerned about public safety. The thing that keeps parole board members awake at night is the fear that they will release someone and that person will commit a serious crime. . . . Validated, actuarial risk assessment tools can significantly increase your ability to assess risk more accurately. The tradition of good risk assessment tools goes back a long way. . . . Indeed, the technology grows from the same techniques that have been used with great success in the insurance industry for years, and in many other industries that are placing increasing focus on empirical risk analysis. When you buy an insurance policy, your rates are determined by empirically verifiable factors—age, health history, occupation, smoking status, etc.—that have been carefully researched, not on what your agent thinks when he interviews you. . . . In this day and age, making parole decisions without benefit of a good, research-based risk assessment instrument clearly falls short of accepted best practice.[29]

Over and over again, the insurance analogy was deployed to placate concern. Here is George Vold, again in 1931:

> The principle of predicting future human conduct, in the mass, from the record of the past, on the assumption that "other things will remain constant," seems sound and worthwhile. Insurance companies have built up large business enterprises on this principle of predicting the future from the past. The present study, in common with those of Burgess and of the Gluecks, seems to establish the validity of that general principle for other phases of human conduct as well.[30]

Here is Monachesi, also inspired by the ideal of insurance: "Insurance companies sometimes take individuals who are not normal risks but require a greater premium from those individuals who are poorer risks."[31] Van Vechten in 1935 similarly opens his study with a bow to the insurance industry:

> There is nothing new about the idea of evaluating the probability of a future happening on the basis of past experience. Insurance, which depends upon actuarial ratings worked out with more or less precision, dates back at least to Roman times; Quetelet and other early statisticians were impressed by the fact that they could predict from past experience the total number of such infrequent occurrences as suicides which would happen in a given year.

The attempt to use actuarial procedure for the evaluation of social risks by welfare agencies is distinctly new, however, and has been largely confined to the study of paroles.[32]

And Walter Argow wrote, in 1935, "This idea is not totally new or peculiar to our field, for insurance companies have been using a similar device to compute the 'probable life-range' of an individual on the basis of data regarding others in similar circumstances."[33]

The structural shift in the use of actuarial measures in criminal law during the twentieth century—namely, the focus on prior criminality as the best predictor of future dangerousness—also mirrors the larger structural transformation in the approach to risk and responsibility in the insurance context. Tom Baker and Jonathan Simon refer to this shift under the rubric "embracing risk"; Nikolas Rose describes this shift under the label "advanced liberalism."[34] What they have in mind is a paradigm shift from the idea of using insurance to "spread risk" during the early part of the twentieth century—whether through workmen's compensation laws, social security programs, Medicare, or Medicaid—to the use of insurance methods to "assign responsibility" at the turn of the twenty-first century. Assigning responsibility corresponds to "various efforts to make people more individually accountable for risk":[35] efforts to use insurance methods "as an incentive that can reduce individual claims on collective resources."[36] In contrast to an earlier period marked by insurance methods that spread risk over larger portions of the population, the newer paradigm seeks to "place more risk on the individual and to dismantle the large risk pools that socialized risk" previously.[37]

In this sense, the nature of the urge to insure was itself transformed significantly in the twentieth century. It served different masters. And, just as naturally, it met with some resistance. Not everyone expressed the desire, and, with regard to parole, some argued against the analogy to insurance. So, for instance, the United States Attorney General wrote in 1939 that "while insurance companies and paroling authorities may both be interested in predicting the future from the past, the purpose for which the life-experience tables used by insurance companies were designed is radically different than that to which parole prediction tables must necessarily be put."[38] He went on to emphasize that

[i]n insurance, life-experience tables are used primarily to determine the amount of premium which should be charged to persons in the various probability groups. The probability of living or dying is, after all, entirely indepen-

dent of the amount of premium charged. In other words, the decision to charge a certain premium to persons in a specific age group cannot, of itself, change the existing probability that persons within the group will die at a certain age. On the other hand, the uses proposed for parole-prediction devices are not independent of the probabilities of success or failures on parole.[39]

Clearly, there was contestation here too, as with the desire to categorize. There was resistance. But again, the resistance seemed to fuel, rather than deter, the attraction to the insurance model, at least within the scientific community.

The Structural Transformations of the Criminal Law

The desire to know, to categorize, to insure deeply influenced the course of parole decision making. What the twentieth century witnessed was not simply the creation and emergence of an actuarial approach to criminal law but, more important, a narrowing and refinement of the variables used in the models, which first narrowed the predictive models onto fewer and fewer variables and then embraced more efficient, multipurpose, and multifactored instruments. Much of the development of the statistical models focused on certain key predictors of crime—most specifically, the prior criminal history of the accused—and by the end of the twentieth century many of the statistical instruments relied primarily on prior delinquency and offense characteristics, rather than on the social, familial, and neighborhood background variables that had been such an integral part of the rehabilitative models. Many, but not all; others compensated for their complexity by serving multiple purposes.

The statistical models reflect the turn to individualization in the early twentieth century, which was inextricably linked to the normal curve. In this sense, the structural transformation of the criminal law over the course of the twentieth century did not reflect evolution from a romantic ideal of individualism to the actuarial paradigm. It reflected, instead, the development and refinement of an actuarial approach to criminal law that was the kernel of the focus on individualization at the turn of the twentieth century, that initially took the shape of a clinical model by default, and that gradually matured into the style of criminal law that is characteristic of the early twenty-first century. The thirst for knowledge and desire for prediction, in this sense, contributed to the structural transformation of the criminal law.

The refinement of the actuarial model also contributed to the more fundamental theoretical shift during the late twentieth century from re-habilitation to incapacitation theory. The desire to model and verify fa-cilitated and promoted an incapacitation approach. In the parole context, we observe a delicate shift from using the new science of crime to find the right rehabilitative treatment to using probabilities to predict success and failure on parole. This is reflected in the evolution from a rehabilita-tive aspiration, which was terribly hard to operationalize, to a functioning parole-prediction system—one that was far more easy to operationalize precisely because of the parole-prediction instruments. Actuarial meth-ods made possible the turn to incapacitation.

Of course, it was not just the technical knowledge. The technical knowl-edge had to be sowed in the right soil—in the right cultural context. Ian Hacking's research on the earlier probabilistic turn is insightful here. As he suggests, the proliferation of printed numbers alone was not enough to trigger the taming of chance. The probabilistic turn developed more in Western Europe (France and England), and far less in Eastern Eu-rope (Prussia) because of different political sensibilities—the West being, crudely, more individualistic, atomistic, and libertarian, the East more community-oriented and collectivist. These sensibilities helped laws of chance flourish in the West, but inhibited their development in the East. Historian of science Deborah Coen demonstrates the contrast in her re-search on Imperial Austria, where she shows how the probabilistic turn was deployed to promote tolerance and liberalism. "In Austria," Coen writes, "liberals embraced probability not as a tool for intervention from above, but rather as a strategy of self-cultivation and self-discipline."[40] Hacking traces the difference to cultural sensibilities. In a world of col-lectivist sensibilities, he suggests, the laws of regularity are more likely to be associated with culture than with individual behavior. In contrast, in a more atomistic world guided by Newtonian physics, social mathematics were more likely to flourish. Thus, Hacking concludes, "Without the ava-lanche of numbers set in motion by the Duvillards, there would have been no idea of statistical laws of society. But without the a priori belief that there are Newtonian laws about people, probabilistic laws would never have been read into those numbers."[41]

We need to focus, then, not only on the rise of technical knowledge, but also on the moral, political, and intellectual sensibilities that have marked our epoch. How is it, after all, that purported correlations between prior incarceration and future criminality have led us to profile prior criminal history for purposes of sentencing and law enforcement rather than to conclude that there is a problem with prisons, punishment, or the lack of reentry programs? What conclusions should we draw from the observation that certain groups may be offending at higher rates than others with regard to specific crimes? The numbers, the correlations, the actuarial methods themselves do not answer the questions. It is, again, what we *do* with the numbers that is far more telling.

Displacing Theories of Punishment

What we *have done*, in essence, is to displace earlier conceptions of just punishment with an actuarial optic. Today, the criminal sentence is related, primarily, to prior criminal history as a proxy for future offending or, better yet, to measures on the LSI-R or the Salient Factor Score. These actuarial instruments allow for a level of determinacy that cannot be matched by retribution, deterrence theory, or the harm principle. The prediction of future dangerousness has begun to colonize our theories of punishment.

This is remarkable because it flips on its head the traditional relationship between social science and the legal norm. The prediction instruments were generated, created, driven by sociology and criminology. They came from the social sciences. They were exogenous to the legal system. They had no root, nor any relation to the jurisprudential theories of just punishment. They had no ties to our long history of Anglo-Saxon jurisprudence—to centuries of debate over the penal sanction, utilitarianism, or philosophical theories of retribution. And yet they fundamentally redirected our basic notion of how best and most fairly to administer the criminal law.

The same distortion afflicts the field of policing, especially criminal profiling. The central goal of policing, after all, is to reduce crime. It is not, primarily, efficient policing. It is not to increase the number of successful searches, to boost the hit rate, or to collar more criminals. It is instead to reduce the number of crimes committed in society—efficiency is entirely subservient to that primary law enforcement objective. The quest for prediction, however, has distorted our conception of just policing by emphasizing efficiency over crime minimization. Profiling has become second nature because of our natural tendency to favor economic efficiency.

Criminal profiling also distorts our sense of justice by making us feel, gradually and over time, more justified about investigating and punishing members of a profiled group. They are, of course, more prone to criminality. They are, after all, guilty. They seem to display, at the very least, a propensity to commit crime. We begin to feel that they are more legitimate targets of punishment, not because they offend more than others, but because of *who they are*. So, for example, in the case of profiling drywall contractors for IRS audits, at some point the lines begin to blur, and we begin to feel morally righteous about going after those contractors because we begin to associate the profiled trait with suspicion. Not everyone, of course, does this. But there is a tendency. And as this tendency grows, it further alleviates our scruples. We become just a little bit less disturbed, a little less troubled by the collateral consequences, precisely because we begin to perceive these groups as *more criminal*.

Suppose we had a thermometer to measure intent. Just imagine, for a moment, that biomedical experts had set their sights on developing such a thermometer and had succeeded—a thermometer that could tell us how intentional a person is or was at a particular time. Or perhaps a biochemical test on a hair sample that could determine a person's level of intent at any prior time—much like the hair-sample tests that reveal prior drug use. How different would our conceptions of just punishment be today? Wouldn't the element of *mens rea* (mental state at the time of the offense) play a greater role in the sentencing decision—or in our very conception of just punishment?

But no. What developed instead was a test to predict future dangerousness. And, not surprisingly, the prediction of future dangerousness became the heart of just punishment. We have become, in this sense, the slaves of probability.

Reshaping Reality, Producing Conformity

It would be interesting to explore further what we associate today with repeat offending and how we characterize the recidivist. Today, I suggest, repeat offending is associated with the prediction of future dangerousness and future offending. It is a signal of future behavior—a semiotic shaped by the new technology of prediction. A prior criminal record communicates, more than anything, a higher likelihood of future offending. This is largely due to the rise of actuarial methods that have helped create and reinforce the idea that prior criminality is the best predictor of recidivism. In earlier times, however, the associations were different, and pointed instead to a more organic or primal link, and in other periods to medical models—

the associations related to the dirtiness or taint or filth of the recidivist. Or they revolved around a disease paradigm—one of contagion. John Pratt has done groundbreaking work in this area, especially in his book *Governing the Dangerous: Dangerousness, Law and Social Change,* and describes well how recidivism was associated more, in the nineteenth century, with notions of "fearful slime": [42] the habitual offender was viewed as "amoral," "immoral," "incorrigible," and "degenerate," both "mentally and bodily diseased." An 1895 text refers to recidivists, for example, as a "stain on our civilisation." [43] A fascinating treatise from 1908, entitled *Recidivism: Habitual Criminality, and Habitual Petty Delinquency,* spoke about the habitual offender in terms of degeneracy, avarice, malice, and lust. [44] These earlier writings suggest an association between the habitual offender and a more primal or organic repulsion, having to do with the dirtiness and degeneracy of the recidivist—as well as with a medical model that Foucault, Pratt, and others have so well documented. It may be possible to trace a history in which the dirt and disease models and associations have gradually been replaced today by prediction—by the actuarial.

Rethinking the actuarial in this way raises important and troubling questions. The use of actuarial methods tends to accentuate the prejudices and biases that are built into the penal code and into criminal law enforcement. This is, naturally, all for the good when we are on the winning side, when we are the enforcers, and when we punish the most heinous offenders. But it is problematic in the gray area of the criminal law, in the mass of cases that engulf the criminal justice system—the drug users, the quality-of-life offenders, the tax cheats, the embezzlers. There, things are less clear. The prejudices and biases of the penal law in those cases are more questionable. What actuarial methods do, in effect, is to leverage any structural tilt and exploit any association between crime and group characteristic. It magnifies correlations into carceral distortions. Racial profiling on the highways is a good example of this, but it is by no means the only example. The same holds true for other forms of actuarial justice, whether in parole or sentencing.

The criminal law is by no means a neutral set of rules. It is a moral and political set of rules that codifies social norms, ethical values, political preferences, and class hierarchies. The use of actuarial methods serves only to accentuate the ideological dimensions of the criminal law. It hardens the purported race, class, and power relations between certain offenses and certain groups. It exacerbates any correlation, reinforcing the public perception that certain groups are more prone to crime than others. In this sense, it polarizes social and political divisions, rather than defusing them. Again, this is perhaps acceptable if we are dealing with child molesters, terrorists, and serial killers. But the criminal law is by no means limited to these heinous and egregious crimes.

The use of actuarial methods has a way of producing social conformity. In each case, there is an imputation of bad character on the group trait itself. Take, for example, traffic stops to search for contraband. If racial profiling is prohibited, state troopers may decide to seek consent to search cars driven by persons who speed. (Assume for a moment that speeders—people who habitually drive over the speed limit—have a slightly higher offending rate for possession and trafficking of illicit drugs.) Targeting speeders will likely produce a ratchet effect along the lines of speeding. It will produce a disproportional correctional population of speeders in relation to their representation of the criminal offending population—a ratchet that will tend to communicate that speeders are, for instance, affiliated with the drug trade or more prone to use drugs. And this, in all likelihood, will discourage deviance through stigma. Similarly, in the bail context, the use of statistical discrimination will produce a prison population that communicates that "drifters"—who are, after all, more likely to flee the jurisdiction—are dangerous people. These forms of actuarial justice will inevitably produce conformity through a stigmatizing effect. They will, of course, produce resistance as well; but they will produce a type of normalization. Profiling even on innocuous traits has the effect of marginalizing anyone who deviates from the norm and thereby imposes normalizing pressure on them.

Now, some will rightly respond: "But that's what we want, right? To eliminate speeding, for instance?" And the response is that, here too, as in the case of just punishment, we should be making independent judgments about the penal law—independent of the unintended consequences of prediction. We may indeed decide that we want to criminalize speeding or discourage drifting. But if so, it should be a decision about speeding or about drifters, and not the by-product of an effort to criminalize drug trafficking—not because speeding predicts drug trafficking or because drifters are more likely to flee a jurisdiction. We need to reach the decision *independently*. Actuarial methods should not reshape or distort our conceptions of justice, nor should they indirectly—by accident—discourage difference and stifle eccentricity.

Paradoxically, we were drawn to the actuarial because it promised to bring us closer to the truth. It seemed that it would help mirror social fact.

The use of statistical discrimination, we believed, might help align our punishment and policing practices with the reality of crime and offending. But, surprisingly, quite the opposite has taken place. Social reality aligns with our carceral and police practices. The reliance on actuarial methods actually ends up shaping reality and changing our social world. And it does so by accentuating and aggravating the correlations between group traits and criminality. The repeat offender, who may indeed be more likely to reoffend, is stigmatized by the profiling and has an even harder time with reentry, resulting in an even greater probability of reoffending. The black male youth, who may indeed have a higher risk of offending, is also stigmatized by the profiling and has an even harder time obtaining legitimate employment, resulting in an even greater probability of delinquency. The actuarial methods begin to reshape our social environment—not always for the better.

PART III
Toward a More General Theory of Punishing and Policing

Today, we deploy the general *in order to individualize*—in order to make a better judgment in the case of "any given man."[1] In order to devise the right punishment "for each man about to be paroled."[2] We place people in categories and assess risk factors in order to know the individual better. The actuarial did not grow out of a desire to disregard the individual. It did not grow out of a preference for the general over the particular. To the contrary, it grew out of our lust to *know* the individual. To know *this* individual. To tailor punishment to the particularities and probabilities of each man. This is, paradoxically, the triumph of the individualization of punishment. Today, we generalize to particularize.

Tragically, though, we are blinded by our lust for knowledge, for prediction, for science. We ignore the complexity of elasticities in order to indulge our desire for technical expertise. We make simplifying assumptions. And we model—incorrectly. What we need to do, instead, is to rigorously analyze the actuarial in much the same way that it analyzes us. And when we do that, we will be surprised to learn that its purported efficiencies are *probably* counterproductive—that they may increase rather than decrease the overall rate of targeted crime; that they may produce distortions in our prison populations with a ratchet effect on the profiled groups; and that they may blind us to our own sense of justice and just punishment.

Carol Steiker captures this dilemma well by analogy to "the old chestnut about the man looking for his car keys under a street lamp yards away from his car. When asked why he is looking all the way over there, he replies, 'Because that's where the light is.'"[3] As Steiker suggests, the appropriate question may be "Why are so many in the world of criminal justice clustering under the street lamp of predicting dangerousness?"

In this final part, I step back from the details of the three critiques to generalize about the force of the argument. I set forth a more general framework for analyzing the particular uses of actuarial instruments in the criminal law. I begin by exploring the specific cases of racial profiling on the highways in chapter 7 and of the 1960s bail-reform initiatives in chapter 8, as vehicles to elaborate the more general framework. In the concluding chapter, I discuss the virtues of randomization.

CHAPTER SEVEN

A Case Study on Racial Profiling

In the actuarial field, the case of racial profiling on the highways has received perhaps the most attention from social scientists, legal scholars, and public policymakers. As a result, it is the subfield with the most abundant empirical data and economic models. It seems only fair to ask, at this point, what the empirical evidence shows: Does racial profiling on the roads reduce the overall incidence of drug possession and drug trafficking on the nation's highways? Does it produce a ratchet effect on the profiled population? And does it distort our shared conceptions of just punishment?

Unfortunately, as noted in chapter 3, the new data on police searches from across the country do not provide reliable observations on the key quantities of interest necessary to answer these questions precisely. Specifically, the data do not contain measures of comparative offending or elasticity, nor of natural offending rates within different racial groups. Nevertheless, it is possible to make reasonable conjectures based on both the best available evidence and conservative assumptions about comparative offending rates and elasticities. Let's proceed, then, cautiously.

Comparative Drug-Possession and Drug-Trafficking Offending Rates

The term *offending rate* can be defined in several ways. First, it can refer to the rate of actual offending in the different racial groups, given the existing distribution of police searches. This I will call the "real offending rate." It is calculated by dividing the total number of members of a racial group on the road who are carrying drug contraband by the total number of persons of that racial group on the road. This is a quantity of interest for which we do not have a good measure. Second, the offending rate may be defined as the actual rate of offending in a racial group *when the police are sampling randomly*—that is, when they are engaged in color-blind policing. This I will call the "natural offending rate." Now, it is not entirely natural because, if offending is elastic, it will depend on the amount of policing. But it is natural in the sense that, *as between racial groups,* there is no racial profiling effect. This definition of the offending rate can be measured only under conditions of random sampling. While hard to measure, it represents the only proper way to obtain a metric that we can use to compare offending among different racial groups.

Under assumptions of elasticity, the "real offending rate" will fluctuate with policing. The "real offending rate," by definition, will be the same as the "natural offending rate" when the police engage in random searches. If the police stop and search more minority motorists, then the real offending rate for minorities will be smaller than their natural offending rate—again, assuming elasticity. Under assumptions of low or no elasticity, changes in policing will cause little to no fluctuation in the real offending rate. The real offending rate will equal the natural offending rate no matter how disproportionate the policing—no matter how much profiling takes place.

In all of this, naturally, the offending rate must be distinguished from the "hit rate"—the rate of successful searches for drug contraband. The two are related because the offending rate feeds the search success rates. However, the hit rate is generally going to be much higher than the offending rate because the police search selectively and identify likely offenders.

With these definitions in mind, it is important to clarify the expression "minority motorists have higher offending rates than white motorists." When someone who believes in rational-action theory makes this claim, then they must be talking about higher *natural* offending rates. Certainly, this is true of economists. The whole idea behind the economic model of racial profiling is that disproportionate searches of minority motorists will, as a result of elasticity, bring down their *real* offending rate to the same level as that of white motorists. When the hit rates are equal, the real offending rates should be equal as well. Yet even when the real rates of offending are the same, the assumption is that minority motorists have higher *natural* rates of offending. This explains the need for disproportionate searches of minorities.[1]

In contrast, when someone who believes that individuals are inelastic to policing makes the claim that "minority motorists have higher offending rates than white motorists," then the term *offending rate* can refer either to real or natural offending rates because the two are essentially identical.

Now, under assumptions of elasticity, might the different offending rates of different racial groups nevertheless intersect at some point? Perhaps, though this is a point of ambiguity. When an economist says, "minority motorists have higher offending rates," it simply is not clear whether they mean "at each and every comparative degree of searching" or only "for the most part." In other words, the offending rates could possibly intersect at higher rates of searches. In effect, the offending rates could look like either of the two graphs—or any permutation of these graphs—shown in figures 7.1 and 7.2.

These two graphs depict very different elasticities of offending to policing between members of the different racial groups, and the different

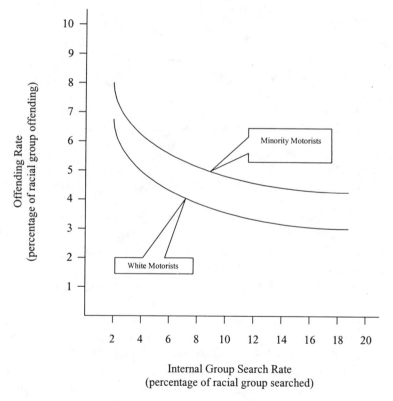

FIGURE 7.1 Consistently higher offending among minority motorists

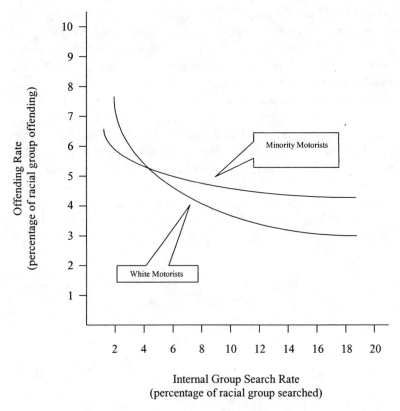

FIGURE 7.2 Mostly higher offending among minority motorists

elasticities affect whether the natural offending rates are consistently or mostly greater for minority motorists. This in turn has important implications for whether racial profiling reduces the amount of profiled crime and for the extent of the ratchet effect on the profiled population.

To estimate natural offending rates, it is also important to distinguish between types of violators: persons carrying drugs for personal use versus drug traffickers. We may also need to explore offending rates by different illicit drugs, given that there may be significant racial differences depending on the specific type of drug being seized on the roads. The place to begin, then, is by estimating natural carrying rates for personal consumption by drug. Here, we can turn to data on personal consumption rates, including various self-report surveys of students and adults, such as the Monitoring the Future Project, the Youth Risk Behavior Surveillance System, and the National Household Survey on Drug Abuse, public health data on drug abuse hospitalizations, and, very carefully, some criminal justice data.

Carrying Drug Contraband for Personal Use

SELF-REPORT STUDIES. The Monitoring the Future Project (MFP) is a cohort self-report study of high school seniors conducted by the University of Michigan's Institute for Social Research. The survey data have been collected since 1975 based on a sample of 120–146 public and private high schools intended to be representative of the entire U.S. high school population. Since 1991, the survey has been extended to include eighth- and tenth-graders, and includes racial and ethnic comparisons.

The MFP data reveal that, for almost all drugs, African American students report lower use than their white and Hispanic cohorts at all grade levels, suggesting that the effect is not due to different dropout rates for users and nonusers. By the twelfth grade, white students have the highest lifetime, annual, and thirty-day reported use of marijuana, inhalants, hallucinogens, amphetamines, sedatives, and tranquilizers in relation to their African American and Hispanic counterparts. White twelfth-graders also report higher lifetime, annual, and thirty-day use of cocaine, heroin, methamphetamines, and steroids than their African American counterparts.[2] Table 7.1 presents the 2003 and 2004 responses combined.

The Youth Risk Behavior Surveillance System (YRBSS) is a national survey of male and female high school students (grades 9–12) conducted by the Center for Disease Control, which tracks high-risk behavior for purposes of studying youth mortality rates. The study includes reported lifetime ("having ever tried") and current ("used once or more in the last 30 days") use of several drugs, including marijuana, cocaine, inhalants, heroin, methamphetamine, and other intravenous drugs. In 2003, white high school students, in contrast to African American students, report higher lifetime and current use of cocaine and inhalants, and higher lifetime use of methamphetamine and intravenous drugs. African American high school students report higher lifetime and current use of marijuana and the same use of heroin as white students. Hispanic students report higher use than white or African American students of cocaine and higher lifetime use of methamphetamine and intravenous drugs.[3] Table 7.2 shows the 2003 YRBSS data, including the percentage of students reporting a given behavior and a 95 percent confidence interval.

TABLE 7.1 Monitoring the Future Project data for 2003 and 2004

Grade:	Any illicit drug[a]			Any illicit drug other than marijuana[a]			Marijuana			Inhalants[b,c]			Hallucinogens[c]			LSD			Hallucinogens other than LSD		
	8th	10th	12th	8th	10th	12th	8th	10th	12th	8th	10th	12th	8th	10th	12th	8th	10th	12th	8th	10th	12th
Lifetime																					
White	20.4	40.1	53.4	12.8	21.2	31.4	15.1	35.1	48.2	16.7	13.4	12.3	3.8	7.7	11.6	1.8	3.6	5.8	3.2	6.9	10.2
Black	23.4	41.4	41.7	8.1	7.7	9.6	19.9	38.0	39.1	12.0	7.7	6.0	2.2	1.4	1.7	1.5	0.6	1.1	1.4	1.1	1.4
Hispanic	30.7	46.4	49.6	18.2	23.6	26.8	23.7	39.9	42.7	19.9	14.3	9.9	5.3	7.4	8.3	3.1	3.5	4.9	4.0	6.4	6.7
Annual																					
White	14.9	32.2	42.0	8.7	15.7	22.8	11.5	28.2	37.3	9.6	6.5	4.7	2.5	4.9	7.0	1.1	1.9	2.2	2.2	4.4	6.4
Black	14.6	29.3	27.7	4.4	4.6	6.5	12.8	27.0	25.5	5.4	2.1	1.3	1.2	0.8	1.2	0.8	0.4	0.8	0.8	0.7	0.9
Hispanic	20.9	34.5	34.4	10.4	15.1	16.2	16.7	29.8	29.5	10.6	5.7	2.9	2.9	3.8	4.1	1.8	1.7	1.7	2.2	3.2	3.7
30-day																					
White	8.4	19.3	25.7	4.4	8.0	11.8	6.2	16.5	22.1	4.3	2.6	1.7	1.0	1.8	2.0	0.4	0.6	0.6	0.8	1.6	1.7
Black	9.1	17.5	16.8	2.6	2.3	4.0	7.7	16.3	15.2	3.0	0.9	0.9	0.6	0.4	0.7	0.5	0.2	0.6	0.3	0.3	0.5
Hispanic	12.1	20.0	19.9	5.9	7.5	8.6	9.3	17.1	16.6	4.9	2.3	0.9	1.7	1.3	1.4	1.0	0.7	0.7	1.3	1.0	1.2
Daily																					
White	—	—	—	—	—	—	0.7	3.5	6.3	—	—	—	—	—	—	—	—	—	—	—	—
Black	—	—	—	—	—	—	1.2	2.8	3.2	—	—	—	—	—	—	—	—	—	—	—	—
Hispanic	—	—	—	—	—	—	1.1	2.9	4.0	—	—	—	—	—	—	—	—	—	—	—	—

Source: Johnston et al. 2005, 129−32, table 4.9.

Notes: To derive percentages for each racial subgroup, data for the specified year and the previous year have been combined to increase subgroup sample sizes and thus provide more stable estimates. Sample sizes are based on the 2003 and 2004 surveys combined:

Dashes indicate data not available.

[a] 8th and 10th grades only: The use of other narcotics and barbiturates has been excluded because these younger respondents appear to overreport use (perhaps because they include the use of nonprescription drugs in their answers). 12th grade only: Use of "any illicit drug" includes any use of marijuana, LSD, other hallucinogens, crack, other cocaine, or heroin, or any use of other narcotics, amphetamines, barbiturates, or tranquilizers not under a doctor's orders.

[b] 12th grade only: Data based on three of six forms; n is one-half of N indicated.

[c] Unadjusted for known underreporting of certain drugs.

Grade:	MDMA[d,e]			Cocaine			Crack			Other cocaine[f]			Heroin			Heroin with a needle[b]			Heroin without a needle[b]		
	8th	10th	12th	8th	10th	12th	8th	10th	12th	8th	10th	12th	8th	10th	12th	8th	10th	12th	8th	10th	12th
Lifetime																					
White	3.0	5.2	8.6	3.1	5.3	8.5	2.2	2.4	3.7	2.4	4.8	7.5	1.5	1.6	1.4	0.9	0.8	0.6	1.0	1.1	1.6
Black	2.5	1.6	2.9	2.1	1.1	1.8	1.5	0.7	1.5	1.4	0.9	1.7	1.0	0.6	0.9	0.7	0.4	0.6	0.7	0.5	1.0
Hispanic	4.1	5.8	7.8	6.8	9.5	10.5	4.7	5.4	5.4	5.1	8.3	9.1	3.4	1.8	1.4	2.4	1.2	0.9	2.0	1.3	1.2
Annual																					
White	1.9	3.1	4.7	1.9	3.7	5.6	1.3	1.6	2.2	1.5	3.4	4.8	0.9	0.8	0.7	0.6	0.4	0.3	0.5	0.6	0.7
Black	1.6	0.9	1.6	1.0	0.8	1.2	0.8	0.4	1.3	0.8	0.7	1.1	0.7	0.4	0.7	0.5	0.2	0.5	0.5	0.3	0.7
Hispanic	2.3	3.0	3.7	3.6	5.8	5.5	2.6	3.1	3.0	2.8	5.1	4.8	1.7	1.2	1.0	1.3	0.8	0.7	1.0	0.9	0.7
30-day																					
White	0.7	1.0	1.3	0.8	1.5	2.3	0.5	0.7	0.9	0.6	1.3	2.0	0.4	0.4	0.3	0.3	0.2	0.2	0.2	0.2	0.3
Black	0.8	0.5	0.8	0.6	0.5	0.9	0.5	0.3	1.1	0.5	0.4	0.9	0.3	0.3	0.6	0.2	0.2	0.4	0.1	0.2	0.5
Hispanic	1.5	1.0	1.2	1.8	2.8	2.5	1.4	1.4	1.3	1.4	2.4	2.1	0.8	0.5	0.4	0.7	0.4	0.3	0.5	0.3	0.3
Daily																					
White	—	—	—	—	—	—	—	—	—	—	—	—	—	—	—	—	—	—	—	—	—
Black	—	—	—	—	—	—	—	—	—	—	—	—	—	—	—	—	—	—	—	—	—
Hispanic	—	—	—	—	—	—	—	—	—	—	—	—	—	—	—	—	—	—	—	—	—

(*continued*)

Source: Johnston et al. 2005, 129–32, table 4.9.

Notes: To derive percentages for each racial subgroup, data for the specified year and the previous year have been combined to increase subgroup sample sizes and thus provide more stable estimates. Sample sizes are based on the 2003 and 2004 surveys combined:

Dashes indicate data not available.

[d] 8th and 10th grades only. Data based on two of four forms; *n* is one-half of *N* indicated.

[e] 12th grade only. Data based on two of six forms; *n* is one-third of *N* indicated.

[f] 12th grade only. Data based on four of six forms; *n* is two-thirds of *N* indicated.

TABLE 7.1 (continued)

Grade:	Other narcotics[g]			Amphetamines[g]			Meth-amphetamine[e,h]			Crystal meth. (ice)[e]			Sedatives (barbiturates)[g]			Methaqualone[g,i]			Tranquilizers[g]		
	8th	10th	12th	8th	10th	12th	8th	10th	12th	8th	10th	12th	8th	10th	12th	8th	10th	12th	8th	10th	12th
Lifetime																					
White	—	—	15.9	8.7	14.7	17.0	3.5	5.6	6.7	—	—	3.9	—	—	10.7	—	—	1.1	4.3	9.0	12.3
Black	—	—	3.5	3.9	4.5	4.0	0.9	1.0	2.0	—	—	2.4	—	—	3.4	—	—	0.2	2.5	2.0	2.5
Hispanic	—	—	8.5	9.0	11.5	11.5	4.6	7.8	7.2	—	—	4.7	—	—	8.0	—	—	0.9	5.4	8.2	8.2
Annual																					
White	—	—	11.2	5.9	10.6	11.6	2.2	3.4	3.5	—	—	2.0	—	—	7.4	—	—	0.6	2.8	6.5	8.4
Black	—	—	2.7	2.1	2.7	2.4	0.6	0.8	1.8	—	—	0.7	—	—	2.4	—	—	0.2	1.2	1.3	1.7
Hispanic	—	—	5.5	5.4	7.3	7.0	3.0	4.6	3.4	—	—	2.6	—	—	4.7	—	—	0.7	3.4	4.5	4.5
30-Day																					
White	—	—	5.0	2.8	5.0	5.5	0.9	1.4	1.5	—	—	0.7	—	—	3.3	—	—	0.3	1.3	2.9	3.4
Black	—	—	1.5	0.9	1.2	1.5	0.3	0.3	1.7	—	—	0.6	—	—	1.2	—	—	0.2	0.7	0.7	1.0
Hispanic	—	—	2.3	2.7	3.3	3.5	1.4	2.2	1.5	—	—	0.9	—	—	2.3	—	—	0.6	2.0	1.8	2.3
Daily																					
White	—	—	—	—	—	—	—	—	—	—	—	—	—	—	—	—	—	—	—	—	—
Black	—	—	—	—	—	—	—	—	—	—	—	—	—	—	—	—	—	—	—	—	—
Hispanic	—	—	—	—	—	—	—	—	—	—	—	—	—	—	—	—	—	—	—	—	—

Source: Johnston et al. 2005, 129–32, table 4.9.

Notes: To derive percentages for each racial subgroup, data for the specified year and the previous year have been combined to increase subgroup sample sizes and thus provide more stable estimates. Sample sizes are based on the 2003 and 2004 surveys combined:

Dashes indicate data not available.

[g] Only drug use not under a doctor's orders is included here.

[h] 8th and 10th grades only: Data based on one form; n is one-third of N indicated.

[i] 12th grade only: Data based on one of six forms; n is one-sixth of N indicated.

Grade:	Alcohol			Been drunk[e]			5 + drinks[j]			Cigarettes			Half-pack or more			Smokeless tobacco[d,j]			Steroids[e]		
	8th	10th	12th	8th	10th	12th	8th	10th	12th	8th	10th	12th	8th	10th	12th	8th	10th	12th	8th	10th	12th
Lifetime																					
White	43.6	66.0	79.3	20.4	46.0	64.1	—	—	—	27.3	42.6	56.1	—	—	—	12.2	16.9	20.7	2.1	2.9	3.6
Black	46.9	61.0	66.7	15.5	29.5	33.9	—	—	—	28.8	36.7	39.4	—	—	—	7.4	7.5	4.1	1.7	1.7	2.0
Hispanic	52.6	71.6	77.4	24.4	44.5	54.7	—	—	—	32.1	45.9	53.3	—	—	—	9.2	10.0	8.8	2.9	2.9	3.1
Annual																					
White	36.9	61.0	73.9	15.4	39.5	56.0	—	—	—	—	—	—	—	—	—	—	—	—	1.3	1.8	2.4
Black	33.6	50.1	55.9	9.4	19.6	24.4	—	—	—	—	—	—	—	—	—	—	—	—	0.9	0.7	1.3
Hispanic	44.0	64.3	69.6	16.6	34.5	41.5	—	—	—	—	—	—	—	—	—	—	—	—	1.7	1.6	2.4
30-day																					
White	19.2	37.8	52.2	6.8	21.7	36.4	—	—	—	10.0	18.7	28.2	—	—	—	4.4	6.1	8.2	0.6	0.9	1.4
Black	16.2	24.6	29.2	4.1	8.3	14.3	—	—	—	6.9	9.2	10.1	—	—	—	3.0	2.7	0.6	0.4	0.4	1.1
Hispanic	23.5	39.5	45.4	8.1	17.0	24.1	—	—	—	10.1	13.9	18.5	—	—	—	4.0	3.3	3.9	0.9	0.9	1.8
Daily																					
White	0.5	1.5	3.2	0.1	0.5	1.8	11.3	24.0	32.5	4.7	10.0	18.3	1.9	4.7	10.0	0.9	2.1	3.2	—	—	—
Black	0.6	0.5	1.2	0.2	0.2	0.8	9.8	11.6	11.4	2.7	4.4	5.2	1.1	1.0	1.6	0.5	0.6	0.0	—	—	—
Hispanic	1.4	1.7	2.7	0.6	0.6	1.8	16.1	26.9	26.0	3.5	6.0	8.2	1.4	1.5	2.9	0.9	0.9	1.1	—	—	—

Source: Johnston et al. 2005, 129–32, table 4.9.

Notes: To derive percentages for each racial subgroup, data for the specified year and the previous year have been combined to increase subgroup sample sizes and thus provide more stable estimates. Sample sizes are based on the 2003 and 2004 surveys combined:

Dashes indicate data not available.

j This measure refers to having five or more drinks in a row in the last two weeks.

TABLE 7.2   **Youth Risk Behavior Surveillance System data for 2003**

	White (%)	Black (%)	Hispanic (%)
Lifetime marijuana use	39.8 (±3.4)	43.3 (±4.1)	42.7 (±3.8)
Current marijuana use	21.7 (±2.3)	23.9 (±3.1)	23.8 (±2.3)
Lifetime cocaine use	8.7 (±1.3)	3.2 (±1.1)	12.5 (±2.1)
Current cocaine use	3.8 (±0.9)	2.2 (±0.8)	5.7 (±1.2)
Lifetime inhalant use	12.8 (±1.5)	7.0 (±1.4)	12.7 (±2.1)
Current inhalant use	3.6 (±0.7)	3.0 (±1.0)	4.3 (±1.3)
Lifetime heroin use	2.6 (±0.6)	2.6 (±1.4)	3.9 (±0.9)
Lifetime methamphetamine use	8.1 (±1.1)	3.1 (±1.0)	8.3 (±1.9)
Lifetime IV drug use	2.5 (±1.3)	2.4 (±1.1)	3.9 (±2.1)

Source: Center for Disease Control and Prevention 2004, 57–63 (tables 28, 30, 32, 34).

The National Household Survey on Drug Abuse (NHSDA) is issued by the U.S. Department of Health and Human Services, Substance Abuse and Mental Health Services Administration. The survey, conducted since 1991, samples household residents and persons in non-institutionalized group quarters over the age of 12 (excluding only homeless persons who do not use shelters, active military personnel, and residents of institutional group quarters, such as jails and hospitals). The NHSDA data place drug use by minorities at approximately the same level as by whites, although usage varies by drug. For 2003, overall thirty-day drug use stood at 8.3, 8.7, and 8.0 percent for whites, African Americans, and Hispanics, respectively.[4] In 2003, white respondents reported slightly higher lifetime use of marijuana, cocaine, and hallucinogens. African American respondents reported higher lifetime use of crack cocaine and higher annual use rates for marijuana. Table 7.3 summarizes yearly data regarding the major drugs for the period 1997–2003.

Overall, these surveys consistently reflect, in terms of overall illicit drug use, lower use rates among African Americans and Hispanics as compared to whites. With regard to the use of marijuana, two of the surveys show whites using more than African Americans or Hispanics, and one shows African Americans using more than Hispanics or whites. With regard to total cocaine consumption, all three surveys show whites and Hispanics consuming more per capita than African Americans; though for crack cocaine, there are higher rates of usage among African Americans.[5]

Although these general survey studies are widely considered a better measure of the nature and extent of drug use than arrest statistics or ethnographies,[6] their reliability is naturally open to question. Researchers have tested the validity of survey data by comparing self-reported drug use with other, presumably more accurate measures of drug use. The three primary tests are internal validity tests,[7] external validation tests,[8] and biological testing.[9]

For our purposes, the relevant question is whether any evidence shows that self-reporting by members of minority groups is less reliable than by whites. On this question, one recent study found that, while self-reporting grossly under-represents the prevalence of drug use in a population,

TABLE 7.3   **Percentages reporting lifetime, past year, and past month use of illicit drugs among persons aged twelve or older by demographics**

	1997	1998	1999	2000	2001	2002	2003
Any illicit drug							
Lifetime							
White (%)	38.17	38.17	42	41.5	44.5	48.5	49.2
Black (%)	31.14	33.16	37.7	35.5	38.6	43.8	44.6
Hispanic (%)	25.9	26.56	31.2	29.9	31.9	38.9	37.0
Annual							
White (%)	11.28	10.43	11.4	11.2	12.9	14.9	14.9
Black (%)	12.12	12.99	13.2	10.9	12.2	16.8	15.5
Hispanic (%)	9.87	10.51	11	10.1	11.9	15.0	14.7
Past 30 Days							
White (%)	6.41	6.09	6.2	6.4	7.2	8.5	8.3
Black (%)	7.48	8.23	7.5	6.4	7.4	9.7	8.7
Hispanic (%)	5.86	6.12	6.1	5.3	6.4	7.2	8.0
Marijuana							
Lifetime							
White (%)	35.55	35.51	37.1	37	40.1	43.5	44.1
Black (%)	28.53	30.25	32.1	30.8	33.1	38.2	38.9
Hispanic (%)	22.33	23.16	25.3	24.2	25.6	30.1	28.9
Annual							
White (%)	9.09	8.45	8.7	8.6	9.8	11.2	10.9
Black (%)	9.9	10.61	10	8.6	9.4	12.9	11.8
Hispanic (%)	7.46	8.19	7.7	6.6	7.3	9.0	8.7
Past 30 Days							
White (%)	5.17	4.98	4.7	4.9	5.6	6.5	6.4
Black (%)	6.1	5.57	5.9	5.2	5.6	7.4	6.7
Hispanic (%)	4.04	4.47	4.2	3.6	4.2	4.3	4.9
Cocaine							
Lifetime							
White (%)	11.84	11.44	12.5	12.4	13.5	15.7	16.1
Black (%)	6.48	8.45	9.5	7.4	8.51	12.2	11.1
Hispanic (%)	7.33	8.86	9.2	8.8	10.8	12.1	12.5
Annual							
White (%)	1.89	1.7	1.7	1.5	1.9	2.5	2.5
Black (%)	2.43	1.87	1.5	1.3	1.5	2.8	2.4
Hispanic (%)	2.01	2.26	2.3	1.7	2.4	2.6	3.0

(*continued*)

TABLE 7.3   (*continued*)

	1997	1998	1999	2000	2001	2002	2003
Past 30 Days							
White (%)	0.59	0.69	0.7	0.6	0.7	0.8	0.9
Black (%)	1.36	1.26	0.9	0.7	0.8	1.6	1.3
Hispanic (%)	0.82	1.31	0.8	0.8	1	0.8	1.1
Crack							
Lifetime							
White (%)	1.87	1.77	—	—	—	3.4	3.3
Black (%)	3.11	4.2	—	—	—	5.8	4.7
Hispanic (%)	1.58	1.86	—	—	—	2.7	2.8
Annual							
White (%)	0.56	0.29	—	—	—	0.5	0.5
Black (%)	1.41	1.31	—	—	—	1.6	1.5
Hispanic (%)	0.39	0.7	—	—	—	0.5	0.5
Past 30 Days							
White (%)	0.22	0.09	—	—	—	0.1	0.2
Black (%)	0.77	0.86	—	—	—	1.1	0.9
Hispanic (%)	0.17	0.25	—	—	—	0.1	0.2
Hallucinogens							
Lifetime							
White (%)	11.33	11.49	13.1	13.7	14.7	17.0	17.0
Black (%)	2.78	4.84	4.9	5	5.1	7.4	6.5
Hispanic (%)	5.66	5.31	7.8	6.9	8.1	9.0	9.6
Annual							
White (%)	2.08	1.82	1.6	1.8	2.3	2.3	1.8
Black (%)	0.74	0.44	0.4	0.6	0.9	1.0	0.9
Hispanic (%)	1.67	1.55	1.4	1.2	1.6	1.4	1.7
Past 30 Days							
White (%)	0.87	0.77	0.5	0.5	0.6	0.6	0.5
Black (%)	0.37	0.15	0.1	0.2	0.3	0.4	0.3
Hispanic (%)	0.48	0.72	0.5	0.3	0.5	0.3	0.5

Source: U.S. Department of Health and Human Services, Substance Abuse and Mental Health Services Administration 2005, tables 1.28B, 1.33B, 1.38B, 1.43B, 1.48B.

under-reporting does not correlate with race. The researchers used respondent demographics to create a logistic regression and mined the data for demographic factors correlated with confirmedly honest self-reporting. The researchers found that African American arrestee crack users were significantly more likely to make a truthful self-report about use than either white or Hispanic arrestee crack users.[10] On the other hand, Hispanic opiate users were significantly more likely to make an accurate self-report about use than African American arrestee opiate users. No statistically significant race effects were found in the validity of self-reporting on marijuana and amphetamine use. Another study found no race effect

TABLE 7.4   **Drug Abuse Warning Network emergency department (ED) data for selected drugs for third and fourth quarters of 2003**

	Drug episode	Marijuana mention	Cocaine mention	Heroin mention
White	169,841 (55.96%)	47,175 (59.22%)	62,581 (49.70%)	25,209 (52.96%)
Black	72,137 (23.77%)	17,644 (22.15%)	40,184 (31.91%)	10,194 (21.39%)
Hispanic	27,271 (8.99%)	7,574 (9.51%)	11,264 (8.95%)	4,515 (9.48%)
Other	4,426 (1.46%)	1,180 (1.48%)	2,005 (1.59%)	428 (0.90%)
Race unknown	29,804 (9.82%)	6,092 (7.65%)	9,887 (7.85%)	7,258 (15.25%)

Source: U.S. Department of Health and Human Services 2004, 39 (table 7).

when comparing the reliability of self-reported drug use by a former drug-treatment sample with their charges upon admission to treatment.[11] Other research, however, has reached the opposite conclusion—namely, that African Americans are less likely than whites to make true and accurate self reports about drug use.[12] One such study found, for example, that although the total rate of recanting on previous self-reports of drug use is quite low, African Americans recant at a significantly higher rate than whites when reporting lifetime use of marijuana and cocaine for the MFP.[13] Naturally, my purpose here is not to certify or invalidate any of the survey results, but simply to present them with all the available evidence and in their full context. Clearly, more research and more empirical evidence is necessary here when reading the survey results on differentials in offending.[14]

PUBLIC HEALTH DATA.   Another approach is to look at public health data. The Drug Abuse Warning Network (DAWN), for instance, is a government program that collects data on drug-related visits to nonfederal hospital emergency rooms across the nation. The assigned DAWN reporter, usually an emergency room physician, reviews the medical charts of all patients and reports drug-related hospitalizations by drug. Table 7.4 presents DAWN data for the third and fourth quarters of 2003, with additional percentage calculations.

These data suggest disproportionately higher offending among African Americans and Hispanics for most drugs. Here again, though, there are important differences by drug, so it would be important to specify offending rate by drug type for the particular drugs that are being interdicted on the highway in the specific geographic locations where racial profiling is taking place. And here too, there are questions about the validity of any inferences concerning real drug use. Drug-related emergency room visits may correlate with socioeconomic status more directly than race. African American and Hispanic users may have less access to private doctors and individualized health care, and therefore may rely more on emergency room medical assistance. Naturally, this correlation would skew the data.

SEARCH DATA.   There are significant questions about the reliability of search, arrest, and other criminal justice data, given that they may be the products of racially disproportionate policing and thus fail to reflect natural offending rates. Despite these possible distortions in the data, the *internal* rates (within each racial group) of persons carrying drugs can be compared and may offer suggestive evidence.

The Maryland data are useful in this regard. Along the I-95 corridor, the Maryland police conducted 2,146 searches from 1995 to 2000. Of the total, 33.3 percent involved white motorists (about 715), 59.7 percent involved African American motorists (about 1,281), and 5.9 percent involved Hispanic motorists (about 127). In other words, setting aside the small number of Hispanic motorists searched (given that the sample is so small and under-representative), the police practices provide a sample of about 715 white motorists and about 1,281 African American motorists.

Samuel Gross and Katherine Barnes break down those searches by race. What their tables reveal is that the searches netted a greater proportion of persons carrying drugs for personal use among white motorists. While African American motorists had a lower internal rate of carrying for personal use, they had a higher rate of carrying evincing drug trafficking or dealing (which I discuss in greater length next). These data tend to corroborate the self-report surveys in revealing evidence of slightly lower personal drug use among African Americans than among white motorists. The Gross and Barnes tables reveal the internal rates of offending shown in table 7.5.

TABLE 7.5   **Internal rates of offending from Maryland search data (%)**

	White motorists	African American motorists	All searches
Total searches	100	100	100
No drugs	59.7	62.2	62.7
Any drugs	40.3	37.8	37.3
Trace or personal use quantities of drugs	36.2	22.4	26.1
Small, medium, or large dealer quantities of drugs	4.2	15.4	11.2

Source: Adapted from Gross and Barnes 2002, 703, table 17.

Drug Trafficking and Drug Couriers

The racial breakdown of drug traffickers, drug sellers, and drug couriers is harder to gauge. Practically all of the data stem from law enforcement operations and are therefore potentially biased by the disproportionate attention to minority trafficking. In addition, there is every reason here to be even more skeptical of self-report data—the little that there is.

Human Rights Watch reports that the National Household Survey on Drug Abuse (NHSDA) instrument, discussed earlier, contained questions about drug-selling during the period 1991–1993. According to Human Rights Watch, "On average over the three year period, blacks were 16 percent of admitted sellers and whites were 82 percent."[15] Given that African Americans represented 11.5 percent of the United States civilian, non-institutionalized population in 1992,[16] the NHSDA survey shows higher drug-selling among African Americans. Naturally, all the same questions about the reliability of self-report studies apply—if anything even more saliently. The more serious the activity surveyed, the less reliable the data;[17] however, there is debate, again, over the comparative reliability by race.

One of the very few other data points, then, is the search data itself. As the Gross and Barnes data (table 7.5) suggest, the internal rate of drug trafficking is higher within the sample of African American motorist searches: 15.4 percent of African American motorists searched are transporting quantities of drugs that suggest dealing, in contrast to 4.2 percent of white motorists. The difference is actually most pronounced among medium and large dealer quantities, where 12.2 percent of African American versus 2.4 percent of white motorists are transporting contraband.[18] As Gross and Barnes explain,

> Black motorists who were searched on I-95 north of Baltimore were more than three-and-a-half times as likely as whites to be dealers, and five times as likely to be medium or large dealers. . . . Of the whites who were found with any drugs on I-95, 10% were dealers and 6% were medium or large dealers; of the blacks with drugs, 40% were dealers and 32% were medium and large dealers.[19]

Clearly, this area requires more sustained research. Reading all the data conservatively, though, it is fair to speculate that African Americans may have a higher offending rate than whites for dealing and selling drugs—though how much higher is not clear—but a similar rate for personal use, resulting in a slightly higher offending rate overall.

One final caveat. The goal in this part was to measure natural offending rates for drug crimes. The estimates may be biased, though, if racial profiling is already prevalent and most people believe that the police are in fact profiling based on race. Survey data suggest that this is true. In a Gallup Poll conducted in late 1999, 59 percent of total respondents indicated that they believe that racial profiling by police officers is "widespread."[20] This perception is even more pervasive among African American respondents: 77 percent believe the practice is widespread.[21] Moreover, among African American respondents more generally, 42 percent have felt that they were "stopped by the police just because of [their] race or ethnic background."[22] If there is a generalized perception of racial profiling, then the existing data on drug use and other crimes would already reflect possible elasticity, if any, resulting from racial profiling or the perception of racial profiling, and in this sense, might indicate *real* as opposed to *natural* offending rates. As a result, we may need to discount existing drug-use offending rates. How this survey data affects offending rates, naturally, depends on whether and to what extent offending is elastic to policing. Assuming elasticity, though, the survey data suggest that the existing offending rates for members of minority groups would actually reflect slightly higher natural offending if the racial profiling is deterring, or slightly lower natural offending if the profiling is delegitimizing the criminal justice system.

The Comparative Elasticity of Offending to Policing

Elasticity of offending to policing is the product of at least two major mechanisms: deterrence and incapacitation. Increased policing may deter some motorists from carrying drugs on their person or in their cars when they are on the road out of fear of being searched. Incapacitation, in the case of highway searches, would most likely be a function of cherry-picking: if the police select motorists based on multiple factors (tinted windows, marijuana stickers, smoky interiors), the hit rate will be high. As the police search proportionally more motorists, however, they will relax their selectivity, and the hit rate will therefore fall. In the latter case, the resulting lower offending rate is not the product of a rational response by motorists—it is not a deterrence effect. Rather, it is a cherry-picking effect—or what we might call an incapacitation effect.

The cherry-picking effect is likely to be negligible. The data from Indianapolis road-block searches—which netted drug possession in 4.7 percent of the total number of stops—suggest that there is unlikely to be much incapacitation.[23] The police in Washington State, for instance, searched only 3.5 percent of the cars stopped, for a total of only 23,393 searches for the period March 2002–October 2002—which is, one can only assume, infinitesimal as compared to the number of motorists on the Washington state highways during the period.[24] It is extremely doubtful that such a small number of searches as compared to the entire motorist population (with drug possession in the range of 5 percent) is going to have any cherry-picking reduction on offending rates. As a result, most of the elasticity, if any, will be the product of rational-choice deterrence.

The deterrence effect is difficult to measure. Most research on deterrence has been conducted in areas where there is likely to be an incapacitation effect, and as a result researchers have not yet been able to distinguish deterrence from incapacitation. The National Academy of Sciences appointed a blue-ribbon panel of experts to examine the problem of measuring deterrence in 1978—led by Alfred Blumstein, Jacqueline Cohen and Daniel Nagin—but the results were disappointing: "[B]ecause the potential sources of error in the estimates of the deterrent effect of these sanctions are so basic and the results sufficiently divergent, no sound, empirically based conclusions can be drawn about the existence of the effect, and certainly not about its magnitude."[25]

Little progress has been made since then. As economist Steve Levitt stated in 1998, "[F]ew of the empirical studies [regarding deterrence of adults] have any power to distinguish deterrence from incapacitation and therefore provide only an indirect test of the economic model of crime."[26]

More specifically, few studies address the elasticity of illicit drug consumption to price or policing. Price elasticities have not been empirically estimated for marijuana, cocaine, or heroin.[27] As a result, the literature is all over the place. Stephen Schulhofer, for example, writes that "[a]vailable estimates nearly all find modest to substantial inelasticity in the overall demand for heroin and cocaine, especially in the short run";[28] yet the study that Schulhofer refers to, authored by Peter Reuter and Mark Kleiman, assumes that "the aggregate demand for heroin may have quite a high elasticity."[29] Reuter and Kleiman argue that it is fair to assume that "the elasticity of demand is moderately high for heroin, a little lower for cocaine, and quite low for marijuana."[30] This inelasticity may partly explain, in their words, the "apparent lack of response of cocaine and marijuana consumption to the increased federal enforcement effort."[31] According to a 1972 study, the demand for marijuana among full-time college students at UCLA is relatively elastic: a 1 percent price increase causes a decrease as great as 1.5 percent in consumption.[32] Schulhofer suggests, however, that "some estimates find that marijuana demand—largely derived from non-addict, recreational users—is also inelastic, possibly because mari-juana expenditures, even at currently inflated prices, remain a small part of the user's income."[33] Given the lack of research in this area, it is difficult to come to firm conclusions.

Another major problem—perhaps *the* major problem—is determining the relative or comparative elasticities between different racial groups. Do minority and white motorists have similar or different elasticities of offending to policing? There are reasons to suspect that they may be different. As noted earlier, elasticity will depend on the existence of legitimate work alternatives, and there may be cause to believe that minority motorists as a group have lower job opportunities.[34] Another issue relates to the perception among minority motorists of the police and the criminal justice system. Perceptions of the legitimacy—or illegitimacy—of the police may affect criminal behavior.[35] This too may produce different rates of elasticity between racial groups.

The bottom line, on the issue of comparative elasticities, is a paucity of good evidence one way or the other. As Nicola Persico observes, there is practically no literature on the relative elasticity of different groups.[36]

If I were forced to speculate, the most conservative position in the drug-possession and trafficking area would be to assume relatively low elasticity across the board, with slightly lower elasticity for minority motorists. Given that most of the successful searches for drug contraband on the highway involve quantities of marijuana that reflect at most personal use—68 percent in Maryland, for example[37]—and that the elasticity of marijuana is either low or average, it seems fair to assume conservatively that overall elasticities are relatively low. Furthermore, African American motorists probably have lower elasticity than white motorists because of lower employment opportunities and other market alternatives.

The Likely Consequences of Racial Profiling

The Long-Term Effect on the Profiled Crime

Based on reasonably conservative assumptions including, first, relatively low elasticity of offending to policing, second, slightly lower elasticity of offending to policing for minority motorists, and third, slightly higher natural offending rates among minority motorists, it is fair to infer that racial profiling on the highways may increase the total number of persons transporting drug contraband on the roads. From equation (6) in chapter 4, we know that, assuming minority motorists are 20 percent of the motorist population and have lower elasticity, racial profiling will increase crime if the ratio of white elasticity to minority elasticity is greater than the ratio of minority offending to white offending—in other words, if the elasticity differential is greater than the differential in offending. Given the paucity of evidence on both relative elasticities and offending, any conclusion is tentative, but under conservative assumptions, racial profiling on the roads probably increases the profiled crime.

This certainly seems to be the case in Maryland based on the little data we have. As noted earlier, if minority motorist elasticity is lower in Maryland, then social costs are minimized only if the search rate of minority motorists is less than .34/.32 or 1.0625 times the search rate of white motorists. Given that approximately 63 percent of searches are of minority motorists, this condition likely does not obtain. Naturally, it would be crucial to do a more nuanced analysis with better comparative data, exploring the different types of drugs being transported in the particular geographic location. It would also be important to develop better data on elasticity, comparative elasticity, and offending. But on a conservative estimate, racial profiling on the highways probably decreases social welfare.

The Ratchet Effect

Racial profiling on the highways also probably has a significant distortion effect on the profiled population. From the earlier analysis of the basic racial profiling models, it is clear that the police may have to subject a disproportionate number of minority motorists to criminal justice supervision to equalize offending rates. In all likelihood, this is exactly what is happening in Maryland. It is hard to imagine, even if we assume that minority motorists are offending at a higher natural rate than white motorists, that minority offenders represent 60 percent of all offenders under natural conditions of offending (that is, if the police are engaged in color-blind policing). After all, 84 percent of motorists in Maryland found with drugs had trace or personal-use amounts, and 68 percent had trace or personal-use quantities of marijuana only; and the survey data seem to suggest that personal consumption of drugs is relatively even across racial lines. Even if we assume that all the other 16 percent of seizures—those seizures involving large hauls of drugs—consist *entirely* of minority motorists,[38] then minority offenders would still represent only approximately 31 percent of offenders.[39]

The most likely explanation for the disjunction between this extreme hypothesized offending differential in Maryland (30/70) and the actual apprehension differential under present conditions of racial profiling (60/40) is that, continuing to assume elasticity, it takes a lot of profiling to bring the hit rates down to the same level. The result is a significant imbalance in negative contact with the police—whether the seizure of drug contraband results in a fine, an arrest, probation, or imprisonment. This represents a distortion effect that has a significant cost to minority families and communities.

In the end, if we make reasonably conservative assumptions from available evidence, it becomes clear that racial profiling on the highways probably does *not* reduce overall crime. Minority motorists, in all likelihood, have slightly lower elasticity of offending to policing than white motorists because of reduced employment opportunities, and they have slightly higher offending rates when drug trafficking is included. Under these conditions, racial profiling on the highways may increase the amount of profiled crime and the costs associated with police searches, resulting in numerically more white motorists offending because of a perceived sense of immunity.

Conceptions of Justice

In all this, I have not even addressed the third critique concerning conceptions of justice. The central question here is, How can it be that our collective social desire to stamp out the use and trafficking of illicit drugs gives us license to impose the burden of our search policies on the African American and Hispanic communities? How can we have allowed our war on drugs to turn into an offensive against black and Hispanic drivers? The answer, naturally, is the desire to maximize the efficiency of our policing resources—assuming higher natural offending within minority communities. But just as naturally, one of the victims of this misguided thirst for efficiency is the fundamental notion of justice that inheres in the idea that all criminal offenders, regardless of race, ethnicity, gender, class or national origin, should face the same likelihood of being apprehended and punished for engaging in criminal behavior. As a society, we have collectively sacrificed our fundamental notion of justice in our pursuit for actuarial precision. And we have done so, most probably, at a net cost to society in crime.

CHAPTER EIGHT

Shades of Gray

"The problems with racial profiling . . . are not problems of profiling, with race being merely an example," Frederick Schauer writes in *Profiles, Probabilities, and Stereotypes*. "Rather . . . the problem is about race and not about profiling."[1] Many people, perhaps even most people, agree and as a result favor criminal profiling in general.

But the exact opposite is true: the problem with racial profiling is about the profiling, not about race. The problems relate to the actuarial method more generally, not simply the racial category. As the analysis in chapter 7 demonstrates, the problems relate to comparative elasticities, relative offending rates, and the ratchet effect—factors that plague criminal profiling schemes more generally, not just racial profiling. In the context of racial profiling on the highway, the central problems are the likely adverse long-term effects on overall drug use and the likely ratchet effect on minority communities. These are concerns that can undermine any profiling scheme, whether based on race, gender, wealth, class, or physical demeanor. Although practically everyone in the criminal justice field endorses criminal profiling as a law enforcement technique outside the racial profiling context, the fact is that criminal profiling advances the larger interest of crime reduction only under very specific circumstances.

What about the cases, then, where the uses of actuarial methods seem to have benefited society and promoted a public interest? What about the prediction of parole violation, or better yet, of violent sexual predation? What about the use of actuarial measures that clearly benefit poor and disadvantaged communities? How should we analyze these apparent victories of the actuarial turn, and what do they tell us about the force of the three critiques presented in this book? As a foil to racial profiling, let's begin then by examining one instance of actuarial progress that unquestionably has benefited poor and minority communities.

The Manhattan Bail Project

The Vera Foundation, New York University School of Law, and the Institute of Judicial Administration initiated the Manhattan Bail Project in October 1961 in an effort to create risk-assessment criteria that would allow judges and magistrates to determine quickly whether defendants could be released on their own recognizance pending trial.[2] The project was largely a response to the plight of poor and indigent defendants who could not afford bail. A study conducted by law students at the University of Pennsylvania in the mid-1950s had found that New York's bail system discriminated against the poor: bail was often set too high with no variations based on individual differences.[3] National surveys in the early 1960s similarly revealed that for most people arrested for a misdemeanor or felony, money bail was set in amounts that were often prohibitive. Two-thirds of all people arrested for a misdemeanor had bond set at five hundred dollars or more, and three-quarters of all people arrested for a felony had bond set at a thousand dollars or more.[4]

The Manhattan Bail Project set out to remedy these problems with the help of actuarial methods—believing that "more persons can be successfully released on parole if verified information concerning their character and roots in the community is available to the court at the time of bail determination."[5] The idea was to facilitate release on personal recognizance—release without posting bail based only on a promise to appear—by providing more information to the deciding magistrates.

NYU law students, working under the supervision of the Vera Foundation, interviewed defendants arriving at the Criminal Court of the Borough of Manhattan to determine the strength of their community ties and their prior criminal histories.[6] The interviews lasted about fifteen minutes, and were based on a questionnaire that related to the following five main factors thought to be relevant to pretrial release:

1. Present or recent residence at the same address for six months or more.
2. Current employment or recent employment for six months or more.
3. Relatives in New York City with whom [the defendant] is in contact.
4. No previous conviction of a crime.
5. Residence in New York City for ten years or more.[7]

In the case of any defendant who responded affirmatively to one of these questions—or partially so to two or more questions—the NYU students tried to verify the information through third parties, such as family or friends, or by field investigation if necessary. The verification process would take about an hour. Using the information from the interviews and third-party verification, the students assigned each defendant a numerical score, with one point for each affirmative factor. The higher the score, the lower the chances that the defendant would fail to appear for trial. For each defendant in the experimental group, as opposed to the control, the NYU students then presented the bail magistrates with a recommendation based on the individual's score.[8]

Follow-up research on the 1961–1962 parole experiment revealed, first, that the courts followed the recommendations: in 60 percent of the cases recommended for pretrial parole (or 215 of the 363 recommendations), the court paroled the defendant.[9] That represented four times the number of persons in the control group who were granted bail. And of that number, only three parolees jumped parole, and two were rearrested on new charges.[10] In sum, the rate of parole jumping was lower than the previous rate of bail-jumping before the experiment began.[11] In addition, "The experimental group released on nothing more than their promise to return had twice the appearance rate of those released on bail."[12] All in all, "failure-to-appear (FTA) rates among project participants were, on average, lower than those of the control group who had posted bond."[13]

The Manhattan Bail Project was perceived by most observers as a great success. As Malcolm Feeley recounts, "During the several years following this initial effort [by Vera], interest in bail reform grew at an exponential rate. Additional support from the Ford Foundation allowed Vera to expand its pretrial release operations to other boroughs and to aid civic leaders in Des Moines, San Francisco, and other cities in establishing ROR projects."[14] New York City government adopted the method as a permanent part of the city's criminal justice system—and to this date continues to perform risk-assessment interviews.[15] "In New York, the same basic system of interviewing defendants, testing their community ties, making release recommendations, and monitoring the results is continued today by the Criminal Justice Agency, a private organization created by the city government and Vera in 1977."[16] Following the success in New York, federal and state courts throughout the nation adopted similar bail-reform measures, culminating in the passage of the federal Bail Reform Act of 1966.[17] As Feeley explains, the Bail Reform Act was "extremely liberal in encouraging nonmonetary release" and "served as a model for many state reform acts."[18] The rest is history:

> Within eighteen months after the 1964 [National Conference on Bail and Criminal Justice], 61 new pretrial release projects had sprung up around the country. By 1969 this number had jumped to 89, and in 1973 the number of projects was 112. It is estimated that there are now well over 200 specialized pretrial release projects. Vera's original Manhattan project served as the model for most of these new programs.[19]

The Manhattan Bail Project is regarded as an example of the ways the problems with bail (especially as they relate to minorities and the poor) can be addressed. Because of the project's age, its place in today's literature is generally fixed as the starting point of efforts to reform bail in the American criminal justice system.[20]

Assessing the Manhattan Bail Project

How then should we think about the Manhattan Bail Project? Clearly, the fact that the Vera Foundation's risk-assessment criteria benefited poor and minority communities cannot be the determinative factor. There is no political or class litmus test for the critiques of actuarial methods. The IRS Discriminant Index Function, after all, also benefits the less wealthy. Yet it is equally problematic as a form of criminal profiling: if the groups profiled by the IRS are less elastic to the audits, the IRS profiling will likely increase overall tax evasion and cost society dearly. The fact that the Discriminant Index Function may benefit the poor, who are not being profiled, is irrelevant to the critique. Similarly, the fact that bail reform helps the poor should not weigh in the balance. There is no ideological tilt to the critiques of the actuarial. The arguments apply to predicting future dangerousness *but also* to predicting future rehabilitation—the flip side of recidivism. The critiques undermine selective incapacitation, but also correction and rehabilitation. In this sense, the arguments advanced in this book do not have a necessary political valence. The Manhattan Bail Project, it turns out, is subject to the same criticisms—though perhaps, in some areas, in a slightly different shade.

The Mathematical Critique

The first critique applies with equal force. If there are in fact different elasticities between low-risk and high-risk pretrial detainees, then profiling the high-risk detainees may well increase the rate at which low-risk detainees fail to appear at trial, ultimately increasing the raw number of defendants who abscond from trial. The analysis is identical from a rational-choice perspective. Pretrial detention is a cost. Increasing the likelihood of that cost will deter some high-risk offenders and reduce the rate at which the profiled group fails to appear for trial. But it simultaneously decreases the cost to low-risk offenders and therefore increases their failure rate. The ultimate effect on the total number of persons who fail to appear for trial will, again, depend on relative elasticities and natural offending rates.

In the case of pretrial detention, there is an added dimension. Like the case of criminal sentencing, pretrial detention is also a pure cost of committing crime. In this sense, the case of bail reform also presents a straightforward application of the economic model of crime regarding sentencing. If the defendants who are at low risk of fleeing perceive that the total cost of offending—including pretrial detention—has decreased, then they are likely to offend more. In other words, they are likely not just to fail to appear for trial, but to actually commit more crimes. Their total cost of committing crimes has fallen. And if they are more elastic to policing than high-risk offenders, then their offending will probably outweigh the reduced offending of the profiled group. Again, this is just a straightforward application of the rational-action model, and therefore simply requires the basic assumptions of rationality and deterrence.

The bottom line is that, in the long run, bail reform may cause higher failure-to-appear rates or higher crime rates depending on group elasticities and offending. If so, then clearly the costs outweigh any efficiency gains in terms of the better detection of high-risk pretrial detainees.

More generally, the key questions regarding the first critique revolve around elasticities and offending rates. There is no good reason to believe that the bail-reform example deviates much from the case of racial profiling. High-risk pretrial detainees are probably less elastic to the policing than low-risk detainees, given that they probably have less education and lower employment opportunities. To be sure, this may not hold in certain identifiable other cases. So, for example, in the traditional case of stranger rape, there may be very low elasticity of offending to policing among women, so that profiling the higher-offending group (males) may make sense. But in more ordinary cases of differential offending, and certainly in cases where the profiled population is less elastic to the policing, the first critique militates against the use of actuarial measures.

The Ratchet Effect

The second critique also applies, though perhaps with slightly different force. Profiling members of the group most likely to flee will aggravate the disparity in the distribution of certain traits between the offending and the carceral populations. In all likelihood, high risk will either correlate with, or be directly related to, say, being unattached, unemployed, or unskilled. As a result, profiling on higher risk will undoubtedly result in the overrepresentation of these traits—being unattached, unemployed, or unskilled—among the jailed population compared to the distribution of those same traits among the actual group of people who fail to appear at trial. Profiling will have the same ratchet effect. Again, the extent of the ratchet will depend on the actual disparity in failure-to-appear rates and elasticities between the two groups; but on conservative assumptions, profiling will undoubtedly ratchet the representation of the unattached, unemployed, and unskilled in the jail population, with detrimental symbolic influence on those persons.

Of course, everyone does not necessarily care—or care as much—about the unattached adult, the unemployed, or the unskilled. Here, the analysis of racial profiling may differ. Many tend to view certain forms of discrimination as less troublesome than others. Many consider discrimination against blacks, Hispanics, Jews, women, or gay men and lesbians as qualitatively worse than discrimination against high-school dropouts or unattached adults. There is in this sense a spectrum of group traits—and not all are treated alike.

For purposes of analyzing actuarial methods, it may be appropriate to conceptualize group traits as running along a spectrum where, at one end, we have the criminal activity itself, narrowly defined, and at the other end, we have the broadest categories of race, gender, religion, class, and wealth, with traits like being an unattached adult or unskilled laborer in the middle. The closer the particular trait is to the criminal act itself, the more comfortable people tend to be with the use of prediction. Profiling on the group of individuals who are actively engaged in killing or raping victims naturally does not present much of a problem. Of course, identifying persons who are active in that group is not easy, since the crimes are most often conducted in private. But the idea of targeting that group does not raise any concern. Moving away slightly from this extreme example, profiling people who are running down the street with a TV in a shopping cart or who have a bicycle without a seat and front wheel, is also less troubling. Certainly, it is less troubling to most than using race or gender as a proxy for suspicion. On the other hand, the closer the trait is to the broad categories of race, gender, religion or class, the more uncomfortable many tend to be with the predictive method. Profiling African Americans, women, Muslims, or the rich is more troubling to most of us. Profiling unattached adults, the unemployed, or the unskilled—or for that matter, adults with children, the well-employed, or the technically skilled—is also troubling to many of us, though for some less so than profiling race, nationality, and gender.

It is important to recognize this spectrum and acknowledge that the second critique may apply with more strength at one end of that spectrum—where predictions are based on the broader categories of race, gender, or wealth—categories that do not seem relevant to criminality. These broader categories are not inherently related to the dominant criminal justice objectives, which are, for instance, to prevent crime or determine the length of a criminal sentence.

Nevertheless, while acknowledging the different force of the arguments, we should bear in mind that there are still problems and concerns with most—practically all—forms of profiling. Even when law enforcement uses an innocuous trait, profiling tends derivatively, rather than directly, to create stigma along unintended dimensions. In the case of bail reform, for instance, using a risk-assessment tool will likely produce an outcome that stigmatizes "drifters" by symbolically portraying them as dangerous people who need to be detained. Profiling those higher-risk defendants will also stigmatize being unattached, unemployed, or unskilled. And it will stigmatize these characteristics derivatively, in an unintended manner. Stigma, in and of itself, is not bad. The very purpose of bail and pretrial detention stigmatizes the act of failing to appear at trial. That stigma is, in truth, intended. But what is not intended, what is not a primary goal of the actuarial method, is the derivative stigma that attaches to the drifter and the unattached adult. And this is a cost to society—one that leads inextricably to greater conformity in society.

Just Punishment

With regard to the third critique, the bail-reform initiatives present a relatively unique situation: the decision whether to grant bail depends precisely on a prediction whether the accused is likely to flee the jurisdiction to avoid trial. The embedded criminal justice standard is all about prediction. In other words, the standard of just punishment here is tied specifically to predicting whether the individual is at high risk of offending. There is no separate or independent criterion of justice to guide the decision whether to release or detain pretrial. The decision turns entirely on whether the individual is likely to show for trial or flee the jurisdiction.

The use of actuarial methods in the context of bail is a weak candidate for a third critique precisely for this reason: in the case of bail, the standard embedded in the criminal justice determination—risk of flight— maps onto prediction *perfectly*. There has been no slippage to prediction, no metamorphosis of the criminal justice objective. Here, the criminal justice outcome is precisely the prediction of future behavior—skipping bail and fleeing the jurisdiction.

Notice that this is *not* the case with the other illustrations of actuarial methods. Criminal profiling aims at reducing crime, not at predicting the higher incidence of the commission of crime. Parole determinations and sentencing more generally aim at imposing just criminal punishment, not necessarily at predicting future violations or dangerousness. IRS enforcement seeks to reduce tax evasion, not predict the likely tax evader. In all these other situations, the prediction of criminal behavior is being substituted for a larger criminal justice end. In the case of bail determinations, though, the goal itself is to predict who is a risk for flight pretrial.

In this sense, determining bail is precisely and specifically about prediction. It does not use prediction as a means toward some other end (fighting crime or just punishment)—it is all about prediction. And in this context, many of us believe that the more accurate the prediction, the better. What could possibly be wrong with having a jail filled with defendants who are more likely to flee the jurisdiction? That is the whole point of detaining them, after all. Using a predictive instrument is only going to improve our ultimate predictions, and these predictions represent the desired criminal justice outcome.

When the criminal justice standard itself, then, is originally and entirely focused on the prediction of criminal offending, there can be no distortion of our conception of just punishment. The key here, then, for purposes of the third critique, is to distinguish cases where the standard has shifted toward actuarial prediction from cases where it originally was centered on prediction. In the former case—where the law has gravitated toward prediction—the third critique is at its strongest. The shift necessarily involves a displacement of an earlier, independent judgment that is rarely, if ever, necessary. In practically all of these cases—fighting crime, determining parole, sentencing a convicted criminal—there are and were earlier solutions that avoided using prediction. There were independent metrics that satisfied the criminal justice goal. In the latter case—where the criminal justice objective originally entailed prediction—the third critique is far weaker.

But even here there is practically always an easy way to avoid the use of actuarial methods—which may be necessary if the first two critiques apply with full force. In the context of pretrial detention, for instance, magistrates could determine bail based on the gravity of the offense charged. The categories that would determine bail, then, would be the classification of felonies and misdemeanors. And if magistrates are concerned about wealthy defendants skipping town because the amount set is too low, then the gravity-of-offense scale can be adjusted for annual salary or total assets. Similarly, in the case of prison classification—another example of a classification where the prediction of future dangerousness seems so central to the criminal justice determination—prison authorities could also use the seriousness of the crime for which the person has been convicted: persons guilty of first-degree murder would get one form of custody—say, the equivalent of our maximum security facilities—and persons convicted of auto theft would get a different form of custody—say, minimum security custody. It is practically always possible to find an independent metric that satisfies the purpose of the classification. In these two examples, the proposed alternatives relate to the crime charged, and as a result, the stigma goes only to the crime—not derivatively to some other category, such as the drifter or the speeder.

A General Framework for Analyzing the Use of Actuarial Methods

There are, then, several different dimensions to keep in mind in evaluating the use of actuarial methods. The first and perhaps most important dimension involves the comparative elasticities and offending rates between the two groups. If there are no differences in offending as between the profiled and nonprofiled groups, then the profiling itself is spurious, and the use of actuarial methods, naturally, is entirely inappropriate. If there are different offending rates, then two questions arise: first, how great are the differences, and, second, what are the comparative elasticities? The overall effect on crime—the overall social cost of using actuarial methods—will depend on the answers to these two questions and the relationship between them.[21]

As demonstrated in the discussion of racial profiling, where the differential in offending is small, and lower elasticity is also likely among the profiled group, actuarial measures will likely increase overall crime. At the other end of the spectrum, however, if the profiled group is offending at a far greater rate and the nonprofiled population is inelastic to policing, the use of actuarial measures will not likely increase overall crime. This is the case with stranger rape: first, the offending population is disproportionately male. Men represent 98 percent of persons convicted of rape in state courts,[22] and approximately 96.5 percent of reported rape offenders, according to crime victimization surveys.[23] Second, the nontargeted group (women) is not very elastic to policing. Under these conditions, profiling men for stranger rape is not likely to increase the total number of such rapes over the long run. Similarly, if we developed a new instrument using genetic information to predict with 95 percent accuracy who would commit sex offenses, and (because it is genetic) we do not believe there is much elasticity among the nonprofiled group, then the first critique simply does not apply.

A second important dimension concerns the type of group trait that is being profiled. This goes to the ratchet effect. Even on the assumption that using actuarial methods decreases overall crime, we must still weigh the countervailing costs against the crime reduction. Those costs are greater when the trait being profiled lies on the spectrum closer to race, ethnicity, and gender. In contrast, the closer the trait lies to the actual commission of the offense—for instance, people walking around with burglar tools—the less we tend to value the costs of a ratchet.

A third dimension consists of the crime itself—the crime targeted by actuarial methods. When that crime is murder, rape, violent and sexual assault, and other physically harmful offenses, the benefits of crime reduction take on added importance. The ratchet effect is, naturally, a cost that must be balanced against any potential crime reduction, and that reduction will be measured by the extent of the harm caused. Disorderly conduct violations should be treated differently than homicides.

Finally, a fourth dimension relates to whether the original criminal justice outcome called for prediction or not—which relates to the third critique and the effect on our shared conceptions of just punishment. If the criminal justice goal originally called for the use of prediction, then the use of actuarial methods may be less problematic. If, on the other hand, the criminal justice standard has gravitated toward prediction, we may have more reason to pause.

When we apply this framework to the different cases of actuarial criminal justice, it becomes clear that the critique developed here has different force in different contexts. The critique of the actuarial is at its strongest in the case of racial profiling on the highways and streets as part of the war on drugs. First, the differentials in offending, if any, are relatively slim, and we have good reason to believe that the profiled group may be less elastic to policing than the white population. As a result, such targeted policing may stimulate more crime overall, reflecting a displacement effect onto other offenders who may begin to feel relatively immune from investigation. Second, the likely ratchet operates on the most troubling group characteristic, namely, race and ethnicity. These traits are far from the criminal activity itself and highly unrelated. Third, the other side of the ledger—the war on drugs—is controversial at the very least. There is a lot of debate about the value of drug-interdiction policies. Although proponents of the war on drugs catalogue serious harms associated with the trade and use of illicit drugs, including homicides resulting from drug turf battles, there are undoubtedly more questions surrounding drug policy than, say, efforts to reduce homicide or rape. Finally, racial profiling for purposes of drug interdiction shifts the criminal justice goal from the traditional law enforcement objective of fighting crime to an efficiency concern about the police searches, distorting in the process our shared conceptions of just punishment. In sum, racial profiling presents the strongest case for the critique of actuarial methods.

The same holds true for IRS profiling of, say, drywall contractors. Here again, the offending differentials are likely to be relatively slim and there is good reason to believe that other tax filers—bankers, accountants, doctors, CEOs, and other well-paid professionals and executives—may be more elastic to policing. Second, the ratchet effect operates on class and wealth, and creates significant blue-collar stigma. Third, the benefits, if any, are purely monetary. The cost-benefit analysis is a simple, lump-sum dollar equation, involving no physical harm or personal injury. In all likelihood, there probably is no monetary gain for the United States Treasury since drywall contractors are probably not withholding from the system as much as the more elastic, nonprofiled group that includes bankers and corporate executives. Finally, the IRS profiling again undermines our shared conception of justice, namely, that all tax evaders should face the same probability of being detected regardless of class.

In the case of other forms of criminal profiling, a lot will turn on the first question concerning differentials in offending and elasticity. Where we have good reason to believe that a significant differential in offending exists concerning a serious crime, such that one group is doing practically all the offending, and where we have good reason to believe that the non-offending group is very inelastic to policing—as in the case of stranger rape—then the first critique will simply not apply, and the second critique, concerning the ratchet effect, may not carry sufficient weight to outweigh the benefits in terms of lower crime. Where uncertainty exists regarding elasticities or differentials in offending, then the strength of the critiques will turn on the other three dimensions: Where does the group trait fall on the spectrum? What are the potential benefits in terms of the crime equation? And is the standard one that seems to call naturally for prediction?

With regard to parole prediction, criminal sentencing, and selective incapacitation, the strength of the critiques depends heavily on the comparative elasticities. If the first critique applies with full force—if the disparities in offending are slim and the profiled groups less elastic—then the arguments are extremely strong. After all, these situations involve homicide, rape, sexual and physical assault, and other serious crimes. If using actuarial measures actually increases these serious offenses, we have little reason even to address the second or third critiques. But, for the same reason, the reverse is true as well: if the first critique fails, the second and third are much less powerful on their own. We are dealing here with potentially serious criminal conduct, and any benefits on the crime side may potentially outweigh the hidden costs of a ratchet or distortions of our shared conceptions of justice. But again, the force of the arguments will turn centrally on comparative elasticities and offending rates.

There are certainly cases where actuarial methods can be put to good use, even in the field of criminal justice. One area, for instance, is the allocation of resources regarding parole supervision. Actuarial data suggest that convicts released from prison are more likely to reoffend, if they do, in the twelve months after their release. A number of studies by the Bureau of Justice Statistics (BJS), going back to the 1980s, consistently document this trend. One BJS study of prisoners released in 1983 revealed that approximately two-thirds of all rearrests during the three-year follow-up period occurred during the first twelve months.[24] A similar study of prisoners released from prison in fifteen states in 1994 revealed that 44.1 percent were rearrested within one year; within three years, the number had only gone up, cumulatively, to 67.5 percent.[25] These numbers favor intensifying post-release supervision during the first twelve months after release. Some evidence from the existing intensive-probation diversionary programs that have been adopted around the country indicates that intensifying supervision can reduce the incidence of rearrests for more serious offenses. Much of the evidence is mixed, and intensive supervision, if misdirected, can often produce higher rates of technical violations, but there is little evidence that intensified supervision causes higher rates of serious crime.[26] So we have little reason not to allocate more of supervisory resources to the earlier period following release. This seems like a clear case where actuarial methods can lead to useful public policies. But this is the rare case.

Two final points—perhaps the most important: first, this framework works at an abstract level. It identifies a number of important dimensions and allows for an analysis at a level of generality that applies to all forms of actuarial justice. In this sense, the problems with stereotyping and profiling are not problems about race; they are problems about the use of actuarial methods. The critiques developed in these pages apply across the board. They are not reserved for the cases of race or gender profiling.

Second, because of the uncertainties along the first dimension and the potential costs associated with actuarial measures, the burden of proof and persuasion must rest on the proponents of profiling. If the predictor is race—as in racial profiling—then the constitutional standard of strict scrutiny requires that the government carry the burden. But, I would suggest, precisely because of the ratchet effect, the same should be true in the case of classifications based on gender, class, wealth, and other troubling distinctions. The potential costs are so problematic that they warrant shifting the burden of proof and persuasion to the proponents of the actuarial.

A Coda on Profiling as a Defensive Counterterrorism Measure

One of the most pressing and controversial issues today involves the profiling of young Muslim men in the domestic struggle against international terrorism. In this final section, I turn to racial profiling in the counterterrorism context as a way to illustrate how the framework developed in this chapter can resolve an important issue of national security.

Both sides of the debate are well represented. In the immediate aftermath of the London bombings in July 2005, Paul Sperry of the Hoover Institution at Stanford University defended the police profiling of young

Muslim men in New York City subways as a matter of simple common sense. Writing in the pages of the *New York Times,* Sperry argued that any future terrorist offender is likely to be young, male, and Muslim: "Young Muslim men bombed the London tube, and young Muslim men attacked New York with planes in 2001. From everything we know about the terrorists who may be taking aim at our transportation system, they are most likely to be young Muslim men." It makes no sense, Sperry contends, to search old ladies or children. Instead, the police should target the high-risk population. Profiling, Sperry writes, is "based on statistics. Insurance companies profile policyholders based on probability of risk. That's just smart business. Likewise, profiling passengers based on proven security risk is just smart law enforcement."[27] A similar column appeared in the *Washington Post* the next day, arguing that "politically correct screenings won't catch Jihadists": "It is a simple statistical fact. Yes, you have your shoe-bomber, a mixed-race Muslim convert, who would not fit the profile. But the overwhelming odds are that the guy bent on blowing up your train traces his origins to the Islamic belt stretching from Mauritania to Indonesia." Using random bag searches in the New York subways, the column concludes, "is simply nuts."[28]

New York City police commissioner Raymond Kelly could not disagree more. "Look at the 9/11 hijackers," Kelly exclaims. "They came here. They shaved. They went to topless bars. They wanted to blend in. They wanted to look like they were part of the American dream. These are not dumb people. Could a terrorist dress up as a Hasidic Jew and walk into the subway, and not be profiled? Yes. I think profiling is just nuts." Racial profiling is ineffective, in Kelly's opinion, because it assumes that terrorists are not going to adapt to changing circumstances, and, as a result, it puts the police one step behind the enemy. Racial profiling focuses on an "unstable" trait—a trait that can easily be switched—which, as Malcolm Gladwell explains, is precisely "what the jihads seemed to have done in London, when they switched to East Africans because the scrutiny of young Arab and Pakistani men grew too intense." Plus, Kelly adds, in New York City it's simply impracticable. "If you look at the London bombings, you have three British citizens of Pakistani descent. You have Germaine Lindsay [the fourth London suicide bomber], who is Jamaican. You have the next crew [in London], on July 21st, who are East African. You have a Chechen woman in Moscow in early 2004 who blows herself up in the subway station. So whom do you profile? Look at New York City. Forty per cent of New Yorkers are born outside the country. Look at the diversity here. Who am I supposed to profile?"[29]

So, is racial profiling post-9/11 "just smart law enforcement" or is it "just nuts"? Theoretically, both sides are partly right. Racial profiling may increase the detection of terrorist attacks *in the short term* but create the possibility of dangerous substitutions *in the long run*. Defensive counterterrorism measures are notoriously tricky and can easily backfire. The installation of metal detectors in airports in 1973, for instance, produced a dramatic reduction in the number of airplane hijackings, but it also resulted in a proportionally larger increase in bombings, assassinations, and hostage-taking incidents. Target hardening of U.S. embassies and missions abroad produced a transitory reduction in attacks on those sites, but an increase in assassinations. The evidence shows that some defensive counterterrorism measures do not work, and some may even increase the likelihood of terrorist acts. And there is no empirical evidence whatsoever on the use of racial profiling as a counterterrorism measure.

As a practical matter, then, racial profiling in the counterterrorism context is neither "just" smart nor "just" nuts. The truth is, we simply have no idea whether racial profiling would be an effective counterterrorism measure or would lead instead to more terrorist attacks. As a result, there is no good reason to make the rights trade-offs that would be associated with racial profiling in the counterterrorism context.

The four dimensions for evaluating the use of actuarial methods discussed earlier lead to this conclusion. As a preliminary step, it is important to identify precisely the type of measure under consideration. Broadly speaking, there are two types of counterterrorist initiatives. The first are called defensive or deterrence-based counterterrorist policies. These are the type of policies that aim at preventing or blocking a successful terrorist attack or reducing the likelihood that an attack will cause injuries. These defensive policies include the development and deployment of technology-based barriers, such as metal or explosives detectors at airports and the hardening of potential targets such as embassies and foreign missions. In contrast, proactive or preemptive policies aim at dismantling terrorist organizations by means of infiltration, preemptive strikes, or invasion of supportive states.[30] Profiling can be used in either type of measure. The profiling of young Muslim men in the New York City subways involves the former—a type of defensive counterterrorism measure. But profiling can also be used in proactive strategies, as when, for example, the FBI engages in targeted interviews of Muslim and Arab Americans in order to collect intelligence. I address here racial profiling by the police in defensive counterterrorism operations and will begin with the first dimension—offending differentials and comparative elasticities.

Offending Differentials

The first question to ask is whether there is an offending differential between profiled and nonprofiled group members. For purposes of the police officer on the street, young Muslim men would include young men of apparent Arab descent; young men who look Middle Eastern, Southeast Asian, or North African; or, more generally, young men of color (excluding young men from East Asia). The nonprofiled group would consist of all women, older men, and young white, African American, or East Asian men.

The answer to this first question surely is yes. Of the total population in the United States, there are extremely few persons of European, American, African American, or East Asian descent who have committed or appear prepared to commit suicide bombings or similar mass terrorist acts against Americans. Richard Reid, the "shoe bomber," who was traveling to the United States on a British passport, and Jose Padilla, a Hispanic American arrested at Chicago's O'Hare airport and accused of plotting a terrorist attack, are the two people who come immediately to mind—out of a population of about 200 million (excluding children, the elderly, and young men of color). In contrast, the number of young men of Arab descent who have engaged in terrorist activities on American soil is larger and includes the nineteen men who participated in the 9/11 terrorist attacks, as well as those who engaged in the earlier car bombing of the World Trade Center on February 26, 1993. In addition, the denominator is much smaller: according to the 2000 U.S. Census, there are 1,189,731 persons living in the United States who have one or more Arab ancestors, and approximately 10 percent of those (or about 120,000) are young men between the ages of 15 and 30.[31] Naturally, many young men of color may appear to be of Arab descent, so the denominator is probably higher. But even if we assume that it is one hundred or more times bigger, there is still an offending differential in the range of at least 1:100 for nonprofiled versus profiled group members. It would be crucial to get a better handle on this first quantity of interest—but there is, in all likelihood, a significant offending differential.

Given the offending differential, there is no doubt that the likelihood of detecting a terrorist attack in the New York subways should increase in the *immediate* aftermath of implementing racial profiling. This is simply the inexorable product of probabilities: if the police dedicate more resources to investigating and searching members of a higher-offending group, they will inevitably increase the detection of terrorist activities within the profiled group and in society as a whole *in the immediate aftermath*. This goes back, again, to sampling more from a higher-offending pool. And it is precisely what gives rise to the claim, among proponents of racial profiling, that it is "based on statistics" and that "[i]t is a simple statistical fact." These claims are theoretically correct at least in the narrow time period immediately following the implementation of a profiling method.

Practically speaking—within the context of the *immediate* aftermath of implementing a profiling measure—the likelihood of realizing any tangible benefits from racial profiling will depend entirely on the frequency of the profiled event. The higher the frequency of the event, the more likely that profiling will immediately detect those events. A good illustration is mandatory screening at airports—an initiative that, to be sure, does not involve profiling, but does involve increased sampling. Implemented in 1973, mandatory screening in the United States detected 4,783 firearms and 46,318 knives in 1975, and, according to the Federal Aviation Administration, prevented approximately thirty-five potential hijackers that year. To put that number in perspective, that same year there were six domestic hijackings in the United States.[32]

Low base-rate events, however, are far more difficult to predict[33] and as a result much harder to detect, for several reasons. First, it is extremely hard to predict where, when, or how the low base-rate offense will occur. Second, low frequency affords more time to adjust to any counterterrorism measure. A terrorist attack in the New York City subway qualifies as a low base-rate event—fortunately, there have not been any such attacks—but as a result, there is a lot of time between events and opportunity for a terrorist organization to adjust to profiling. In the case of low-frequency events, the real question is whether the increased likelihood of detection associated with the *immediate* implementation of a profiling measure will result in the *actual* detection of planned terrorist activity or instead in the rapid substitution of persons who do not meet the profile or alternative acts that are not as easily profiled.

Comparative Elasticities

The second question is how the elasticities of the profiled and nonprofiled groups compare. This will affect the long-term impact on terrorist attacks. It is precisely the *comparative* elasticities that give rise to the possibility of "substitution"—to the possibility that, in response to profiling, terrorist organizations will either recruit more individuals from nonprofiled groups, thereby expanding the overall pool of potential terrorists, or substitute different types of terrorist attacks that are more immune to profiling and yet more devastating in terms of deaths and injuries.

We know that substitution occurs. It happened in Israel, for instance, starting in 2002 when young girls and women became suicide bombers. As Jonathan Tucker, a counterterrorism expert, explains, "At first, suicide terrorists [in Israel] were all religious, militant young men recruited from Palestinian universities or mosques. In early 2002, however, the profile began to change as secular Palestinians, women, and even teenage girls volunteered for suicide missions. On March 29 2002, Ayat Akhars, an 18-year-old Palestinian girl from Bethlehem who looked European and spoke Hebrew, blew herself up in a West Jerusalem supermarket, killing two Israelis. Suicide bombers have also sought to foil profiling efforts by shaving their beards, dyeing their hair blond, and wearing Israeli uniforms or even the traditional clothing of orthodox Jews."[34]

This is why the opponents of racial profiling also are correct—and supported by "statistical fact." If we assume elasticity among rational actors, then profiling will *increase* offending among members of the nonprofiled group. This has led some counterterrorism experts and practitioners to avoid profiling on traits that can substitute easily. As Malcolm Gladwell explains, "It doesn't work to generalize about a relationship between a category and a trait when that relationship isn't stable—or when the act of generalizing may itself change the basis of the generalization."[35]

The fact that there may be elasticity among the nonprofiled and therefore substitution, however, does not end the debate. The mere fact that there is substitution does not mean that profiling is ineffective. Some substitution is inevitable. The question is, how much will there be? If the profiled group members are *less* elastic than the nonprofiled group, then racial profiling will ultimately *increase* the amount of terrorism in the long run. On this central question, there is no reliable empirical evidence. There is no empirical research on elasticities in the terrorism context—absolute or comparative—or on substitution effects in the racial profiling context. The only forms of substitution that have been studied empirically in the counterterrorism context involve substitution between different methods of attack and intertemporal substitution.

Rigorous empirical research in the terrorism context traces to a 1978 paper by my colleague at the University of Chicago, William Landes, that explores the effect of installing metal detectors in airports on the incidence of aircraft hijackings. Extending the rational choice framework to terrorist activities, Landes found that "increases in the probability of apprehension, the conditional probability of incarceration, and the sentence are associated with significant reductions in aircraft hijackings in the 1961-to-1976 time period," and he estimated that between 41 and 67 fewer aircraft hijackings occurred on planes departing from the United States following mandatory screening and the installation of metal detectors in U.S. airports.[36]

Subsequent research built on Landes's framework to explore possible substitution effects. Jon Cauley and Eric Im used interrupted time series analysis in their research to explore the impact of the installation of metal detectors on different types of terrorist attacks. They found that, although the implementation resulted in a permanent decrease in the number of hijackings, it produced a proportionally larger increase in other types of terrorist attacks.[37] In their 1993 article "The Effectiveness of Antiterrorism Policies," Walter Enders and Todd Sandler also revisited mandatory screening and similarly showed that, although mandatory screening coincided with a sharp decrease in hijackings, it also coincided with increased assassinations and other kinds of hostage attacks, including barricade missions and kidnappings.

These researchers have also looked at other forms of substitution. Retaliatory strikes, like the U.S. strike on Libya on April 15, 1986, resulted in "*increased* bombings and related incidents";[38] but such incidents tended to level off later. As Enders and Sandler explain, "The evidence seems to be that retaliatory raids induce terrorists to *intertemporally* substitute attacks planned for the future into the present to protest the retaliation. Within a relatively few quarters, terrorist attacks resumed the same mean number of events."[39] Enders and Sandler also found that the fortification of U.S. embassies and missions in October 1976 resulted in a reduction of terrorist attacks against U.S. interests, but produced a substitution effect of more assassinations.[40] Cauley and Im also analyzed the effect of target hardening of U.S. embassies and found that they had an "abrupt but transitory influence on the number of barricade and hostage taking events."[41]

The fact is, defensive counterterrorism measures are tricky. The existing empirical evidence tends to show a potential for significant substitution effects. The evidence, though, is slim. The most recent and thorough review of the empirical literature identifies only seven rigorous empirical studies from over 20,000 studies on terrorism. The review concludes: "there is little scientific knowledge about the effectiveness of most counter-terrorism interventions. Further, from the evidence we were able to locate, it appears that some evaluated interventions either didn't work or sometimes *increased* the likelihood of terrorism and terrorism-related harm."[42] None of the evidence addresses racial profiling.

At the theoretical level, there is no good reason to assume that young Muslim men are as or more responsive to policing than members of the nonprofiled group. The two groups, after all, have *different* offending rates, and we have to assume there is a reason for that—whether it is due to different religious beliefs, educational backgrounds, or upbringing. If members of the profiled group are offending more because they are more religious, for example, then that may also affect their elasticity to policing. There is no a priori reason why a group that offends more should be more or less elastic than a group that offends less.

The Type of Group Trait

The second dimension addresses the type of group trait to be profiled, which in this case involves the most sensitive group characteristics, namely, ethnicity, national origin, youth, and gender. All four, but especially the first two, are the most problematic of group traits. For this reason, the use of racial profiling may actually aggravate the situation: it may soften the elasticity of the nonprofiled group and harden the elasticity of the profiled group by reinforcing the perception that the United States is anti-Muslim. There is good reason to believe, for instance, that the 2004 Abu-Ghraib torture scandal has served as a recruitment tool for terrorist organizations. As Charles Anderton and John Carter suggest, "It is likely that the degrading images of Iraqi prisoners hardened the preferences of terrorists against the United States. It may have also created terrorist preferences among some individuals who previously had flat indifference curves [as to terrorist activities]. Hence, the prisoner abuse scandal can be seen as a form of 'negative advertising' that may have reshaped terrorist preferences toward more terrorism."[43] In the same way, the profiling of young Muslim men in New York City may serve as a form of "negative advertising" that may undermine efforts to eradicate terrorism. Profiling on those sensitive traits may also have a detrimental effect on the criminal justice system as a whole, especially on general obedience to the law (again, according to the work of Tom Tyler).

The Targeted Crime

The crime targeted by counterterrorism profiling is of the most serious kind—large-scale murder, devastation, and havoc. As a result, it is unlikely that the other costs of profiling would amount to much in comparison to the benefits, if terrorist acts were actually reduced. It is, of course, not entirely clear that a ratchet would even obtain under these conditions. The offending differential is so large that there is likely little room for a ratchet on the carceral population. But even if there were a ratchet, it would be insignificant in the face of a successful reduction in the incidence of terrorist acts.

The Lure of Prediction

On the final dimension—whether the outcome originally called for prediction—the analysis is strikingly similar to the earlier discussion of racial profiling on the highways. The primary objective is to eliminate terrorism or reduce it as much as possible over the long term. The goal is to reduce the overall number of deaths and injuries caused by terrorism over the next decades—not just to police terrorism more efficiently in the next month or two. To be sure, the long-term objective has a predictive element. But if the profiling practices fuel more terrorism over the long term, then the current efficiencies are ultimately counterproductive. Here too we should not allow the pull of the actuarial to distort our objective.

Minding the Gap

The central question, then, is whether racial profiling of young Muslim men in the New York subways will likely detect a terrorist attack or instead lead to the recruitment of nonprofiled persons and the substitution of other more deadly acts for subway attacks. Given the seriousness of the offense and of the group traits that are profiled, the analysis turns narrowly on the likely effectiveness and long-term impact of racial profiling. On this question, there is simply no reliable empirical evidence, or any solid theoretical reason to believe that racial profiling is an effective counterterrorism measure. The possibility of recruiting outside the profiled group and of substituting different modes of attack renders racial profiling in the counterterrorism context suspect.

Does this mean that the New York City police department should not harden targets like the subway system—targets that are attractive to terrorists because of the number of potential victims? No. It is better to divert terrorist attacks away from large groups of people, if possible. But it probably does mean that the police should harden those types of targets without deploying a racial profile. Putting police officers at subway entrances and searching bags already increases the cost of a subway terrorist attack. There is no point in triggering the potential substitution effects associated with racial profiling.

There is a larger lesson here as well. Defensive counterterrorism measures need to be evaluated closely. Measures that raise the price of one and only one specific activity, such as airplane hijackings, are likely to produce troubling substitution effects. Measures that raise the price of *all* terrorist acts or, conversely, reduce the resources of terrorists are less problematic and are likely to increase the use of nonterrorist activities as compared to illegal terrorist activities without producing unanticipated substitution.[44] The optimal strategy to combat terrorism is to reduce terrorists' resources across the board. It is for this reason that intelligence and proactive counterterrorism operations are generally viewed as a priority. As General Meir Dagan, former head of the Bureau for Counterterrorism in the Israeli prime minister's office, explains, "Investments in intelligence are invisible, whereas increased security is visible but often wasteful. The first priority must be placed on intelligence, then on counterterrorism operations, and finally on defense and protection."[45] And where there is no evidence in favor of those defensive counterterrorism measures and some reason to believe that they might actually *increase* the incidence of terrorist attacks, they should be avoided.

CHAPTER NINE

The Virtues of Randomization

The use of actuarial methods in the criminal law may be counterproductive to the central law enforcement objective of reducing crime. Even on very conservative assumptions entirely consistent with rational-choice theory, the use of prediction tools may backfire: given the reasonable possibility that differentials in offending go hand in hand with different elasticities to policing, there is good reason to believe—again from a rational-action perspective—that actuarial methods will increase rather than decrease the overall amount of crime in society. In addition, the use of actuarial methods will aggravate social disparities and tend to distort our conceptions of just punishment.

The critiques set forth in this book reflect problems with the actuarial approach *more generally*—not just with specific types of stereotyping or profiles. What the ratchet effect does, for instance, is violate a core intuition of just punishment—the idea that anyone who is committing the same crime should face the same likelihood of being punished regardless of their race, sex, class, wealth, social status, or other irrelevant categories. When prediction *works*—when it targets a higher-offending population—it likely violates this fundamental idea by distributing the costs of the penal system along troubling lines such as race, gender, class, and the like. The only way to achieve our ideal of criminal justice is to avoid actuarial methods and to police and punish color-blind, gender-blind, or class-blind. To police and punish, in essence, *prediction-blind*. Naturally, race is what makes racial profiling on the highways so controversial in public debate and, at least at the level of public rhetoric, so condemned. But it is important to rethink racial profiling through the lens of the actuarial.

What, then, should we do? Where do we go if we forsake the actuarial? Do we return to clinical judgment? No. Clinical judgment is merely the human, intuitive counterpart to the actuarial. It is simply the less rigorous version of categorization and prediction—the hunch rather than the regression. We should not return to the clinical. Instead, we should look inward. We should look to our own, most central intuition of just punishment: the idea that any person committing a criminal offense should have the same probability of being apprehended as similarly situated offenders. The only way to achieve this goal, surprisingly, is to engage in more random law enforcement.

Randomization, it turns out, is the only way to achieve a carceral population that reflects the offending population. Randomization in this context is a form of random sampling: random sampling on the highway, for instance, is the *only way* that the police would obtain an accurate reflection of the offending population. And random sampling is the central virtue behind randomization. What randomization achieves, in essence, is to neutralize the perverse effects of prediction, both in terms of the possible effects on overall crime and of the other social costs.

Randomization translates into different practices in the policing and sentencing contexts. In the policing context, randomization is relatively straightforward: the IRS could assign a number to each tax return and audit on a lottery basis—or, for that matter, randomly select based on social security numbers. At the airport, the security details could search all passengers or employ a randomized program to select passengers to search. On the highway, the state patrol could deploy random numerical ordering to seek consent to search cars. In fact, one radical idea would be to draw social security numbers by lottery and then have a full investigation of the person's life—audit their taxes, take a hair and urine sample for drugs, clock their driving habits, determine whether they pay social security taxes on their housekeeper, and so forth. This would represent the ultimate random criminal check—an interesting experiment in randomization.

In the sentencing area, randomization means something quite different. Randomization does *not* mean drawing names out of a hat in deciding who to parole or how long to sentence. *It means eliminating the effect of predictions of future dangerousness.* So we impose a sentence based, for instance, on the harm associated with the offense, or proportionally to the degree of the conviction, *and then we stick by it*. We neither enhance nor decrease the punishment based on predictions of future dangerousness. We do not allow prediction to infect the decision-making process. Similarly, the prison authorities would classify inmates for security purposes according to the degree of the felony conviction. This would neutralize the perverse effects of prediction in the sentencing context.

Just like the term *actuarial,* which I define in a narrow, precise, and limited manner in the introduction to this book, the concept of *randomization* is also a term of art. It is used here in a narrow way, with a precise meaning. It does not mean sentencing arbitrarily, but using an independent metric such as the seriousness of the offense or amount of harm caused—independent of the prediction of future dangerousness—that effectively distributes punishment more randomly along the dimension of prediction. It represents the effort to eliminate the unintended consequences of using actuarial methods and the perverse effects of predictions of future dangerousness by eliminating the use of such predictions in postconviction processes, including sentencing, prison classification, parole, and other punishments.

Randomization is already a feature of our law in a number of areas.[1] It should become part of the law of punishing and policing. Nothing in my argument suggests that we should stop researching and theorizing prediction instruments. It is not even clear that we could. It is difficult to imagine quenching our thirst for technical knowledge in the human sciences—especially because of the astounding accomplishments we have achieved in the natural sciences. Human progress in communication, transportation, and medicine are models of success, and the advances we have made in those areas are simply remarkable. From the first flight to the first steps on the moon, from the telegraph to wireless Internet connections, from vaccines to atomic energy, our technical discoveries have led to awe-inspiring heights. And yet, the human sciences—the study of our political, social, and economic organization—though dazzling at times, have not produced such results. Certainly, they have not helped avoid massive human suffering—whether measured in terms of world wars, genocide, hunger, or malnutrition. Is it that we have not yet built the right model? Have we not yet discovered the correct variable? Have we not yet designed the right test? Possibly. Or perhaps it has something to do with the difference, ultimately, between the natural and the human. Whatever the difference, it should be possible, at the very least, to quell the desire to put these prediction instruments to use. It should be possible to resist implementation—particularly since we are implementing them in the most devastating area of social life, in the field of crime and punishment.

Randomizing punishment and policing *v. Abbr.* **Randomization.** *Law.* The effort to eliminate the unintended consequences and perverse effects of employing actuarial methods in the criminal law by (1) using random sampling in police practice and (2) eliminating the use of predictions of future dangerousness in postconviction processes, including sentencing, prison classification, parole, and other punishments. [From random sampling procedure in the social sciences used to achieve a more accurate reflection of social reality.]

Acknowledgments

This project grew out of a haunting realization that the increasingly pervasive use of actuarial measures in the criminal law was beginning to shape our conception of just punishment. It also grew out of my deep concern over the issue of racial profiling in the United States. It became clear to me that the two matters were linked by the concept of statistical discrimination, and that it would be impossible to unpack one without fully understanding the other. As the project took shape, I had the enormous good fortune of spending time at several universities, each of which contributed in special ways to the ultimate production of this book. Martha Minow and Carol Steiker at Harvard University generously offered guidance, much criticism, and even more support throughout the entire project and helped bring this book to fruition. For that, I am deeply grateful.

As I focused more and more on the emerging data on police practices from across the country, I turned my attention to the new economic models of racial profiling that were being developed simultaneously in the United States and abroad. I owe a great debt of gratitude to Gary Becker at the University of Chicago for working through my models with me with chalk and pen, and for giving me extensive comments, guidance, and feedback. I am also extremely grateful to Nicola Persico at the University of Pennsylvania for generous comments and exchanges, especially, I recall fondly, by e-mail as we separately prepared Thanksgiving dinner in November 2004. Fred Schauer generously debated my criticisms and challenged me to rethink my central arguments.

My colleagues at the University of Chicago were instrumental in refining my analysis, especially Richard Posner, Tracey Meares, Tom Miles, Geoffrey Stone, and David Weisbach. Martha Nussbaum and Cass Sunstein offered extensive reactions and rich discussion, particularly in the context of the 2004–2005 Workshop on Law and Philosophy, which focused on the topic of race. Lani Guinier, Randall Kennedy, Dan Meltzer, and Bill Stuntz at Harvard, as well as all the participants in the 2005 Criminal Justice Roundtable, helped me see the strengths and weaknesses of my argument. Richard Revesz and Lewis Kornhauser at New York University Law School were instrumental in pushing me to refine my critique of the economic models, as well as my discussion of the ratchet effect. From all these conversations, it became clear to me that the problems that plague racial profiling on the highways are not just about race, but have to do with a number of dimensions, including differentials in elasticities and offending, the seriousness of the offense, the group trait, and the criminal justice objective itself. I came to realize that these different dimensions were generalizable to the use of all actuarial methods and that it might be possible to generate a larger mechanical understanding of actuarial methods that could apply to the use of any such method—a larger framework for analyzing claims for using the actuarial. As a result, this work is an elaboration and extension of my concerns about racial profiling to the larger and more abstract concept of actuarial methods.

As I traced the genealogy of the actuarial, I became fascinated by the first prediction instruments and their early implementation in Illinois. I was fortunate to find myself at their very birthplace—literally—thanks to my colleague and friend, Andrew Abbott, one of the most insightful scholars of the Chicago School of sociology. As fate would have it, Andrew Abbott is the current occupant of the office in the sociology department that Ernest Burgess occupied in the first half of the twentieth century—Social Science 313. It was extraordinarily stimulating to spend late afternoons with Andrew Abbott in his and Burgess's office, rethinking the role of prediction in sociological thought and reworking the central contributions of Ernest Burgess. I am also deeply grateful to Iris Marion Young for lengthy discussions and feedback about the impact of the actuarial on our conceptions of just punishment; to David Garland for guidance regarding the historical trajectory of the actuarial; and to Dan Kahan, Jonathan Simon, and John Monahan for pushing me to refine my concept of the actuarial.

In writing and finalizing this manuscript, I benefited greatly from dialogue, guidance, comments, and criticisms from Al Alschuler, Rachel Barkow, Alfred Blumstein, Adam Cox, Jeffrey Fagan, Malcolm Feeley, Michael Gottfredson, Benjamin Goold, Jeff Grogger, Jim Jacobs, Jack Katz, Ian Loader, Jens Ludwig, Calvin Morrill, Norval Morris, John Pfaff,

Leonard Post, Dorothy Roberts, Adam Samaha, Robert Sampson, Steve Schulhofer, Michael Tonry, Loïc Wacquant, Robert Weisberg, Lucia Zedner, and Frank Zimring. I am immensely grateful to all of them. Portions of this book were presented at workshops at the University of Chicago, Harvard University, New York University, and the Universities of Florida and Oregon, and I am grateful as well for the comments and reactions I received there.

Many outstanding students helped me with this project. Jennifer Miller of the University of Chicago conducted remarkable research on the early history of parole prediction. Marylynne Hunt-Dorta of Princeton University, now at Harvard Law School, performed outstanding research on the current use of prediction instruments. Ranjit Hakim and Tim Karpoff assisted brilliantly in the original formulations of the arguments. I am also deeply grateful to Stephen Cowen, Kate Levine, Aaron Simowitz, Justin Hurwitz, Brian Mikulencak, Hitesh Aidasani, and Zac Callen at the University of Chicago for outstanding research, as well as Sarah Nolan and Bryn Dodge at New York University who helped launch this project. Dan Montgomery and Sam Lim at the Illinois Mathematics and Science Academy provided excellent assistance at several junctures of the project. I also thank Judith Wright, Margaret Schilt, and Greg Nimmo, librarians at the University of Chicago, for their assistance.

This book benefited greatly from many intense and insightful conversations with my editor at the University of Chicago Press, J. Alex Schwartz, and for that and for his encouragement and support, I am deeply grateful. I also thank Nicholas Murray, Christine Schwab, and Parker Smathers for outstanding assistance at every juncture of the editorial process. Mia Ruyter and our children, Isadora and Léonard, participated in every aspect of this book, for which I am, as always, eternally grateful.

Appendix A

RETRACING THE PAROLE-PREDICTION DEBATE AND LITERATURE

1918 Pinter, R., and J. C. Reamer. "Mental Ability and Future Success of Delinquent Girls." *Journal of Delinquency* 3:74–89.

1920 Fernald, M. R., M. H. S. Hayes, and A. Dawlet. *A Study of Women Delinquents in New York State.* New York: Century.

1922 Barnes, H. E. "Some Leading Phases of the Evolution of Modern Penology." *Political Science Quarterly* 37:251–80.

1923 Hart, H. "Predicting Parole Success." *Journal of the American Institute of Criminal Law and Criminology* 41 (3): 405–13.

   Warner, S. B. "Factors Determining Parole from the Massachusetts Reformatory." *Journal of Criminal Law and Criminology* 14:172–207.

1925 Lindsey, E. "Historical Sketch of the Indeterminate Sentence and Parole System." *Journal of Criminal Law and Criminology* 16:9.

   Witmer, H. L. "The Development of Parole in the United States." *Social Forces* 4:318–25.

1926 Bramer, J. P. *A Treatise Giving the History, Organization, and Administration of Parole.* New York: Irving Press.

1927 Witmer, H. L. "Some Factors in Success or Failure on Parole." *Journal of Criminal Law and Criminology* 17:384–403.

1928 Borden, H. G. "Factors for Predicting Parole Success." *Journal of Criminal Law and Criminology* 19:328–36.

   Bruce, A. A., E. W. Burgess, and A. Harno. *The Workings of the Indeterminate-Sentence Law and the Parole System in Illinois: A Report to Hinton G. Clabaugh, Chairman, Parole Board of Illinois.* Springfield: State of Illinois Board of Parole and Pardon.

   Harno, A. J. "The Workings of the Parole Board and Its Relation to the Court." In *The Workings of the Indeterminate-Sentence Law and the Parole System in Illinois.* Repr., Springfield: State of Illinois Board of Parole and Pardon, 1979.

1929 Bramer, J. P. "Is Prediction Feasible in Social Work? An Inquiry Based upon a Sociological Study of Parole Records." *Social Forces* 7:533–45.

Cobb, J. C. "A Study of Social Science Data and Their Use." *American Journal of Sociology* 35:80–92.

1930 Brown, R. M. "Crime and Its Treatment." *Social Forces* 8:591–95.

Glueck, S., and E. T. Glueck. *Five Hundred Criminal Careers.* New York: Alfred A. Knopf.

1931 Gehlke, C. E. "Testing the Work of the Prison." *Annals of the American Academy of Political and Social Science* 157:121–30.

Tibbitts, C. "Success and Failure on Parole Can Be Predicted." *Journal of Criminal Law and Criminology* 22:11–50.

Vold, G. B. "Do Parole Prediction Tables Work in Practice?" *Publications of the American Sociological Society* 25 (2): 136–38.

———. *Prediction Methods and Parole: A Study of the Factors Involved in the Violation or Non-violation of Parole in a Group of Minnesota Adult Males.* Hanover, NH: Sociological Press.

Wood, A. E. "Crime and Penology." *American Journal of Sociology* 36: 1017–29.

1932 Mead, B. "Evaluating the Results of Correctional Treatment." *Journal of the American Statistical Association* 27:30–39.

Monachesi, E. D. *Prediction Factors in Probation.* Hanover, NH: Sociological Press.

Tibbitts, C. "Reliability of Factors Used in Predicting Success or Failure on Parole." *Journal of Criminal Law and Criminology* 22: 844–53.

1933 Taft, D. R. "Testing the Selective Influence of Areas of Delinquency." *American Journal of Sociology* 38:699–712.

1935 Chamberlin, H. B. "Concerning Parole in Illinois." *Journal of Criminal Law and Criminology* 26:487–516.

Fenton, N. *The Delinquent Boy and the Correctional School.* Claremont, CA: Claremont Colleges Guidance Center.

Klein, C. R. "Success and Failure on Parole: A Study of 160 Girls Paroled from the State Training School at Geneva, Illinois." Master's thesis, School of Social Service Administration, University of Chicago.

Lanne, W. F. "Parole Prediction as a Science." *Journal of Criminal Law and Criminology* 26:377–400.

Laune, F. F. "A Technique for Developing Criteria of Parolability." PhD diss., Department of Sociology, Northwestern University.

Sanders, B. S. "Testing Parole Prediction." Paper presented at the sixty-fifth annual congress of the American Prison Association.

Van Vechten, C. C., Jr. "A Study of Success and Failure of One Thousand Delinquents Committed to a Boy's Republic." PhD diss., Department of Sociology, University of Chicago.

1936 Laune, F. F. "The Application of Attitude Tests in the Field of Parole Prediction." *American Sociological Review* 1:781–96.

———. *Predicting Criminality: Forecasting Behavior on Parole.* Northwestern University Studies in the Social Sciences, no. 1. Evanston, IL: Northwestern University Press.

Schiedt, R. *Ein Beitrag zum Problem der Rueckfallsprognose.* Munich: Muenchener Zeitungs Verlag.

1937 Horner, H. "Bill Affecting Parole in Illinois: The Governor's Veto." *Journal of Criminal Law and Criminology* 28:318–26.

Sanders, B. S. "Consistency of Recording Statistical Data from Prison Files." *Journal of the American Statistical Association* 32:323–36.

1939 Kersey, L. C. *A Parole and Probation Officers' Manual.* St. Paul, MN: State Board of Parole.

Morse, W. *U.S. Attorney General's Survey of Release Procedures.* Washington, DC: U.S. Government Printing Office.

1941 Bell, M., ed. *Probation and Parole Progress.* Yearbook. New York: National Probation Association.

Guttman, L. "An Outline of Statistical Theory of Prediction." In *The Prediction of Personal Adjustment,* ed. P. Horst. New York: Social Science Research Council.

Monachesi, E. D. "An Evaluation of Recent Major Efforts at Prediction." *American Sociological Review* 6:478–86.

Wish, H. "Altgeld and the Progressive Tradition." *American Historical Review* 46:813–31.

1942 Allen, R. M. "A Review of Parole Prediction Literature." *Journal of Criminal Law and Criminology* 32:548–54.

Clemmer, D. "Probation and Parole Progress: Yearbook, National Probation Association, 1941." *American Sociological Review* 7:584–86.

Clinard, M. B. "The Process of Urbanization and Criminal Behavior." *American Journal of Sociology* 48:202–13.

Jenkins, R. L. "Prediction of Parole Success: Inclusion of Psychiatric Criteria." *Journal of Criminal Law and Criminology* 33:38–46.

Redden, E. "Embezzlement: A Study of One Kind of Criminal Behavior with Prediction Tables Based on Fidelity Insurance Records." PhD diss., Department of Sociology, University of Chicago.

1943 Gillin, J. L. "Prediction of Parole Success in Wisconsin." *Journal of Criminal Law and Criminology* 34:236–39.

Glueck, S., and E. T. Glueck. *Criminal Careers in Retrospect.* New York: Commonwealth Fund.

Hathaway, S. R., and J. C. McKinley. *Manual for the Minnesota Multiphasic Personality Inventory.* New York: Psychological Corporation.

Weeks, H. A. "Predicting Juvenile Delinquency." *American Sociological Review* 8:40–46.

1945 Glueck, S., and E. T. Glueck. *After-conduct of Discharged Offenders*. London: Macmillan.

Hakeem, M. "Glueck Method of Parole Prediction Applied to 1,861 Cases of Burglars." *Journal of Criminal Law and Criminology* 36:97.

Monachesi, E. D. "A Comparison of Predicted with Actual Results of Probation." *American Sociological Review* 10 (1): 26–31.

1947 Allen, R. M. "Problems of Parole." *Journal of Criminal Law, Criminology, and Police Science* 38:7–13.

1948 Hakeem, M. "The Validity of the Burgess Method of Parole Prediction." *American Journal of Sociology* 53 (5): 376–86.

1949 Lunday, G. A. "A Study of Parole Prediction." PhD diss., Department of Sociology, University of Chicago.

Ohlin, L. E., and O. D. Duncan. "The Efficiency of Prediction in Criminology." *American Journal of Sociology* 54:441–51.

Reiss, A. J., Jr. "The Accuracy, Efficiency, and Validity of a Prediction Instrument." PhD diss., Department of Sociology, University of Chicago.

Vold, G. B. "Comment on 'The Efficiency of Prediction in Criminology.'" *American Journal of Sociology* 54:451–52.

1950 Everson, F. C. "A Study in the Prediction of Criminal Careers from the Case Histories of Eighty-three Nondelinquent Social Histories." Master's thesis, Department of Sociology, University of Chicago.

Lunday, G. A. "Vulnerable Parolees." *Journal of Criminal Law, Criminology, and Police Science* 40:620–21.

1951 Caldwell, M. G. "Preview of a New Type of Probation Study Made in Alabama." *Federal Probation* 15 (June): 3–15.

Dressler, D. *Practice and Theory of Probation and Parole*. New York: Columbia University Press.

Johnson, N. B. *A Reconsideration of Certain Factors in the Prediction of Success or Failure on Parole from the Illinois State Penitentiary, Joliet*. Master's thesis, Department of Sociology, University of Chicago.

Ohlin, L. E. *Selection for Parole: A Manual of Parole Prediction*. New York: Russell Sage Foundation.

Powers, E., and H. Witmer. *An Experiment in the Prevention of Delinquency: The Cambridge-Somerville Youth Study*. New York: Columbia University Press.

Reiss, A. J., Jr. "The Accuracy, Efficiency, and Validity of a Prediction Instrument." *American Journal of Sociology* 56 (6): 552–61.

Schnur, A. "The Validity of Parole Selection." *Social Forces* 29:322–28.

1952 Black, B. J., and S. J. Glick. *Recidivism at the Hawthorne-Cedar Knolls School*. New York: Jewish Board of Guardians.

Gillin, John Lewis. *Predicting Criminal Behavior*. Madison: University of Wisconsin Press.

Ohlin, L. E., and R. A. Lawrence. "A Comparison of Alternative Methods of Parole Prediction." *American Sociological Review* 17:268–74.

1953 Duncan, O. D., L. E. Ohlin, A. J. Reiss, and H. R. Stanton. "Formal devices for making selection decisions." *American Journal of Sociology* 58:573–84.

1954 Glaser, D. "A Reconsideration of Some Parole Prediction Factors." *American Sociological Review* 19:335–41.

———. "A Reformulation and Testing of Parole Prediction Factors." PhD diss., Department of Sociology, University of Chicago.

Meehl, P. *Clinical versus Statistical Prediction.* Minneapolis: University of Minnesota Press.

Schuessler, K. F. "Parole Prediction: Its History and Status." *Journal of Criminal Law and Criminology* 45:425–31.

1955 Glaser, D. "The Efficacy of Alternative Approaches to Parole Prediction." *American Sociological Review* 20 (3): 283–87.

Mannheim, H., and L. T. Wilkins. *Prediction Methods in Relation to Borstal Training.* London: H. M. Stationery Office.

1956 *Parole in Principle and Practice: A Manual and Report.* Second National Conference on Parole, Washington, DC. New York: National Probation and Parole Association.

1957 Arkoff, A. "Prison Adjustment as an Index of Ability to Adjust on the Outside." *Journal of Correctional Education* 9:1–2.

1958 Hayner, N. S. "Why Do Parole Boards Lag in the Use of Prediction Scores?" *Pacific Sociological Review* 1 (2): 73–76.

1959 Beattie, R. H. "Sources of Statistics on Crime and Correction." *Journal of the American Statistical Association* 54:582–92.

Giardini, G. I. *The Parole Process.* Springfield, IL: Charles C Thomas.

1961 Gottfredson, D. M. "Comparing and Combining Subjective and Objective Parole Predictions." *California Department of Corrections Research Newsletter,* 11–17.

Hakeem, M. "Prediction of Parole Outcome from Summaries of Case Histories." *Journal of Criminal Law, Criminology, and Police Science* 52: 145–56.

1962 England, R. W., Jr. "Some Dangers in Parole Prediction." *Crime and Delinquency* 8:265–69.

Evjen, V. H. "Current Thinking on Parole Prediction Tables." *Crime and Delinquency* 8:215–24.

Glaser, D., and V. O'Leary. "Prediction Tables as Accounting Devices for Judges and Parole Boards." *Crime and Delinquency* 8:239–58.

Grant, J. D. "It's Time to Start Counting." *Crime and Delinquency* 8:259–64.

Johnson, B. M. *An Analysis of Predictions of Parole Performance and Judgments of Supervision in the Parole Research Project.* Sacramento, CA: Department of Youth Authority, Research Report 32.

Panton, J. H. "Use of the M.M.P.I. as an Index to Successful Parole." *Journal of Criminal Law, Criminology, and Police Science* 53:484–88.

1963 Craig, M. M., and S. J. Glick. "Ten Years' Experience with the Glueck Social Prediction Table." *Crime and Delinquency* 9:249–61.

Gottfredson, D. M., and K. B. Ballard. *Predictive Attribute Analysis and Prediction of Parole Performance.* Vacaville, CA: Institute for the Study of Crime and Delinquency.

——. *The Validity of Two Parole Prediction Scales: An Eight Year Follow-up Study.* Vacaville, CA: Institute for the Study of Crime and Delinquency.

Gottfredson, D. M., K. B. Ballard, and L. Lane. *Association Analysis in a Prison Sample and Prediction of Parole Performance.* Vacaville, CA: Institute for the Study of Crime and Delinquency.

Metzner, R., and G. Weil. "Predicting Recidivism." *Journal of Criminal Law, Criminology, and Police Science* 54:307–16.

Voss, H. L. "The Predictive Efficiency of the Glueck Social Prediction Table." *Journal of Criminal Law, Criminology, and Police Science* 54: 421–30.

1964 Glaser, D. *The Effectiveness of a Prison and Parole System.* Indianapolis: Bobbs-Merrill.

Mueller, P., and D. Coon. *Parole Outcome Prediction for Male Opiate Users in Los Angeles Area.* Research Report 18. Sacramento, CA: Department of Corrections.

Stott, D. H. "Prediction of Success or Failure on Probation." *International Journal of Social Psychiatry* 10:301–40.

Wilkins, L. T., and P. McNaughton-Smith. "New Prediction and Classification Methods in Criminology." *Journal of Research in Crime and Delinquency* 1:19–32.

Wisconsin Division of Corrections. *Adult Base Expectancies.* Research Bulletin C8. Madison, WI: Division of Corrections.

1965 Gough, H. G., E. A. Wenk, and V. V. Rozynko. "Parole Outcome as Predicted from the C.P.I., the M.M.P.I., and a Base Expectancy Table." *Journal of Abnormal Psychology* 70 (6): 432–41.

Takagi, P. *Criminal Types and Parole Prediction.* Research Report 14. Sacramento, CA: Department of Corrections.

Vichert, B., and W. Zahnd. "Parole: Low and High Risk Parolees." *Canadian Journal of Corrections* 7:39–48.

Wisconsin Division of Corrections. *Juvenile Base Expectancies, Wisconsin School for Girls.* Research Bulletin C9. Madison, WI: Division of Corrections.

1966 Cowden, J. E. "Predicting Institutional Adjustment and Recidivism in Delinquent Boys." *Journal of Criminal Law, Criminology, and Police Science* 57:39–44.

Glaser, D. *The Sentencing and Parole Process, Parole Decision Making.* Washington, DC: National Parole Institutes, U.S. Department of Health, Education, and Welfare.

Glaser, D., and V. O'Leary, eds. *Personal Characteristics and Parole Outcome.* Washington, DC: National Parole Institutes, U.S. Department of Health, Education, and Welfare.

Grygier, T. "The Effect of Social Action: Current Prediction Methods and Two New Models." *British Journal of Criminology* 6:269–93.

MacSpeiden, T. R. "The Influence of Scholastic and Vocational Training Programs on the Rate of Parole Violation." PhD diss., Purdue University.

Mandel, N., and A. Barron. "The MMPI and Criminal Recidivism." *Journal of Criminal Law, Criminology, and Police Science* 57:35–38.

1967 Carney, F. J. "Predicting Recidivism in a Medium Security Correctional Institution." *Journal of Criminal Law, Criminology, and Police Science* 58: 338–48.

Johns, D. *Institutional Program Patterns, Parole Prognosis and Outcome.* Research Report 52. Sacramento, CA: Department of Youth Authority.

Taylor, A. J. W. "Prediction for Parole." *British Journal of Criminology* 7: 418–23.

1968 Babst, D. V., D. M. Gottfredson, and K. B. Ballard. "Comparison of Multiple Regression and Configural Analysis Techniques for Developing Base Expectancy Tables." *Journal of Research in Crime and Delinquency* 5:72–80.

Dean, C. W. "New Directions for Parole Prediction Research." *Journal of Criminal Law, Criminology, and Police Science* 59:214–18.

Evans, R., Jr. "The Labor Market and Parole Success." *Journal of Human Resources* 3:201–12.

Jaman, D. *Behavior during the First Year in Prison.* Research Report 32. Sacramento, CA: Department of Corrections.

Rogers, J. W., and N. S. Hayner. "Optimism and Accuracy in the Perception of Selected Parole Prediction." *Social Forces* 46:388–400.

Ward, P. G. "The Comparative Efficiency of Differing Techniques of Prediction Scaling." *Australian and New Zealand Journal of Criminology* 1: 109–12.

1969 Dean, C. W., and T. Duggan. "Statistical Interaction and Parole Prediction." *Social Forces* 48:45–49.

Mack, J. "The MMPI and Recidivism." *Journal of Abnormal Psychology* 74: 612–14.

1970 Grygier, T. "Treatment Variables in Non-linear Prediction." In *The Sociology of Punishment and Correction,* ed. N. Johnston, L. Savitz, and M. E. Wolfgang. New York: Wiley.

La Brie, R. A. "Verification of the Glueck Prediction Table by Mathematical Statistics Following a Computerized Procedure of Discriminant

Function Analysis." *Journal of Criminal Law, Criminology, and Police Science* 61:229–34.

Robison, J., and P. T. Takagi. "The Parole Violator as an Organization Reject." In *Probation and Parole: Selected Readings,* ed. R. M. Carter and L. T. Wilkins. New York: John Wiley & Sons.

1971 Grygier, T. "Decision and Outcome: Studies in Parole Prediction." *Canadian Journal of Criminology* 13:133.

Kassebaum, G., D. Ward, and D. Wilner. *Prison Treatment and Parole Survival: An Empirical Assessment on Group Counseling.* New York: John Wiley & Sons.

Simon, F. H. *Prediction Methods in Criminology: Including a Prediction Study of Young Men on Probation.* London: H. M. Stationery Office.

Taylor, C. V. *The Early Violators—Who Are They?* Springfield: Illinois Department of Corrections.

Veverka, M. "The Gluecks' Social Prediction Table in Czechoslovak Research." *British Journal of Criminology* 11:187–90.

Wilkins, L. T. *Why Are Inefficient Statistics Best for Parole Research?* Albany, NY: School of Criminal Justice. Photocopy.

1972 Jenkins, W. O. *The Measurement and Prediction of Criminal Behavior and Recidivism: The Environmental Deprivation Scale and the Maladaptive Behavior Record.* Elmore, AL: Rehabilitation Research Foundation.

O'Leary, V. *The Organization of Parole Systems in the United States.* Washington, DC: National Council on Crime and Delinquency.

O'Leary, V., and D. Glaser. "The Assessment of Risk in Parole Decision-Making." In *The Future of Parole,* ed. D. West. London: Duckworth.

Simon, F. H. "Statistical Methods of Making Prediction Instruments." *Journal of Research in Crime and Delinquency* 9:46–53.

1973 Avi-Itzhak, B., and R. Shinnar. "Quantitative Models in Crime Control." *Journal of Criminal Justice* 1:185–217.

Bottomley, K. A. "Parole Decisions in a Long-Term Closed Prison." *British Journal of Criminology* 13:26–40.

Carlson, K. "Some Characteristics of Recidivists in an Ontario Institution for Adult Male First Incarcerates." *Canadian Journal of Criminology and Corrections* 15:397–409.

Ganzer, V., and I. Sarason. "Variables Associated with Recidivism among Juvenile Delinquents." *Journal of Consulting and Clinical Psychology* 40:1–5.

Gottfredson, D. M. *Parole Decision Making Study.* 10 vols. Davis, CA: National Council on Crime and Delinquency Research Centre.

Schumacher, M. "Predicting Subsequent Convictions for Individual Male Prison Inmates." *New Zealand Statistician* 8:26–34.

1974 Blumstein, A., and J. Cohen. "Estimation of Individual Crime Rates from Arrest Records." *Journal of Criminal Law and Criminology* 70:561–85.

Challinger, D. "A Predictive Device for Parolees in Victoria." *Australian and New Zealand Journal of Criminology* 7:44–54.

Eysenck, S. B. G., and H. J. Eysenck. "Personality and Recidivism in Borstal Boys." *British Journal of Criminology* 14:386–87.

Hoffman, P. B., and J. L. Beck. "Parole Decision-Making: A Salient Factor Score." *Journal of Criminal Justice* 2:195–206.

O'Leary, V. *Parole Administration*. Chicago: Rand McNally.

Payne, C., S. McCabe, and N. Walker. "Predicting Offender-Patients' Reconvictions." *British Journal of Psychiatry* 125:60–64.

Stollmack, S., and C. M. Harris. "Failure Rate Analysis Applied to Recidivism Data." *Operations Research* 22:1192–1205.

Waller, I. *Men Released from Prison*. Toronto: University of Toronto Press.

Weis, K. "The Glueck Social Prediction Table: An Unfulfilled Promise." *Journal of Criminal Law and Criminology* 65:397–404.

1975 Aitchison, J., and I. R. Dunsmore. *Statistical Prediction Analysis*. Cambridge: Cambridge University Press.

Ferfusson, D. M., A. A. Donnell, S. W. Slater, and J. K. Fifield. *The Prediction of Juvenile Offending: A New Zealand Study*. Wellington: L. A. R. Shearer, Government Printer.

Gottfredson, D. M. "Diagnosis, Classification, and Prediction." In *Decision-Making in the Criminal Justice System: Reviews and Essays,* ed. D. M. Gottfredson. Rockville, MD: National Institute of Mental Health.

Moos, R. *Evaluating Correctional and Community Settings*. New York: John Wiley & Sons.

"Parole Release Decision-Making and the Sentencing Process." Special issue. *Yale Law Journal* 84.

1976 Friedman, J., and F. Mann. "Recidivism: The Fallacy of Prediction." *International Journal of Offender Therapy* 20:153–64.

Heilbrun, A. B., I. J. Knopf, and P. Bruner. "Criminal Impulsivity and Violence and Subsequent Parole Outcome." *British Journal of Criminology* 16:367–77.

Palmer, J. R., and P. Carlson. "Problems with the Use of Regression Analysis in Prediction Studies." *Journal of Research in Crime and Delinquency* 13:64–81.

Robuck, B. E. *A Study of Inmate Outcome in Kentucky*. Ann Arbor, MI: University Microfilms.

Solomon, H. "Parole Outcome: A Multidimensional Contingency Table Analysis." *Journal of Research in Crime and Delinquency* 13:107–26.

1977 Abadinsky, H. *Probation and Parole*. Upper Saddle River, NJ: Prentice Hall.

Inciardi, J., and D. McBride. "The Parole Prediction Myth." *International Journal of Criminology and Penology* 5:235–44.

Kantrowitz, N. "How to Shorten the Follow-up Period in Parole Studies." *Journal of Research in Crime and Delinquency* 14:222–36.

Nuttal, C. P., et al. *Parole in England and Wales*. London: H. M. Stationery Office.

Witte, A. D., and P. Schmidt. "An Analysis of Recidivism: Using the Truncated Lognormal Distribution." *Applied Statistics* 26:302–11.

1978 Brown, L. D. "The Development of a Parolee Classification System Using Discriminant Analysis." *Journal of Research in Crime and Delinquency* 15:92–108.

Brown, R. C., C. A. D'Agostino, and R. A. Craddick. "Prediction of Parole Outcome Based on Discrimination Function." *Corrective and Social Psychiatry and Journal of Behavior Technology, Methods and Therapy* 24:93–101.

Gottfredson, D. M., C. A. Cosgrove, L. T. Wilkins, J. Wallerstein, and C. Rauh. *Classification for Parole Decision Study*. Washington, DC: National Institute of Law Enforcement and Criminal Justice.

Holland, T. R., N. Holt, and D. L. Brewer. "Social Roles and Information Utilization in Parole Decision-Making." *Journal of Social Psychology* 106:111–20.

Lancucki, L., and R. Tarling. "The Relationship between Mean Cost Rating and Kendall's Rank Correlation Coefficient." In *Guidelines for Parole and Sentencing*, ed. D. M. Gottfredson, L. T. Wilkins, and P. B. Hoffman. Lexington, MA: Heath.

McGurk, B. J., N. Bolton, and M. Smith. "Some Psychological, Education, and Criminological Variables related to Recidivism in Delinquent Boys." *British Journal of Social and Clinical Psychology* 17:251–54.

Van Alstyne, D. J., and M. R. Gottfredson. "A Multidimensional Contingency Table Analysis of Parole Outcome: New Methods and Old Problems in Criminological Predictions." *Journal of Research in Crime and Delinquency* 15:172–93.

1979 Bohnstedt, M. *Classification Instrument Dissemination Project: General Information*. Sacramento, CA: American Justice Institute with the National Council on Crime and Delinquency.

Carlson, E. *Contemporary United States Parole Board Practices*. San Jose, CA: San Jose State University Foundation.

Nuffield, J. *Parole Guidelines*. Preliminary version, 3rd draft (revised).

Phillpotts, G. J. O., and L. B. Lancucki. *Previous Convictions, Sentence and Reconvictions: A Statistical Study of a Sample of 5,000 Offenders Convicted in January 1971*. London: H. M. Stationery Office.

Pritchard, D. A. "Stable Predictors of Recidivism: A Summary." *Criminology* 17:15–21.

Underwood, B. D. "Law and the Crystal Ball: Predicting Behavior with Statistical Inference and Individualized Judgment." *Yale Law Journal* 88:1408–48.

Von Hirsch, A., and K. Hanrahan. *The Question of Parole: Retention, Reform or Abolition.* Cambridge, MA: Ballinger.

1980 Fuchs, C., and J. Flanagan. "Stepwise Fitting out of Logit Models with Categorical Predictors in the Analysis of Parole Outcomes: On the Van Alstyne and Gottfredson Study." *Journal of Research in Crime and Delinquency* 17:273–79.

Gendreau, P., P. G. Madden, and M. Leipciger. "Predicting Recidivism with Social History Information and a Comparison of Their Predictive Power with Psychometric Variables." *Canadian Journal of Criminology* 22: 328–36.

Gottfredson, M. R., and D. M. Gottfredson. *Decisionmaking in Criminal Justice: Toward the Exercise of Rational Discretion.* Cambridge, MA: Ballinger.

Greenwood, P. W. "Career Criminal Prosecution." *Journal of Criminal Law and Criminology* 71:85–88.

Larntz, K. "Linear Logistic Models for the Parole Decision Making Problem." In *Indicators of Crime and Criminal Justice,* ed. S. E. Fienberg and A. J. Reiss. Washington, DC: U.S. Government Printing Office.

Rothman, D. *Conscience and Convenience: The Asylum and Its Alternative in Progressive America.* Boston: Little, Brown.

1981 Baird, S. C. "Probation and Parole Classification: The Wisconsin Model." *Corrections Today* 43:36–41.

Fischer, D. R. *The Use of Actuarial Methods in Early Release Screening.* Des Moines, IA: Statistical Analysis Center, Office for Planning and Programming, State of Iowa.

Graham, S. A. "Predictive and Concurrent Validity of the Jesness Inventory Asocial Index." *Journal of Consulting and Clinical Psychology* 5: 740–42.

Harris, C. M., A. R. Kaylan, and M. D. Maltz. "Advances in Statistics of Recidivism Measurement." In *Mathematical Frontiers in Criminology,* ed. J. A. Fox. New York: Academic Press.

Rolph, J., J. Chaiken, and R. Houchens. *Methods for Estimating Crime Rates for Individuals.* Santa Monica, CA: Rand Corporation.

1982 Blumstein A., and E. Graddy. "Prevalence and Recidivism in Index Arrests: A Feedback Model." *Law and Society Review* 16:265–90.

Cavendar, G. *Parole: A Critical Analysis.* New York: Kennikat Press.

"Criminal Sentencing Symposium." Special issue. *Loyola University Chicago Law Journal* 13.

Nuffield, J. *Parole Decision Making in Canada: Research towards Decision Guidelines.* Ottawa: Supply and Services Canada.

Tarling, R. "Comparison of Measures of Predictive Power." *Education and Psychological Measurement* 42:479–87.

1983   Farrington, D. P., and A. M. Morris. "Sex, Sentencing, and Reconviction."
          British Journal of Criminology 23:229–48.

         Hanson, R. W., C. S. Moss, R. E. Hosford, and M. E. Johnson. "Predicting
          Inmate Penitentiary Adjustment: An Assessment of Four Classificatory
          Methods." *Criminal Justice and Behavior* 10:293–309.

         Louscher, P. K., R. E. Hosford, and C. S. Ross. "Predicting Dangerous Be-
          havior in a Penitentiary Using the Megargee Typology." *Criminal Justice
          and Behavior* 10:269–84.

1984   Casper, J. D. "Symposium: Prison Crowding: Determinate Sentencing and
          Prison Crowding in Illinois." *University of Illinois Law Review* 1984:
          231–52.

         Chaiken, M. R., and J. M. Chaiken. "Offender Types and Public Policy."
          Crime and Delinquency 30:195–226.

         Copas, J., and R. Tarling. "Some Methodological Issues in Making Predic-
          tions." Paper prepared for the National Academy of Sciences Panel on
          Research on Criminal Careers.

         Loeber, R., and T. Dishion. "Early Predictors of Male Delinquency: A Re-
          view." *Psychological Bulletin* 94:68–99.

         Loeber, R., T. Dishion, and G. R. Patterson. "Multiple Gating: A Multistage
          Assessment Procedure for Identifying Youths at Risk for Delinquency."
          Journal of Research in Crime and Delinquency 21:7–32.

         Maltz, M. D. *Recidivism.* Orlando, FL: Academic Press.

         Palmer, J. R. *Parole Selection, Abolishment and Determinate Sentencing
          Creation: Role and Influence in the Change Process.* Washington, DC:
          National Institute of Corrections.

         Quinsey, V. L. "Institutional Release Policy and the Identification of Dan-
          gerous Men: A Review of the Literature." *Criminology* 17:53–78.

         Star, D., and J. E. Berecochea. "Rationalizing the Conditions of Parole."
          In *Probation, Parole, and Community Corrections,* ed. R. M. Carter, D.
          Glaser, and L. T. Wilkins. New York: John Wiley & Sons.

         Wright, K. N., T. R. Clear, and P. Dickson. "Universal Applicability of Proba-
          tion Risk-Assessment Instruments: A Critique." *Criminology* 22:113–34.

1985   Bonta, J., and L. Motiuk. "Utilization of an Interview-Based Classification
          Instrument: A Study of Correctional Halfway Houses." *Criminal Justice
          and Behavior* 12:333–52.

         Farrington, D. P., and R. Tarling. *Prediction in Criminology.* Albany: State
          University of New York Press.

         Gottfredson, S. D., and D. M. Gottfredson. "Screening for Risk among Pa-
          rolees: Policy, Practice, and Method." In *Prediction in Criminology,* ed.
          D. P. Farrington and R. Tarling. Albany: State University of New York
          Press.

         Wilbanks, W. L. "Predicting Failure on Parole." In *Prediction in Criminol-*

ogy, ed. D. P. Farrington and R. Tarling. Albany: State University of New York Press.

1986 Andrews, D. A., J. J. Kiessling, S. Mickus, and D. Robinson. "The Construct Validity of Interview-Based Risk Assessment in Corrections." *Canadian Journal of Behavioural Science* 18:460–71.

Baird, S. C., and D. Lerner. *A Survey of the Use of Guidelines and Risk Assessments by State Parole Boards.* Washington, DC: U.S. Government Printing Office.

Gabor, T. *The Prediction of Criminal Behavior: Statistical Approaches.* Toronto: University of Toronto Press.

Gottfredson, S. D., and D. M. Gottfredson. "The Accuracy of Prediction Models." In *Criminal Careers and "Career Criminals,"* ed. A. Blumstein, J. Cohen, J. Roth, and C. Visher. Washington, DC: National Academy Press.

1987 Barnett, A., A. Blumstein, and D. P. L. Farrington. "Probabilistic Models of Youthful Criminal Careers." *Criminology* 25:83–107.

Burke, P. *Structuring Parole Decisionmaking: Lessons from Technical Assistance in Nine States.* Washington, DC: National Institute of Corrections.

Dutile, F. N., and C. H. Foust. *The Prediction of Criminal Violence.* Springfield, IL: Charles C Thomas.

Linster, R. L., and E. B. Patterson. *Probability Models of Recidivism: An Exploration.* Washington, DC: U.S. Department of Justice.

Nietzel, M. T., and M. J. Himelein. "Probation and Parole." In *Behavioral Approaches to Crime and Delinquency: A Handbook of Application, Research, and Concepts,* ed. E. K. Morris and C. J. Braukmann. New York: Plenum Press.

Petersilia, J., and S. Turner. "Guidelines-Based Justice: Prediction and Racial Minorities." In *Prediction and Classification,* ed. D. Gottfredson and M. Tonry. Chicago: University of Chicago Press.

Tonry, M. "Prediction and Classification: Legal and Ethical Issues." *Crime and Justice: An Annual Review of Research* 9:367–414.

1988 Burke, P. *Current Issues in Parole Decisionmaking: Understanding the Past, Shaping the Future.* Washington, DC: National Institute of Corrections.

Schmidt, P., and A. D. Witte. *Predicting Recidivism Using Survival Models.* New York: Springer-Verlag.

1989 Rhine, E. E., W. Smith, R. Jackson, and L. Rupp. "Parole: Issues and Prospects for the 1990s." *Corrections Today* 51:78–83.

1990 Bonta, J., and L. Motiuk. "Classification to Halfway Houses: A Quasi-experimental Evaluation." *Criminology* 28:497–506.

Bottomley, K. A. "Parole in Transition: A Comparative Study of Origins, Developments, and Prospects for the 1990s." In *Crime and Justice:*

A Review of Research, ed. M. Tonry and N. Morris. Chicago: University of Chicago Press.

1991 Keve, P. W. *Prisons and the American Conscience: A History of U.S. Federal Corrections.* Carbondale: Southern Illinois University Press.

Laub, J. H., and R. J. Sampson. "The Sutherland-Glueck Debate: On the Sociology of Criminological Knowledge." *American Journal of Sociology* 96:1402–40.

Rhine, E. E., W. Smith, R. Jackson, P. Burke, and R. LaBelle. *Paroling Authorities: Recent History and Current Practice.* Laurel, MD: American Correctional Association.

1992 Ellermann, R., S. Pasquale, and J. M. Tien. "An Alternative Approach to Modeling Recidivism Using Quantile Residual Life Functions." *Operations Research* 40:485–504.

Hann, R. G., and W. G. Harman. *Predicting General Release Risk for Canadian Penitentiary Inmates.* Ottawa, Ontario: Secretariat of the Ministry of the Solicitor General of Canada.

McCleary, R. *Dangerous Men: The Sociology of Parole.* New York: Harrow & Heston.

Motiuk, M. S., L. L. Motiuk, and J. Bonta. "A Comparison between Self-Report and Interview-Based Inventories in Offender Classification." *Criminal Justice and Behavior* 19:143–59.

1993 Simon, J. *Poor Discipline: Parole and the Social Control of the Underclass, 1890–1990.* Chicago: University of Chicago Press.

1994 Hoffman, P. B. "Twenty Years of Operational Use of a Risk Prediction Instrument: The U.S. Parole Commission's Salient Factor Score." *Journal of Criminal Justice* 22:477–94.

Runda, J. C., E. E. Rhine, and R. E. Wetter. *The Practice of Parole Boards.* Lexington, MA: Association of Paroling Authorities, International.

1995 Burke, P. *Abolishing Parole: Why the Emperor Has No Clothes.* Lexington, MA: American Probation and Parole Association.

Hood, R., and S. Shute. *Paroling with New Criteria.* London: Home Office.

Richards, S. C. *The Structure of Prison Release: An Extended Case Study of Prison Release, Work Release, and Parole.* New York: McGraw-Hill.

1997 Berkerian, D., and J. L. Jackson, eds. *Offender Profiling: Theory, Research, and Practice.* New York: John Wiley & Sons.

Clear, T., and G. Cole. *American Corrections.* Belmont, CA: Wadsworth.

Hoffman, P. B. "History of the Federal Parole System: 1910–1972." Pt. 1. *Federal Probation* 61:23–31.

———. "History of the Federal Parole System: 1973–1997." Pt. 2. *Federal Probation* 61:49–57.

Zamble, E., and V. Quinsey. *The Criminal Recidivism Process.* Cambridge: Cambridge University Press.

1998 Cohn, E. G., D. Farrington, and R. Wright. *Evaluating Criminology and Criminal Justice*. Ed. M. Wolfgang. London: Greenwood Press.

Dodge, L. M. "'Her Life Has Been an Improper One': Women, Crime, and Prisons in Illinois, 1835–1933." PhD diss., Department of Sociology, University of Illinois, Chicago.

Holt, N. "The Current State of Parole in America." In *Community Corrections: Probation, Parole, and Intermediate Sanctions*, ed. J. Petersilia. New York: Oxford University Press.

Lynch, M. "Waste Managers? New Penology, Crime Fighting, and the Parole Agent Identity." *Law and Society Review* 32:839–69.

Walker, S. *A History of American Criminal Justice*. New York: Oxford University Press.

1999 Cromwell, P. F., and R. del Carmen. *Community Based Corrections*. Belmont, CA: West/Wadsworth.

Ditton, P., and D. J. Wilson. *Truth in Sentencing in State Prisons*. Washington, DC: U.S. Department of Justice, Bureau of Justice Statistics.

Petersilia, J. "Parole and Prisoner Reentry in the United States." In *Crime and Justice: A Review of Research*. Chicago: University of Chicago Press.

2000 Hood, R., and S. Shute. *The Parole System at Work: A Study of Risk Based Decision-Making*." London: Home Office.

Padfield, N., A. Liebling, and H. Arnold. *An Exploration of Decision-Making at Discretionary Lifer Panels*. London: Home Office.

2002 Dodge, M. L. *Whores and Thieves of the Worst Kind: A Study of Women, Crime, and Prisons, 1835–2000*. DeKalb: Northern Illinois University Press.

Appendix B

To make these proofs as accessible as possible to a general audience, I discuss elasticity in terms of changes in magnitude rather than derivatives. This allows me to present the equations using simple algebra instead of calculus. The logic and results, however would be identical using derivatives and point elasticity. For the most precise model using derivatives, see pages 132–33 above.

Under Conditions of Equal and Constant Elasticity of Offending to Policing

Assuming resource constraint, racial profiling will decrease the profiled crime under conditions of equal and constant elasticity of offending to policing if the minority-motorist offending rate is greater than the white-motorist offending rate. This can be derived from the definition of elasticity.

For purposes of notation, let $r \in \{M, W\}$ denote the race of the motorists, either minority or white. Let Pop_r denote the representation of each racial group in the total population. Let O_r denote the offending rate of each racial group. Let ΔO_r denote the *absolute value* of the change in the offending rate of the racial group from Time 1 (no racial profiling) to Time 2 (racial profiling). Let I_r denote the internal search group rate for each racial group. Let ΔI_r denote the *absolute value* of the change in the internal search rate for each racial group from Time 1 to Time 2. Let S denote the search rate for the total population.

From the definition of elasticity, if minority and white motorists have the same and constant elasticity, then the following is true:

$$\frac{(\Delta O_M/O_M)}{(\Delta I_M/I_M)} = \frac{(\Delta O_W/O_W)}{(\Delta I_W/I_W)} \tag{A1}$$

Given that at Time 1 the police are engaged in color-blind policing, the internal group search rates are going to be the same for both racial groups. In other words, we know that

$$S = I_M = I_W. \tag{A2}$$

We also know that the changes in internal search rates between the different racial groups will offset each other since we are assuming a resource constraint such that there are fixed law enforcement resources. This implies that S is a constant: the total number of searches does not vary, and the police merely distribute their searches between white and minority motorists. Hence the search rate of minority motorists is related to the search rate of white motorists. We can determine the relationship between the change in the internal search rate for each racial group as follows, given that the Time 1 total search rate will be the same as the Time 2 total search rate:

$$Pop_M I_M + Pop_W I_W = Pop_M(I_M + \Delta I_M) + Pop_W(I_W - \Delta I_W). \tag{A3}$$

If we work this through the same way we worked through equation (1) in chapter 4, this implies that

$$\Delta I_M = \frac{Pop_W}{Pop_M} \Delta I_W. \tag{A4}$$

Given that we are assuming a minority-motorist representation of 20 percent, equation (A4) is the same as

$$\Delta I_M = 4\Delta I_W. \tag{A5}$$

Using equations (A2) and (A5), we can substitute values for the denominator in equation (A1). Since we know from equation (A2) that I_M equals I_W and, from equation (A5), that ΔI_M equals four times ΔI_W, then we know that one denominator in equation (A1) is simply one-fourth of the other. Thus, from the definition of elasticity, if minority and white motorists have the same and constant elasticity, then the following is true:

$$(\Delta O_M/O_M) = 4(\Delta O_W/O_W). \tag{A6}$$

We can rewrite equation (A6) as follows:

$$(\Delta O_W/\Delta O_M) = 0.25(O_W/O_M). \tag{A7}$$

We know from equation (3) in chapter 4 that racial profiling decreases crime only if

$$0.25 > \frac{\Delta O_W}{\Delta O_M}.$$ (A8)

If we substitute from equation (A7), this holds true only if

$$0.25 > 0.25 \ \frac{O_W}{O_M}.$$ (A9)

To simplify:

$$O_M > O_W.$$ (A10)

In other words, racial profiling will decrease crime under these conditions only if the offending rate of minority motorists exceeds that of white motorists.

Under Conditions of Lower but Constant Elasticity of Offending to Policing for Minority Motorists

Assuming resource constraint and lower but constant elasticity of offending to policing for minority motorists, racial profiling will decrease the profiled crime only under very specific conditions concerning the relationship between elasticities and offending. We can derive this relationship, again, from the definition of elasticity.

If minority motorists have lower elasticity than white motorists, then the following is true:

$$x \ \frac{(\Delta O_M / O_M)}{(\Delta I_M / I_M)} \ = \ \frac{(\Delta O_W / O_W)}{(\Delta I_W / I_W)} \ , \text{where } x > 1.$$ (A11)

If we let E_r denote the elasticity of offending to policing for each racial group, this is equivalent to saying that

$$x = E_W / E_M.$$ (A12)

Using equations (A2) and (A5), we can substitute values for the denominator in equation (A11). Since we know from equation (A2) that I_M equals I_W and, from equation (A5), that ΔI_M equals four times ΔI_W, then we know that one denominator in equation (A11) is simply one-fourth of the other. Thus, from the definition of elasticity, the following is true:

$$x\,(\Delta O_M / O_M) = 4(\Delta O_W / O_W).\tag{A13}$$

If we work this through, equation (A13) is the same as the following:

$$(\Delta O_W / \Delta O_M) = 0.25x(O_W / O_M).\tag{A14}$$

We know from equation (3) in chapter 4 that racial profiling decreases crime only if

$$0.25 > \frac{\Delta O_W}{\Delta O_M}.\tag{A15}$$

If we substitute from equation (A14), this holds true only if

$$0.25 > 0.25\,x\,\frac{O_W}{O_M}.\tag{A16}$$

To simplify:

$$O_M > xO_W.\tag{A17}$$

In other words, racial profiling will decrease crime under these conditions only if minority motorists' offending exceeds white motorists' offending times their elasticity differential, x, which from equation (A12) we know is E_W / E_M.

Under Conditions of Lower but Constant Elasticity of Offending to Policing for White Motorists

Assuming resource constraint and lower but constant elasticity of offending to policing for white motorists, racial profiling will decrease the profiled crime if minority motorists' offending is higher than white motorists' offending. This can be derived, again, from the definition of elasticity.

If white motorists have lower elasticity, then the following is true:

$$\frac{(\Delta O_M / O_M)}{(\Delta I_M / I_M)} = x\,\frac{(\Delta O_W / O_W)}{(\Delta I_W / I_W)}\text{ , where }x > 1.\tag{A18}$$

Using equations (A2) and (A5), we can substitute values for the denominator in equation (A18). Since we know from equation (A2) that I_M equals I_W and, from equation (A5), that ΔI_M equals four times ΔI_W, we also know that one denominator in equation (A18) is simply one-fourth of the other. Thus, from the definition of elasticity, the following is true:

$$(\Delta O_M / O_M) = 4x(\Delta O_W / O_W). \tag{A19}$$

To simplify:

$$(\Delta O_W / \Delta O_M) = \frac{O_W}{4x O_M} \cdot \tag{A20}$$

We know from equation (3) in the chapter 4 that racial profiling decreases crime only if

$$0.25 > \frac{\Delta O_W}{\Delta O_M}. \tag{A21}$$

If we substitute from equation (A20), this holds true only if

$$0.25 > \frac{O_W}{4x O_M} \cdot \tag{A22}$$

To simplify:

$$O_M > \frac{O_W}{x} \cdot \tag{A23}$$

But since x is greater than 1, this will be true whenever minority motorists' offending exceeds white motorists' offending. In other words, racial profiling will decrease crime under these conditions if minority motorists' offending is greater than white offending.

Notes

Prologue

1. Bruce, Burgess, and Harno 1928, 284.
2. Burgess and Sellin 1951, 12–13.

Chapter One

1. Biggs 2003. *See generally* Moon 2004.
2. *See* Austin and Hardyman 2004.
3. *See* Kansas Senate Bill 123, New Section 1(b)(2) (2003), available at the Web site of the Kansas Legislature, Session of 2003, Senate Bill No. 123, by Special Committee on Judiciary: http://www.kslegislature.org/bills/2004/123.pdf.
4. *See* Moon 2004; Biggs 2003. The cost of treatment over that period has been approximately $14,155 per person.
5. *See generally* Austin et al. 2003.
6. "Washington's Parole System Summarized" on the Web site of the State of Washington Indeterminate Sentence Review Board, available at http://www.srb.wa.gov/summary.html.
7. *See* the Web site of the North Dakota State Government, North Dakota Legislative Council, Minutes of the Corrections Committee, Tuesday, September 3, 2002: http://www.legis.nd.gov/assembly/57-2001/interim-info/minutes/cor090302.html.
8. Michael Stark, Alaska parole board member, telephone interview by Marylynne Hunt-Dorta, June 29, 2004.
9. Vermont parole department, telephone interview by Marylynne Hunt-Dorta, June 30, 2004.
10. *See* Ronald J. Ward, Director, Oklahoma Department of Corrections, "Statutory Termination of Supervision" available at the Web site of the Oklahoma Department of Corrections: http://www.doc.state.ok.us/Offtech/op160111.htm.

11. Association of Paroling Authorities International and the National Institute of Corrections, *Handbook for New Parole Board Members* (April 2003), 35. Available at the Web site of the Association of Paroling Authorities International: http://www.apaintl.org/Handbook.html.

12. This proportion is down from 1 in 78 in the late 1990s. *See* Taylor 2003.

13. Lerner 2000.

14. IRS spokesman Bill Knight, St. Paul, MN, as reported in Lerner 2000.

15. *Federal Tax Course* 1991, 1344–45; Slemrod and Bakija 2000, 157; Russell 2004, 10; Taylor 2003; Ambrose 2001; Lerner 2000; Smith 1999, 137; Schauer 2003.

16. Scherreik 2000 (the IRS used the DIF to select 29 percent of returns audited in 1998); Smith 1999 (estimating about 20 percent of returns audited selected by DIF). The rest of the audits come from tips from state agencies, citizen information, or targeting of certain professions. According to Lerner (2000), "A congressional study in 1999 found that the IRS singled out drywall contractors, car dealers and gamblers in the mid-1990s" (D3).

17. *See* Kern and Farrar-Owens 2004, 165; *see generally* Virginia Criminal Sentencing Commission 2004 (hereafter VA Annual Report 2004).

18. VA Annual Report 2004, 39.

19. *See* Kern and Farrar-Owens 2004; VA Annual Report 2004, 39. For general discussion of these actuarial initiatives, see Monahan 2004; Monahan and Silver 2003; Brian J. Ostrom et al. 2002; John Monahan et al. 2005; John Monahan et al. 2001; Chanenson 2003, 1 (focusing on Virginia's nonviolent risk-assessment methodology); Kuhn 2005, 1507 (discussing Virginia's voluntary system as one which survives Blakely, and its success relative to other states' voluntary systems, in the context of adopting a voluntary guidelines system in Minnesota); Wilhelm and Turner 2002, 41 (using Virginia to consider the effect that budgets have on sentencing policy, and suggesting that Virginia's nonviolent offender risk-assessment program has been implemented, in part, because it is cheaper than incarceration).

20. Ostrom et al. 2002, 1.

21. *See* VA Annual Report 2004, 39.

22. Ibid., 39.

23. Kern and Farrar-Owens 2004; VA Annual Report 2004, 39.

24. VA Annual Report 2004, 39.

25. Ibid.

26. Ibid., 40–41.

27. Correspondence from John Monahan, July 31, 2005. *See also* Monahan 2004.

28. Sexually Violent Predators Act, Virginia Acts, Chapter 989 (2003), codified at Virginia Code Section 37.2-900 through 37.2-919 (effective Oct. 1, 2005); *see generally* Monahan and Walker 2006, 400–401; *Commonwealth v. Allen,* 269 Va. 262, 609 S.E.2d 4 (2005) (discussing VSPA's actuarial aspects); *Shivaee v. Com-*

monwealth, 270 Va. 112, 613 S.E.2d 570 (2005) (upholding SVPA against constitutional challenges); *Kansas v. Hendricks,* 521 U.S. 346 (1997) (upholding Kansas's sexually violent predator statutes).

29. *See* Monahan and Walker 2006, 400.

30. Ibid. For background on this instrument, see Hanson 1997; Hanson and Thornton 2000.

31. *See generally* Barbaree et al. 2000.

32. *See generally* Monahan and Silver 2003, 1–6. The COVR software is designed to be used in the context of making discharge decisions from civil mental health facilities. According to John Monahan, the software can place a person into one of five categories of risk for committing a serious violent act to others over the next several months. The categories represent a 1, 8, 26, 56, or 76 percent likelihood of violence. The software incorporates a total of forty risk factors, but since it uses a "tree" structure, many fewer risk factors may be used in a given case (Monahan and Silver 2003, 3).

33. *See* Monahan 2004; Steiker 1997, 775, 776 n. 5. *See also* Fitch 2003; Fitch and Hammen 2003; Schulhofer 1996; Blacher 1995.

34. Steiker 1997, 776 n. 51; *see generally* Blacher 1995.

35. *Kansas v. Hendricks,* 521 U.S. 346 (1997).

36. Monahan 2004, 21.

37. Fitch and Hammen 2003.

38. Monahan 2004, 21.

39. Harris 2002; Becton 1987, 426, 433–34.

40. Becton 1987, 426.

41. Ibid., 430 n. 72.

42. *See* ibid., 417 n. 2, 417–18.

43. *United States v. Mendenhall,* 446 U.S. 544, 547 n. 1 (1980).

44. *See* Zedlewski 1984.

45. Monahan and Walker 2006, 452–53.

46. *See generally* Zimring, Hawkins, and Kamin 2001; Nourse 2004.

47. Jonathan Simon, forthcoming (draft on file with author, p. 2).

48. By clinical, I am referring to a model of prediction or diagnosis that relies primarily on the subjective judgment of experienced decision makers. *See generally* Meehl 1954, 4; Underwood 1979, 1420; Janus and Prentky 2003, 1453–58. *Clinical* here is opposed to *statistical* or *actuarial,* by which I mean a model of prediction that relies on statistical analysis of large datasets. *See generally* Meehl 1954, 3.

49. Meehl 1954, 3.

50. Underwood 1979, 1420.

51. Tribe 1971b, 1330 n. 2. Tribe's article addressed the use of explicit mathematical tools and models (such as Bayesian statistical evidence) in the trial process and argued that the introduction of such expertise would undermine the values served by the presumption of innocence and the reasonable doubt standard, and

would dehumanize justice. The article formed part of an important debate over the use of mathematical tools in jury trials. *See* Finkelstein and Fairley 1970; Tribe 1971a; Nesson 1979. This debate focused on jury trials, not on criminal justice procedures, such as policing or sentencing, and therefore does not speak directly to the issues in this book. For more recent writings about the role of social science prediction and probabilities in constitutional criminal procedure, see Meares and Harcourt 2000.

52. *See* Foucault 1976; Rothman 1971; Beckett 1997, 10; Cohen 1985; Feeley and Simon 1992, 450–52; Garland 2001; Pratt 1997; Brown and Pratt 2000; Rose 2002; Scheingold 1998, 866–69, 882–86; Wacquant 1998; 2005; Alschuler 2003, 12; Robinson 2001.

53. Baker and Simon 2002, 1.

54. Several scholars have written about the shift from the welfare to the penal state, especially Loïc Wacquant, Jonathan Simon, Nikolas Rose, Alan Hunt, and Katherine Beckett. *See, e.g.,* Beckett 1997; Wacquant 1998; 2005; and the articles collected in the symposium issue titled "De l'État Social à l'État Pénal" in *Actes de la recherche en sciences sociales* 124 (September 1998); Burchell, Gordon, and Miller 1991; Rose and Miller 1992; Hunt and Wickham 1994. For discussion of the separate thesis of the rise of the prison-industrial complex, see, for example, Donziger 1996, 85–87.

In the early 1990s, Malcolm Feeley and Jonathan Simon identified the trend and dubbed it "The New Penology." *See, e.g.,* Feeley and Simon 1992 (suggesting that a new paradigm for the management of dangerous persons has emerged in the late twentieth century, accompanied by a new language of penology); Simon 1993 (exploring this "new penology" through the historical development of parole in California); Scheingold 1998, 866–69 (discussing the role of the "new penology"); Alschuler 2003 (discussing the "new penology" and suggesting that "one can discern this new penology in sentencing guidelines and mandatory minimum sentences that allocate punishment wholesale rather than retail" [12]). Stanley Cohen (1985) described many of its features in his seminal book, *Visions of Social Control*. John Pratt has also studied, identified and written extensively about the trend. *See, e.g.,* Brown and Pratt 2000. More recently, David Garland (2001) refers to it in terms of the new focus on risk and describes many of its related features in his book *Culture of Control*.

To be sure, the actuarial is not the only aspect described in these works, but forms part of the overall texture of our new penal mechanisms. My point here is simply to disclaim any originality in identifying the trend. Many before me—from Foucault to Garland—have done that. I discuss the trend in some of my earlier work, including Harcourt 2003a and 2003c.

55. The leading studies include Knowles, Persico, and Todd 2001; Hernández-Murillo and Knowles 2003; Persico 2002; Dominitz and Knowles 2005; Manski 2005; Borooah 2001.

56. Schauer 2003, ix.

57. Ibid., 197–98.

58. Ibid., ix.

59. David Harris, the most vocal opponent of racial profiling on the highways, for instance, writes about criminal profiling in glowing terms: "In practical terms, there simply aren't enough police officers or resources to keep every person and every place under surveillance . . . so officers welcome any tool to help them identify the most likely lawbreakers. Profiles enable the police to create portraits of criminals using facts instead of gut instinct or wishful thinking. Profiles can systematically pool collective police experience into information that is comprehensive, solid, and accurate—something much better than the selectively remembered war stories of individual officers. Compiling this information into a real picture of criminal activity on the street should offer a better basis for suspicion than simple intuition" (Harris 2002, 16). Harris argues that certain kinds of profiling are dangerous—namely, the informal, "less rigorous and less structured" types of profiling (26)—but not that criminal profiling itself raises any problems. He argues that the danger of informal profiling is that the profiles are most often wrong. "Drawing on only a small, unrepresentative sample of events," Harris explains, "these less formal profiles can easily become dangerously inaccurate" (27). He contrasts these inaccurate, informal profiles based on hunches to formal profiles "based on hard data accumulated methodically over time" (26). The problem, according to Harris, is the increased reliance on the informal and inaccurate profiles. "When informal profiling is the norm, evidence that supports a view other than the prevailing wisdom will not change what an officer thinks, even if, in any fair and objective sense, it strongly contradicts these beliefs. Thus the use of informal profiling presents a stark and real danger" (27–28). This dichotomy between accurate and inaccurate profiles, however, is off the mark. An inaccurate profile is, obviously, useless and dangerous. The question is whether an accurate profile also has consequences. Harris's essay, I argue, has two important and troublesome consequences: first, the use of the profile may in fact increase long-term crime trends. Second, the use of profiles per se creates social distortions. These apply to profiling especially when the profiles *are* reliable.

60. Underwood 1979, 1442.

61. Lerner 2000.

62. U.S. Bureau of Justice Statistics 2001a, table 6.27; 2002, 2.

63. Levitt 2004.

64. *See* Spelman 2000, 123.

65. For present purposes, I am using the hypothetical example in Harcourt 2003c, 121–22.

66. Roberts 1999, 805.

67. Tom Tyler has done the most far-reaching research in this area. *See generally* Tyler's masterful book *Why People Obey the Law* (1990), and his writings on

procedural fairness and institutional legitimacy, including his essay "Trust and Democratic Governance" (1998).

68. *See generally* Harcourt 2001, 166–75.

69. The NAACP Legal Defense Fund, for instance, has done a study in Mississippi looking at the cost of pretrial detention to the community in terms of lost income of the prisoners and loss of ability to support their families.

70. In this sense, I am arguing here against the model of "modified desert" proposed by John Monahan in 1982—the idea that any independent principle of just punishment would be improved by allowing "some role to such crime control devices as predictions of recidivism"; *see* Monahan 1982, 103. The concept of randomization neutralizes precisely the modification to the principles of just desert that Monahan advocates in that piece.

Part One Introduction

1. *See* Warner 1923.

2. Hart 1923.

3. Ibid., 411.

4. Ibid.

5. In discussing his first parole-prediction study, Burgess noted, "Although Professor Sam Warner had made a similar attempt with negative results, a review of his work by Professor Hornell Hart indicated possibilities of success in a new venture" (Burgess 1928, 534).

6. Reiss 1949.

7. Ohlin 1951.

8. Glaser 1954.

9. Vold 1931.

10. Van Vechten 1935.

11. Laune 1936, dedication page.

12. Klein 1935.

13. Lunday 1949.

14. Saleilles 1898.

15. Ibid., 12–13.

16. *See generally* Garland 1985.

17. Ibid., 14; emphasis in original.

18. The ideology of punishment was closely connected to that of the liberal political state, which ideally does not intervene to cure or rehabilitate, but performs the minimal state task of meting out punishment for violations of a social compact. *See generally* Garland 1985, 18.

19. *See* Garland 1995.

20. Garland 1985, 24; emphasis in original.

21. Ibid., 28; emphasis in original.

22. Wigmore 1911; *see generally* Green 1995, 1949–64.

23. Wigmore 1911, vii.

24. *See* Pound 1911, xv–xvii; emphasis in original.

25. Hacking 1990, 1–8.

26. Rose 2002, 214.

27. Ibid.

28. Naturally, the probabilistic turn did not uniformly aim for individual control. The cultural context matters, and as historian of science Deborah Coen demonstrates in her research on nineteenth-century imperial Austria, the probabilistic turn there promoted liberalism and tolerance, as opposed to the control sought by the Catholic Church. *See* Coen 2004.

29. Hacking 1990, 1.

30. Ibid., 105.

31. Pearson 1919, ix, xii–xiii; emphasis in original.

32. Quoted in Hacking 1990, 41 (this, she concluded, demonstrates that "events which depend on a multitude of diverse combinations have a periodic recurrence, a fixed proportion, when the observations result from a large number of chances" [ibid.]). *See generally* Deguise 1981.

33. Hacking 1990, 160–69. As Jack Katz (1988, 43) similarly has suggested, these categories took hold as products of historical and political-institutional forces; rarely, if ever, did they arise from causal social theory.

34. Wigmore 1911, vii.

35. *See* Tonry 1996.

Chapter Two

1. Vold 1931, 103.

2. Bruce, Burgess, and Harno 1928, 271.

3. Abbott and Sparrow 2005, 6. For excellent discussion of the Chicago School, see Abbott 1997 and 1999.

4. Warner 1923.

5. *See* Pinter and Reamer 1918 (study of twenty-six delinquent girls linking success to coefficient of mental ability); Clark 1921 (study of 301 paroled delinquent boys linking success to intelligence); Heacox 1917 (study of 143 paroled delinquent boys for correlations with race, age, prior criminal record, home conditions, length of stay in reformatory, and mental intelligence). These studies are discussed and reviewed in Vold 1931, 10–12.

6. The process was not exactly randomized. Warner started with prisoners whose name started with a *J* and examined every folder thereafter until he got to his 680 total count. *See* Warner 1923, 176 n. 3.

7. Ibid., 187.

8. These are the sixty-six factors that Warner examined: (1) character of father, (2) character of mother, (3) marital relations of parents, (4) education of father, (5) education of mother, (6) financial circumstances of parents, (7) religion of parents, (8) religion of prisoner, (9) life with parents, (10) heredity, (11) color, (12) citizen, (13) nativity of parents, (14) residence of parents, (15) number of states in which resided, (16) education of prisoner, (17) alcohol, (18) tobacco, (19) drugs, (20) gambling, (21) sexual indulgence, (22) age at time of crime, (23) marital condition, (24) lived with parent, wife, etc., (25) character of home, (26) corresponds with relatives, (27) character of associates, (28) sweetheart's character, (29) church attendance, (30) extent of occupation, (31) financial circumstances, (32) life insurance, (33) contributes to the support of others, (34) the crime, (35) sentence, (36) plea and admission of guilt, (37) means of commission, (38) association in commission, (39) loss occasioned by acquisitive crimes, (40) amount recovered, (41) restitution mode, (42) intention as to restitution, (43) crimes committed without being arrested, (44) criminal record, (45) criminal record (vis-à-vis both the above), (46) physique, (47) mental condition, (48) evidence of disease, (49) serious illness, (50) surgical operations, (51) heredity, (52) number of cases in which no report of any sort appears, (53) report, (54) intramural descriptive designations, (55) alienist diagnosis, (56) conduct in reformatory, (57) disposition in reformatory, (58) willing to work in reformatory, (59) ability to earn living on outside, (60) conduct in school of reformatory, (61) work in reformatory school, (62) number of times guilty of misconduct, (63) number of persons guilty of various offenses at the reformatory, (64) number of persons losing marks in the reformatory, (65) actual time served to first parole, (66) time served to first parole by prisoners having five-year sentences.

9. Warner 1923, 199, table 3.15.

10. Ibid., 191.

11. Ibid., 196.

12. Hart 1923, 411.

13. Glueck and Glueck 1939, 280 n. 2.

14. Argow 1935, 562-63.

15. Hart 1923, 405.

16. Ibid., 409-10. Hart's list of thirty factors, with Warner's table number, is as follows: (1) men guilty of "other crimes" (38); (2) partly support unnamed persons (37); (3) guilty of assault and battery (38); (4) occupation "none" (34); (5) no criminal record (49); (6) accidental offenders (58); (7) religion "other" (12); (8) extent of occupation "regular" (34); (9) "responsible" and "normal" offenders (58); (10) used fraud to commit crime (41); (11) using cigarettes (22); (12) character of associates "bad" (31); (13) guilty of larceny (38); (14) men with three or more criminal records (49); (15) claim to be contributing to parents (37); (16) guilty of misconduct six or more times in reformatory (66); (17) served one or more jail

sentences (48); (18) claim parents own property (10); (19) guilty of breaking and entering (38); (20) claim to attend church regularly (33); (21) evidence of disease not answered (52); (22) men with reformatory records (49); (23) marital relations of parents "fair," "unpleasant," or "questionable" (7); (24) serious illness not answered (53); (25) surgery not answered (54); (26) uses drugs (23); (27) character of home "bad" (29); (28) mother drank (6); (29) father served jail sentence (14); (30) mother arrested or jailed (14).

17. Hart 1923, 411.

18. Witmer 1927, 398–403. The characteristics included the following: (1) age, (2) marital condition, (3) use of alcohol, (4) previous record, (5) previous occupation, (6) offense causing commitment, (7) length of sentence, (8) time spent in reformatory before parole, (9) marks received in the reformatory, (10) grades in the reformatory school, (11) superintendent's recommendations as to parole, (12) place of residence before commitment, (13) type of community to which they were paroled, (14) occupation on parole, (15) amount of monthly earnings.

19. Borden 1928.

20. Ibid., 331.

21. "Letter of Transmission," in Bruce, Burgess, and Harno 1928, 5.

22. Bruce, Burgess, and Harno 1928.

23. Ibid., 42–43, 50, 51; See also Morse 1939, vol. 4 (tracing the history of parole in Illinois from its inception in 1891 to 1939). The Attorney General's survey consists of four volumes, the last of which covers parole procedures; all subsequent references are to vol. 4, hereafter referred to as the *Attorney General's Survey*.

24. Bruce, Burgess, and Harno 1928, 63.

25. Ibid., 53, 57; see also Morse 1939, 310 n. 3.

26. *See* Morse 1939, 311.

27. Bruce, Burgess, and Harno 1928, 57, 84.

28. Laune 1936, 2.

29. Ibid., 85.

30. Ibid., 84.

31. Ibid., 87.

32. Simon 1993.

33. Ibid., 48–49.

34. Ibid., 53.

35. Rothman 1980.

36. Bruce, Burgess, and Harno 1928, 58–59, 90–91.

37. Ibid., 90.

38. Ibid., 93.

39. Ibid., 91 n. 2.

40. Ibid., 94.

41. Ibid., 273.

42. Ibid., 98 n. 1, 99, 100–101.

43. The study took one thousand cases of paroled convicts from each of the three main adult male penal institutions (Illinois State Penitentiary at Joliet, Illinois Southern Penitentiary at Menard, and Illinois State Reformatory at Pontiac). The cases taken were "all consecutive, beginning with December 31, 1924 and going backward until 1,000 had been examined from each institution." According to the report, "Therefore, each man had been released on parole from the institution at least two and one-half years, and, in certain instances, four, five, and even six years at the time the inquiry was made" (Bruce, Burgess, and Harno 1928, 6).

44. The full list of twenty-two factors follows: "(1) nature of offense; (2) number of associates in committing offense for which convicted; (3) nationality of the inmate's father; (4) parental status, including broken homes; (5) marital status of the inmate; (6) type of criminal, as first offender, occasional offender, habitual offender, professional criminal; (7) social type, as ne'er-do-well, gangster, hobo; (8) county from which committed; (9) size of community; (10) type of neighborhood; (11) resident or transient in community when arrested; (12) statement of trial judge and prosecuting attorney with reference to recommendation for or against leniency; (13) whether or not commitment was upon acceptance of lesser plea; (14) nature and length of sentence imposed; (15) months of sentence actually served before parole; (16) previous criminal record of the prisoner; (17) his previous work record; (18) his punishment record in the institution; (19) his age at time of parole; (20) his mental age according to psychiatric examination; (21) his personality type according to psychiatric examination; (22) and psychiatric prognosis" (Bruce, Burgess, and Harno 1928, 257–58).

45. Ibid., 259.

46. Ibid.

47. Bruce, Burgess, and Harno 1928, 271.

48. Ibid., 283.

49. Ibid., 284.

50. Ibid., 305.

51. Laune 1936, 5. *See also* Burgess and Sellin 1951, 11.

52. *See* Tibbitts 1931.

53. Laune 1936, 5.

54. Ibid., 5.

55. Laune 1936.

56. Ibid., title page.

57. Ibid., 5.

58. As Van Vechten would write in his dissertation in 1935, "Burgess's methodology is still the fundamental one in the field; it is also the basis for the work of the Illinois sociologist-actuaries, the only official workers in the field to date" (Van Vechten 1935, 20).

59. Morse 1939, 312.

60. Ibid., 312–13.

61. Ibid., 316.

62. *See* Hoffman and Beck 1974, 197 (describing the federal parole-prediction method and explaining that "the 'Burgess' method was chosen because of its simplicity and ease of calculation in 'field' usage"); *see* Simon 1993, 172 n. 3.

63. *See* Reiss 1951, 561.

64. Ohlin 1951.

65. *See* Simon 1993, 173. One of the four factors was prior commitments; another was race; and the other two were offense type and number of escapes.

66. Glueck and Glueck 1939.

67. For a fascinating discussion and analysis of the lives and work of Sheldon and Eleanor Glueck, with a special focus on their complex interdisciplinary contexts, see Laub and Sampson 1991.

68. Ibid., 1405.

69. In his differential association theory, Sutherland posited that youth become delinquent when they are socialized into an "excess" of values that legitimate the commission of crime and deviance. He and scores of scholars subsequently applied this theory to all forms of criminality, including white-collar crime. *See* Sutherland and Cressey 1978. Sutherland was extremely critical of the Gluecks' work because of their emphasis on the individual, rather than the social. As Laub and Sampson recount, "Sutherland saw the multiple-factor approach, with its inclusion of such individual-level factors as age and mental capacity, as a threat to a substantive version of sociological positivism. . . . [C]rime was viewed by Sutherland as a social phenomenon that could *only* be explained by social (i.e., nonindividual) factors" (Laub and Sampson 1991, 1420).

70. Burgess 1925.

71. Laub and Sampson 1991, 1403.

72. *See generally* ibid., 1408–10.

73. Glueck and Glueck 1939. The seven factors follow: (1) industrial habits, (2) seriousness and frequency of prereformatory crime, (3) arrests for crimes preceding, (4) penal experience preceding, (5) economic responsibility preceding, (6) mental abnormality on entrance, (7) frequency of offences in the reformatory.

74. Ibid., 281 n. 3.

75. Ibid., 280.

76. *See, e.g.,* Monachesi 1945; Hakeem 1948; Reiss 1951; Glaser 1955.

77. Tibbitts 1931. The additional factors include "the use of alcohol, the community to which the individual was to be returned, the last work assignment in the institution, and the first job on parole" (11).

78. Here are the twenty-three factors: (1) nature of the offense, (2) number of associates, (3) nature and length of sentence, (4) length of time served, (5) part of lesser plea, (6) statement of trial judge, (7) previous criminal record, (8) punishment record in the institution, (9) previous work record, (10) employed at time crime committed, (11) type of criminal, (12) age at time of parole, (13) nationality

of his father, (14) social type, (15) size of residential area, (16) resident or transient, (17) type of neighborhood, (18) type of neighborhood into which paroled, (19) first job on parole, (20) last work assignment in the institution, (21) mental age, (22) personality type, (23) psychiatric prognosis.

79. Tibbitts 1931, 40.

80. Ibid., 43.

81. Vold 1931.

82. Ibid., 16.

83. Ibid., 17.

84. Ibid., 18.

85. Ibid., 55.

86. The forty-four factors that Vold tested follow: (1) county received from, (2) prior criminal record, (3) number of associates in offense for which convicted, (4) length of maximum sentence imposed, (5) plea entered, (6) nature of the offense, (7) statement of trial judge, (8) statement of county attorney, (9) size and type of community in which offense was committed, (10) inmate's marital status, (11) number of children, (12) number of siblings, (13) home condition, (14) education of inmate, (15) mobility before conviction, (16) state or county where born, (17) occupation at conviction, (18) Minn. Inst. of Child Welfare class. of occupation at conviction, (19) previous work habits, (20) social type, (21) size and type of community in which brought up, (22) age at conviction, (23) mental age, (24) IQ, (25) height, (26) weight, (27) character traits (work), (28) character traits (honesty), (29) habits: use of liquor, (30) habits: use of drugs, (31) sex habits, (32) prison official's estimate of inmate's mentality, (33) prison official's estimate of prison conduct: deportment, (34) punishment record in institution, (35) months in prison before paroled, (36) whether aid was given dependents while man was in the institution, (37) size and type of community into which paroled, (38) where living on parole in relation to where brought up, (39) where living on parole in relation to where offense was committed, (40) inter-relation of place where brought up, where offense was committed and where placed on parole in terms of communities or neighborhoods, (41) work record on parole, (42) wage received on parole, (43) number of visits to parolee by state parole agent, (44) at which hearing before the board of parole the parole was granted.

87. Vold 1931, 55.

88. Ibid., 84.

89. Ibid., 95.

90. Monachesi 1932.

91. Ibid., vii: "In recent years some studies predicting outcome of parole have been made which are indicative of the methods and techniques that can be used in the field of probation (Burgess in Illinois, the Gluecks in Massachusetts, and Vold in Minnesota). In general, the methods and techniques suggested by these studies have been employed in the present study."

92. The fifty-four categories for the juvenile pre-probation delinquents follow: (1) nativity, (2) sex, (3) size of place in which reared, (4) age at conviction, (5) nativity of parents, (6) economic status of the family, (7) type of home in which reared, (8) marital status of the family prior to probation, (9) age at time of leaving home, (10) causes for leaving home, (11) home difficulties and with whom, (12) age at time of death of father or mother, (13) age at time of divorce or separation of parents, (14) number of other children in the family, (15) rank of probationer in reference to the other children, (16) occupation of father, (17) whether mother was gainfully employed outside of home, (18) religion of mother, (19) religion of father, (20) criminal record of mother, (21) criminal record of father, (22) education, (23) school record, (24) religion, (25) church attendance prior to probation, (26) type of neighbourhood in which reared, (27) type of employment engaged in prior to probation, (28) previous work history, (29) earnings prior to probation, (30) with whom living prior to probation, (31) mobility prior to probation, (32) contact with parents or relatives prior to probation, (33) type of neighbor hood lived in immediately prior to probation, (34) character trait ambition, (35) character trait honesty, (36) habit trait liquor, (37) habit trait masturbation, (38) habit trait sex morality, (39) habit trait drugs, (40) habit trait tobacco, (41) associates prior to probation, (42) use of leisure time prior to probation, (43) social type, (44) previous delinquent record, (45) previous probation record, (46) previous institutional record, (47) nature of offense for which convicted, (48) circumstances leading to committing of offense, (49) number of associates in offense for which convicted, (50) to whom supervision was given, (51) length of probation imposed, (52) number of delinquent notices sent to probationer, (53) number of home visits made, (54) subsequent criminal record.

93. Monachesi 1932, 110.

94. Ibid., 60.

95. Van Vechten 1935. With regard to Sutherland, Van Vechten writes, "I wish especially to express my appreciation for the inspiration and guidance of Dr. Edwin H. Sutherland, teacher, co-worker, critic, and guide, during three years of graduate work and two of professional experience" (ii–iii).

96. Ibid., 3.

97. Ibid.

98. Ibid., 131.

99. Laune 936.

100. The fifty-four factors follow: (1) intelligence, (2) absence of stupidity, (3) timidity, (4) absence of foolhardiness, (5) strength of character, (6) absence of weakness of character, (7) pleasing personality, (8) phlegmaticness, (9) absence of emotional instability, (10) shrewdness, (11) critical qualities, (12) absence of a lack of discrimination, (13) selfishness, (14) absence of altruism, (15) lack of conceit, (16) absence of argumentativeness, (17) absence of love of comfort, (18) religiosity, (19) long view of the future, (20) absence of short view of the future, (21) absence

of a tendency to be an agitator, (22) learned lesson, (23) absence of failure to learn lesson, (24) absence of sharp practices, (25) absence of positive Wasserman reaction, (26) absence of physical defects, (27) industry, (28) absence of laziness, (29) previous work record, (30) trade, (31) working ability, (32) absence of lack of working ability, (33) absence of inordinate desire for clothes, (34) absence of sex craving, (35) absence of desire for white lights, (36) absence of wanderlust, (37) absence of broken family, (38) absence of lack of love for relatives, (39) family ties, (40) rural type, (41) happily married, (42) good outside environment, (43) absence of bad outside environment, (44) absence of criminality in family, (45) absence of previous hoodlum activities, (46) absence of recidivism, (47) absence of good job in prison, (48) absence of gangster status, (49) absence of minor racketeering, (50) favorable age relation, (51) absence of unfavorable age relation, (52) break in criminal record, (53) long time to serve on maximum, (54) absence of short time to serve.

101. Laune created a questionnaire with 1,701 questions grouped by factors. He sought a norm from a fifty-seven-member "truth group." He then administered the questionnaire to groups of fifty-seven inmates (Random Groups A, B, C, and D). Then with the information from all the groups, Laune created a short questionnaire based on thirty-six factors with 161 questions that he thought could be used to create an experience table.

102. *See* Ohlin and Lawrence 1952 (finding that the inmate questionnaires were no more predictive than the Burgess method).

103. The 1939 study was intended to examine the practices of the Federal Parole Board in selecting people for parole. The study reviewed the folders of more than ninety thousand federal inmates and explored the following eighty-two predictive factors: (1) race of father, (2) descent of father, (3) citizenship of father, (4) religion of father, (5) occupation of father, (6) economic status of parents, (7) size of community in which family resided during inmate's adolescence, (8) size of parental family, siblings, (9) size of parental family other than siblings, (10) congeniality of parents, (11) rearing, (12) family history, (13) delinquency and criminality in family, (14) mental and nervous diseases in family, (15) birth rank, (16) birth date, (17) nativity by age at last entry into the united states, (18) citizenship, (19) birthplace, (20) size of community of last permanent residence, (21) mobility, (22) marital status, (23) age at leaving school, (24) age at first marriage, (25) congeniality of marriage, (26) congeniality with parents, (27) number of children, (28) number of dependents, (29) economic status, (30) education, (31) intelligence, (32) habits, (33) age on leaving parents/chief reason for leaving, (34) occupation, (35) occupational stability, (36) periods unemployed, (37) unemployment: preoffense, (38) average earnings: last job, (39) psychiatric classification, (40) general health, (41) venereal disease, (42) charge on first arrest, (43) age at time of first arrest, (44) total arrests, (45) disposition: first arrest, (46) total number of arrests without conviction, (47) total number sentences to penal and correctional institutions, (48) total

time spent in penal and correctional institutions prior to eighteenth birthday, (49) total time spent after eighteenth birthday, (50) escapes, (51) nature of instant offenses, (52) number of associates participating in instant crime, (53) inmate's relationship to associates, (54) inmate's reason for committing instant crime/attitude at time of arrest, (55) residence as compared with place where instant crime was committed, (56) number of aliases, (57) plea entered, (58) number and disposition of previous paroles, (59) age on admission to institution, (60) length of sentence, (61) amount of fine imposed, (62) time served in institution for instant crime, (63) institutional offenses, (64) occupation in institution, (65) number of occupational changes, (66) occupational adjustment, (67) work habits, (68) longest institutional occupation as compared with usual occupation, (69) self-advancement, (70) recommendations for parole, (71) age at time of release, (72) interval from date of eligibility for parole to date of release, (73) length of period between release and expiration of sentence, (74) residence on release as compared to residence prior to incarceration, (75) size of community into which inmate was released, (76) family at time of release, (77) relation to family at time of release, (78) family on release as compared to family prior to incarceration, (79) occupation longest followed on release, (80) occupation on release as compared with institutional occupation, (81) degree of unemployment, (82) advisor.

104. Morse 1939, 541.

105. Jenkins 1942, 40. Jenkins was concerned by the omission of elements that got at personality patterns in traditional predictive studies. He studied the case records of 300 boys at a New York reformatory and from those ended up with a sample of 85 successful cases and 107 failures. He checked their outcomes against the following seventy-four factors, which were weighted from −4 to +4. (Jenkins claimed to have used ninety-five factors; but if we use mutual exclusivity as the criterion for determining whether something is a factor, he actually used seventy-four factors. In the following list, I collapsed the following: age at first court appearance, age on admission, offense for which committed, home, condition of home, economic status, neighborhood, attitude toward school, and educational quotient.)

Here are the seventy-four factors: (1) apathy, (2) assaultive tendencies, (3) awkwardness, (4) bullying, (5) carelessness, (6) cruelty, (7) daydreaming, (8) defiance of authority, (9) disobedience, (10) drug addiction, (11) emotional immaturity, (12) enuresis, (13) homicidal tendencies, (14) impudence, (15) jealousy, (16) lying, (17) obscenity, (18) over activity, (19) over aggressiveness, (20) quarrelsomeness, (21) revengefulness, (22) repeated running away from home, (23) active homosexuality, (24) shamelessness, (25) stealing, (26) aggressive stealing, (27) cooperative stealing, (28) furtive stealing, (29) compulsive stealing, (30) submissiveness, (31) suspiciousness, (32) truancy, (33) age at first court appearance for delinquency, (34) age on admission, (35) past experience in institution for delinquents, (36) past experience in institution for dependants, (37) past experience in institution for defectives, (38) previously in New York house of refuge, (39) offense for which committed, (40) offense committed in company of associates, (41) offense committed as part of a gang, (42) whereabouts of child, (43) condition of home, (44) economic status, (45) alcoholism of parents or substitutes, (46) brutality of parents or substitutes, (47) conflict of parents or substitutes, (48) death or deprivation of parents or substitutes, (49) desertion by parents or substitutes, (50) excessive discipline by parents or substitutes, (51) early marriage (before 23) of parents or substitutes, (52) forced marriage of parents or substitutes, (53) illiteracy of parents or substitutes, (54) neglect by parents or substitutes, (55) rejection by parents or substitutes, (56) sex immorality of parents or substitutes, (57) shielding by parents or substitutes, (58) syphilis of parents or substitutes, (59) illegitimate child, (60) unwanted child, (61) step child, (62) foster child, (63) less favored child, (64) conflict with siblings, (65) illegitimacy of siblings, (66) jealousy toward siblings, (67) neighborhood, (68) past attendance of truant school, (69) past attendance of probationary school, (70) ungraded class, (71) retardation, (72) frequent change of school, (73) attitude toward school, (74) educational quotient.

106. Hakeem (1948) studied 1,108 men paroled from a state prison (probably in Ohio) over a two-year period, six years after they were paroled. He produced unweighted prediction scores based on twenty-seven characteristics that he had developed after studying 9,729 inmates paroled from the same system. He used the Burgess method, including many of the Burgess factors. He concluded that his predictions were remarkably close to the actual outcomes; however, he did not use tests of statistical significance or tests of association. His factors follow: (1) nature of offense, (2) number of associates in the records, (3) nationality of father, (4) parental status, (5) marital status, (6) type of criminal, (7) social type, (8) size of community when arrested, (9) type of neighborhood, (10) resident or transient when arrested, (11) nature and length of sentence, (12) months of sentence actually served, (13) previous criminal record, (14) previous work record, (15) punishment record in the inst., (16) age at time of parole, (17) mental age, (18) personality type, (19) psychiatric prognosis, (20) extent of contact with relatives or friends, (21) whether the subject was employed when he committed the crime, (22) job assignment held in prison, (23) indulgence in drink, (24) presence or absence of history of venereal infection, (25) size of community to which the subject plans to go after release, (26) type of neighborhood to which he will go, (27) type of job he will have upon release.

107. Kirby (1954) used the case files for the U.S. District Court for the Western District of Washington. He chose 455 cases of men who had been released on parole between 1944 and 1949, gathering information on nineteen factors. There were thirty-three variables altogether since each variable basically had to have a binary response. Offense, race, and marital status therefore were divided into a series of variables. Criminal record and work record were also coded as two variables. Kirby prepared an experience table and applied various prediction methods. He concluded that the discriminant-function method was the best method

both for selecting predictor variables and for weighting them for best prediction. Here are his thirty-three factors: (1) offense—selective service, (2) offense—auto transportation, (3) offense—narcotics, (4) offense—forgery, (5) offense—larceny, post office, (6) offense—white slavery, (7) offense—other offenses, (8) race—white, (9) race—negro, (10) race—American Indian, (11) race—oriental, (12) marital status—married, (13) marital status—divorced or separated, (14) marital status—deserted, (15) marital status—widowed, (16) marital status—single, (17) age at first arrest, (18) length of sentence, (19) number of accomplices, (20) criminal record, (21) time previously served, (22) behavior in prison, (23) employment record, (24) work when arrested, (25) age at time of release, (26) veteran status, (27) quality of parental home, (28) interest of family in inmate, (29) personality abnormality, (30) education, (31) intelligence, (32) rating of neighborhood to which parolee moved, (33) type of supervision.

108. Ohlin 1951.

109. *See* ibid., 51–53. The twelve factors follow: (1) type of offense, (2) sentence, (3) type of offender, (4) home status, (5) family interest, (6) social type, (7) work record, (8) community, (9) parole job, (10) number of associates, (11) personality rating, (12) psychiatric prognosis.

110. Burgess and Sellin 1951, 12.

111. Ohlin 1951, 87–88.

112. *See* Reiss 1951, 552–53.

113. Guttman 1941 (discussed in Glaser 1954, 37).

114. Gillin 1950.

115. Glaser 1954, ii. *See also* Glaser 1955, 285; Evjen 1970, 617.

116. Glaser 1954, 262.

117. Ibid., 261–62.

118. The seven factors follow: (1) age at first leaving home for six months or more, (2) social development pattern, (3) work record, (4) most serious previous sentence, (5) total criminal record, (6) schooling completed, (7) use of prison time.

119. Argow 1935, 561–71. Argow reviewed the records for 563 inmates in Connecticut jails. He compared the percentage of known first offenders for each factor with the percentage of known recidivists for each factor. He calculated the ratio of the two and translated it to a scale of 10 (scores above 10 were favorable for non-rearrest; scores below 10 were not). Argow scored each case history and rendered the score as an average. He computed the mean score and then the quotient (by dividing the individual's score by the mean for the group) to produce what he called the Criminal Liability Index (CLI). Argow intended to use a group of fifty from the YMCA as a control group. He made up cards and intended to use the CLI in his work as a welfare worker in the New Haven County jail, although it was never officially adopted. His thirty-seven factors follow: (1) age, (2) place of crime, (3) place of longest residence, (4) age at first arrest, (5) times arrested, (6) time spent in penal institution, (7) criminality in parental family, (8) education,

(9) age on leaving school, (10) truancy, (11) school report, (12) broken home, (13) mother working, (14) reared in institution, (15) parents getting charity, (16) parents own home, (17) with whom subject lived, (18) marital status, (19) subject getting charity, (20) subject owns home, (21) with whom subject lives, (22) occupation of subject, (23) parents' contribution to family income, (24) subjects' contribution to family income, (25) employment prior to 1930, (26) unemployment prior to arrest, (27) personality state, (28) alcoholism, (29) drug addiction, (30) institutional record, (31) industrial record, (32) order in fraternity, (33) race, (34) church attendance, (35) subject's associates, (36) parental economic status, (37) size of parental family.

120. Redden (1942) looked at the records of the United States Fidelity and Guaranty Company for the years 1926–1932. She took every twenty-first file, and her sample included 2,454 embezzlers and 7,756 non-embezzlers. She compared the two groups on twenty-two factors. Twenty of the factors had contingency coefficients that were considered significant. No single factor was of marked significance, but she found it useful to combine the information from several categories into prognostic scores. The twenty-two factors she explored follow: (1) amount of bond, (2) occupation, (3) employer's business, (4) city (not significant), (5) age, (6) sex, (7) marital status, (8) color, (9) nativity, (10) parents living (not significant), (11) parents' residence, (12) dependents, (13) salary basis, (14) monthly salary from bonded positions, (15) source of other income, (16) monthly other income, (17) value of property, (18) debts, (19) bankrupt, (20) declined a bond, (21) number of times bonded previously, (22) length of time in first previous job and length of time in second previous job.

121. Weeks (1943) was interested in predicting juvenile delinquency. He filled out schedules for the 420 males who appeared before the Spokane Juvenile Court in 1937 and those of a comparable group of nondelinquents randomly chosen from the public schools of Spokane. Weeks had put together a questionnaire that he submitted to the public schools, receiving 5,811 responses (93 percent of the student body). He narrowed these down to 2,105 cases, and from these he obtained his control group. Weeks found fourteen factors that separated the delinquents from the nondelinquents. He tried weighted scoring and two versions of unweighted scoring. The first method (weighted scoring) assigned scores for things that were either positively or negatively associated with delinquency. The second method (unweighted scoring) assigned scores only for things positively associated with delinquency. The fourteen factors follow: (1) school advancement or retardation, (2) length of time in country, (3) home ownership, (4) education of mother, (5) education of father, (6) occupation of father, (7) home situation in which child is now living, (8) marital relations of parents, (9) size of family, (10) nativity of mother, (11) religion of mother, (12) nativity of father, (13) rank of sibling, (14) employment.

122. See, e.g., Van Vechten 1935, 22 (discussing the "Burgess 'unweighted, many factors' method" versus the "Glueck 'weighted, few factors' method").

123. Morse 1939, 154.

124. Mannheim and Wilkins 1955, 27 n. 76.

125. *See* Evjen 1970, 616–17.

126. Morse 1939, 539–41.

127. Ibid., 625, 650–59.

128. Ibid., 653–54.

129. *See* Underwood 1979, 1422 n. 38; *see also* Hoffman and Beck 1974, 197–200 (describing nine factors used since November 1, 1973, when it replaced the earlier version).

130. Hoffman and Beck 1974, 196–97.

131. For instance, the researchers eliminated the factor "prior arrests not leading to conviction" even though it was a strong predictor because it would "pose ethical problems," and they eliminated others if they overlapped too much with other predictors. *See* Hoffman and Beck 1974, 197.

132. Ibid., 197–99.

133. Ibid., 200.

134. Ibid.

135. Ibid., 202.

136. *See* Simon 1993, 173.

137. Brown 1978. Brown looked at the records obtained from the National Council on Crime and Delinquency of thirteen thousand inmates from across the country over a two-year period. He split the group in two to test the model and then to validate it. He concluded that multivariate results were superior and used multiple discriminant analysis. The ten factors he used follow: (1) incarceration length, (2) age upon release, (3) sex, (4) admission type, (5) offense type, (6) sentence type, (7) number of prior prison commitments, (8) number of prior non-prison sentences, (9) drug use, (10) alcohol use.

Chapter Three

1. As noted earlier, the Attorney General's 1939 survey revealed that Illinois alone was using a prediction tool (*see* Morse 1939). The survey of the parole boards of the fifty states conducted in August 1961 revealed that two states (Illinois and Ohio) were using predictive models, two states (California and Colorado) were developing prediction statistics, and one other state (Minnesota) had experimented with but was no longer using prediction (*see* Evjen 1970, 616–17). A survey of paroling authorities conducted in 1994 revealed that twenty-six jurisdictions were using actuarial methods. *See* Runda, Rhine, and Wetter 1994. The authors of the 1994 survey report that

> [s]ince the 1970s various risk-assessment instruments have been developed and adopted by various criminal justice and parole decision makers to help them more accurately determine the likelihood of offender recidivism.

As shown in Figure 26, there is an even split between boards that use risk instruments (twenty-six jurisdictions) and those that do not rely on such instruments (twenty-six jurisdictions) to guide their decision-making process. With respect to the former, the results of a formal risk assessment do not mandate a particular decision. They only place an inmate in a particular grouping with a known risk of reoffending. In these jurisdictions, parole boards retain the ultimate authority to deny parole, if there are grounds to override the instrument-based recommendation. (9)

2. The following lists the states *with* parole that use an actuarial method and the date of adoption: (1) Georgia, Parole Decision Guidelines, 1979; (2) Iowa, Iowa Parole Board Risk Assessment, 1981; (3) Tennessee, Parole Grant Prediction Scale and Guidelines, 1982; (4) Alabama, Alabama Risk Assessment Tool, 1985; (5) South Carolina, Parole Risk Assessment, 1985; (6) North Dakota, Level of Services Inventory-Revised (LSI-R), 1990; (7) Missouri, Salient Factor Score, 1991; (8) Michigan, Parole Guidelines, 1992; (9) Colorado, Colorado Actuarial Risk Assessment Scale, 1993; (10) Arkansas, Post-Prison Board Transfer Risk Assessment, 1994; (11) Nevada, Guidelines and Recommended Months to Serve, 1994; (12) Maryland, Uniform Assessment Policy and Uniform Sexual Offense Policy, 1997; (13) New Jersey, LSI-R, 1998; (14) Ohio, Parole Board Guidelines, 1998; (15) Connecticut, Salient Factor Score, 1999; (16) Vermont, LSI-R, 2000; (17) Idaho, LSI-R, 2001; (18) Montana, the Risk Assessment, 2001; (19) Pennsylvania, LSI-R, 2001; (20) Texas, Risk Assessment Instrument, 2001; (21) Utah, LSI-R, 2001; (22) Alaska, Risk Factor, 2002; (23) Kentucky, Kentucky Parole Guidelines Risk Assessment Instrument, 2003.

3. *See* Raynor et al. 2001, 2.

4. *See generally* Austin et al. 2003; "Risk Assessment Instruments," in "Washington's Parole System Summarized" on the Web site of the State of Washington Indeterminate Sentence Review Board, available at http://www.srb.wa.gov/summary.html.

5. Jane Parnell in Washington state, telephone interview by Marylynne Hunt-Dorta, June 30, 2004.

6. John Austin in Washington state, telephone interview by Marylynne Hunt-Dorta, June 29, 2004.

7. *See* Walsh and Walsh 2005, 6–15.

8. Further screening is done on certain people with specific issues (sex offenders, domestic violence, drug issues) to filter them into rehabilitative programs. *See generally* http://www.doc.state.vt.us/policy/371.07-%20Directive-%20Assessments.pdf. A breakdown of the different classifications and what LSI-R scores are associated with different security levels is available on the Vermont Web site: http://www.doc.state.vt.us/custsupr.htm.

9. *See generally* http://www.doc.state.ok.us/Offtech/op160103.htm.

10. Jimmy Wallace, Alaska parole supervisor, telephone interview by Marylynne Hunt-Dorta, July 2, 2004.

11. *See generally* http://www.bi.com/pdfs/BI_ReEntry.pdf.

12. *See* Gendreau, Goggin, and Little 1996 (study comparing different prediction instruments and concluding that "amongst the composite risk measures, the Level of Service Inventory (LSI-R) generated higher correlations with recidivism than did other risk measures (e.g., Salient Factor Score, Wisconsin) and measures of antisocial personality" [3]).

13. Austin et al. 2003, ii.

14. Ibid., iii.

15. Raynor et al. 2001, 2.

16. *See generally* Austin et al. 2003.

17. "Washington's Parole System Summarized," available at http://www.srb .wa.gov/summary.html.

18. *See* http://www.state.nd.us/lr/assembly/57-2001/interim-info/minutes/cor 090302.html.

19. Michael Stark, Alaska parole board member, telephone interview by Marylynne Hunt-Dorta, June 29, 2004.

20. Linda Shambo, Vermont parole department, telephone interview by Marylynne Hunt-Dorta, June 30, 2004.

21. *See generally* http://www.ncjj.org/stateprofiles/profiles/CO02.asp?state5 CO02.asp&topic5Profile.

22. *See generally Handbook for New Parole Board Members* 2003, 38–42.

23. Robinson 2001, 1429, 1432.

24. Greenwood with Abrahamse 1982.

25. Wolfgang, Figlio, and Sellin 1972, 244.

26. Ibid.

27. Ibid., 244–45.

28. Ibid., 248.

29. Figlio, Tracy, and Wolfgang 1990.

30. In other influential research, Alfred Blumstein and Jacqueline Cohen demonstrated that the effectiveness of selective incapacitation would depend on the relationship between the rate of participation and frequency with which persons engage in crime. The overall crime rate, naturally, depends on both: it depends on the number of people who are participating in criminal activity and on the frequency with which they commit crimes. In fact, the crime rate is simply the participation rate *times* the frequency rate. The implications of this relatively straightforward insight, though, are important: if participation is high and frequency low, selective incapacitation is not likely to work well; however, if participation is low and frequency high, then selective incapacitation has potential. *See generally* Blumstein et al. 1986.

31. Williams 1979.

32. "Selective Incapacitation" 1982, 516 n. 96.

33. Greenwood with Abrahamse 1982.

34. Blumstein et al. 1986, 2:viii. The panel ultimately recommended more longitudinal research in order to obtain better estimates of participation and frequency

rates, as well as seriousness of the offenses and career length, triggering a sharp controversy over the value of longitudinal research. *See generally* Laub and Sampson 1991, 1430.

35. Greenwood with Abrahamse 1982, xii.

36. Ibid., xv–xvi.

37. Ibid., 53.

38. Ibid., xiii.

39. Rhodes et al. 1982.

40. "Selective Incapacitation" 1982, 518.

41. Ibid., 518.

42. Marcus 2003, 142.

43. "Selective Incapacitation" 1982, 514–15.

44. Robinson 2001, 1431.

45. Ibid., 1431 n. 7.

46. O'Neill 2001, 301 n. 34.

47. Luna 1998.

48. Ibid., 7 (quoting Marcus 1994, 225).

49. California Penal Code Section 667(b)–(i).

50. Coonen 2001.

51. Luna 1998, 8.

52. "Selective Incapacitation" 1982, 511 n. 1.

53. *See* Nourse 2004.

54. Ibid.

55. "Selective Incapacitation" 1982, 511 n. 2.

56. Ibid., 511 n. 3.

57. Luna 1998, 2.

58. Ibid., 2–3.

59. U.S. Sentencing Commission 1987, 3. Hereafter referred to in the text as the Supplementary Report of 1987.

60. Tonry 1996, 4.

61. Ibid., 6–7.

62. *See generally* U.S. Sentencing Commission 1991; Stith and Cabranes 1998; Frase 1997; Kamisar et al. 2002, 1498–1502; and U.S. Sentencing Commission 1987. The focus on categories (and subtypes) of crime, rather than on individual causes of crime, is captured well by the federal firearm enhancement statute, 18 U.S.C. § 924(c). The statute provides in part that any person who carries a firearm in connection with a crime of violence or drug trafficking shall be sentenced to an additional enhancement of, for instance, not less than ten years if the firearm is "a short-barreled rifle, short-barreled shotgun, or semiautomatic assault weapon," and not less than thirty years if the firearm is "a machinegun or a destructive device, or is equipped with a firearm silencer or firearm muffler"; *see* 18 U.S.C. § 924(c)(1)(B)(i) and (ii) (2003). A second or subsequent conviction involving

the latter type of firearm is to be punished by life imprisonment; *see* 18 U.S.C. § 924(c)(1)(C)(ii) (2003).

63. *See* Tonry 1996, 84. The idea of a commission that would fix sentencing guidelines is one of the only surviving models of the massive reforms that took place in the 1970s. As Tonry suggests, "After nearly two decades of experimentation, the guideline-setting sentencing commission is the only reform strategy that commands widespread support and continues to be the subject of new legislation" (28).

64. Ibid., 86.

65. U.S. Sentencing Commission 1987, 13. The commission wrote, "The Commission's early efforts, which were directed at devising such a comprehensive guideline system, encountered serious and seemingly insurmountable problems. The guidelines were extremely complex, their application was highly uncertain, and the resulting sentences often were illogical" (14).

66. Ibid., 13.

67. "The list of potentially relevant sentencing factors is long," the commission noted. "The fact that they can occur in multiple combinations means that the list of possible permutations of factors is virtually endless. . . . The introduction of crime-control considerations makes the proper interrelationship among sentencing factors even more complex" (13–14).

68. Tonry 1996, 87.

69. U.S. Sentencing Commission 1987, 14.

70. Andrew von Hirsch, quoted in Tonry 1996, 88.

71. O'Neill 2001, 301.

72. Breyer 1988, 7.

73. In terms of empirical data, the commission relied primarily on estimates of current practices focusing on a small number of relevant variables. The actual methodology is somewhat mysterious; the methodological appendix to the sentencing guidelines does not meet social science standards, and seems almost deliberately intended to obfuscate discussion of the methods used. In fact, the Supplementary Report of 1987 has a number of inconsistencies. At page 9 for instance, we are told that the research staff used "summary reports of 40,000 federal convictions and a sub-sample of 10,000 augmented presentence reports." At page 16, the report indicates that the data contained "detailed data drawn from more than 10,000 presentence investigations, [and] less detailed data on nearly 100,000 federal convictions during a two-year period." At page 21, it refers to presentence reports from a sample of 10,500 cases. And at page 22, the report indicates that the data essentially consisted of "40,000 defendants convicted during 1985." The report never bothers to clarify the exact size of the detailed and less-detailed datasets. Surprisingly little has been written about the scientific method, and most of the discussions rely entirely on the Supplementary Report.

74. U.S. Sentencing Commission 1987, 22.

75. U.S. Sentencing Commission 1987, 23.

76. Ibid., 43.

77. Ibid.

78. Ibid.

79. Ibid., 41.

80. Ibid., 42 (quoting Gottfredson and Gottfredson 1986, 2:239–40).

81. Ibid.

82. Ibid. (quoting ABA Standards of Criminal Justice, § 18-2.2 commentary at 68 [1979]).

83. Ibid. (quoting Hoffman 1983, 543).

84. Ibid.; *see also* O'Neill 2001, 303.

85. U.S. Sentencing Guideline Manual, chap. 4, pt. A, 4A1.1(a)–(c).

86. O'Neill 2001, 305–6.

87. Ibid., 19.

88. Ibid., 18.

89. Tonry 1996, 15.

90. O'Neill 2001, 301 n. 34.

91. Ibid.

92. 408 U.S. 238 (1972).

93. *See Jurek v. Texas,* 428 U.S. 262 (1976). Subsequently, as a result of the controversy surrounding the imposition of death sentences on persons with mental retardation, the Texas statute was modified to add a fourth, more general question on whether the totality of the mitigating circumstances warrant a sentence of life imprisonment rather than death. *See* Tex. Crim. Proc. Code Ann. art. 37.071, § 2(e)(1) (Vernon 2001). For excellent background on the Texas statute and the development of aggravating factors, see generally Steiker and Steiker 1992, 862–66; and 1995.

94. 428 U.S. 262 (1976).

95. 463 U.S. 880 (1983).

96. *See generally* Cunningham and Reidy 1998; Sorensen and Pilgrim 2000; La Fontaine 2002; Beecher-Monas 2003; Regnier 2004; Solomon 1999; Albertson 1989; Texas Defender Service 2004.

97. *See* Cunningham and Reidy 1998, 71; Sorensen 2000, 1252; La Fontaine 2002, 228.

98. *See* La Fontaine 2002, 228.

99. Robinson 2001, 1430 n. 4.

100. *See generally* Blume, Garvey, and Johnson 2001.

101. La Fontaine 2002, 209.

102. *Barefoot v. Estelle,* 463 U.S. at 918 (Blackmun, J., dissenting).

103. La Fontaine 2002, 208. Dr. Grigson was ultimately expelled from the American Psychiatric Association (APA). However, he has been called to testify by the prosecution since that time (ibid., 210).

104. *See United States v. Barnette,* 211 F.3d 803 (4th Cir. 2000).

105. *See Barnette* at 815; *see generally* Beecher-Monas 2003, 363.

106. *See Barnette* at 811.

107. Ibid., 816.

108. The Fifth Circuit, in *Martinez v. Dretke,* 99 Fed. Appx. 538, 2004 WL 1161957 (May 24, 2004), and the Eighth Circuit, in *United States v. Lee,* 274 F.3d 485 (8th Cir. 2002), held admissible PCL-R evidence. *See generally* Walsh and Walsh 2005, 9−11.

109. Cunningham and Reidy 1998, 92.

110. *See, e.g.,* Heumann and Cassak 2001, 916 ("Profiling as a separate and distinct law enforcement technique began in the mid-twentieth century and developed along two lines").

111. *See generally* Harris 2002, 10−11, 17−26.

112. The "hijacker profile," which would trigger an examination with a magnetometer, was discontinued in 1973 when the Federal Aviation Administration required all passengers to go through metal detectors. In 1980, however, the FAA started using the profile again in order to target suspects bringing gasoline on board planes. *See generally* McGinley and Downs 1972, 302−3; Dailey 1973, 1008; Monahan and Walker 2006, 430−37; Becton 1987, 423 n. 45; Heumann and Cassak 2001; Harris 2002, 10−11, 17−26.

113. Becton 1987, 424−25.

114. Skolnick and Fyfe 1993, 43−48, 174−84.

115. *See generally* Harcourt 2001.

116. Some commentators use *criminal profiling* to refer exclusively to criminal suspect profiling—the type of reactive, after-the-crime type of profiling intended to create a profile of a suspect. *See* Heumann and Cassak 2001, 915−19. I am referring to criminal profiling here as the umbrella category.

117. In this book, I emphasize the turn to the actuarial, which I define in terms of the use of statistical rather than clinical analyses, and the use of actuarial prediction instruments. Of course, developments have occurred in the clinical area as well. A good example of a clinical (nonactuarial) profile that developed in the late twentieth century is the school-shooter profile. A word about that profile seems appropriate here, with a preliminary caveat as well. The architects of the school-shooter threat-assessment model emphatically stress that it is *not* a criminal profile. The first page of the FBI report entitled *The School Shooter: A Threat Assessment Perspective* states, "This model is not a 'profile' of the school shooter or a checklist of danger signs pointing to the next adolescent who will bring lethal violence to a school. Those things do not exist. . . ." *See* U.S. Department of Justice 2000. With that in mind, let's look at the assessment.

The school-shooter model is based on an empirical case-study approach. The National Center for the Analysis of Violent Crime (NCAVC) developed the model as a way to study school shooters "from a behavioral perspective." The NCAVC worked with law enforcement officers, school teachers and administrators, mental health professionals, and "experts in disciplines including adolescent violence, mental health, suicidology, school dynamics, and family dynamics." The model was based primarily on an analysis of eighteen school-shooting cases from across the United States—including fourteen cases where shootings occurred and four cases in which shootings were planned and prepared but prevented. In addition, the analysts considered an undisclosed number of cases in which a threat assessment was being prepared. The data consisted of information provided by the school and law enforcement officials, including summary investigative reports, interviews of the offenders, witness statements, interviews with people who knew the offenders and families, crime scene photographs and videos, counseling and psychiatric reports, examples of the offenders' writings, drawings, essays, letters, poems, songs, videos and tapes, school records and school work of the offenders, trial psychiatric reports, and "other pertinent case materials" (U.S. Department of Justice 2000, 35; *see generally* ibid., 34–35).

The model focuses first on the type of threat presented—whether it is a direct, specific threat with highly plausible details identifying the potential victims and locations or, at the other extreme, a vague and indirect threat with inconsistent or implausible details and content suggesting that the student is unlikely to carry it out. Next, the model proposes a four-prong assessment of the student making the threat, focusing on the student's personality and the family, school, and social dynamics surrounding the youth. The model lists "warning signs" in these four categories—traits or circumstances that might lead an assessor to believe that the threat is credible.

For prong one—personality traits and behavior—the list includes such things as "leakages," which reveal clues to violent or macabre feelings or fantasies, "low tolerance for frustration," "poor coping skills," "lack of resilience," "failed love relationship," "nurs[ing] resentment over real or perceived injustices," "signs of depression," "narcissism," "alienation," "lack of empathy," "attitude of superiority," "exaggerated or pathological need for attention," "intolerance," "inappropriate humor," "lack of trust," "change of behavior," or "rigid and opinionated." For prong two—family dynamics—the list includes "turbulent parent-child relationship," parental "acceptance of pathological behavior," "lack of intimacy" within the family, "few or no limits on the child's conduct," or "no limits or monitoring of TV or Internet." The third prong—school dynamics—includes the student being detached from school, bullying and inequitable discipline as part of the school culture, or a prevalent "code of silence" among the students. Finally, the list for the fourth prong—social dynamics—includes a violent or extremist peer group, drug and alcohol use, or "copycat behavior" that may mimic school violence elsewhere.

Despite the caveat and protest, then, the school-shooter threat-assessment model is a method to determine the seriousness of school threats that depends largely on a four-prong analysis of the personality traits and relationships of the threatening youth—in other words, on a profile of the more likely school shooter. Clearly it is based on a clinical, rather than actuarial approach.

118. Becton 1987, 429–30.

119. Harris 2002, 20; Becton 1987, 426, 433-34.

120. Becton 1987, 426.

121. Ibid., 430 n. 72.

122. *See* ibid., 426-27.

123. Ibid., 427.

124. Petition for Writ of Certiorari in *United States v. Mendenhall,* 446 U.S. 544 (1980), at 17-18 n. 17 (quoted in Becton 1987, 433).

125. *See, e.g.,* Cole 1999, 48-49; Becton 1987, 421.

126. Becton 1987, 433-34.

127. *United States v. Mendenhall,* 446 U.S. 544, 562 (1980) (Powell, J., concurring, joined by Burger, C.J., and Blackmun, J.).

128. *Reid v. Georgia,* 448 U.S. 438, 440 (1980) (per curiam).

129. *Florida v. Royer,* 460 U.S. 491, 507 (1983).

130. Cole 1999, 47.

131. *See* Zedlewski 1984.

132. *See generally* John Monahan et al. 2001. (discussing superiority of actuarial over clinical methods of prediction); Grove et al. 2000 (finding that actuarial methods are about ten percent more accurate than clinical methods); Barbaree et al. 2000; Gottfredson 1987; Cunningham and Reidy 1998, 72; Quinsey et al. 1998 (calling on clinicians in the mental health area to use actuarial methods: "What we are advising is not the addition of actuarial methods to existing practice, but rather the complete replacement of existing practice with actuarial methods" [171]); Janus and Prentky 2003.

133. Meehl 1954; 1986.

134. Quinsey et al. 1998, 30.

135. Janus and Prentky 2003, 1455.

136. Ostrom et al. 2002, 28.

137. Monahan et al. 2001, 7.

138. Litwack 2001, 409.

139. *See, e.g.,* Litwack 2001, 410 (arguing that for assessments of dangerousness actuarial methods have not been proven more accurate than clinical methods); Melton et al. 1997 (concluding that "the bottom line is that the research has not delivered an actuarial equation suitable for clinical application in the area of violence prediction").

140. Simon 2005, 4.

Part Two Introduction

1. Schauer 2003, ix.

2. Alschuler 1991, 904.

3. Ibid., 904-5.

4. *See* Feeley and Simon 1992. *See also* Simon and Feeley 1995, 163–69; Simon 1993. This idea of a new actuarial paradigm thesis met with some resistance and criticism at first. *See, e.g.*, Garland 1995, 181, 201 (suggesting that increased managerialism or actuarial analysis most likely attributable to the growth and maturation of the carceral system—a natural maturation process—rather than a shift in approaches). Nevertheless, the thesis has continued to weave its way into contemporary debates and literature; *see, e.g.*, Scheingold 1998, 866–69, 882–86; Beckett 1997, 9–11; Shichor 1997. Katherine Beckett, for example, in her insightful book *Making Crime Pay*, takes for granted the emergence of this new actuarial and managerial approach. She refers to "managerial criminology" as "technocratic, behaviorist, and 'realistic' in tone," and describes it as a field in which "the language of probability and risk supercedes any interest in clinical diagnosis" (1997, 9, 103). "These 'risk assessments,'" Beckett writes, "are based not on knowledge of the individual case but on actuarial or probabilistic calculations" (103).

5. *See* Feeley and Simon 1992, 450, 452; emphasis added.

6. Schauer 2003, ix.

7. *See* Pound 1911, xvii; *see also* Wigmore et al. 1911.

Chapter Four

1. Becker 1996.

2. The leading studies include Knowles, Persico, and Todd 2001; Hernández-Murillo and Knowles 2003; Persico 2002; Borooah 2001; Dominitz and Knowles 2005; and Manski 2005. For fruitful discussions of the difference between statistical discrimination and naked bigotry, compare Borooah 2002 and Chakravarty 2002.

3. Knowles, Persico, and Todd 2001, 206; emphasis in original.

4. I take full responsibility for this graphical representation. The economists developing the models of racial profiling have not attempted to translate their equations into graphs.

5. Figure 4.1 makes many simplifying assumptions about the comparative elasticities among different racial groups, about the comparative offending rates of racial groups, about the selectiveness with which race is used in the searching process, and about several other complicating matters. I discuss these and other matters later.

6. Hernández-Murillo and Knowles 2003, 3. *See also* Knowles, Persico, and Todd 2001, 212 ("Our model assumes that motorists respond to the probability of being searched").

7. Knowles, Persico, and Todd 2001, 208. *See generally* Becker 1996.

8. Knowles, Persico, and Todd 2001, 206; emphasis in original.

9. Ibid., 227; emphasis in original. *See also* Borooah 2001, 35 ("If the likelihood of being stopped was the same for blacks and whites, then the likelihood of being arrested after a stop would be substantially higher for blacks").

10. One important point here is that when the economists investigate data revealing disproportionate searches of minority motorists, their models do not attempt to explain away the disproportionality by holding constant other search criteria. Instead, they essentially assume that the imbalance is intentional and attempt to test the data to explain whether the inequality is due to statistical discrimination or racial bigotry. In this sense, the economists' approach differs significantly from the more traditional, multiple-regression approach of political scientists—represented, for example, by the work of Mitchell Pickerill, Clayton Mosher, Michael Gaffney, and Nicholas Lovrich. These political scientists are focusing their research on identifying the other possible traits that may account for police searches to determine whether the contribution of race vanishes when other nonracial factors are held constant. *See* Pickerill et al. 2003 (explaining the empirical model).

11. *See* Mosher, Miethe, and Phillips 2002, 186 ("As of March 2001, more than 400 law enforcement agencies in the United States were gathering information on the race/ethnicity of those stopped"). *See also* Russell 2001, 68–71 (listing jurisdictions that have enacted data-collection mandates); Garrett 2001, 81–83 (reviewing data-collection efforts); Ramirez, McDevitt, and Farrell 2000 (describing the data-collection systems in California, New Jersey, North Carolina, and Great Britain). For the most recent data, legislation, and news, see the Northeastern University Center on Racial Profiling Web site: http://www.racialprofilinganalysis.neu.edu (visited June 5, 2004). *See also* the Web site of the Institute on Race and Poverty at the University of Minnesota: http://www1.umn.edu/irp/publications/racialprofiling.html (visited June 5, 2004).

12. The controversy over the definition of the term *racial profiling* has been rehearsed in several leading articles on racial profiling. In this book, the term denotes the practice of stopping and searching minority motorists at a rate in excess of their representation on the road, on the assumption that they are more likely to be transporting contraband. The term *racial profiling* is of recent vintage. *See generally* Skolnick and Caplovitz 2001 (discussing the history of the expression). For discussions of the controversy over the definition of racial profiling, see, for example, Russell 2001, 65–68; Alschuler 2002, 168–73 and n. 24; Gross and Barnes 2002, 738 and nn. 278–82. For a careful definition of the term, see Risse and Zeckhauser 2004.

13. *See* Gross and Barnes 2002, 651. Other leading articles and books that describe the data include Harris 2002; Rudovsky 2001; Gross and Livingston 2002; and Maclin 2001.

14. Gross and Barnes 2002, 664. Cited hereafter in the following discussion parenthetically in the text.

15. *See generally* Harris 2002, 62–64; Rudovsky 2001, 300; Russell 2001, 73.

16. *See generally* Rudovsky 2001, 300–301; Harris 2002, 64–66. *See also Chavez v. Illinois State Police*, 251 F3d 612, 634–48 (7th Cir 2001) (reviewing the empirical evidence of racial profiling and rejecting the equal protection claim).

17. *See State v. Soto,* 734 A.2d 350, 353 (N.J. Super. Ct. 1996). *See generally* Harris 2002, 53–60; Rudovsky 2001, 299–300; Russell 2001, 74–75. Civil liberties advocates also refer to Philadelphia, where the ACLU analyzed police stops of motorists and pedestrians in several districts in the late 1990s and found significant disparities. *See generally* Rudovsky 2001, 301; Russell 2001, 73–74. "For a one-week period in July, 1999, for car and pedestrian stops made in predominantly white police districts, the ratio of African-Americans who were stopped was up to ten times higher than one would expect from population data" (Rudovsky 2001, 301). Data from the Richmond, Virginia Police Department from 2000 reveal that the percentage of automobile stops that resulted in a search was most likely determined by location in a predominately African American neighborhood. *See* Petrocelli, Piquero, and Smith 2003, 7. Data from San Diego for the year 2001 reveal that "[o]n average, Black/African American drivers had about a 60% greater chance of being stopped during the year than White drivers; the comparable figure for Hispanic drivers was about 37% greater than for White drivers" (Cordner, Williams, and Velasco 2002). Data from the San Jose Police Department for 2001 reveal that Hispanic and African American motorists are stopped at a higher rate than their demographic representation. *See* San Jose California Police Department 2002; *Racial Profiling: Limited Data Available on Motorist Stops* 2000 (reviewing five early racial profiling studies and finding that, although the studies contain methodological limitations, "the cumulative results of the analyses indicate that in relation to the populations to which they were compared, African American motorists in particular, and minority motorists in general, were proportionately more likely than whites to be stopped on the roadways studied").

18. *See, e.g.,* Harcourt 2001, 166–72 (discussing New York City stop-and-frisks).

19. Knowles, Persico, and Todd 2001, 208.

20. A number of other studies also explore the Maryland data. *See* Gross and Barnes 2002, 662–95; Lamberth 1996.

21. Knowles, Persico, and Todd 2001, 218. Cited parenthetically in the text for the rest of this discussion.

22. "The lower guilty rate for Hispanics is suggestive of prejudice against this group" (Knowles, Persico, and Todd 2001, 222).

23. Hernández-Murillo and Knowles 2003, 4 and n. 4.

24. Ibid., 31, table 1.

25. Ibid., 4–5.

26. Ibid.

27. Ibid., 26.

28. Borooah 2001, 35, 36.

29. Borooah 2001, 19.

30. Borooah 2001, 27. Shanti Chakravarty, in a critique of Borooah, takes Borooah to task for failing to recognize that bigotry and business necessity may be commingled. Chakravarty argues that the data may be contaminated because, if

both groups have the same likelihood of offending, the bigotry in the selection of persons to stop and search is not wiped away by the similarity of the offending rates (2002, 605). In reply, Borooah calls this a "fairly obvious" point. The "whole point of my paper," he argues, is that under conditions of elasticity, the similar success rates show non-prejudice. The data suggest that "Blacks have a greater mean probability of offending than Whites" (2002, 607). Because the rates of success are the same, the data show no bigotry. As a result, the argument against racial profiling, Borooah explains, does not go to the effectiveness of policing, but to the costs of stopping more blacks. It is about "the *consequences* of policing in terms of harassing the innocent and, as a corollary, in terms of the broader message that is issued to the Black community at large" (608; emphasis in original).

31. Knowles, Persico, and Todd 2001, 205; emphasis added.

32. Ibid., 205−6 ("Our model assumes that the police maximize the number of successful searches, net of the cost of searching motorists").

33. Many other commentators who discuss policing efficiency make the same error and draw on a similarly narrow definition of success. John Derbyshire, for instance, also focuses narrowly on the police officer trying to maximize his arrests: "A policeman who concentrates a disproportionate amount of his limited time and resources on young black men is going to uncover far more crimes—*and therefore be far more successful in his career*—than one who biases his attention to, say, middle-aged Asian women" (2001, 39; emphasis added). *See also* Will 2001 (attributing disproportion in stops of minority motorists to effective policing, and noting the "truism" that "minority groups dominate . . . [drug] trafficking"); Toby 1999 (arguing that "if drug traffickers are disproportionately black or Hispanic, the police don't need to be racist to stop many minority motorists; they simply have to be efficient in targeting potential drug traffickers"). *See generally* Callahan and Anderson 2001, 37 (noting, in the context of discussing commentators' diverse reactions to racial profiling, that "[i]f police have a goal of maximizing drug arrests, they may indeed find that they can achieve this most easily by focusing on minorities").

34. Persico 2002, 1474.

35. Meares 2000, 400.

36. *See generally* Tyler 1990; and 1998 (explaining that legitimacy stems from trust relations, which turn on expectations of reciprocity and perceived status as inferred from treatment by group authorities); Tyler and Huo 2002 (exploring the empirical basis and explicating the conceptual structure of the interplay between trust and authority); Lind and Tyler 1988. *See also* Leitzel 2001, 39−40 (attributing the parallel stereotyping of police as racists and minorities as lawbreakers to race-based policing and arguing that the concomitant police-minority hostility undermines efficacious crime control).

37. Most of the economists recognize fully that the goal of narrow efficiency may be offset by other social ends. "Statistical discrimination, even if not due to

prejudice, may be considered unfair because innocent drivers experience different probabilities of being searched depending on their race" (Knowles, Persico, and Todd 2001, 228). Borooah also recognizes that statistical discrimination "may be reprehensible to society" and that "society may prefer its police to implement a 'colour-blind' policy" (2001, 19).

38. Special thanks to Gary Becker for helping me think through this model.

39. We assume here that the social cost is the same for all incidents, regardless of the type of drugs, the quantity, or the race of the carrier. This is, naturally, a simplifying assumption, given that the transportation of drugs for personal use and for drug trafficking have very different costs for society as a whole.

40. Here too we assume that the social cost is the same for all searches, regardless of the type of car, search, or the race of the motorist.

41. To put this another way, it is easy to come up with a counterexample to the argument that the police should seek to equalize the hit rates between white and minority motorists—in other words, that minimizing the costs of drug carrying would imply equal hit rates for racial groups. If we assume equal elasticity of offending to policing between white and minority motorists and higher search rates for minority motorists, then this implies that, at equilibrium, minimizing social costs will require *higher* offending rates for minority motorists—not equal hit rates. So if in Maryland, for example, minority and white motorists have equal elasticities, the higher search rates for minority motorists would imply that, to minimize total social costs, there should be greater hit rates among minority motorists. The data showing higher search rates but relatively equal hit rates in Maryland translate into *higher* social costs. If we assume lower elasticity among minority motorists in Maryland, it is also likely that the disproportionate searches of minority motorists do not minimize social costs. If minority motorist elasticity is lower, then social costs are minimized only if the search rate of minority motorists is less than .34/.32, or 1.0625 times the search rate of white motorists. Given that approximately 63 percent of searches are of minority motorists, this condition likely does not obtain.

42. Nicola Persico (2002), for instance, recognizes that maximizing the search success rates may lead to maximizing crime. Jeff Dominitz and John Knowles (2005) also recognize this. Charles Manski (2005) also recognizes the conflict between crime minimization and hit rate maximization.

43. Dominitz and Knowles 2005, 4.

44. Ibid., 16. The authors go on to develop the further assumptions necessary to infer bias, or more specifically "that joint restriction on the quantile-quantile plot g and the densities φ_r will be necessary for such inference" (16). As they recognize, "[e]mpirical verification of these conditions, however, poses a serious challenge" (21). This makes it extremely difficult, if not impossible, to imagine implementing their revised test.

45. *See* Gross and Barnes 2002, 682–84 (discussing differential subsearches).

46. Knowles, Persico, and Todd 2001, 215.

47. In this context, it is important to note the difficulty of identifying what counts as "racist." From one perspective, applying more subsearch techniques (canine sniffing, heavy-handed interrogation, closer visual inspections) to one set of motorists is *more* fair toward that set of motorists, because it decreases the number of innocent motorists in that group who are subjected to full-scale searches. If we are more careful in this manner with white motorists, fewer white motorists will be unnecessarily searched; minority motorists, as a whole, will be subjected to comparatively more futile searches. From another perspective, though, the subsearch techniques themselves are often intrusive, invasive, and, for innocent motorists, may well feel like full-blown searches. In this view, the subsearch techniques count as searches, and their disproportionate application appears racist against the beneficiary—against the group subject to the practices. Moreover, the use of additional subsearch techniques creates a perception that the beneficiary group is more crime prone. Thus, it is difficult to know how to label the police officer who subjects white motorists to a canine sniff. Is she racist against African American motorists because she is less careful and causing more unsuccessful searches of innocent minority motorists, or racist against white motorists because she is subjecting white motorists to intrusive canine searches and jacking up their collective hit rate, thus painting them as drug dealers? I leave this question unresolved, but flag it to emphasize the complexity of interpreting hit rates.

48. Knowles, Persico, and Todd list the following characteristics from a training manual for the Illinois State Police: "tinted windows, cell phones, leased vehicles, religious paraphernalia used to divert suspicion, and attorney business cards" (2001, 204 n 2).

49. *See* Michelson 2001.

50. Knowles, Persico, and Todd 2001, 222, table 2 (listing proportion of vehicles searched found to be carrying drugs, broken down by race).

51. *See City of Indianapolis v. Edmond,* 531 U.S. 32, 35 (2000) (noting that 55 drug-related arrests were made during a total of 1,161 stops). The Indianapolis road block in 1998 involved random stops without police discretion whether to stop or search. The selected car would be stopped, the driver would be asked to produce a license and registration, and a dog would sniff the outside of the car. A search was to be conducted upon consent or based on a specified amount of particularized suspicion.

52. *See* Hernández-Murillo and Knowles 2003, 31, table 1.

53. The only way to address the issue of subsearches or search-selection criteria is to get the relevant data—offending or hit rates—holding all other factors constant and holding constant subsearch processes. That would be difficult, but not impossible. It would require asking the police officer to report all grounds of suspicion and to report all subsearch processes administered. It would then be possible to hold these other factors constant in the offending and hit rates. Political scientists at Washington State University—Pickerill, Mosher, Gaffney, and Lovrich—are

attempting to do this, but for slightly different purposes. Their research, which involves a more traditional multiple-regression approach, seeks to identify all factors that may contribute to searches in order to determine whether any of those factors neutralize the role of race.

In their research, Pickerill et al. find that some of these other factors affect the racial disparities. The strongest predictor of a search is the seriousness of the violation associated with the stop. The influence of race is mitigated by other variables, including the age of the driver, geographical location, time of day, and the seriousness of the violation triggering the traffic stop. Most important, they find that the disparities in searches do not vary much between searches that are nondiscretionary (which they define as searches incident to arrest, "impound searches," and "warrant searches") and those that are discretionary (which they define as canine searches, consent searches, and pat down searches); see Pickerill et al. 2003, 18. They infer from this that "this is one indicator that while there may be racial disparities in search rates, those disparities do not appear to be the result of intentional discrimination by the officers" (18).

Their data consist of every stop made by a Washington State Patrol officer from March 2002 through October 2002, which amounts to 677,514 cases (Pickerill et al. 2003, 17). Of those, 23,393 (or 3.5 percent) resulted in searches. Their findings are preliminary, but what they also find is that race plays an important role in the incidence of searches by the Washington State Police. "Even when we control for other factors that influence whether or not searches are conducted after motorists are contacted by the WSP, we find that race still has an impact on the likelihood of a search" (26). Specifically, Native Americans are searched at much higher rates than whites, African Americans and Hispanics are searched at moderately higher rates than whites, and Asians are searched at slightly lower rates than whites. Whereas 3 percent of white motorists who were stopped were searched, the search rates were 15 percent, 7.6 percent, 6.7 percent, and 2.5 percent respectively for Native Americans, African Americans, Hispanics, and Asians (21). Although Pickerill and his colleagues do not develop an economic model of racial profiling focused on hit rates, they do nevertheless report the hit rates from the data. They find that, overall, white motorists are the most likely to be found with contraband. The disparities are greater with regard to discretionary searches—not surprisingly. Adding both types of searches, it turns out that the hit rates are 24.8 percent for whites, 18.9 percent for African Americans, 21.4 percent for Native Americans, 16.7 for Hispanics, and 12.2 percent for Asians (34, table 4).

Their primary purpose is to test whether the consistently disproportionate searches of minority motorists are an artifact of some other *nonracial* factor—in other words, whether the race correlations would vanish if some other variable were held constant. As they explain,

> While virtually every extant study of such data indicate that racial profiling *may* be occurring, it is important to stress that these studies do not

provide *proof* that biased policing exists. Without appropriate "denominator" data keyed to specific racial and ethnic populations, and without the addition of appropriate contextual information concerning traffic stops to multivariate analyses, it is not possible to distinguish biased policing from entirely appropriate, but demographically disproportionate, enforcement outcomes with respect to racial and ethnic characteristics. (Pickerill et al. 2003, 11; emphasis in original)

See also Michelson 2001 (suggesting that the existing studies do not prove discriminatory impact because they fail to account for proportions of drivers excessively speeding and do not measure the extent to which police officers can discern motorists' race); *but see New Jersey v. Soto,* 734 A.2d at 354-57 (recounting plaintiffs' experts addressing these and other concerns).

54. Tribe 1971b, 1346.

55. U.S. Bureau of Justice Statistics 2002b, table 4.19.

56. U.S. Bureau of Justice Statistics 2000a, 9-10, tables 1.17 and 1.20.

57. U.S. Bureau of Justice Statistics 2002b, table 6.42.

Chapter Five

1. *See* Levitt 2004.

2. *See* Spelman 2000, 123.

3. According to the United States Department of Justice, "The average annual operating cost per State inmate in 2001 was $22,650, or $62.05 per day. Among facilities operated by the Federal Bureau of Prisons, it was $22,632 per inmate, or $62.01 per day." *See* U.S. Bureau of Justice Statistics 2001b.

4. This is a simplified model that does not account for the slight incapacitation effect resulting from the additional members of the higher-offending group incarcerated as a result of the profiling. But even when we account for that, there is still a ratchet. In fact, even if we run the model with complete incapacitation— meaning that every offender who is apprehended is incapacitated and no offender is ever released—there is still a ratchet effect. It is slightly tempered, but functions nonetheless to continually increase the carceral imbalance. I run such a model in my article, "From the Ne'er-Do-Well to the Criminal History Category" (Harcourt 2003a, 138-46).

5. *See, e.g.,* Roberts 1999, 808-10. This is also the sense in which David Harris argues that racial profiling is a "self-fulfilling prophecy" (2002, 223-25). His argument is not that racial profiling is too effective. On the contrary, he argues that the evidence shows that it is ineffective and results in lower hit rates for minorities: "Racial profiling is neither an efficient nor an effective tool for fighting crime" (79). His argument that racial profiling is nevertheless a self-fulfilling prophecy is, instead, that police will find crime wherever they look. If they spend more time

in minority communities, they will find more crime there: "[W]hom they catch depends on where they look" (224).

6. *See* Verniero 1999, 68.

7. Meares 1998; Roberts 1999; Cole 1999; Tonry 1995; Wacquant 2005.

8. Shaw and McKay 1969.

9. Meares 1998, 206.

10. Ibid., 209–10.

11. Ibid., 206–8.

12. Roberts 1999, 805.

13. Ibid.

14. Johnson 1984, 949.

15. Roberts 1999, 806.

16. Ibid., 813, fig. 2.

17. Ibid., 799–801.

18. Sampson and Laub 1993, 255.

19. U.S. Bureau of Justice Statistics 1989.

20. Langan and Levin 2002, 3, table 2.

21. *See generally* Austin and Hardyman 2004, table 3.

22. *See, e.g.,* Travis 2000, 3.

23. *See also, e.g., United States v. Villamonte-Marquez,* 462 U.S. 579 (1983): otherwise valid warrantless boarding of vessel by customs officials not rendered illegal by ulterior motive of accompanying state police officer; *United States v. Robinson,* 414 U.S. 218 (1973): traffic violation stop not rendered illegal because it was a pretext for drug search; *Gustafson v. Florida,* 414 U.S. 260 (1973): same.

24. U.S. Bureau of Justice Statistics 2001a, table 6.2.

25. For excellent discussions of these trends, see Tonry 1995, 28–31, 56–68. *See also* Justice Policy Institute 2002.

26. Tyler 1998, 289. *See also* Tyler 1990.

27. *See generally* Harcourt 2001, 166–75.

28. Gould and Mastrofski 2004.

29. Gould and Mastrofski's aggregate findings are troubling. But even more troubling than the aggregate numbers, are the individual cases. Buried in an appendix to Gould and Mastrofski's article is a field note about a police-civilian encounter that illustrates the unquantifiable harms we are dealing with in the context of actuarial policing. It involves a cavity search of an African American man conducted *in public*—on the side of the road. I describe this extremely troubling incident in my essay, "Unconstitutional Police Searches and Collective Responsibility" (Harcourt 2004b).

30. Although Gould and Mastrofski do not disclose the site of their research for purposes of confidentiality, I have been told that the research was conducted in Richmond, Virginia. The African American population in the city of Richmond is 57.2 percent of the total population according to the 2000 U.S. Census. *See* http://

quickfacts.census.gov/qfd/states/51/51760lk.html. This is consistent with the little information that Gould and Mastrofski offer, namely, that "many of the city's residents were African American, and many experienced concentrated disadvantage" (2004, 324). It would represent a 26.8 percent disparity in the search rates.

Chapter Six

1. *See, e.g.,* Beckett 1997, 10 (discussing "the effort to replace social welfare with social control as the principle of state policy"); Wacquant 1998, 7. For discussion of the separate thesis of the rise of the prison-industrial complex, see, for example, Donziger 1996, 85–87.

2. *See, e.g.,* Feeley and Simon 1992, 450–52 (suggesting that a new paradigm for the management of dangerous persons has emerged in the late twentieth century, accompanied by a new language of penology); Simon 1993 (exploring this "new penology" through the historical development of parole in California); Scheingold 1998, 866–69, 882–86 (discussing the role of the "new penology"); Alschuler 2003, 12 (discussing the "new penology" and suggesting that "one can discern this new penology in sentencing guidelines and mandatory minimum sentences that allocate punishment wholesale rather than retail").

3. Hacking 1990, 2.

4. Wigmore et al. 1911, vii.

5. Ibid.

6. Burgess 1928.

7. Laune 1936, 2.

8. Burgess and Sellin 1951, 11.

9. Lohman 1951, 7.

10. Glueck and Glueck 1939, 280.

11. Vold 1931, 19.

12. Hart 1923, 413.

13. Bruce, Burgess, and Harno 1928, 285.

14. Burgess and Sellin 1951, 12–13.

15. Vold 1931, 103.

16. Laune 1936, 3.

17. Ibid., 5.

18. Ibid., 9.

19. Argow 1935, 565.

20. Morse 1939, 658 (all references are to vol. 4, *Parole*).

21. Vold 1931, 16.

22. Ibid., 70.

23. Laune 1936, 7.

24. Ohlin 1951, 53–54.

25. Ibid., 53-54.
26. Ibid., 127.
27. Glaser 1954, 268.
28. Bruce, Burgess, and Harno 1928, 285.
29. *Handbook for New Parole Board Members* 2003, 35.
30. Vold 1931, 103.
31. Monachesi 1932, 110.
32. Van Vechten 1935, 19.
33. Argow 1935, 562.
34. Baker and Simon 2002a, 1; Rose 1999, and 2002, 209.
35. Baker and Simon 2002a, 1.
36. Ibid., 3-4.
37. Ibid., 17.
38. Morse 1939, 654-55.
39. Ibid.
40. Coen 2004, 9.
41. Hacking 1990, 46.
42. Pratt 1997, 39 (quoting Jack London, *The People of the Abyss* [1903]).
43. Ibid., 39, 44 (quoting an 1870 text), and 31 (quoting an 1895 report of the Departmental Committee on Prisons).
44. Sutherland 1908.

Part Three Introduction

1. Vold 1931, 5.
2. Ernest Burgess, quoted in Bruce, Burgess, and Harno 1928, 283.
3. Personal correspondence from Carol Steiker to author, 2005.

Chapter Seven

1. This is what Borooah means when he writes that "[i]f the likelihood of being stopped was the same for blacks and whites, then the likelihood of being arrested after a stop would be substantially higher for blacks" (2001, 35).
2. Johnston et al. 2005, table 4.9.
3. Center for Disease Control and Prevention 2004, 57–63, tables 28, 30, 32, 34.
4. U.S. Department of Health and Human Services, Substance Abuse and Mental Health Services Administration 2005, tables 1.28B, 1.33B, 1.38B, 1.43B, 1.48B.
5. These statistics concern only illegal drugs. If we include prescription mood-altering drugs, such as Prozac or Valium, the disproportionality may be far greater. The use of legal mood-altering drugs exploded in the 1990s. As Joseph Kennedy

reports, "Between 1987 and 1997, the percentages of outpatient psychotherapy patients using prescribed antidepressant medications, mood stabilizers, and stimulants tripled" (2003, 173). The consumption of such drugs tends to correlate with higher-income white consumers, which suggests that, in reality, whites may consume drugs at a far higher rate than minorities. I thank Richard Posner for this insight.

6. Harrison 1997, 17–18.

7. Internal validity is determined by looking at a respondent's answers to related items on a survey. For instance, a survey response would be internally inconsistent if the respondent claimed to have smoked marijuana in the last thirty days in response to one question and in a later question denied ever having used any illicit drugs over the course of his lifetime. On the other hand, researchers interpret the high correlation between estimates of friends' drug use and aggregate self-reported drug use as evidence of the MFP's high internal validity. Both the NHSDA and the MFP have a high degree of internal consistency. *See* Harrison 1997, 19–20. *See also* Johnston and O'Malley 1997, 59.

8. External validity is demonstrated by consistency between self-reports and an official record, polygraph test, or confirmation from interviews of friends or family. Researchers have found that the external validity of self-reported drug use varies with the type of drug involved, but not with the race of the respondents. *See* Harrell 1997, 37, 46–48, 53.

9. In biological testing, urine and hair samples are analyzed for evidence of drug metabolites and used to impeach or confirm self-reports. Several of these studies suggest that the validity of self-reporting is lower than hoped for. *See* Cook, Bernstein, and Andrews 1997, 247 (estimating actual prevalence to be 51 percent higher than self-reports indicate). Validity varies for different population groups (arrested offenders versus office workers) and also for different types of drugs. *See generally* Harrison 1997, 26–28, 31–32.

10. Lu, Taylor, and Riley 2001.

11. Harrell 1997, 53.

12. *See, e.g.,* Gray and Wish 1999, 100–101 ("The odds of self-reporting recent cocaine use by whites were almost twice the odds of nonwhites"); Fendrich and Xu 1994, 977–82; Falck et al. 1992; Page et al. 1977, 445–49.

13. *See* Johnston and O'Malley 1997, 72–74.

14. There is also the question whether school and home survey data on drug consumption are reliable, given that they may overlook homeless drug users and school dropouts. However, roadway searches probably target persons with cars and more than subsistence income.

15. Human Rights Watch 2000, chap. 7.

16. U.S. Department of Health and Human Services, Substance Abuse and Mental Health Services Administration 1995, 17, table 1.3.

17. *See* Harrison 1997, 29 (observing that self-report studies are more accurate for the least-stigmatized drugs and least accurate for the most-stigmatized drugs).

18. Gross and Barnes 2002, 703.

19. Ibid.

20. U.S. Bureau of Justice Statistics 1999, 111, table 2.33 (defining racial profiling as occurring when "some police officers stop motorists of certain racial or ethnic groups because the officers believe that these groups are more likely than others to commit certain types of crimes"), citing Gallup and Gallup 1999, 23.

21. Ibid.

22. Ibid., table 2.32, citing Gallup and Gallup 1999, 18–19.

23. *See City of Indianapolis v. Edmond,* 531 U.S. at 34–35.

24. *See* Pickerill et al. 2003, 20.

25. Blumstein, Cohen, and Nagin 1978, 42. *See also* Nagin 1978, 95, 135 (deeming current empirical evidence insufficient to confirm the existence of a deterrent effect and "woefully inadequate" for estimating its magnitude). *See generally* Spelman 2000, 97 (reviewing the literature on the deterrence hypothesis and noting the studies' inability to separate deterrence from incapacitation or rehabilitation).

26. Levitt 1998, 1158 n. 2.

27. *See* Reuter and Kleiman 1986, 289, 299.

28. Schulhofer 1994, 207, 223.

29. Reuter and Kleiman 1986, 300, as cited in Schulhofer 1994, 223 n. 51.

30. Ibid., 300.

31. Ibid., 290.

32. Schulhofer 1994, 223 n. 50 (citing Nisbet and Vakil 1972, 474–75).

33. Ibid., 223.

34. Persico 2002, 1474–75.

35. *See generally* Meares 2000, 400; Tyler 1990; Tyler 1998 (explaining that legitimacy stems from trust relations, which turn on expectations of reciprocity and perceived status as inferred from treatment by group authorities); Tyler and Huo 2002 (exploring the empirical basis and explicating the conceptual structure of the interplay between trust and authority); Lind and Tyler 2001, 39–40 (attributing the parallel stereotyping of police as racists and minorities as lawbreakers to race-based policing and arguing that the concomitant police-minority hostility undermines efficacious crime control).

36. While no studies have been conducted domestically, Bar-Ilan and Sacerdote (2001) found that "as the fine is increased for running a red light in Israel, the total decrease in tickets is much larger for Jews than for non-Jews" (Persico 2002, 1476).

37. Gross and Barnes 2002, 697.

38. Note that this would be an unreasonably conservative assumption. A more reasonable assumption from the Maryland data is that approximately 84 percent of the dealer population is African American. *See* Gross and Barnes 2002, 703.

39. Assuming that 18 percent of the motorists are minorities, if minorities and whites offend at the same rate with regard to 84 percent of the offenses (personal use seizures) and minorities comprise all of the other 16 percent of the offenders,

then minority motorists represent 31.12 percent of all offenders. (The equation is $[18/100 \times 84/100] + [16/100 \times 1] = .1512 + .16 = .3112$.)

Chapter Eight

1. Schauer 2003, 197–98.

2. *See generally* Vera Institute 2003, 2; Ares, Rankin, and Sturz 1963, 68; Feeley 1983, chap. 2; Harmsworth 1996.

3. Ares, Rankin, and Sturz 1963, 71. This study culminated in the famous 1956 New York City Bail Study.

4. Feeley 1983, 41–42.

5. Ares, Rankin, and Sturz 1963, 68.

6. They focused on persons charged with robbery and burglary, *excluding* those charged with (or who had a previous record of) drug offenses, homicide, "forcible rape, sodomy involving a minor, corrupting the morals of a child, carnal abuse, and assault on a police officer"; *see* Ares, Rankin, and Sturz 1963, 72 (this exclusion was based on the inherently higher-risk nature of such defendants).

7. Ibid.

8. Ibid., 73. For a thorough explanation of the project's method of using control groups versus experimental groups, see p. 74; for a sample questionnaire, see pp. 93–95.

9. Ibid., 86.

10. Ibid.

11. Ibid.

12. Vera Institute 2003, 2.

13. Feeley 1983, 46.

14. Ibid.

15. It is interesting to note in this case that community ties appear to be the critical link to success in the prediction process. The only unsuccessful application of the program that the Vera Institute itself cites is its Bronx Bail Bond Agency, shut down in 1994, which had difficulty with higher pretrial monitoring costs and, especially, found that its participants were less likely to have sufficient community ties to be reliable on their own recognizance, relative to other boroughs. *See* Vera Institute 2003, 3 (noting that other factors eroding the agency's success in the Bronx included higher rates of drug use and lower employment prospects).

16. Ibid., 2.

17. Ibid.

18. Feeley 1983, 47.

19. Ibid.

20. *See, e.g.,* Bak 2002 (cautiously concluding that "a persuasive case can be made for the continued release of defendants whom the [US attorney] wishes to

detain"). Other articles are even more effusive. *See, e.g.,* Harmsworth 1996 (providing an analysis of the project and other bail-reform efforts and noting that "[a]fter the Manhattan Bail Project . . . the entire focus of pretrial custody changed" [text at n. 17]).

21. To be sure, the overall impact on crime is not determinative and does not end the discussion; but certainly, an increase in crime undermines any argument *for* using actuarial methods from a law enforcement perspective. If actuarial methods ultimately increase criminal activity, no law enforcement purpose is served.

22. *See* Matthew R. Durose and Patrick A. Langan, *State Court Sentencing of Convicted Felons, 2002, Statistical Tables,* table 2.1 at 19 (May 2005). Available at the Web site of the U.S. Department of Justice, Office of Justice Programs, Bureau of Justice Statistics, on the page entitled State Court Sentencing of Convicted Felons—Statistical Tables: http://www.ojp.usdoj.gov/bjs/pub/pdf/scscf02st.pdf.

23. *Criminal Victimization in the United States, 2003, Statistical Tables,* table 38 ("Personal Crimes of Violence, 2003: Percent distribution of single-offender victimizations, by type of crime and perceived gender of offender"). Available at the Web site of the U.S. Department of Justice, Office of Justice Programs, Bureau of Justice Statistics, on the page entitled Criminal Victimization in the United States—Statistical Tables: http://www.ojp.usdoj.gov/bjs/pub/sheets/cvsprshts.htm #table38.

24. U.S. Bureau of Justice Statistics 1989.

25. Langan and Levin 2002, 3, table 2; *see generally* Austin and Hardyman 2004.

26. For the most part, the studies examine the pervasive use of intensive supervision as a diversionary alternative to incarceration—a slightly different issue. For a review of the existing evidence, see Petersilia and Turner 1991; Byrne, Lurigio, and Baird 1989; United States General Accounting Office 1993; Petersilia 1998.

27. Sperry 2005.

28. Krauthammer 2005.

29. Gladwell 2006.

30. *See generally* Enders and Sandler 1993; Faria 2006.

31. Brittingham and de la Cruz 2005.

32. Landes 1978, 24 n. 41, and 3, table 1.

33. Rosen 1954.

34. Tucker 2003.

35. Gladwell 2006.

36. Landes 1978, 28–29.

37. Cauley and Im 1988.

38. Enders and Sandler 1993, 835.

39. Enders and Sandler 2004, *16.

40. Enders and Sandler 1993, 842.

41. Cauley and Im 1988, 30.

42. Lum, Kennedy, and Sherley 2006, 3.

43. Anderton and Carter 2004, 10.

44. *See* Enders and Sandler 2004, *10.

45. Tucker 2003, *2.

Chapter Nine

1. Several states statutorily prescribe a flip of the coin to resolve election ties and a number of courts partition disputed land by lot or chance. Wisconsin law, for instance, provides that "[i]f 2 or more candidates for the same office receive the greatest, but an equal number of votes, the winner shall be chosen by lot in the presence of the board of canvassers charged with the responsibility to determine the election"; *see* Wis. Stat. Ann. § 5.01(4) (2005). Similarly, Louisiana law expressly states that "[i]n case of a tie, the secretary of state shall invite the candidates to his office and shall determine the winner by the flip of a coin"; *see* La. Rev. Stat. 46: § 1410(C)(3) (2005). *See generally* Choper 2001, 340 n. 22 (collecting other sources); *Huber v. Reznick,* 437 N.E.2d 828, 839 (Ill. App. Ct. 1982) (holding that trial court did not err in choosing a coin flip as the method of determining the winner of the tie vote by lot); "Election 2000; The Presidency; High Stakes; If Vote Is Tied in New Mexico, Poker Hand Could Settle It," *Newsday,* November 15, 2000, A05 (describing practice of using "one hand of five-card poker"). In addition, in a number of jurisdictions, courts resolve land disputes by lot. *See generally* Zitter 1999. Special thanks to Adam Samaha for these insights.

References

Abbott, Andrew. 1997. "Of Time and Space: The Contemporary Relevance of the Chicago School." *Social Forces* 75 (4): 1149–82.

———. 1999. *Department and Discipline: Chicago Sociology at One Hundred.* Chicago: University of Chicago Press.

Abbott, Andrew, and James T. Sparrow. 2005. "Hot War, Cold War: The Structures of Sociological Action, 1940–1955." Unpublished ms. on file with author, dated July 6.

Albertson, Mark David. 1989. "Can Violence Be Predicted? Future Dangerousness: The Testimony of Experts in Capital Cases." *Criminal Justice* 3 (Winter): 18–48.

Alschuler, Albert W. 1991. "The Failure of Sentencing Guidelines: A Plea for Less Aggregation." *University of Chicago Law Review* 58:901–51.

———. 2002. "Racial Profiling and the Constitution." *University of Chicago Legal Forum* 2002:163–269.

———. 2003. "The Changing Purposes of Criminal Punishment: A Retrospective on the Past Century and Some Thoughts about the Next." *University of Chicago Law Review* 70:1–22.

Ambrose, Eileen. 2001. "Surviving a Tax Audit's Scrutiny." *Chicago Tribune,* June 5, sec. N.

Anderton, Charles H., and John R. Carter. 2004. "Applying Intermediate Microeconomics to Terrorism." College of the Holy Cross, Department of Economics Faculty Research Series, Working Paper no. 04-12 (August).

Anwar, Shamena, and Hanming Fang. 2005. "An Alternative Test of Racial Prejudice in Motor Vehicle Searches: Theory and Evidence." National Bureau of Economic Research Working Paper 11264. Available at http://www.nber.org/papers/w11264.

Ares, Charles E., Anne Rankin, and Herbert Sturz. 1963. "The Manhattan Bail Project: An Interim Report on the Use of Pre-Trial Parole." *New York University Law Review* 38:67–95.

Argow, Walter Webster. 1935. "A Criminal Liability-Index for Predicting Possibility of Rehabilitation." *Journal of Criminal Law and Criminology* 26:561–77.

Austin, James, Dana Coleman, Johnette Peyton, and Kelly Dedel Johnson. 2003. *Reliability and Validity Study of the LSI-R Risk Assessment Instrument, Final*

Report Submitted to the Pennsylvania Board of Probation and Parole. Available at the Web site of the Pennsylvania Commission on Crime and Delinquency, Center for Research, Evaluation, and Statistical Analysis: http://www.pccd. state.pa.us/pccd/cwp/view.asp?A51390&Q5574731.

Austin, James, and Patricia L. Hardyman. 2004. "The Risks and Needs of the Returning Prisoner Population." *Review of Policy Research* 21:13–29.

Ayres, Ian. 2002. "Outcomes Tests of Racial Disparities in Police Practices." *Justice Research and Policy* 4:131–42.

Bak, Thomas. 2002. "Pretrial Release Behavior of Defendants Whom the US Attorney Wished to Detain." *American Journal of Criminal Law* 30:45–74.

Baker, Tom, and Jonathan Simon. 2002a. "Embracing Risk." In Baker and Simon 2002b, 1–25.

———, eds. 2002b. *Embracing Risk: The Changing Culture of Insurance and Responsibility.* Chicago: University of Chicago Press.

Banks, R. Richard. 2003. "Beyond Profiling: Race, Policing, and the Drug War." *Stanford Law Review* 56:571–602.

Barbaree, Howard E., Michael C. Seto, Calvin M. Langton, and Edward J. Peacock. 2000. "Evaluating the Predictive Accuracy of Six Risk Assessment Instruments for Adult Sex Offenders." *Criminal Justice and Behavior* 28 (August): 490–521.

Bar-Ilan, Avner, and Bruce Sacerdote. 2001. "The Response to Fines and Probability of Detection in a Series of Experiments." National Bureau of Economic Research Working Paper no. 8638. Available at http://papers.nber.org/papers/w8638.pdf.

Becker, Gary. 1996. *Accounting for Tastes.* Cambridge, MA: Harvard University Press.

Beckett, Katherine. 1997. *Making Crime Pay: Law and Order in Contemporary American Politics.* New York: Oxford University Press.

Becton, Charles L. 1987. "The Drug Courier Profile: 'All Seems Infected That th' Infected Spy, as All Looks Yellow to the Jaundic'd Eye.'" *North Carolina Law Review* 65:417–81.

Beecher-Monas, Erica. 2003. "The Epistemology of Prediction: Future Dangerousness Testimony and Intellectual Due Process." *Washington & Lee Law Review* 60:353–416.

Biggs, Patricia. 2003. *SB 123 Background and Offender Flow.* Report and Presentation Prepared by Patricia Biggs, Executive Director of the Kansas Sentencing Commission (on file with author).

Blacher, Raquel. 1995. "Comment: Historical Perspective of the 'Sex Psychopath' Statute: From the Revolutionary Era to the Present Federal Crime Bill." *Mercer Law Review* 46:889–920.

Blume, John H., Stephen P. Garvey, and Sheri Lynn Johnson. "Future Dangerousness in Capital Cases: Always 'At Issue.'" *Cornell Law Review* 86:397–410.

Blumstein, Alfred, Jacqueline Cohen, and Daniel Nagin. 1978. "Report of the Panel on Research on Deterrent and Incapacitative Effects." In *Deterrence and Incapacitation: Estimating the Effects of Criminal Sanctions on Crime Rates,* ed. Alfred Blumstein, Jacqueline Cohen, and Daniel Nagin. Washington, DC: National Academy of Sciences.

Blumstein, Alfred, Jacqueline Cohen, Jeffrey A. Roth, and Christy A. Visher, eds. 1986. *Criminal Careers and "Career Criminals."* 2 vols. Washington DC: National Academy Press.

Borden, Howard G. 1928. "Factors for Predicting Parole Success." *Journal of Criminal Law and Criminology* 19:328–36.

Borooah, Vani K. 2001. "Racial Bias in Police Stops and Searches: An Economic Analysis." *European Journal of Political Economy* 17:17–37.

———. 2002. "Economic Analysis of Police Stops and Searches: A Reply." *European Journal of Political Economy* 18:607–8.

Breyer, Stephen. 1988. "The Federal Sentencing Guidelines and the Key Compromises upon Which They Rest." *Hofstra Law Review* 17:1–50.

Brittingham, Angela, and G. Patricia de la Cruz. 2005. *We the People of Arab Ancestry in the United States: Census 200 Special Reports.* Washington DC: United States Department of Commerce, Economics and Statistics Administration (March).

Brown, Lawrence D. 1978. "The Development of a Parolee Classification System Using Discriminate Analysis." *Journal of Research in Crime and Delinquency* 15:92–108.

Brown, Mark, and John Pratt, eds. 2000. *Dangerous Offenders: Punishment and Social Order.* London: Routledge.

Bruce, Andrew A., Ernest W. Burgess, and Albert M. Harno. 1928. "A Study of the Indeterminate Sentence and Parole in the State of Illinois." *Journal of the American Institute of Criminal Law and Criminology* 19, no. 1, pt. 2 (May): 1–306. (This study was reprinted in book form by the State of Illinois Board of Parole and Pardon in 1928 under the title *The Workings of the Indeterminate-Sentence Law and the Parole System in Illinois: A Report to the Honorable Hinton G. Clabaugh, Chairman, Parole Board of Illinois.*)

Burchell, Graham, Collin Gordon, and Peter Miller, eds. 1991. *The Foucault Effect: Studies in Governmentality.* London: Harvester Wheatsheaf.

Burgess, Ernest W. 1925. "The Growth of the City: An Introduction to a Research Project." In Park and Burgess 1925, chap. 2.

———. 1928. "Is Prediction Feasible in Social Work? An Inquiry Based upon a Sociological Study of Parole Records." *Social Forces* 7:533–45.

Burgess, Ernest W., and Thorsten Sellin. 1951. "Introduction." In Ohlin 1951.

Byrne, James M., Arthur J. Lurigio, and Christopher Baird. 1989. "The Effectiveness of the New Intensive Supervision Programs." *Research in Corrections* 2 (2): 1–48.

Callahan, Gene, and William Anderson. 2001. "The Roots of Racial Profiling: Why Are Police Targeting Minorities for Traffic Stops?" *Reason,* August–September, 37.

Carter, Robert M., and Leslie T. Wilkins, eds. 1970. *Probation and Parole: Selected Readings.* New York: John Wiley & Sons.

Cauley, Jon, and Eric I. Im. 1988. "Intervention Policy Analysis of Skyjackings and Other Terrorist Incidents." *American Economic Review* 78:27–31.

Center for Disease Control and Prevention. 2004. "Youth Risk Behavior Surveillance—United States, 2003." *Surveillance Summaries* 53, no. SS-2. Available at http://www.cdc.gov/HealthyYouth/yrbs/index.htm. Visited July 28, 2005.

Chakravarty, Shanti P. 2002. "Economic Analysis of Police Stops and Searches: A Critique." *European Journal of Political Economy* 18:597–605.

Chanenson, Steven L. 2003. "Sentencing and Data: The Not-so-Odd Couple." *Federal Sentencing Reporter* 16:1–7.

Choper, Jesse H. 2001. "Why the Supreme Court Should Not Have Decided the Presidential Election of 2000." *Constitutional Commentary* 18:335–57.

Clark, W. W. 1921. "Supervised Conduct Response of Delinquent Boys." *Journal of Delinquency* 6 (May): 387–401.

Coen, Deborah Rachel. 2004. *A Scientific Dynasty: Probability, Liberalism, and the Exner Family in Imperial Austria*. Ann Arbor, MI: UMI Dissertation Services.

Cohen, Stanley. 1985. *Visions of Social Control: Crime, Punishment and Classification*. Cambridge: Polity Press.

Cole, David. 1999. *No Equal Justice: Race and Class in the American Criminal Justice System*. New York: New Press.

Cook, Royer F., Alan D. Bernstein, and Christine M. Andrews. 1997. "Assessing Drug Use in the Workplace: A Comparison of Self-Report, Urinalysis, and Hair Analysis." In Harrison and Hughes 1997.

Coonen, Rose A. 2001. "*United States v. Gatewood*: Does the Three Strikes Statute Violate Due Process and Undermine the Presumption of Innocence?" *American Journal of Criminal Law* 29:83–113.

Cordner, Gary, Brian Williams, and Alfredo Velasco. 2002. "Vehicle Stops in San Diego: 2001." San Diego Police Department. Available at http://www.sandiego.gov/police/pdf/stoprpt.pdf. Visited June 8, 2004.

Cunningham, Mark D., and Thomas J. Reidy. 1998. "Integrating Base Rate Data in Violence Risk Assessments at Capital Sentencing." *Behavioral Sciences and the Law* 16:71–95.

Dailey, John T. 1973. "Development of a Behavioral Profile for Air Pirates." *Villanova Law Review* 18:1004–11.

Deguise, Alix. 1981. *Trois femmes: Le Monde de Madame de Charrière*. Geneva: Slatkine.

"De l'État Social à l'État Pénal." 1998. Special issue. *Actes de la recherche en sciences sociales* 124 (September).

Derbyshire, John. 2001. "In Defense of Racial Profiling." *National Review* 53 (3): 38–40.

Dominitz, Jeff, and John Knowles. 2005. "Crime Minimization and Racial Bias: What Can We Learn From Police Search Data?" PIER Working Paper 05-019 (February 18). Available at the Social Science Research Network Web site: http://ssrn.com/abstract5719981.

Donziger, Steven A., ed. 1996. *The Real War on Crime: The Report of the National Criminal Justice Commission*. New York: HarperCollins.

Dressler, David. 1969. *Practice and Theory of Probation and Parole*. 2nd ed. New York: Columbia University Press.

Durose, Matthew R., and Patrick A. Langan. 2005. *State Court Sentencing of Convicted Felons, 2002, Statistical Tables*. Available at the Web site of the U.S. Department of Justice, Office of Justice Programs: http://www.ojp.usdoj.gov/bjs/abstract/scsc02st.htm.

Dutile, Fernand N., and Cleon H. Foust, eds. 1987. *The Prediction of Criminal Violence*. Springfield, IL: Charles C Thomas.

Enders, Walter, and Todd Sandler. 1993. "The Effectiveness of Antiterrorism Policies: A Vector-Autoregression Intervention Analysis." *American Political Science Review* 87:829–44.

———. 2004. "What Do We Know about the Substitution Effect in Transnational Terrorism?" In *Researching Terrorism: Trends, Achievements, Failures*, ed. Andrew Silke and G. Ilardi. London: Frank Cass.

Ericson, Richard, and Kevin Haggerty. 1997. *Policing the Risk Society*. Oxford: Oxford University Press.

Evjen, Victor H. 1970. "A Current Thinking on Parole Prediction Tables." In Carter and Wilkins 1970. Orig. pub. in *Crime and Delinquency* 8 (July 1962): 215–24.

Ewald, François. 1986. *L'Etat Providence*. Paris: Grasset.

———. 1991. "Insurance and Risk." In Burchell, Gordon, and Miller 1991.

———. 2002. "The Return of Descartes's Malicious Demon: An Outline of a Philosophy of Precaution." In Baker and Simon 2002b, 273–301.

Falck, Russel, H. A. Siegal, M. A. Forney, J. Wang, and R. G. Carlson. 1992. "The Validity of Injection Drug Users Self-Reported Use of Opiates and Cocaine." *Journal of Drug Issues* 22:823–32.

Faria, João Ricardo. 2006. "Terrorist Innovations and Anti-Terrorist Policies." *Terrorism and Political Violence* 18:47–56.

Federal Tax Course. 1991. Upper Saddle River, NJ: Prentice Hall.

Feeley, Malcolm M. 1983. *Court Reform on Trial: Why Simple Solutions Fail*. New York: Basic Books.

Feeley, Malcolm M., and Jonathan Simon. 1992. "The New Penology: Notes on the Emerging Strategy of Corrections and Its Implications." *Criminology* 30: 449–74.

Fendrich, Michael, and Yanchun Xu. 1994. "The Validity of Drug Use Reports from Juvenile Arrestees." *International Journal of Addictions* 29:971–85.

Figlio, Robert M., Paul E. Tracy, and Marvin E. Wolfgang. 1990. "Delinquency in a Birth Cohort, pt. 2: Philadelphia, 1958–1986." [Computer files]. 3rd ICPSR version. Philadelphia, PA: Sellin Center for Studies in Criminology and Criminal Law and National Analysts, Division of Booz-Allen and Hamilton, Inc. [producers], 1990. Ann Arbor, MI: Inter-University Consortium for Political and Social Research [distributor], 1994.

Finkelstein, Michael O., and William B. Fairley. 1970. "A Bayesian Approach to Identification Evidence." *Harvard Law Review* 83:489–517.

Fitch, W. Lawrence. 2003. "Sex Offender Commitment in the United States: Legislative and Policy Concerns." In *Sexually Coercive Behavior: Understanding and Management*, ed. Robert A. Prentky, E. Janus, and M. Seto. New York: New York Academy of Sciences.

Fitch, W. Lawrence, and Debra A. Hammen. 2003. "The New Generation of Sex Offender Commitment Laws: Which States Have Them, and How Do They Work?" In *Protecting Society from Sexually Dangerous Offenders*, ed. Bruce J. Winick and John Q. LaFond. Rice, ME: American Psychological Association.

Foucault, Michel. 1976. *Discipline and Punish: The Birth of the Prison*. New York: Vintage Books.

Frase, Richard S. 1997. "Sentencing Guidelines Are 'Alive and Well' in the United States." In *Sentencing Reform in Overcrowded Times—A Comparative Perspective,* ed. Michael Tonry and Kathleen Hatlestad. New York: Oxford University Press.

Gallup, George, and Alec Gallup. 1999. *The Gallup Poll Monthly* 411 (December).

Garland, David. 1985. *Punishment and Welfare*. Gower, UK: Aldershot.

———. 1995. "Penal Modernism and Postmodernism." In *Punishment and Social Control: Essays in Honor of Sheldon L. Messinger,* ed. Thomas G. Blomberg and Stanley Cohen. New York: Aldine de Gruyter.

———. 2001. *The Culture of Control: Crime and Culture in Contemporary Society*. Chicago: University of Chicago Press.

Garrett, Brandon. 2001. "Remedying Racial Profiling." *Columbia Human Rights Law Review* 33:41–148.

Gendreau, Paul, Claire Goggin, and Tracy Little. 1996. "Predicting Adult Offender Recidivism: What Works!" Ottawa: Public Safety and Emergency Preparedness Canada.

Georgakopoulos, Nicholas L. 2004. "Self-Fulfilling Impressions of Criminality: Unintentional Race Profiling." *International Review of Law and Economics* 24:169–90.

Gillin, J. L. 1950. "Predicting Outcome of Adult Probationers in Wisconsin." *American Sociological Review* 15 (August): 550–53.

Gladwell, Malcolm. 2006. "Troublemakers: What Pit Bulls Can Teach Us about Profiling." *New Yorker,* February 6. Available at http://www.newyorker.com/fact/content/articles/060206fa_fact.

Glaser, Daniel. 1954. "A Reformulation and Testing of Parole Prediction Factors." PhD diss., Department of Sociology, University of Chicago.

———. 1955. "The Efficacy of Alternative Approaches to Parole Prediction." *American Sociological Review* 20 (3): 283–87.

Glueck, Sheldon, and Eleanor Glueck. 1939. *Five Hundred Criminal Careers*. New York: Alfred A. Knopf. Repr., New York: Kraus Reprint, 1954. Orig. pub. in 1930. Citations are to the 1954 reprint edition.

———. 1943. *Criminal Careers in Retrospect*. New York: Commonwealth Fund.

———. 1945. *After-Conduct of Discharged Offenders: A Report to the Department*. London: Macmillan.

Gottfredson, Don M., and Michael Tonry. 1987. *Prediction and Classification: Criminal Justice Decision Making*. Vol. 9 of *Crime and Justice: A Review of Research*. Chicago: University of Chicago Press.

Gottfredson, Stephen. 1987. "Statistical and Actuarial Considerations." In Dutile and Foust 1987, 71–81.

Gottfredson, Stephen, and Don Gottfredson. 1986. "The Accuracy of Prediction Models." In Blumstein et al. 1986, 2:212–90.

Gould, Jon B., and Stephen D. Mastrofski. 2004. "Suspect Searches: Assessing Police Behavior Under the U.S. Constitution." *Criminology and Public Policy* 3 (3): 315–62.

Gray, Thomas A., and Eric D. Wish. 1999. "Correlates of Underreporting Recent Drug Use by Female Arrestees." *Journal on Drug Issues* 29:91–105.

Green, Thomas A. 1995. "Freedom and Criminal Responsibility in the Age of Pound: An Essay on Criminal Justice." *Michigan Law Review* 93:1915–2053.

Greenwood, Peter W., with Allan Abrahamse. 1982. *Selective Incapacitation.* Santa Monica, CA: Rand Corporation.

Gross, Samuel R., and Katherine Y. Barnes. 2002. "Road Work: Racial Profiling and Drug Interdiction on the Highway." *Michigan Law Review* 101:651–753.

Gross, Samuel R., and Debra Livingston. 2002. "Racial Profiling under Attack." *Columbia Law Review* 102:1413–38.

Grove, William M., David H. Zald, Boyd S. Lebow, Beth E. Snitz, and Chad Nelson. 2000. "Clinical Versus Mechanical Prediction: A Meta-Analysis." *Psychological Assessment* 12:19–30.

Guinier, Lani, and Susan Sturm. 1996. "The Future of Affirmative Action: Reclaiming the Innovative Ideal." *California Law Review* 84 (4): 953–1036.

Guttman, Louis. 1941. "An Outline of the Statistical Theory of Prediction." In *The Prediction of Personal Adjustment,* ed. Paul Horst. New York: Social Science Research Council.

Hacking, Ian. 1990. *The Taming of Chance.* New York: Cambridge University Press.

Hakeem, Michael. 1948. "The Validity of the Burgess Method of Parole Prediction." *American Journal of Sociology* 53 (5): 376–86.

Handbook for New Parole Board Members. 2003. Association of Paroling Authorities International and the National Institute of Corrections. Available at http://www.apaintl.org/Handbook.html.

Hanson, R. Karl. 1997. *The Development of a Brief Actuarial Risk Scale for Sexual Offense Recidivism.* Department of the Solicitor General of Canada. Available at the Web site of Public Safety and Emergency Preparedness Canada: http://www.psepc-sppcc.gc.ca/publications/corrections/199607_e.asp.

Hanson, R. Karl, and David Thornton. 2000. "Improving Risk Assessment for Sex Offenders: A Comparison of Three Actuarial Scales." *Law and Human Behavior* 24:119–56.

Harcourt, Bernard E. 2001. *Illusion of Order: The False Promise of Broken Windows Policing.* Cambridge, MA: Harvard University Press.

———. 2003a. "From the Ne'er-Do-Well to the Criminal History Category: The Actuarial in Criminal Law." *Law and Contemporary Problems* 66:99–151.

———, ed. 2003b. *Guns, Crime, and Punishment in America.* New York: New York University.

———. 2003c. "The Shaping of Chance: Actuarial Models and Criminal Profiling at the Turn of the Twenty-first Century." *University of Chicago Law Review* 70: 105–28.

———. 2004a. "Rethinking Racial Profiling: A Critique of the Economics, Civil Liberties, and Constitutional Literature, and of Criminal Profiling More Generally." *University of Chicago Law Review* 71 (4): 1275–1381.

———. 2004b. "Unconstitutional Police Searches and Collective Responsibility." *Criminology and Public Policy* 3 (3): 363–78.

———. 2006a. *Language of the Gun: Youth, Crime, and Public Policy.* Chicago: University of Chicago Press.

———. 2006b. "Muslim Profiles Post 9/11: Is Racial Profiling an Effective Counterterrorism Measure and Does It Violate the Right to Be Free from Discrimination?" Paper presented at the Oxford Colloquium on Security and Human Rights, Oxford University, March 17.

———. 2006c. "*United States v. Brignoni-Ponce* and *United States v. Martinez-Fuerte*: The Road to Racial Profiling." In *Criminal Procedure Stories,* ed. Carol Steiker. New York: Foundations Press.

Harmsworth, Esmond. 1996. "Bail and Detention: An Assessment and Critique of the Federal and Massachusetts Systems." *New England Journal on Criminal and Civil Confinement* 22:213–90.

Harrell, Adele V. 1997. "The Validity of Self-Reported Drug Use Data: The Accuracy of Responses on Confidential Self-Administered Answered Sheets." In Harrison and Hughes 1997.

Harris, David A. 2002. *Profiles in Injustice: Why Racial Profiling Cannot Work.* New York: New Press.

Harrison, Lana. 1997. "The Validity of Self-Reported Drug Use in Survey Research: An Overview and Critique of Research Methods." In Harrison and Hughes 1997.

Harrison, Lana, and Arthur Hughes, eds. 1997. *The Validity of Self-Reported Drug Use: Improving the Accuracy of Survey Estimates.* Washington, DC: United States Department of Health and Human Services.

Hart, Hornell. 1923. "Predicting Parole Success." *Journal of the American Institute of Criminal Law and Criminology* 41 (3): 405–13.

Heacox, F. L. 1917. "A Study of One Year's Parole Violators Returned to Auburn Prison." *Journal of Criminal Law and Criminology* 7 (July): 233–58.

Hernández-Murillo, Rubén, and John Knowles. 2003. "Racial Profiling or Racist Policing? Testing in Aggregated Data." University of Pennsylvania, Department of Economics working paper.

Heumann, Milton, and Lance Cassak. 2001. "Profiles in Justice? Police Discretion, Symbolic Assailants, and Stereotyping." *Rutgers Law Review* 53:911–78.

Hoffman, Peter B. 1983. "Screening for Risk: A Revised Salient Factor Score (SFS 81)." *Journal of Criminal Justice* 11:539–47.

Hoffman, Peter B., and James L. Beck. 1974. "Parole Decision-Making: A Salient Factor Score." *Journal of Criminal Justice* 2:195–206.

Human Rights Watch. 2000. *Punishment and Prejudice: Racial Disparities in the War on Drugs.* New York: Human Rights Watch. Available at http://www.hrw.org/reports/2000/usa/. Visited July 27, 2004.

Hunt, Alan, and Gary Wickham. 1994. *Foucault and Law: Towards a Sociology of Law as Governance.* London: Pluto Press.

Janus, Eric S., and Robert A. Prentky. 2003. "Forensic Use of Actuarial Risk Assessment with Sex Offenders: Accuracy, Admissibility and Accountability." *American Criminal Law Review* 40:1443–99.

Jenkins, R. L. 1942. "Prediction of Parole Success: Inclusion of Psychiatric Criteria." *Journal of Criminal Law and Criminology* 33:38–46.

Johnson, Sheri Lynn. 1984. "Cross-Racial Identification Errors in Criminal Cases." 69 *Cornell Law Review* 934–87.

Johnston, Lloyd D., and Patrick M. O'Malley. 1997. "The Recanting of Earlier Reported Drug Use by Young Adults." In Harrison and Hughes 1997.

Johnston, Lloyd D., Patrick M. O'Malley, Jerald G. Bachman, and John E. Schulenberg. 2005. *Monitoring the Future: National Survey Results on Drug Use, 1975–2004.* Vol. 1. *Secondary School Students.* NIH Publication No. 05-5727. Bethesda, MD: National Institute on Drug Abuse.

Justice Policy Institute. 2002. *Cellblocks or Classrooms? The Funding of Higher Education and Corrections and Its Impact on African American Men.* Available at http://www.justicepolicy.org/coc1/corc.htm. Visited January 5, 2003.

Kamisar, Yale, Wayne R. Lafave, Jerold H. Israel, and Nancy J. King. 2002. *Modern Criminal Procedure: Cases, Comments and Questions.* 10th ed. St. Paul, MN: Thompson/West.

Katz, Jack. 1988. *Seductions of Crime: Moral and Sensual Attractions in Doing Evil.* New York: Basic Books.

Kennedy, Joseph E. 2003. "Drug Wars in Black and White." *Law and Contemporary Problems* 66 (Summer): 153–82.

Kern, Richard P., and Meredith Farrar-Owens. 2004. "Sentencing Guidelines with Integrated Offender Risk Assessment." *Federal Sentencing Reporter* 16: 165–69.

Kirby, Bernard C. 1954. "Parole Prediction Using Multiple Correlation." *American Sociological Review* 6:539–50.

Klein, C. R. 1935. "Success and Failure on Parole: A Study of 160 Girls Paroled from the State Training School at Geneva, Illinois." Master's thesis, School of Social Service Administration, University of Chicago.

Knowles, John, Nicola Persico, and Petra Todd. 2001. "Racial Bias in Motor Vehicle Searches: Theory and Evidence." *Journal of Political Economy* 109:203–29.

Krauthammer, Charles. 2005. "Give Grandma a Pass." *Washington Post,* July 29, A23. Available at http://www.washingtonpost.com/wp-dyn/content/article/2005/07/28/AR2005072801786.html.

Kuhn, Matthew. 2005. "Note: The Earthquake That Will Move Sentencing Discretion Back to the Judiciary? *Blakely v. Washington* and Sentencing Guidelines in Minnesota." *William Mitchell Law Review* 31:1507–44.

La Fontaine, Eugenia T. 2002. "A Dangerous Preoccupation with Future Danger: Why Expert Predictions of Future Dangerousness in Capital Cases Are Unconstitutional." *Boston College Law Review* 44:207–43.

Lamberth, John. 1996. "Report of John Lamberth on the Incidence and Significance of Police Searches along the I-95 Corridor." Available at the American Civil Liberties Union Web site: http://archive.aclu.org/court/lamberth.html. Visited June 6, 2004.

Landes, William M. 1978. "An Economic Study of U.S. Aircraft Hijacking, 1961–1976." *Journal of Law and Economics* 21 (1): 1–31.

Langan, Patrick A. 1985. "Racism on Trial: New Evidence to Explain the Racial Composition of Prisons in the United States." *Journal of Criminal Law and Criminology* 76:666–83.

Langan, Patrick A., and David J. Levin. 2002. *Recidivism of Prisoners Released in 1994*. Washington, DC: Bureau of Justice Statistics, U.S. Department of Justice. Available at http://www.ojp.usdoj.gov/bjs/pub/pdf/rpr94.pdf. Visited September 19, 2005.

Laub, John H., and Robert J. Sampson. 1991. "The Sutherland-Glueck Debate: On the Sociology of Criminological Knowledge." *American Journal of Sociology* 96 (May): 1402–40.

Laune, Ferris F. 1936. *Predicting Criminality: Forecasting Behavior on Parole*. Northwestern University Studies in the Social Sciences, no. 1. Evanston, IL: Northwestern University.

Leitzel, Jim. 2001. "Race and Policing." *Society* 38 (3): 38–42.

Lerner, Maura. 2000. "Who Gets Audited up to Science." *Arkansas Democrat-Gazette*, April 17, sec. D. (Also in the *Minneapolis-St. Paul Star Tribune*, April 17, 2000.)

Levitt, Steven D. 1998. "Juvenile Crime and Punishment." *Journal of Political Economy* 106 (6): 1156–85.

———. 2004. "Understanding Why Crime Fell in the 1990s: Four Factors That Explain the Decline and Six That Do Not." *Journal of Economic Perspectives* 18: 163–90.

Lind, E. Allan, and Tom R. Tyler. 1988. *The Social Psychology of Procedural Justice*. New York: Plenum Press.

Litwack, Thomas R. 2001. "Actuarial Versus Clinical Assessments of Dangerousness." *Psychology, Public Policy, and Law* 7:409–43.

Lohman, Joseph. 1951. "Preface." In Ohlin 1951.

Lu, Natalie T., Bruce G. Taylor, and K. Jack Riley. 2001. "The Validity of Adult Arrestee Self-Reports of Crack Cocaine Use." *American Journal on Drug and Alcohol Abuse* 27:399–420.

Lum, Cynthia, Leslie W. Kennedy, and Alison J. Sherley. 2006. "The Effectiveness of Counter-Terrorism Strategies: A Campbell Systematic Review." Campbell Collaboration working paper (January). Available at http://www.campbellcollaboration.org/CCJG/reviews/CampbellSystematicReviewOnTerrorism02062006FINAL_REVISED.pdf.

Luna, Erik G. 1998. "Foreword: Three Strikes in a Nutshell." *Thomas Jefferson Law Review* 20:1–96.

Lunday, G. A. 1949. "A Study of Parole Prediction." PhD diss., Department of Sociology, University of Chicago.

Maclin, Tracey. 2001. "The Fourth Amendment on the Freeway." *Rutgers Race and Law Review* 3:117–90.

Mannheim, Hermann, and Leslie Wilkins. 1955. *Prediction Methods in Relation to Borstal Training*. London: H. M. Stationery Office.

Manski, Charles. 2005. "Search Profiling with Partial Knowledge of Deterrence." National Bureau of Economic Research Working Paper no. 11848. Available at http://www.nber.org/papers/W11848.

Marcus, Michael H. 2003. "Comments on the Model Penal Code: Sentencing Preliminary Draft No. 1." *American Journal of Criminal Law* 30:135–70.

Marcus, Rebecca. 1994. "Racism in Our Courts: The Underfunding of Public Defenders and Its Disproportionate Impact upon Racial Minorities." *Hastings Constitutional Law Quarterly* 22:219–67.

McGinley, Patrick W., and Stephen F. Downs. 1973. "Airport Searches and Seizures: A Reasonable Approach." *Fordham Law Review* 41:293–324.

Meares, Tracey L. 1998. "Social Organization and Drug Law Enforcement." *American Criminal Law Review* 35:191–227.

———. 2000. "Norms, Legitimacy and Law Enforcement." *Oregon Law Review* 79: 391–416.

Meares, Tracey L., and Bernard E. Harcourt. 2000. "Foreword to Supreme Court Review: Transparent Adjudication and Social Science Research in Constitutional Criminal Procedure." *Journal of Criminal Law and Criminology* 90: 733–98.

Meehl, Paul E. 1954. *Clinical versus Statistical Prediction: A Theoretical Analysis and a Review of the Evidence.* Minneapolis: University of Minnesota Press.

———. 1986. "Causes and Effects of My Disturbing Little Book." *Journal of Personality Assessment* 50:370–75.

Melton, Gary B., John Petrila, Norman G. Poythress, and Christopher Slobogin. 1997. *Psychological Evaluations for the Courts.* 2nd ed. New York: Guilford Press.

Michael, Jerome, and Mortimer J. Adler. 1933. *Crime, Law, and Social Science.* New York: Harcourt, Brace.

Michelson, Stephan. 2001. "Driving While Black: A Skeptical Note." *Jurimetrics* 44:161–80.

Monachesi, Elio D. 1932. *Prediction Factors in Probation.* Hanover, NH: Sociological Press.

———. 1945. "A Comparison of Predicted with Actual Results of Probation." *American Sociological Review* 10 (1): 26–31.

Monahan, John. 1982. "The Case for Prediction in the Modified Desert Model of Criminal Sentencing." *International Journal of Law and Psychiatry* 5:103–13.

———. 2004. "Forecasting Harm: The Law and Science of Risk Assessment among Prisoners, Predators, and Patients." Available at the Web site of the Berkeley Electronic Press: http://law.bepress.com/expresso/eps/410.

———. 2005. "Risk and Race: An Essay on Violence Forecasting and the Civil/ Criminal Distinction." Working paper on file with author.

Monahan, John, and Eric Silver. 2003. "Judicial Decision Thresholds for Violence Risk Management." *International Journal of Forensic Mental Health* 2 (1): 1–6.

Monahan, John, Henry J. Steadman, Pamela Clark Robbins, Paul Appelbaum, Steven Banks, Thomas Grisso, Kirk Heilbrun, Edward P. Mulvey, Loren Roth, and Eric Silver. 2005. "An Actuarial Model of Violence Risk Assessment for Persons with Mental Disorders." *Psychiatric Services* 56 (7): 810–15.

Monahan, John, Henry J. Steadman, Eric Silver, Paul Appelbaum, Pamela Clark Robbins, Edward P. Mulvey, Loren Roth, Thomas Grisso, and Steven Banks. 2001. *Rethinking Risk Assessment: The MacArthur Study of Mental Disorder and Violence.* New York: Oxford University Press.

Monahan, John, and Laurens Walker. 2006. *Social Science in Law: Cases and Materials.* 6th ed. Westbury, NY: Foundation Press.

Moon, Chris. 2004. "Governor Proposes Spending More on Drug Treatment for Offenders." *Topeka Capital-Journal* (Kansas), January 27.

Morse, Wayne L., ed. 1939. *The Attorney General's Survey of Release Procedures. U.S. Dept. of Justice. Vol. 4. Parole.* 4 vols. Washington, DC: U.S. Government Printing Office.

Mosher, Clayton J., Terance D. Miethe, and Dretha M. Phillips. 2002. *The Mismeasure of Crime.* Thousand Oaks, CA: Sage.

Nagin, Daniel. 1978. "General Deterrence: A Review of the Empirical Evidence." In *Deterrence and Incapacitation: Estimating the Effects of Criminal Sanctions on Crime Rates, Report of the Panel of Deterrence and Incapacitation,* ed. Alfred Blumstein, Jacqueline Cohen, and Daniel Nagin. Washington DC: National Academy of Sciences.

Nesson, Charles R. 1979. "Reasonable Doubt and Permissive Inferences: The Value of Complexity." *Harvard Law Review* 92:1187–1225.

Nisbet, Charles T., and Firouz Vakil. 1972. "Some Estimates of Price and Expenditure Elasticities of Demand for Marijuana among UCLA Students." *Review of Economics and Statistics* 54:473–75.

Nourse, Victoria F. 2004. "Rethinking Crime Legislation: History and Harshness." *Tulsa Law Review* 39:925–40.

Ohlin, Lloyd E. 1951. *Selection for Parole: A Manual of Parole Prediction.* New York: Russell Sage Foundation.

Ohlin, Lloyd E., and Richard A. Lawrence. 1952. "A Comparison of Alternative Methods of Parole Prediction." *American Sociological Review* 17:268–74.

O'Leary, Vincent, and Joan Nuffield. 1973. "A National Survey of Parole Decision-Making." *Crime and Delinquency* 19 (1): 378–93.

O'Malley, Pat. 1999. "Volatile and Contradictory Punishment." *Theoretical Criminology* 3:175–96.

———. 2002. "Imagining Insurance: Risk, Thrift, and Life Insurance in Britain." In Baker and Simon 2002b.

O'Neill, Michael Edmund. 2001. "Abraham's Legacy: An Empirical Assessment of (Nearly) First-Time Offenders in the Federal System." *Boston College Law Review* 42 (March): 291–348.

Ostrom, Brian J., Matthew Kleiman, Fred Cheesman, Randall M. Hansen, and Neal B. Kauder. 2002. *Offender Risk Assessment in Virginia: A Three-Stage Evaluation.* Williamsburg, VA: National Center for State Courts and the Virginia Criminal Sentencing Commission.

Page, W. F., J. E. Davies, R. A. Ladner, and J. Alfassa. 1977. "Urinalysis-Screened vs. Verbally Reported Drug Use: The Identification of Discrepant Groups." *International Journal on Addictions* 12:439–50.

Park, Robert E., and Ernest W. Burgess. 1925. *The City.* Chicago: University of Chicago Press.

Pearson, Karl. 1919. "Charles Goring and his Contributions to Criminology." In *The English Convict: A Statistical Study,* ed. Karl Goring. Belmont, CA: Wadsworth.

Persico, Nicola. 2002. "Racial Profiling, Fairness, and Effectiveness of Policing." *American Economic Review* 92 (5): 1472–97.

Persico, Nicola, and Petra Todd. 2004. "Using Hit Rates to Test for Racial Bias in

Law Enforcement: Vehicle Searches in Wichita." Working paper on file with author (November 18).

Petersilia, Joan, ed. 1998. *Community Corrections: Probation, Parole, and Intermediate Sanctions.* New York: Oxford University Press.

——. 2003. *When Prisoners Come Home: Parole and Prisoner Reentry.* New York: Oxford University Press.

Petersilia, Joan, and Susan Turner. 1991. "An Evaluation of Intensive Probation in California." *Journal of Criminal Law and Criminology* 82 (3): 610–58.

Petrocelli, Matthew, Alex R. Piquero, and Michael R. Smith. 2003. "Conflict Theory and Racial Profiling: An Empirical Analysis of Police Traffic Stop Data." *Journal of Criminal Justice* 31:1–11.

Pickerill, J. Mitchell, et al. 2003. "Search and Seizure, Racial Profiling, and Traffic Stops on Washington State Highways." Unpublished paper prepared for annual meeting of the Law and Society Association. Pittsburgh, PA. Available from the author.

Pinter, R., and J. C. Reamer. 1918. "Mental Ability and Future Success of Delinquent Girls." *Journal of Delinquency* 3:74–89.

Pound, Roscoe. 1911. "Introduction to the English Version." In Saleilles 1911.

Pratt, John. 1997. *Governing the Dangerous: Dangerousness, Law and Social Change.* Sydney: Federation Press.

Quinsey, Vernon L., Grant T. Harris, Marnie E. Rice, and Catherine A. Cormier. 1998. *Violent Offenders: Appraising and Managing Risk.* Washington, DC: American Psychological Association.

Racial Profiling: Limited Data Available on Motorist Stops. 2000. Report of the Government Accounting Office (GAO). Washington, DC (March). Available at http://www.gao.gov/new.items/gg00041.pdf. Visited June 8, 2004.

Ramirez, Deborah, Jack McDevitt, and Amy Farrell. 2000. "A Resource Guide on Racial Profiling Data Collection Systems: Promising Practices and Lessons Learned." U.S. Department of Justice. Washington, DC: U.S. Government Printing Office.

Raynor, Peter, Jocelyn Kynch, Colin Roberts, and Simon Merrington. 2001. "Two Risk and Need Assessment Instruments Used in Probation Services: An Evaluation." Findings 143, United Kingdom Home Office. Available at http://www.homeoffice.gov.uk/rds/pdfs/r143.pdf.

Redden, Elizabeth. 1942. "Embezzlement: A Study of One Kind of Criminal Behavior with Prediction Tables Based on Fidelity Insurance Records." PhD diss., Department of Sociology, University of Chicago. Private edition, University of Chicago Libraries.

Regnier, Thomas. 2004. "Barefoot in Quicksand: The Future of 'Future Dangerousness' Predictions in Death Penalty Sentencing in the World of Daubert and Kumho." *Akron Law Review* 37:469–507.

Reiss, Albert J., Jr. 1949. "The Accuracy, Efficiency, and Validity of a Prediction Instrument." PhD diss., Department of Sociology, University of Chicago. September.

——. 1951. "The Accuracy, Efficiency, and Validity of a Prediction Instrument." *American Journal of Sociology* 56 (6): 552–61.

Resnik, Judith. "Procedure's Projects." *Civil Justice Quarterly* 23:273–308.

Reuter, Peter, and Mark A. R. Kleiman. 1986. "Risks and Prices: An Economic Analysis of Drug Enforcement." In *Crime and Justice: An Annual Review of Research,* ed. Michael Tonry and Norval Morris. Chicago: University of Chicago Press.

Rhodes, William, Herbert Tyson, James Weekly, Catherine Conly, and Gustave Powell. 1982. *Developing Criteria for Identifying Career Criminals.* Unpublished paper. Institute for Law and Social Research, Washington, DC.

Risse, Mathias, and Richard Zeckhauser. 2004. "Racial Profiling." *Philosophy and Public Affairs* 32:131.

Roberts, Dorothy E. 1999. "Foreword: Race, Vagueness, and the Social Meaning of Order-Maintenance Policing." *Journal of Criminal Law and Criminology* 89: 775–836.

Robinson, Paul H. 2001. "Punishing Dangerousness: Cloaking Preventive Detention as Criminal Justice." *Harvard Law Review* 114:1429–56.

Rose, Nikolas. 1999. *Powers and Freedom.* Cambridge: Cambridge University Press.

———. 2002. "At Risk of Madness." In Baker and Simon 2002b.

Rose, Nikolas, and Peter Miller. 1992. "Political Power Beyond the State: Problematics of Government." *British Journal of Sociology* 43 (2): 173–205.

Rosen, Albert. 1954. "Detection of Suicidal Patients: An Example of Some Limitations of the Prediction of Infrequent Events." *Journal of Consulting Psychology* 18:397–403.

Rothman, David J. 1971. *The Discovery of the Asylum: Social Order and Disorder in the New Republic.* Boston: Little, Brown.

———. 1980. *Conscience and Convenience: The Asylum and Its Alternatives in Progressive America.* Boston: Little, Brown.

Rudovsky, David. 2001. "Law Enforcement by Stereotypes and Serendipity: Racial Profiling and Stops and Searches without Cause." *University of Pennsylvania Journal of Constitutional Law* 3:296–366.

Runda, John C., Edward E. Rhine, and Robert E. Wetter. 1994. *The Practice of Parole Boards.* Lexington, KY: Host Communications Printing.

Russell, Katheryn K. 2001. "Racial Profiling: A Status Report of the Legal, Legislative, and Empirical Literature." *Rutgers Race and Law Review* 3:61–82.

Russell, Roger. 2004. "IRS Examination Program Undergoes Re-Engineering." *Accounting Today* 18 (12): 10–15.

Saleilles, Raymond. 1898. *L'Individualisation de la peine: Étude de criminalité sociale.* Paris: F. Alcan.

———. 1911. *The Individualization of Punishment.* Trans. Rachel Szold Jastrow. Boston: Little, Brown.

Sampson, Robert J., and John H. Laub. 1993. *Crime in the Making: Pathways and Turning Points through Life.* Cambridge, MA: Harvard University Press.

San Jose, California, Police Department. 2002. "Vehicle Stop Demographic Study." Available at http://www.sjpd.org/pdf%20file%20for%206-14-2002%20annual%20report.pdf. Visited June 8, 2004.

Schauer, Frederick. 2003. *Profiles, Probabilities, and Stereotypes.* Cambridge MA: Harvard University Press.

Scheingold, Stuart A. 1998. "Constructing the New Political Criminology: Power, Authority, and the Post-Liberal State." *Law and Social Inquiry* 23:857–95.

Scherreik, Susan. 2000. "The Tax Man Still Biteth." *Business Week*, February 28, 162.

Schulhofer, Stephen J. 1994. "Solving the Drug Enforcement Dilemma: Lessons from Economics." *University of Chicago Legal Forum* 1994:207–36.

———. 1996. "Two Systems of Social Protection: Comments on the Civil-Criminal Distinction, with Particular Reference to Sexually Violent Predator Laws." *Journal of Contemporary Legal Issues* 7:69–96.

"Selective Incapacitation: Reducing Crime Through Predictions of Recidivism" [Note]. 1982. *Harvard Law Review* 96:511–33.

Shaw, Clifford R., and Henry D. McKay. 1969. *Juvenile Delinquency and Urban Areas: A Study of Rates of Delinquency in Relation to Differential Characteristics of Local Communities in American Cities*. Chicago: University of Chicago Press.

Shichor, David. 1997. "Three Strikes as a Public Policy: The Convergence of the New Penology and the McDonaldization of Punishment." *Crime and Delinquency* 43:470–92.

Simon, Frances H. 1971. *Prediction Methods in Criminology: Including a Prediction Study of Young Men on Probation*. London: Her Majesty's Stationery Office.

Simon, Jonathan. 1993. *Poor Discipline: Parole and the Social Control of the Underclass*. Chicago: University of Chicago Press.

———. Forthcoming. "Reversal of Fortune: The Resurgence of Individual Risk Assessment in Criminal Justice." *Annual Review of Law and Social Science*.

Simon, Jonathan, and Malcolm M. Feeley. 1995. "True Crime: The New Penology and Public Discourse on Crime." In *Punishment and Social Control: Essays in Honor of Sheldon L. Messinger*, ed. Thomas G. Blomberg and Stanley Cohen. Hawthorne, NY: Aldine de Gruyter.

Skolnick, Jerome H., and Abigail Caplovitz. 2001. "Guns, Drugs, and Profiling: Ways to Target Guns and Minimize Racial Profiling." *Arizona Law Review* 43:413–38.

Skolnick, Jerome H., and James J. Fyfe. 1993. *Above the Law: Police and the Excessive Use of Force*. New York: Free Press.

Slemrod, Joel, and Jon Bakija. 2000. *Taxing Ourselves*. Cambridge, MA: MIT Press.

Slobogin, Christopher. 1996. "Dangerousness as a Criterion in the Criminal Process." In *Law, Mental Health and Mental Disorder*, ed. Bruce Sales and S. W. Shuman. Pacific Grove, CA: Brooks/Cole.

Smith, Kelly. 1999. "Audits Are Down But Your Number May Be Up." *Money* 28 (August): 137–38.

Solomon, Jason J. 1999. "Future Dangerousness: Issues and Analysis." *Capital Defense Journal* 12:55–75.

Sorensen, Jonathan R., and Rocky L. Pilgrim. 2000. "An Actuarial Risk Assessment of Violence Posed by Capital Murder Defendants." *Journal of Criminal Law and Criminology* 90:1251–70.

Spelman, William. 2000. "The Limited Importance of Prison Expansion." In *The Crime Drop in America*, ed. Alfred Blumstein and Joel Wallman. New York: Cambridge University Press.

Sperry, Paul. 2005. "When the Profile Fits the Crime." *New York Times*, July 28.

Steadman, Henry J. 1972. "The Psychiatrist as a Conservative Agent of Social Control." *Social Problems* 20:263–71.

———. 1987. "Mental Health Law and the Criminal Offender: Research Directions for the 1990s." *Rutgers Law Review* 39:81–95.

Steiker, Carol S. 1995. "Sober Second Thoughts: Reflections on Two Decades of Constitutional Regulation of Capital Punishment." *Harvard Law Review* 109: 355–438.

———. 1997. "Punishment Theory and the Criminal-Civil Procedural Divide." *Georgetown Law Journal* 85:775–819.

Steiker, Carol, and Jordan Steiker. 1992. "Let God Sort Them Out? Refining the Individualization Requirement in Capital Sentencing." *Yale Law Journal* 102: 835–70.

Stith, Kate, and Jose A. Cabranes. 1998. *Fear of Judging: Sentencing Guidelines in the Federal Courts*. Chicago: University of Chicago Press.

Sutherland, Edwin H., and Donald R. Cressey. 1978. *Principles of Criminology*. 10th ed. Philadelphia, PA: J. B. Lippincott.

Sutherland, J. F. 1908. *Recidivism: Habitual Criminality, and Habitual Petty Delinquency: A Problem in Sociology, Psycho-Pathology and Criminology*. Edinburgh: William Green & Sons.

Taylor, Paul. 2003. "Be Afraid, Be Very Afraid—Unless You Can Avoid An Audit." *Financial Times,* February 13.

Texas Defender Service. 2004. *Deadly Speculation: Misleading Texas Capital Juries with False Predictions of Future Dangerousness*. Houston, TX: Public Defender Service.

Tibbitts, Clark. 1931. "Success or Failure on Parole Can Be Predicted." *Journal of Criminal Law and Criminology* 22:11–50.

Toby, Jackson. 1999. "Racial Profiling Doesn't Prove Cops Are Racist." *Wall Street Journal,* March 11.

Tonry, Michael. 1995. *Malign Neglect: Race, Crime, and Punishment in America*. New York: Oxford University Press.

———. 1996. *Sentencing Matters*. New York: Oxford University Press.

Travis, Jeremy. 2000. "But They All Come Back: Rethinking Prisoner Reentry." *Papers From the Executive Sessions on Sentencing and Corrections,* No. 7, Research in Brief, Washington, DC: National Institute of Justice, U.S. Department of Justice.

Tribe, Laurence H. 1971a. "The Continuing Debate over Mathematics in the Law of Evidence: A Further Critique of Mathematical Proof." *Harvard Law Review* 84:1810–20.

———. 1971b. "Trial by Mathematics: Precision and Ritual in the Legal Process." *Harvard Law Review* 84:1329–93.

Tucker, Jonathan B. 2003. "Strategies for Countering Terrorism: Lessons from the Israeli Experience." (March) Available at the U.S. Homeland Security Department Institute web site at http://www.homelandsecurity.org/journal/Articles/tucker-israel.html.

Tyler, Tom R. 1990. *Why People Obey the Law*. New Haven, CT: Yale University Press.

———. 1998. "Trust and Democratic Governance." In *Trust and Governance*, ed. Valerie Braithwaite and Margaret Levi. New York: Russell Sage Foundation.

Tyler, Tom R., and Yuen J. Huo. 2002. *Trust in the Law: Encouraging Public Cooperation with the Police and the Courts.* New York: Russell Sage Foundation.

Underwood, Barbara. 1979. "Law and the Crystal Ball: Predicting Behavior with Statistical Inference and Individualized Judgment." *Yale Law Journal* 88: 1408–48.

U.S. Bureau of Justice Statistics. 1989. *Recidivism of Prisoners Released in 1983.* U.S. Department of Justice. Washington, DC: U.S. Government Printing Office.

———. 1997. "Correctional Populations in the United States, 1995." U.S. Department of Justice. Washington, DC: U.S. Government Printing Office.

———. 1999. *Sourcebook of Criminal Justice Statistics.* Ed. Ann L. Pastore and Kathleen Maguire. United States Department of Justice. Washington, DC: U.S. Government Printing Office.

———. 2000a. "Correctional Populations in the United States, 1997." U.S. Department of Justice. Washington, DC: U.S. Government Printing Office.

———. 2000b. *Sourcebook of Criminal Justice Statistics.* Ed. Ann L. Pastore and Kathleen Maguire. U.S. Department of Justice. Washington, DC: U.S. Government Printing Office.

———. 2001a. *Sourcebook of Criminal Justice Statistics 2000.* Ed. Ann L. Pastore and Kathleen Maguire. U.S. Department of Justice. Washington, DC: U.S. Government Printing Office.

———. 2001b. *State Prison Expenditures.* U.S. Department of Justice. Washington, DC: U.S. Government Printing Office.

———. 2002a. *Prisoners in 2001.* U.S. Department of Justice. Washington, DC: U.S. Government Printing Office.

———. 2002b. *Sourcebook of Criminal Justice Statistics.* Ed. Ann L. Pastore and Kathleen Maguire. U.S. Department of Justice. Washington, DC: United States Department of Justice.

U.S. Department of Health and Human Services, Substance Abuse and Mental Health Services Administration. 1995. *National Household Survey on Drug Abuse: Main Findings 1992.* Washington, DC: U.S. Government Printing Office.

———. 2004. *Drug Abuse Warning Network, 2003: Interim National Estimates of Drug-Related Emergency Department Visits.* Washington, DC: U.S. Government Printing Office.

———. 2005. *Results from the 2003 National Survey on Drug Use and Health: Detailed Tables.* Washington, DC: U.S. Government Printing Office.

U.S. Department of Justice, Federal Bureau of Investigation. 2000. *The School Shooter: A Threat Assessment Perspective.* Washington, DC: U.S. Government Printing Office.

U.S. Department of Justice, Federal Bureau of Prisons. 2001. *State Prison Expenditures 2001.* Washington, DC: U.S. Government Printing Office.

U.S. General Accounting Office. 1993. *Intensive Probation Supervision: Mixed Effectiveness in Controlling Crime.* Report to the Chairman, Subcommittee on

Crime and Criminal Justice, Committee on the Judiciary, House of Representatives. Washington, DC: U.S. Government Printing Office.

U.S. Sentencing Commission. 1987. *Supplementary Report on the Initial Sentencing Guidelines and Policy Statements*. Washington, DC: U.S. Government Printing Office.

———. 1991. *Mandatory Minimum Penalties in the Federal Criminal Justice System*. Washington, DC: U.S. Government Printing Office.

Van Vechten, Courtlandt Churchill, Jr. 1935. "A Study of Success and Failure of One Thousand Delinquents Committed to a Boy's Republic." PhD diss., Department of Sociology, University of Chicago. Private edition, distributed by the University of Chicago Libraries.

Vera Institute of Justice. 2003. *A Short History of Vera's Work on the Judicial Process*. Available at http://www.vera.org/publications/publications_5.asp?publication_id5119.

Verniero, Peter. 1999. "Interim Report of the State Police Review Team Regarding Allegations of Racial Profiling" (April). Available at http://www.state.nj.us/lps/intm_419.pdf. Visited June 5, 2004.

Virginia Criminal Sentencing Commission. 2004. *2004 Annual Report*. Available at http://www.vcsc.state.va.us/2004FULLAnnualReport.pdf.

Vold, George B. 1931. *Prediction Methods and Parole: A Study of the Factors Involved in the Violation or Non-Violation of Parole in a Group of Minnesota Adult Males*. Hanover, NH: Sociological Press.

Wacquant, Loïc. 1998. "L'ascension de l'État Pénal en Amérique." *Actes de la recherche en sciences socials* 124:7.

———. 2005. *Deadly Symbiosis: Race and the Rise of Neoliberal Penality*. Cambridge: Polity Press.

Walsh, Tiffany, and Zach Walsh. 2005. "The Evidentiary Introduction of Psychopathy Checklist-Revised Assessed Psychopathy in U.S. Courts: Extent and Appropriateness." Paper submitted for publication; on file with author.

Warner, Samuel B. 1923. "Factors Determining Parole from the Massachusetts Reformatory." *Journal of Criminal Law and Criminology* 14:172–207.

Weeks, H. Ashley. 1943. "Predicting Juvenile Delinquency." *American Sociological Review* 8:40–46.

Wigmore, John H., Ernst Freund, Maurice Parmelee, Roscoe Pound, Robert B. Scott, and William W. Smithers. 1911. "General Introduction to the Modern Criminal Science Series." In Saleilles 1911, v–ix.

Wilhelm, Daniel F., and Nicholas R. Turner. 2002. "Is the Budgeting Crisis Changing the Way We Look at Sentencing and Incarceration?" *Federal Sentencing Reporter* 15:41–49.

Will, George. 2001. "Exposing the 'Myth' of Racial Profiling." *Washington Post*, April 19.

Williams, Kristen. 1979. "The Scope and Prediction of Recidivism." Unpublished research monograph. Washington, DC: Institute for Law and Social Research.

Witmer, Helen Leland. 1927. "Some Factors in Success or Failure on Parole." *Journal of Criminal Law and Criminology* 17:384–403.

Wolfgang, Marvin E., Robert M. Figlio, and Thorsten Sellin. 1972. *Delinquency in a Birth Cohort*. Chicago: University of Chicago Press.

Zedlewski, Edwin. 1984. *The DEA Airport Surveillance Program: An Analysis of Agent Activities*. In Monahan and Walker 2006.

Zimring, Franklin E., and Gordon Hawkins. 1995. *Incapacitation: Penal Confinement and the Restraint of Crime*. New York: Oxford University Press.

Zimring, Franklin E., Gordon Hawkins, and Sam Kamin. 2001. *Punishment and Democracy: Three Strikes and You're Out in California*. New York: Oxford University Press.

Zitter, Jay M. 1999. "Judicial Partition of Land by Lot or Chance." *American Law Reports* 32, 4th 909 (Updated March 1999 Annotation).

Index